THE
AUDUBON SOCIETY
GUIDE TO
ATTRACTING
BIRDS

Other Audubon Society/Scribners Books

The Audubon Society Handbook for Birders,
by Stephen W. Kress

The Audubon Society Handbook for Butterfly Watchers,
by Robert Michael Pyle

THE
AUDUBON SOCIETY GUIDE TO
ATTRACTING BIRDS

STEPHEN W. KRESS

ILLUSTRATIONS BY
ANNE SENECHAL FAUST

FOREWORD BY
ROGER TORY PETERSON

Sponsored by the Laboratory of Ornithology, at Cornell University

CHARLES SCRIBNER'S SONS
New York

Library of Congress Cataloging in Publication Data
Kress, Stephen W.
The Audubon Society guide to attracting birds.
Bibliography: p.
Includes index.
1. Birds, Attracting of. I. Title.
QL676.5.K74   1985   639.9'78   85-10813
ISBN 0-684-18362-5

1 3 5 7 9 11 13 15 17 19   F/C   20 18 16 14 12 10 8 6 4 2

All photographs by Stephen W. Kress, unless otherwise indicated.

To my parents,
who share my enthusiasm
for birds

CONTENTS

THE NATIONAL AUDUBON SOCIETY

The National Audubon Society is among the oldest and largest private conservation organizations in the world. With 400,000-plus members and over 450 local chapters across the country, the Society works in behalf of our natural heritage through environmental education and conservation action and research. It protects wildlife in more than 70 sanctuaries from coast to coast. It also operates outdoor education centers, ecology workshops, and publishes the prize-winning *Audubon* magazine, *American Birds* magazine, newsletters, films, and other educational materials. For information regarding membership in the Society, write to the National Audubon Society, 950 Third Avenue, New York, NY 10022.

THE CORNELL LABORATORY OF ORNITHOLOGY

The Laboratory of Ornithology at Cornell University was founded in 1955. The mission of the Laboratory is to increase the knowledge, understanding, and appreciation of living birds. We believe that knowledge comes from research, understanding from education, and appreciation from both. The activities of the Laboratory are intended to provide information and an understanding of that information which will support the preservation of living birds and their habitats. Further, the Laboratory works to facilitate communication between professional and amateur ornithologists in cooperative efforts to contribute to the knowledge of North American birds.

The Laboratory of Ornithology also is a membership organization. Members receive our publication, *The Living Bird Quarterly*, four times each year, along with discounts on items purchased from our bookshop, and advance announcements of birding tours and summer workshops offered exclusively to Laboratory members. For information about membership in the Laboratory, write Cornell Laboratory of Ornithology, Sapsucker Woods, Ithaca, New York 14850.

FOREWORD

No suburban garden is without birds or butterflies, but by imaginative planning you can easily double or triple their numbers. The environmentally oriented gardener can enjoy not only red, orange, yellow, and blue flowers, but also red, orange, yellow, and blue birds such as cardinals, orioles, goldfinches, and jays.

During the past twenty or thirty years birdwatching has become much more sophisticated. So has attracting birds to the house and garden. The state of the art has gone far beyond the window feeder, the wren box, and the birdbath. There have been a number of primers designed for the needs of the white-breasted nuthatch type of bird watcher, but this new book by Stephen Kress goes much further; it opens new vistas. It not only offers more imaginative ideas for making the suburban backyard a Mecca for the local birds, but it also extends coverage to the more expansive acreages of farms, roadsides, and even wild areas.

A recent survey by the U.S. Fish and Wildlife Service arrived at an estimate of more than half a billion dollars spent yearly by Americans for birdseed. I suspect that the figure might be closer to a billion. Although a few critics have questioned whether it is really helpful to the birds to feed them except in periods of stress, I need only point out that a number of species have vastly extended their ranges during the past half century because of our largesse. Cardinals and tufted titmice, formerly regarded as southern, now reside permanently as far north as southern Canada and have established themselves throughout much of New England. Because their winter survival has been enhanced by feeders, mourning doves now winter north to the Maritime Provinces. Evening grosbeaks apparently can recognize a feeding table at a great distance when their nomadic flocks move south-ward from the boreal forests during those years when their natural food supply is insufficient to support them. Virtually confined to the northwest in Audubon's day, they now nest east to New England. If attractive birds such as these have extended their ranges and have become more numerous, how can we say they have not benefited?

We have been cautioned that we should not start feeding birds in the fall or at the onset of winter if we plan a midwinter holiday. It is reasoned that the birds might suffer if their source of food is cut off. This advice is perhaps valid in some parts of the country, but where I live, in Connecticut, everyone up and down our road feeds birds, so if I discontinue for a couple of weeks in January or even for a month, my white-throats, chickadees, and jays will simply go to the neigh-bors—to Mr. Schulze's feeding tray, or to the Kennedys, who also feed birds.

I suspect that if I did not feed birds at all they would manage to survive; the reason I spend so much on hundreds of pounds of bird seed is that I enjoy watch-ing the birds, and the more the merrier. At my studio feeders are visible from both the north and south windows so I can watch the show while I work. At the main house other feeders, facing south and east, have become the dining room for a large company of white-throated sparrows. By careful manipulation of the forsythia I have given them a secure fortress which apparently is used as their social club, and by clumping the rhododendrons and other evergreen shrubs I have given them snug bedroom quarters.

On several occasions over the years a sharp-shinned hawk or a Cooper's hawk has attempted to dine on the diners, but the white-throats' impenetrable social club in the forsythia was their salvation. On the other hand I have known a red-shouldered hawk living near the Washington Cathedral to come regularly to a feeding tray for suet, forcing the chickadees to wait their turn.

My friend, the late Herbert Mills, even operated a feeding station specifically for hawks. He kept a large supply of moribund mice in his refrigerator for just that purpose. He told me that at his feeder in southern New Jersey it was possible to see several evening grosbeaks feeding on sunflower seeds at one end of the feeding board while a red-tailed hawk devoured a mouse at the other.

During the course of my travels I have seen many innovative devices for at-tracting birds that are not described in this book. In Switzerland I watched a man weave a decoy stork's nest in the hopes that it might lure a pair of prospecting storks to the roof of his chalet. With the same thing in mind, another workman was nailing together a platform on the nave of a nearby church. A month later, on an island off the Baltic coast of Finland, I was shown boxes resembling little dog kennels that were being used as nesting boxes by scoters.

Although square wooden platforms on poles are widely used by ospreys, es-pecially near my home in Connecticut, I was quite unprepared to see similar plat forms accepted by merlins in the Canadian arctic. Well known are the small floating platforms and even rubber tires that are anchored offshore in ponds or lakes so that loons and geese may nest unmolested by raccoons and foxes.

The creation and management of spoil islands, sand and shell dredged and dumped from the ship channels, has had incredible success in some states such as North Carolina and Texas in building up populations of colonial birds. But unless high storm tides sweep things clean once in awhile, such islands need management. Sand and shell soon give way to grass, then shrubs. If there are to be terns and black skimmers rather than herons and other long-legged waders, plant succession must be arrested. Choices must be made—terns or herons?

Even the roofs of factories, office buildings, supermarkets, and shopping centers can offer secure nesting places for a few beleaguered species such as nighthawks, least terns, and even skimmers. There is a hazard, however, on roofs covered with pea gravel—least terns making a scrape and getting down to the tar base run the risk of hard-boiled eggs! At Manchester, New Hampshire, a management study is under way to see what can be done to help the nighthawks that are still nesting on some of the office buildings. Rooftop management is a wide-open field for enterprising local clubs. Unfortunately our wood stork does not nest on buildings like its European relative.

The use of decoys was pioneered in Maine by the author of this book, first with puffins, then with common terns. Similar efforts have succeeded in inducing least terns and black skimmers to nest on selected sites along the Gulf coast and elsewhere.

There is no limit to the possibilities with decoys—including human. Let me explain. By erecting a scarecrow and putting the bird seed on its outstretched hand, many of the birds will not seem to know the difference when some days later you remove the scarecrow and substitute yourself in a sneaky sort of way.

Sometimes, quite unintentionally, birds may benefit from human activity in a larger way. In Toronto, when the subway system was being excavated, the earth was transported by dump truck to the edge of Lake Ontario where a long peninsula eventually formed. Initially about 70 pairs of ring-billed gulls took up residence on the sandspit. Today the number of ring-bills is close to 80,000 pairs, each of which raises an average of 2.3 chicks per nest. This means that by summer's end there are a third of a million birds. These multitudes of gulls give life and beauty not only to the Great Lakes but also to the beaches and bays along the entire Atlantic coast during the colder months.

Ring-bills can spot a McDonald's hamburger stand or any similar seaside eating place at the limit of gull vision. Near our home on the Connecticut River we have a very good restaurant called The Gull, the walls of which are adorned with paintings of gulls. I suggested to the management that they could have the real thing— live gulls hovering in front of the picture windows—if they would construct a long narrow box or ledge to hold waste scraps from the kitchen. It would give authenticity to the name of the restaurant. So far my idea has not been adopted.

There is no substitute for ingenuity and imagination. This manual will give you many ideas, but don't hesitate to try new ideas of your own. The birds will decide if they are valid.

Roger Tory Peterson

PREFACE

To some the term bird attraction brings to mind thoughts of feeding backyard land birds. In this book I interpret bird attraction in a much broader sense, based on the idea that the best way to attract birds is to enrich their habitats by improving vegetation, natural foods, water supplies, and nest sites.

When I first considered writing a book about attracting birds, I hesitated because there were already many good books on the topic. There seemed, however, to be a need for a comprehensive book that presented ideas for improving wildlife habitat on large properties, such as farms and estates, as well as backyards. There also was a need to offer ideas for attracting large birds as well as small and to compile many of the ingenious techniques that have proven useful for attracting birds as diverse as hawks, owls, loons, and terns. Finally, I set as my goal the objective of pulling together most of the vast literature about bird attraction from conservation agencies and bird clubs and to assemble ample source lists for plants and bird-attracting products. The pages that follow are my effort to accomplish this goal.

The publications about bird attracting and habitat management were collected from federal and state offices of the Cooperative Extension Service, Soil Conservation Service, Forest Service, and state wildlife agencies. Through a special news release I also requested innovative ideas for feeders, houses, and nuisance animal control from several hundred bird clubs in the United States and Canada.

The plant nursery appendix was compiled to determine dependable sources for often elusive bird-attracting plants.

I could not have written this book without the help and enthusiastic support of many people. I especially thank my wife, Evie, for her helpful comments, suggestions, and encouragement. The manuscript also profited greatly from the helpful comments of many colleagues at Cornell University and elsewhere. For their generous assistance, I thank Jane Bock, Daniel Decker, George Eickwort, Aelred D. Geis, Arthur Gingert, Gene Good, George Good, Daniel Gray, Peter Hyypio, John Kelly, Richard Malecki, Charles Smith, Sally Spofford, and Warren Stiles.

It is my pleasure to again work with Anne Senechal Faust, whose creative line drawings lend feeling and beauty to these pages. I also thank Diane DeLuca and Maryann Saphra for their help researching and compiling data and express my appreciation to Patti Farrell for her patience and great care in typing the manuscript. Finally, I thank all of those generous people who shared their innovative ideas for attracting birds. Space limits permitted me to include only a sample of the ideas received.

STEPHEN W. KRESS
Ithaca, New York

INTRODUCTION

Improving the quality of land for wildlife is the single most constructive step that anyone can take to assist wild bird populations. Happily, it is well within almost everyone's capabilities to improve bird habitats by managing for important food and cover plants. Such management is becoming vitally important because of the frightening loss of natural landscapes in North America.

Recent estimates predict that by the year 2000 approximately 3.5 million acres in the United States and Canada will be covered with pavement for highways and airports and an additional 19.7 million acres of now-undeveloped land will probably be converted to sprawling suburbia, an area equivalent to the states of New Hampshire, Vermont, Massachusetts, and Rhode Island.[1]

Even lands that are not lost to pavement and suburbia are becoming increasingly less attractive to many kinds of birds. The trend toward larger farms with fewer property lines has resulted in the loss of many brushy fencerows, farm woodlots, and wetlands. Such varied habitats are vital to maintaining abundant *and* varied bird populations. Trackless horizons of single crop plantings result in a similar monotony of bird life. In the same way suburban areas often replace natural habitats with sterile lawns and pavement, and since most bird species have minimum territory sizes, even remaining woodlands may no longer be suitable for nesting.

[1]H. Jackson. Testimony presented by Senator Henry Jackson (D, Wash.) in connection with Senate Bill 984. *Congressional Record* 121(36). 6 March 1975.

It is true that some species have clearly benefited by the changes man has brought to the land. Chimney swift, barn owl, and barn swallow even show their long association with human beings in their names, but these are largely incidental relationships in which birds have benefited without intentional management. More often, land developments from city and suburban planning to modern agriculture tend to simplify plant and animal communities, and this means fewer kinds of plants, birds, and other animals.

Expansive, close-cropped lawns, street plantings with the same kind of trees, and vast fields of grain without shrubby fencerows all have the same negative effect on wild bird populations. Monotonous plant communities lead to similarly monotonous bird populations. Air and water pollution further deplete bird numbers by stressing vegetation and thus reduce the variety of natural foods and nesting places available to birds. Some pollution, such as acid rain, may reduce plant and animal numbers hundreds of miles away from the pollution source.

The trend toward a monotonous landscape has already claimed several North American birds, but the toll on plants is even greater. In 1978 the Smithsonian Institution listed close to 10 percent of the 22,200 plant species native to the continental United States as being "endangered" or "threatened." The effects of human disturbance are even greater where human populations are concentrated in plant-rich areas. For example, such human activities as land development and the introduction of exotic plants now threaten or endanger 20 percent of the plant species found in California and 50 percent of Hawaii's native plants.

According to Peter H. Raven, director of the Missouri Botanical Garden, a disappearing plant can take with it ten to thirty dependent species of insects, higher animals, and even other plants. Clearly, protection and management of plant communities are essential if we are to also enjoy varied bird life.

In 1933, Charles Scribner's Sons published Aldo Leopold's *Game Management*. In the Preface of his now-classic work, Leopold observed, "The central thesis of game management is this: game can be restored by the *creative use of* the same tools which have heretofore destroyed it—axe, plow, cow, fire, and gun." Modern technology has verified Leopold's observation. Although we now have chain saws and bulldozers in addition to axes and plows, the motives of those who guide these powerful tools are still what determines whether they will work to replenish or extinguish wildlife.

The opportunity to increase or restore wild bird populations rests on the remarkable ability of most species to quickly replenish their numbers where they find good habitat. For example, in just four years with nothing slowing their increase in ideal habitat, one pair of northern bobwhites could increase to 500 birds. Obviously, such increases never happen, but understanding the reasons that keep them from happening is the basis of good management.

Habitat management is the key to any successful effort to increase wildlife numbers. The number of animals that can survive within any one piece of habitat is determined by one of several restrictions known as limiting factors. These commonly include food, cover, water, and nesting sites, but other factors such as parasites, predators, display areas, or singing posts may also limit populations. The challenge for anyone interested in increasing bird populations is to determine which of these factors keeps a given population from naturally increasing.

When attempting to solve this puzzle, it is important to realize that limiting factors change from one season to the next. Food may limit numbers in the winter but not in the summer. Likewise, cover may be sufficient in the summer but not in the winter. Providing more nesting cover and food may be useless if there is not an adequate supply of open water or suitable nest sites. As soon as one limiting factor is identifed and removed, another comes into play. If this one is then removed, the population will increase still further until something else limits growth. Eventually, such social factors as territoriality will limit bird numbers, but even territory size is not a fixed constraint, for most birds will compromise the size of their territory for quality habitat.

When human-induced changes create limiting factors such as destruction of nesting vegetation or introduction of a nest competitor such as the house sparrow, removal of the limiting factors may quickly result in the return of desired species. However, when *natural* limiting factors are removed, unforeseen and sometimes disastrous consequences may result. For example, limited supplies of natural foods once prevented Canada geese from staying more than a few weeks in the Horicon Marshes of Wisconsin before dispersing south to the Gulf coast. When artificial feeding removed this limit, overcrowding resulted, setting the stage for disease epidemics that threatened the geese and other water birds.

This book rests on the idea that bird populations will increase only when proper action is taken to remove limiting factors. Because the results of management efforts are often difficult to predict, careful planning and follow-up monitoring are essential. The chapters which follow are organized to help identify limits to growth and to offer techniques and resources for improving habitat. Habitat improvement through vegetation manipulation is often slow, but for those with patience and an interest in gardening, there will be a longer and sounder benefit than can be achieved by simply putting out food for birds.

The human presence has become so prevalent on earth that there are few places left where nature can completely take its own course. This is especially true in the cities and suburbs of North America. Without concerted efforts to improve and protect land for birds, there will continue to be loss of native birds at both the continental and local levels, as aggressive generalist species such as house sparrows, starlings, red-winged blackbirds, and herring gulls dominate habitats ecologically simplified by human activities.

Many environmental problems may seem beyond our daily grasp, but the tendency toward monotonous landscapes is something that any property owner can do something about. This book shows how to create and protect plant communities that provide food, cover, and nest sites for birds. Artificial nest boxes, platforms, and watering devices can also make a very real difference where nest sites or scarce water supplies prevent birds from occupying habitat that is otherwise suitable.

Birds brighten our lives with their song, color, and grace, but their well-being cannot be assumed. If we are to leave a heritage for future generations as rich as that which we know today, we must pursue a more active and responsible approach to conservation.

THE
AUDUBON SOCIETY GUIDE TO
ATTRACTING BIRDS

CHAPTER I

LANDSCAPING
FOR BIRDS

The following bird management projects meet the varied needs of wildlife for food, water, cover, and nest sites by fulfilling their demands with as much *variety* as possible. For the small-property owner, increasing vegetation variety usually means replacing expansive, close-cropped lawns with creative landscaping. If care is taken to select plants with high wildlife value and these are landscaped effectively, the result can be a property that is both easier to maintain and more alive with birds. Large-property owners, including farmers, have even more opportunities available for improving habitat for wild birds, and as the following projects suggest, improvements for wildlife can occur without losses in agricultural production. Regardless of property size, the same fundamental principle applies; increase bird variety by manipulating the succession and physical structure of vegetation.

MANAGEMENT PROJECTS

Start with an Inventory and Develop a Plan

Before you attempt to improve your land for birds, conduct an inventory to see which birds currently visit your property. List the kinds of birds, the numbers of each, and whether they breed on your property. Also include a list of your most conspicuous trees, shrubs, and weeds. Map the distribution of your plant communities to create a record of what your property looks like before your management efforts begin. Be sure to include property lines, buildings, wetlands, changes in slope, existing bird feeders, and houses.

With your inventory map complete, begin to plan on paper what changes you might accomplish to improve your property for wildlife. Your plan will depend largely on the size of your property and available finances, but it will also depend on which birds you hope to attract. The regional tables of recommended plants in Chapter II will prove useful in the early stages of your plan. From these you can decide which trees, shrubs, vines, and ground covers should be retained and encouraged and which should be replaced by bird-attracting plants. The structure of plant communities and their arrangement on your property are the keys to successful bird attracting through the seasons.

An inventory map is the first step toward improving land for wildlife.

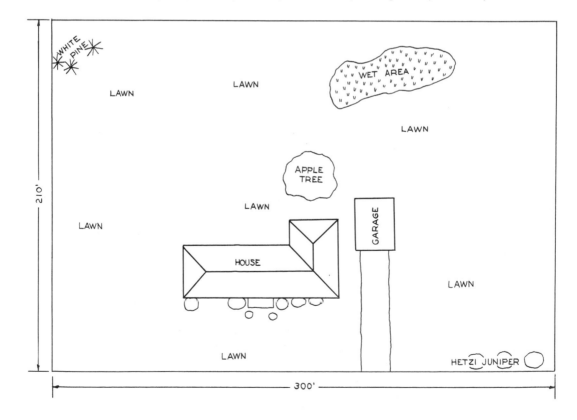

Optimizing Edge

Because of the abundant mix of food, cover, nest sites, perches, and other limiting factors, bird variety is greatest where two or more plant communities come together. This increase is known as edge effect.

Rapid-growing thicket communities frequently thrive at woodland borders, and these are especially high in fruit-producing shrubs and insect populations. Many thicket plants, such as mesquite, juniper, hawthorn, raspberries, and roses, have well-armed stems that deter browsing mammals such as deer and rabbits. Such prickly thickets also provide excellent predator-safe nesting places.

Shrubby edges (hedgerows) are especially important to wild birds because they provide shelter from the extremes of both winter and summer weather, nesting places, protection from such predators as hawks, and abundant foods in the form of insects and fruits throughout most of the year. Thicket-nesting birds and birds

A management plan that outlines the structure and arrangement of plant communities should be drawn up.

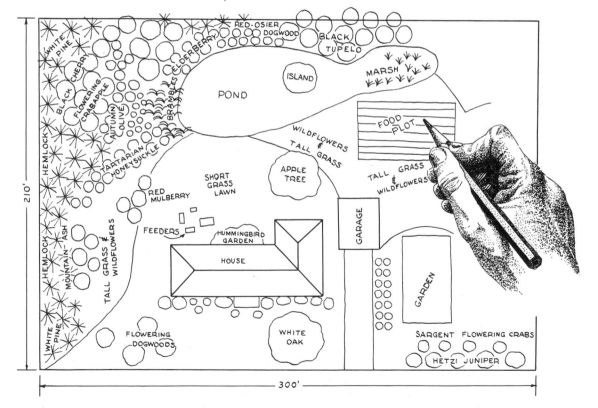

from adjoining habitats, such as meadows and forests, frequently find shelter and food in such hedgerows.

When planting shrubby borders, mix several shrub species to vary the shape and density for a greater selection of nest sites. Also select shrubs for your hedge that fruit at different times to better provide an ample food supply throughout the year.

Hedgerows are also useful for connecting separate woodlots and may increase movements of forest birds between otherwise isolated forest islands. An inexpensive, though slow, technique for developing a shrubby hedgerow is to till the soil where you want the hedge, then stretch a tight wire between posts. Birds will soon perch on the wire, and some will drop shrub seeds in their excrement. A hedgerow of bird favorites like juniper, hawthorn, and rose will eventually develop.

If there is wood cutting on your land, you can increase the proportion of edge and the number of junctions where two or more plant communities come together by adopting a cutting scheme that will permit harvesting of wood and will also maximize the amount of edge. A planned cutting scheme for a large woodland appears in the accompanying illustration. It is organized to maximize the number of junctions where three different areas come together. In this plan, each section is cut once every five years in rotation. The size of the sections depends on the amount of land available. A central strip planted as a food patch or herbaceous cover (grasses and legumes) provides both access to the various sections and additional edge.

The principle of maximizing the number of habitat junctions also applies to agricultural fields. When agricultural fields are laid out in squares, only one habitat junction usually results. In contrast, an area the same size could have as many as nine junctions between three different adjacent crop fields. Although such a plan would be more difficult to cultivate, careful matching of soils and drainage with selected crops may result in increased production of both crops and wildlife.

Maximize Vegetation Levels

Even within the same habitat, different birds show strong preferences for specific elevations in which they feed and nest. This is most apparent in forests, where some species such as tanagers and grosbeaks sing and feed in the canopy level but nest in the subcanopy. Other birds, such as chipping sparrows, may feed on the ground, nest in shrubs, and sing from the highest trees. Such movements suggest that a multileveled plan for wildlife plantings is especially important.

This principle is helpful in many different situations. Bird habitat in woodlots can be improved by planting shade-tolerant shrubs and vines at the bases of large trees to improve food supplies and nesting places. Isolated trees in pastures and

Shrubby hedgerows are one of the best ways to increase the variety of birds on your property. Upper diagram provides a vertical view of a hedgerow; lower diagram presents an aerial view.

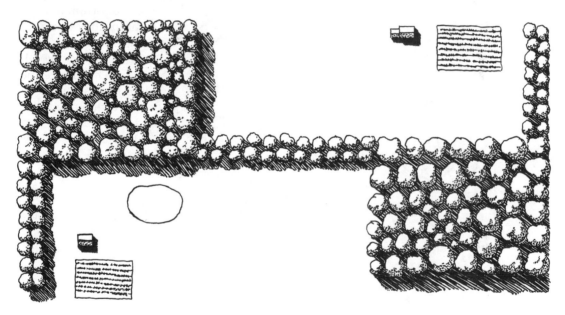

NATURAL WAY TO PLANT A MIXED HEDGE

A wire stretched across a tilled plot of land allows a natural hedgerow to develop from seeds that drop in bird excrement.

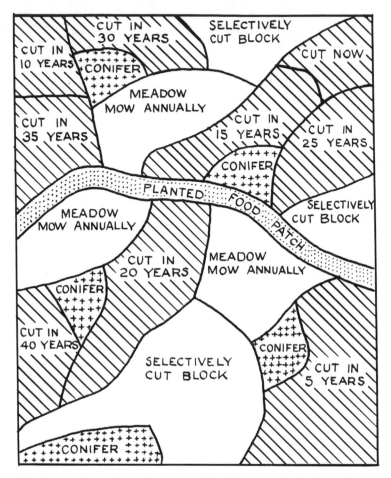

Cutting scheme for a large woodland to maximize junctions where three or more plant communities come together.

backyards will attract more birds if shrubs are planted at their bases, creating vegetation of varied heights. The same principle should be kept in mind when selecting border plantings for yards.

Where space permits, maximize vegetation levels and at the same time provide the most effective visual screening from neighboring properties. First plant the tallest trees such as pines and spruce; then in front of these, plant a bank of subcanopy-level trees such as dogwood or serviceberry, followed by a bank of tall shrubs such as autumn olive and honeysuckle. Further improvements in vegetation levels can be made by planting climbing vines, small shrubs, and ground cover.

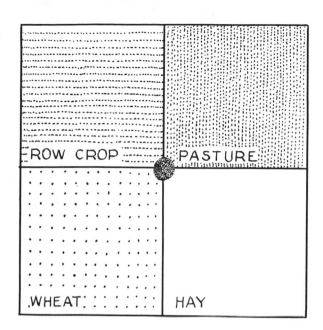

A creative crop-planting scheme (lower diagram) can greatly increase the number of habitat junctions found in a quartered plot of land (upper diagram).

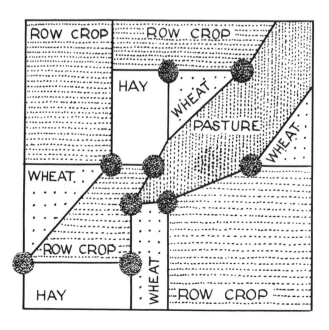

Tall conifers are best located to the rear of your property or to the northern property border so that they provide maximum shelter from winter winds without excessively shading other plantings. Deciduous trees planted on the south side of buildings provide cooling summer shade; in winter, the leafless trees permit warming sunlight to reach buildings.

Compromise Some Lawn for Mixed Ground Cover

A small central patch of well-cropped grassy lawn is useful for viewing backyard birds. Birds that feed and nest in surrounding shrubs and trees will venture out onto the lawn—especially if lured there with feeders, baths, and dusting areas. But lawn itself, especially expansive rolling fields of it, is one of the most destitute bird habitats on earth.

While some birds such as robins feed on earthworms and insects in grassy lawns, others, such as towhees, fox sparrow, and white-throated sparrow, prefer feeding among fallen leaves, where they can scratch and look for hidden insects. Such habitats, however, are too often missing from manicured suburban lawns. A good place to create the leaf-litter preferred by such birds is under shrubs and trees where grasses already have a difficult time growing. Avoid raking these areas clean and even extend them several feet in front of the shrubs. For color, plant bird-attracting flowers and add a border of flagstone or brick to neatly set this off as a managed area rather than out-of-control undergrowth. Enrich your leaf-litter areas each autumn by adding several inches of leaves. By spring they will decompose into rich soil with an abundance of earthworms and insects for ground-feeding spring migrants.

Even robins that so capably pull earthworms from lawns may suffer if lawns are the only feeding habitat available. In West Newton, Massachusetts, a community with spacious lawns and many planted trees around the houses, a recent study found that robins were not producing enough young to balance losses to the adult population. Although West Newton seemed to be ideal robin habitat, a closer examination found that the carefully groomed grounds around the homes had few brushy areas with little available leaf-litter. In April and May, the robins fed successfully in lawns, but in the drier months of June and July, when earthworms were not available in the lawns, the lack of moist leaf-litter among the carefully tended gardens and lawns left the robins with little alternate foods for their young.

Further variety in ground cover can be achieved by planting borders and patches of low-growing perennial plants, such as bearberry, coralberry, and small-leaved cotoneasters, that can compete with invading grasses and yet produce large quantities of bird foods. These plants are more useful to birds than some known ground covers such as Boston ivy, pachysandra, and periwinkle. Although these popular plants are effective alternatives to grasses (especially in shady areas), they provide little food for the wild birds.

The variety of birds will increase when different levels of vegetation are planted, as illustrated here.

A small property with varied plant habitats will help increase bird numbers and variety.

Close-cropped grass lawns make even less sense in dry or desert habitats. Groundcover plants and shrubs that are especially adapted for arid climates make both ecologic and economic common sense (see the section on mountains and deserts in Chapter II for recommended trees, shrubs, vines, and ground covers for arid habitats).

Changes in Slope

Ground-feeding birds such as sparrows, towhees, and wrens are attracted to abrupt changes in slope. In natural habitats birds frequently forage along stream banks, rock outcrops, and tree roots, as these habitats have a myriad of tiny crev-

Properties with expansive lawns and few foundation plantings offer little in the way of food or cover for birds.

ices and crannies in which to dig and probe for hiding insects, worms, and other small-animal life. Breaks in elevation can be used to good advantage when landscaping for birds.

On small properties, artificial changes in slopes can be created by building a gently sloping soil mound with a steep rock face or by creating rock gardens or stone walls. In northern habitats, the steep face of an artificial slope should face south so that the first spring thaw will reveal foraging places previously hidden by snow. On larger properties the opportunities for creating varied slopes are even greater, using a bulldozer rather than a shovel and wheelbarrow for landscaping tools. Here, miniature cliffs landscaped with ground cover, rotting logs, and shrubs will vary the terrain, creating warm south-facing slopes to attract

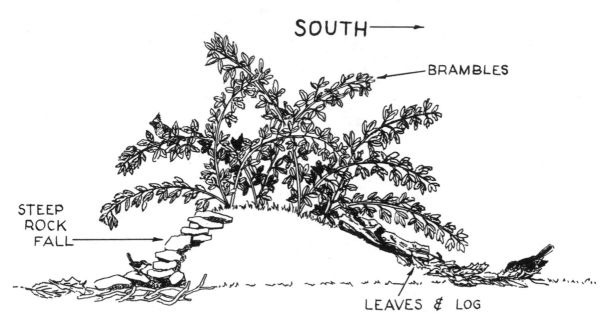

Even a small alteration in slope will help attract such ground-feeding birds as wrens and sparrows.

early spring migrants, and cool, north-facing slopes where summer birds may forage. Changes in slope combined with rock-faced water pools (see Chapter III) are especially attractive.

Dust Bathing

Many kinds of birds, including quail, pheasant, birds of prey, kinglets, and sparrows, enjoy taking a vigorous dust bath. Bathing movements in dust are remarkably like those in water, as birds fluff themselves up and flutter in the dust with their wings. The function of dusting is little understood, but it may help to rid the body of parasites such as feather lice.

This dusting area has attracted quail in search of a cleansing dust bath.

A dusting area is another way to attract birds into an open viewing space. Even small backyards can accommodate a square foot of dusting area. Where space permits, a dusting area 3 feet on each side will accommodate several birds at a time. Excavate soil to create a dust bath about 6 inches deep and line the edge with brick or rocks. To create a suitable dust mix, combine one-third each of sand, loam, and sifted ash.

Natural Food Patches

Wild plants such as ragweed, lamb's-quarter, amaranth, bristle grass, and panicgrass are among the most important wild bird foods. Weed seeds are so abundant that there is usually an ample supply available as soon as the ground is opened by tilling. An excellent way to favor growth of these plants is to establish a wild food patch. Depending on available space, this can be a 100- to 2000-foot-square patch of tilled soil or, if space permits, a rotating series of five strips that are plowed in different years in sequences such as 1–3–5–2–4 or 2–4–1–3–5. By repeating the sequence after the fifth year, the chance of shrub growth is eliminated and the rotation starts back to bare soil. Several long narrow patches are preferred over a single large patch because they will offer more edge. After three

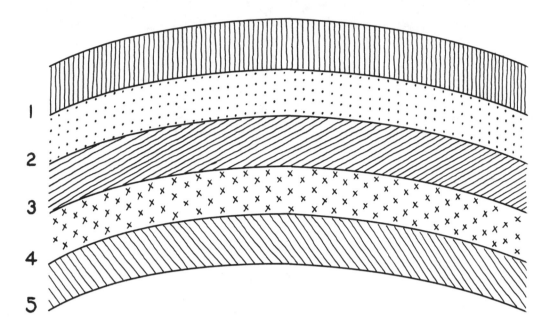

1
2
3
4
5

A five-strip natural food patch is a tilled area of soil where wildflowers and weeds are encouraged. Such plants are important food sources for wild birds.
Planted food patches are similar to giant bird feeders in that both provide concentrated supplies of food.

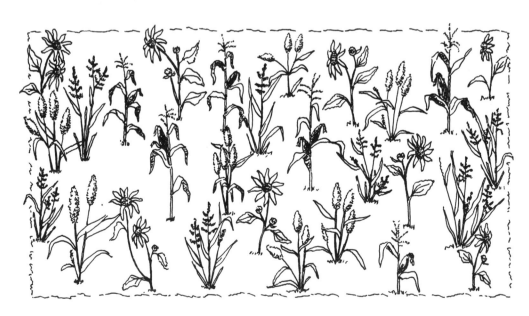

years, the pioneering annual weeds are usually replaced by goldenrod, aster, and perennial grasses. See the last two sections of Chapter II for descriptions of important bird weeds.

Planted Food Patches

Cultivated crops can provide abundant, concentrated food supplies for wild birds. They are also useful for attracting birds to preferred areas. Several small rectangular food patches within the 100- to 2000-foot-square range located near water or good cover are best. A useful goal for density of food patches is one half-acre food patch for every 20 acres of land. The simplest way to establish a food patch is to thoroughly till the soil and then broadcast a mixed bag of millet and sunflower bird seed over the soil. Just 15 pounds of millet and sunflower mix is enough to seed a half-acre plot.

Farmers and owners of other large properties may want to take on more ambitious food-patch planting programs using farm equipment and a wider range of cultivated crops. Sharecropping may be a useful way to establish cultivated food patches on your property without making a substantial investment in machinery, seed, and fertilizer. By this system a nearby farmer cultivates your land and leaves part of the crop standing in return for harvesting the remainder—it is a form of paying rent for use of your property. Under successful sharecropping agreements on Illinois public wildlife lands, sharecroppers were even restricted from plowing corn stubble in the fall and from using herbicides and insecticides.

Most of the cultivated plants listed in the following table for the northeast can also be planted elsewhere in the United States and Canada. Crop mixtures will attract the greatest variety of birds. If it is necessary to cultivate sloping soils, be sure to plant rows with the contour of the slope to reduce erosion. The following tables also recommend additional cultivated plants for the southeastern United States, prairies, plains, western states, and the Canadian provinces. Be sure to check with your county office of the Soil Conservation Service or Cooperative Extension Service to determine planting dates, fertilizer requirements, and specific varieties best adapted to your local conditions.

Food patches should be used as a supplement to natural food supplies from native plant communities such as meadows, thickets, and forests. As with bird feeders and other supplementary food supplies, they are expensive annual investments. The best long-term way to provide dependable sustained food supplies is by maintaining established food-rich plant communities.

CULTIVATED FOOD PATCHES FOR THE NORTHEAST

Crops	Site Requirements*	Sowing Method	Per Acre	Availability Fall	Winter	Birds or Animals Attracted
Buckwheat	Treat with lime and fertilizer as required for local cultivated crops. Plant in 1/8- to 1/2-acre plots, well-drained, with abundant light near good cover	Broadcast	50 lb.	Fair	Poor	Waterfowl, mourning doves, pheasant, quail, Hungarian partridge. Wilts with first frost
Clover, White Clover, Red Alfalfa Trefoil	"	Broadcast on fitted soil; most successful after a rain	2–4 lb. 8–10 lb. 12–20 lb. 5 lb.	Good	Poor	All wildlife; especially good for ruffed grouse, deer, and rabbits
Common Millet	"	Broadcast and light harrow	20 lb.	Fair	None	Songbirds, waterfowl
Corn	"	Rows 3 ft. apart; cultivation at least twice	7 lb.	Good	Good	Pheasant, quail, Hungarian partridge, mourning doves, turkey, deer, raccoon, squirrel, and songbirds
Early Amber Sorghum (milo)	"	Rows 3 ft. apart; sow sparsely	6 lb.	Good (late)	Fair	Quail, pheasant, turkey, and songbirds
Oats	"	Rows 7 in. apart; sow in fall	2 1/2 bu.	Good	Poor	Pheasant, turkey, mourning doves, songbirds, deer
Rye	"	Broadcast in fall	60 lb.	Good	None	Deer, pheasant, quail
Soybeans	"	Rows 2 1/2 ft. apart	50 lb.	Fair	Good	Pheasant, quail, rabbits, deer, mourning doves
Sunflower	"	Rows 3 ft. apart or broadcast	5 lb.	Good	None	Songbirds, pheasant, quail
Wheat	"	Rows 7 in. apart; sow in fall	60 lbs.	Good	Poor	Mourning doves, Hungarian partridge, pheasant, quail, turkey, songbirds, rabbits

CULTIVATED FOOD PATCHES FOR THE NORTHEAST *(cont.)*

Crops	Site Requirements*	Sowing Method	Per Acre	Availability Fall	Winter	Birds or Animals Attracted
Wild Rice	Good soils necessary. Wet soils and soft mud flats, water depth under 3 in.	Broadcast in fall or early spring	2 bu.	Good	Poor	Waterfowl, songbirds, most other wildlife
Corn-Buckwheat Mixture	Same as individual planting. Cultivate twice	Rows 3 ft. apart; broadcast buckwheat after second cultivation	7 lb. corn 30 lb. buckwheat	Good	Good	Pheasant, quail, Hungarian partridge, mourning doves, turkey, deer, raccoon, squirrel, songbirds
Corn-Soybean Mixture	Same as individual planting. Cultivate	Rows 3 ft. apart	4 lb. corn 25 lb. soybeans	Good	Good	Pheasant, quail, Hungarian partridge, mourning doves, turkey, songbirds, deer, rabbits, raccoon, squirrel
Sorghum-Sunflower Mixture	Same as individual planting	Rows 3 ft. apart or broadcast	5 lb. sorghum 3 lb. sunflower	Good	Fair	Quail, pheasant, turkey, songbirds

Source: Adapted from D.J. Decker and J.W. Kelley, *Enhancement of Wildlife Habitat on Private Lands* (undated, Ithaca, N.Y.).

*Planting dates and fertilizer and lime requirements vary depending on latitude and soil conditions within the northeast region. Check with your county office of the Soil Conservation Service, Cooperative Extension Service, or state/provincial wildlife department for planting specifications in your area.

Food Plots for the Southeast

In order of importance, corn, rice, wheat, and oats have the greatest value for feeding wildlife in the southeast region. These and all of the cultivated plants listed for the northeast region can be grown in the southeastern states. See page 18 for cultivation details. In addition to these, the following cultivated plants also provide important wildlife food in the southeast. Check with your county office of the Soil Conservation Service or Cooperative Extension Service to determine planting dates and fertilizer requirements.

CULTIVATED PLANTS THAT PROVIDE IMPORTANT WILDLIFE FOOD IN SOUTHEAST

Crops	Pure stand Seeding Rates/Acre*	Birds or Animals Attracted
Chufa	40 lb.	Nine species of waterfowl, ground dove, and seven species of songbirds; quail
Cowpeas	30 lb.	Quail and mourning dove
Common lespedeza	25 lb.	Quail; occasionally wild turkey
Korean lespedeza	25 lb.	Quail; occasionally wild turkey
Sericea lespedeza	30 lb.	Quail; occasionally wild turkey
Browntop millet	8 lb.; 30-in. rows 30 lb.; broadcast	Quail, dove, and many songbirds
Dove Proso	8 lb.; 36-in. rows 20 lb.; broadcast	Mourning dove, quail, and many songbirds
Partridge pea	16 lb.	Quail
Sorghum-sudan hybrids (milo)	20 lb.	Mallard ducks, doves and wild turkey

*Seeding rates are from Alabama Habitat Management Guide No. AL-6. 1975. Soil Conservation Service.

Food Plots for the Prairies and Plains

Important cultivated plants listed in order of their use by wildlife in the prairie region are corn, sunflower, wheat, oats, sorghum, alfalfa, and barley. These and all of the cultivated plants listed for the northeast region can be grown in food plots for prairie region wildlife. See page 16 for cultivation methods. Your county office of the Soil Conservation Service or Cooperative Extension Service can provide recommendations for specific varieties best adapted for your local conditions.

Food Plots for Western States and Provinces

Important cultivated crops for food plots include wheat, oats, corn, sorghum, barley, and alfalfa. Cultivate these using the methods for northeastern cultivated crops. In addition, the plants in the following chart will provide useful supplemental food. Check with your local Soil Conservation Service office to determine fertilizer requirements for your vicinity.

SOME SUGGESTED PLANTS FOR WESTERN FOOD PLOTS

Name	Establishment/ management	Birds or Animals Attracted
Barnyard grass (wild millet) (*Echinochloa crus-galli*)	Disk and harrow before seeding. Broadcast or drill 20 lb. seed/a. onto wet mud	Mourning dove, quail, ducks, geese, pheasant, and many seed-eating songbirds
Bristle grass (foxtail millet) (*Setaria italica*)	Plant seed by drilling into well-prepared seedbed at the rate of 20 lb./a.	Most song- and game birds
Buckwheats (*Fagopyrum esculentum*) (*Fagopyrum tataricum*)	Broadcast or drill seed on well-prepared seedbed at 30–40 lb./a. Flood with 1–15 in. of water for ducks. After 90 days under water, about 35% of seed deteriorates	Juncos, purple finch, evening grosbeak, wild turkey, mourning doves, and many other landbirds; also dabbling ducks
Delar small burnet (*Sanguisorba minor*)	Mix 2–3 lb./a. with other seed or plant 11 lb./a. for pure stand. Plant by broadcast or drilling. Plants will readily self-sow. Grows well on strip-mined and other poor soils	Many game and nongame birds readily consume the seed.

SOME SUGGESTED PLANTS FOR WESTERN FOOD PLOTS*(cont.)*

Name	Establishment/ management	Birds or Animals Attracted
Japanese barnyard millet (*Echinochloa crus-galli* var. *frumentacea*)	Plant 20–30 lb./a. in May or June. Disk and harrow before seeding. Broadcast or drill seed no more than ¼ in. deep. Flood 1–18 in. for ducks	Mourning dove, California quail, ducks, geese, and nongame, seed-eating landbirds
Proso millet (Broomcorn panic) (*Panicum miliaceum*)	Plant 20 lb./a. in late spring. Prepare soil by plowing or disking. Allow 80 days from seeding to maturity. Flood with 10–15 in. of water for ducks.	Upland game birds and such nongame, seed-eating birds as sparrows
Smartweed (*Polygonum lapathifolium*)	Plant 10 lb./a., covering the seed ½ in. deep from late spring to early summer. Flood from 1–15 in. deep for waterfowl, but plant is not well adapted to extreme alkaline or saline soils	Waterfowl
Bird's-foot trefoil (*Lotus corniculatus*)	Plant 3 lb./a. mixed with grass (such as orchard grass, timothy, or foxtail). Plant by drilling ¼ in. deep in early spring. Creates green, year-round ground cover, and blooms profusely with yellow or red flowers	Canada goose
Tall wheatgrass (*Agropyron elongatum*)	Plant 8 lb./a. Provide light irrigation every 2–3 days. To obtain increased height, plant in wide-spaced rows and cultivate the first year. The best grass for saline or alkaline soils	Upland game birds

Garden Flowers for Songbirds

The seeds of many garden flowers are useful additions to wild bird diets. When selecting flowers for your garden, keep birds in mind and choose some of their favorites. Most of the following garden flowers will grow in moist summer gardens throughout North America. The majority belong to the sunflower family, which helps to explain their attractiveness to songbirds such as goldfinch and native sparrows. Most require an open, sunlit area. For best results fertilize once a month with 1–2 pounds of general-purpose fertilizer per 100 square feet. Water, but don't soak, and use mulch to retain soil moisture and minimize competing weeds. Be sure to let flower heads go to seed for fall and winter food.

BIRD-ATTRACTING GARDEN FLOWERS FOR NORTH AMERICAN SUMMER GARDENS

Asters (*Aster spp.**)
Bachelor's buttons (*Centaurea hirta*);
‡Basket flower (*Centaurea americana*)
Blessed thistle (*Carduus benedictus*)
Calendula (*Calendula officinalis*)
California poppy (*Eschscholzia californica*); choice seed for doves
Campanula (bluebells) (*Campanula spp.*)
China aster (*Callistephus chinensis*)
Chrysanthemum (*Chrysanthemum spp.*)
Coneflowers (*Rudbeckia spp.*) (includes black-eyed Susan)
‡Coreopsis (*Coreopsis spp.*)
Cornflower (*Centaurea cyanus*)
Cosmos (*Cosmos spp.*)
‡Dayflowers (*Commelina spp.*)
Dusty miller (*Centaurea cineraria*)
Love-lies-bleeding (*Amaranthus caudatus*)
Marigolds (*Tagetes spp.*)
Phlox (*Phlox spp.*), especially (*P. drummondii*)
Portulaca (*Portulaca spp.*), especially moss rose (*P. grandiflora*)
Prince's feather (*Celosia cristata*)
Prince's plumes (*Celosia plumosa*)
Rock purslane (*Calandrinia spp.*)
‡Royal sweet sultan (*Centaurea imperialis*)
Silene (*Silene spp.*)
Sunflower (*Helianthus annuus*); seeds eaten by at least 42 bird species
Sweet scabious (*Scabiosa atropurpurea*)
Tarweed (*Madin elegans*)
Verbena (*Verbena hybrida*)
Zinnia (*Zinnia elegans*)

*Abbreviation means that several species are available.
‡Tolerates light shade.

Goldfinches and other seed-eating birds will feed on the mature seeds of zinnia, marigold, and other garden flowers.

Hummingbird Gardens

In the eastern states and provinces, the ruby-throated hummingbird is essentially the only hummingbird except for an occasional western or Caribbean stray, but sometimes twenty or more ruby-throats will frequent the same food patch, working it carefully for nectar and insects. Hummingbirds are much more common in the western and especially the southwestern states. At least fourteen species occur occasionally in this region and some are regular throughout the year.

To attract hummingbirds to your property, plant flower gardens that have bright-colored tubular flowers. In general, orange and red flowers are the most frequently visited, but hummingbirds will also occasionally visit yellow, pink, purple, and even blue flowers. Some trees and vines are also useful for attracting hummingbirds. You should plant flowers in large clumps of similar species to make the most conspicuous display, and select species that will provide a continuous flower display from spring to fall.

An excellent planting design is based on the concept of layered vegetation. Build a cascade of hummingbird-attractive plants on the side of your home by securing a trellis to a wall, then planting trumpet or creeper vines or one of the climbing honeysuckles on the trellis. Layer such shrubs as bush fuschias and low flowering hummingbird herbs in front of the trellis. Or devote a circular patch of yard to your hummingbird garden. Plant tall hummingbird shrubs, such as trumpet honeysuckle, Siberian peashrub, or coralberry, in the center of the circle and ring this core with a colorful selection of hummingbird annuals or perennials from the following lists.

HUMMINGBIRD PLANTS FOR NORTHERN GARDENS

American columbine (*Aquilegia canadensis*); perennial herb
Bee balm (Oswego tea) (*Monarda didyma*); native perennial herb
Bugleweed (*Ajuga reptans*); creeping ornamental carpet
Butterfly milkweed (*Aesclepias tuberosa*); perennial; orange flowers also attract butterflies
Cardinal flower (*Lobelia cardinalis*); perennial herb; requires moist soil, partial shade
Columbine (*Aquilega canadensis*); perennial herb with orange-yellow flowers
Coralberry (*Symphoricarpos orbiculatus*); native shrub with attractive fruits
Dahlias (*Dahlaia spp.**); perennial herb
Four-o'clock (*Mirabilis jalapa*); perennial herb
Fuschias (*Fuscha spp.*); flowering shrub; hang in basket; also ornamental shrubs.
Gladiolus (*Gladiolus spp.*); "Flash" variety is 3–4 ft. tall and bright red
Hibiscus (*Hibiscis spp.*); flowering shrub, especially althaea (*H. syriacus*).
Hollyhocks (*Althea spp.*); perennial herb
Horse chestnut (*Aesculus hippocastanum*); introduced flowering tree
Jewelweeds (*Impatiens spp.*); wildflower; a hummingbird favorite
Larkspur (*Delphinium spp.*); perennial herb
Limber honeysuckle (*Lonicera divica*); shrubby vine
Madrone (*Arbutus menzilsii*); northwestern tree
Morning glory (*Ipomoea spp.*); annual vine
Manzanitas (*Arctostaphylos spp.*); northwestern shrub
Nasturtiums (*Tropalolum majus*); annual herb
Ohio buckeye (*Aesculus glabra*); native flowering tree
Orange honeysuckle (*Lonicera ciliosa*); northwestern shrub
Paintbrushes (*Castilleja spp.*); annual and perennial herbs
Petunias (*Petunia spp.*); annual herb
Phlox (*Phlox spp.*); perennial herb
Evening primrose (*Oenothera spp.*); perennial wildflower
Sage (*Salvia spp.*), especially red garden (*S. officinalis rubriflora*) and scarlet (*S. splendens*)
Siberian pea tree (*Caragana arborescens*); very winter-hardy; introduced shrub
Tiger lily (*Lillium tigrinum*); perennial herb
Trumpet honeysuckle (*Lonicera sempervirens*); twining shrub; flowers March–July
Trumpet vine (*Campsis radicans*); native vine
Zinnia (*Zinnia elegans*); annual herb

*Abbreviation means that several species are available.

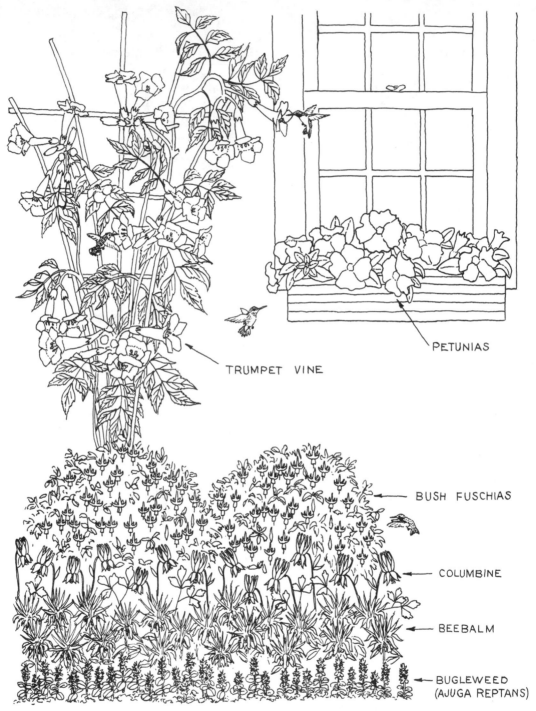

PETUNIAS

TRUMPET VINE

BUSH FUSCHIAS

COLUMBINE

BEEBALM

BUGLEWEED
(AJUGA REPTANS)

Multilevel hummingbird gardens, based on the concept of layered vegetation, are a colorful way to attract many hummingbirds to a small area.

ADDITIONAL HUMMINGBIRD PLANTS FOR SOUTHERN GARDENS

Birds-of-paradise bush (*Poinciana gilliesii*); evergreen shrub; clustered yellow flowers (zones 8–10)

Citrus tree (*Citris spp.*); orange, grapefruit, and lemon tree

Coral bean (*Erythrinia spp.*); southwestern tree

Fire pink (*Silene virginiana*); bright red-flowered herb

Lemon bottlebrush (*Callistemon lanceolatus*); evergreen shrub, 6-in. red flowers (zones 9–10)

Mimosa tree (*Albizzia julibrissin*); introduced flowering tree with pink-to-lilac flowers

Red buckeye (*Aesculus pavia*); small native tree of the southeastern United States with bright red flowers

Scarlet gila (*Gila aggregata*); excellent for southwest

Scarlet runner bean (*Phaseolus coccineus*); cultivated legume vine

Wiegala (*Wiegala spp*); deciduous shrubs with white, pink, or red tubular flowers

Conifer Plantations

A plantation of pine, hemlock, spruce, or other conifers in a corner of your yard or an odd area between agricultural fields adds pleasing variety to the landscape and benefits wild birds for several reasons. Some, such as crossbills, favor conifer seeds over all other foods. Conifers also provide excellent cover from both summer and winter temperature extremes and are favorite roosting and nesting places for owls. Look for regurgitated owl pellets and whitewashed tree trunks to locate favorite owl perches. You can improve conifer stands for birds by leaving or creating snags, by modifying tree branches into owl nest sites (see section on nest platforms in Chapter IV), and by installing artificial nest boxes for barred and screech owls (see about nest boxes in Chapter IV).

Conifer soils are usually too acidic for most understory and groundcover plants adapted to deciduous forest soils. Consequently, conifer plantations often have little layering and few birds inhabit the forest floor and subcanopy levels. Where light levels permit, plant or encourage bird-attracting, acid-tolerant shrubs, such as blueberry and huckleberry, and ground covers, such as bunchberry and bearberry.

Preserving Forest Interiors

Not long ago there was widespread opinion that the best thing one could do to improve large tracts of forest for birds was to create openings in the forest. While the technique remains a well-established and proven method for increasing the variety of birds in forested land, there is growing awareness that this prac-

Conifer plantations offer useful roosting and nesting habitats for owls.

tice may actually reduce populations of forest-interior specialists that require large tracts of forest for nesting.

Recent studies by Chandler Robbins and associates at Patuxent Wildlife Research Center for the U.S. Fish and Wildlife Service demonstrate that some forest birds, such as barred owl, red-shouldered hawk, red-eyed vireo, scarlet tanager, and ovenbird, require large tracts of continuous forest for nesting. Robbins found that in the heavily populated Baltimore–Washington, D.C., area, these species required at least 200 acres of unbroken forest. Smaller areas apparently did not include enough habitat or protection from predators and nest parasites. This and other similar studies throughout forested North America point to an alarming decline in forest-interior birds that appears to be linked to the increasing fragmentation and loss of woodlands caused by spreading suburbs.

The birds most sensitive to fragmented forest share the following characteristics: they migrate to tropical America annually; nest only in forest interiors; are primarily insectivorous; build open nests on or near the ground; have a low reproductive rate (usually one brood per year); and are relatively short-lived. A few examples of area-sensitive birds are worm-eating warbler, ovenbird, red-eyed vireo, scarlet tanager, and great-crested flycatcher.

While these and many other species have seriously declined in some areas since 1940, other birds have either maintained stable populations or have shown increases. Most landbirds with stable or increasing numbers usually show the following characteristics: they are resident or have short migration; inhabit the forest edge; have a varied diet; choose various nest sites; and have a high reproductive rate (often two or more broods a year). Some examples of birds in this group include most sparrows, catbird, mockingbird, robin, jay, crow, wren, and blackbird.

Although unbroken forest might seem to be a uniform habitat, it is actually a mosaic of slightly varied habitats, such as wet and dry forest and north and south slopes. There may also be changes in the age of adjoining woodland sections resulting from earlier disruptions such as storm blowdowns or fire. Forest birds may require more than one habitat in their nesting cycle. By decreasing the size of forests, fragmentation can reduce the variety of habitats within the forest and decrease opportunities for birds to move between different habitats. Unfortunately, so little is known about the patterns of movement within the forest that it is impossible to determine exact habitat requirements for most species.

Another problem that occurs in small fragmented forests is an increase in the number of nest predators and parasites. Fragmentation creates more edge and thus favors edge-nesting birds, such as blue jays and grackles, that will often prey on eggs and nestlings of other species when they have the opportunity. Since neotropical migrants usually nest on or near the ground in open, cup-shaped nests, they are especially vulnerable to such predation. Their nesting habits also make them vulnerable to nest parasitism from the brown-headed cowbird. Recent studies by Stanley Temple, of the University of Wisconsin, demonstrate that birds nesting near the forest edge are more frequently parasitized by cowbirds than those nesting in forest interiors.

Brown-headed cowbirds lay their eggs in other birds' nests and let foster parents, usually warblers, vireos, or sparrows, raise their young. Cowbirds lay a clutch of six or more eggs, usually depositing each egg in a different nest. After a few days, they begin to lay a second clutch and may lay as many as three or four clutches in a season, totaling 11–20 eggs. A single female cowbird may deposit eggs in as many as twenty other birds' nests, often throwing out the host's eggs as she goes. At least 121 other bird species have successfully reared brown-headed cowbird young. Many of these are forest-interior species, such as worm-eating warbler, Kentucky warbler, and red-eyed vireo. These species build open-cup nests on the ground or in low trees and thus are vulnerable to cowbird parasitism, as well as nest predation.

Fragmentation increases the amount of edge, favoring invasion of cowbirds and nest predators into the forest interior. Since most neotropical migrants have only one brood each year, one encounter with a nest predator or parasite will eliminate chances for reproduction for an entire year. To benefit area-sensitive forest birds, it is important to minimize fragmentation and to preserve forest interiors. This can be accomplished by preserving large unbroken tracts of forest—the larger the better. Where some forest must be cut, the remainder will be better

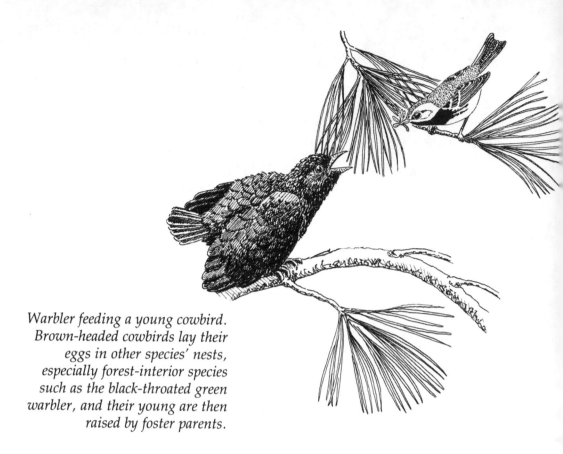

Warbler feeding a young cowbird. Brown-headed cowbirds lay their eggs in other species' nests, especially forest-interior species such as the black-throated green warbler, and their young are then raised by foster parents.

habitat for forest-interior birds if it is preserved in circular rather than oval shapes, as oval patterns greatly increase the amount of edge.

Creating Woodland Openings

Where woodlands are significantly larger than 200 acres, it may be possible to increase the number of edge-nesting birds without eliminating forest-interior species. This can be done by creating an occasional woodland opening. Such openings occur naturally every time a storm downs a large tree, disease kills a stand of spruce, or lightning starts a fire, but manmade openings can serve the same purpose. Openings provide more varied nest sites, increase the amount of fruit-bearing shrubs, and increase the size of insect populations. These conditions soon result in a greater variety of birds as edge species colonize the opening.

One useful technique for creating a forest opening and increasing food production is to select a large healthy forest specimen of cherry, hackberry, oak, or other fruiting tree. Measure the diameter of the tree in inches 4½ feet above the ground, multiply the diameter by three, and substitute feet for inches. This gives the side of a square that should have the selected tree in its center. Then remove all trees within the square except the central tree, making the borders irregular

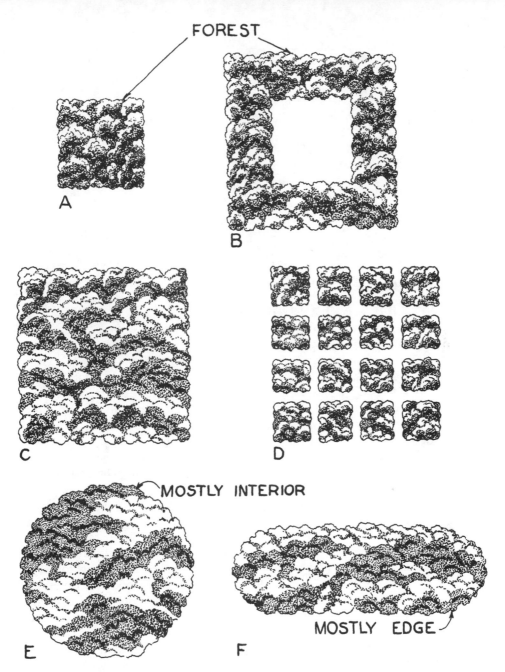

Forest patterns that minimize and favor forest-interior species. A, C, and E min-imize fragmentation of the forest interior, allowing stable nesting sites for forest-interior species and providing protection from predators. Patterns B, D, and F have far more edge and open up the forest to a greater variety of birds, which can lead to increased predation and brood parasitism by cowbirds. Block B covers four times the area of A but has the same amount of forest and three times the edge. Block D has four times the edge of C but covers the same area. Block F's oval pattern has more edge than E's circular shape but both have the same area.

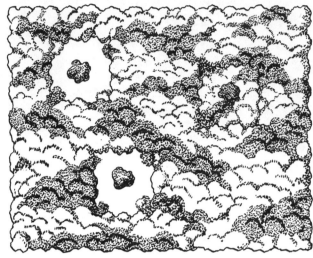

For woodlands more than 200 acres in size, occasional openings around fruit or mast trees can provide additional food and favor certain edge birds.

CREATING WOODLAND CLEARINGS

to give a more natural appearance to the opening. For example, if the central tree had a 20-inch diameter at 4½ feet and this were multiplied by three, you would get 60 inches. Change the 60 inches to 60 feet, and you would get an opening that measures 60 feet on a side. After clearing the area, fruit production on the central tree will increase and abundant shrubs will soon crowd into the sunlit opening. Preferred bird-attracting shrubs could be planted in the clearing to increase food production.

The decision to create woodland openings or preserve forest interiors is clearly a matter of deciding whether an increase in variety and abundance of species should be traded off against possible reductions in the populations of forest-interior birds. The decision to manage one group at the expense of another, and finding ways to preserve significant sized forests, are two of the most difficult challenges for forest managers until more is known about forest birds.

Managing Snags for Cavity-Nesting Birds

Naturally developing forests have a high proportion of dead or partially dead trees known as snags. Studies of upland forests show that 90 percent of the trees that reach an age of 20 years will die during the next 60 years. This abundance of snags gives cavity-nesting birds, ranging in size from the turkey vulture to the prothonotary warbler, ample choices for nesting and roosting.

The abundance of suitable snags has changed dramatically since colonial days. Clearing of vast forests eliminated old-age timber stands with high proportions of snags during the nineteenth century. Farmlands replaced forests throughout much of North America in the mid-1800s and early 1900s, a land use that no doubt greatly benefited open-country birds, including such cavity-nesting birds as tree swallows and bluebirds that nested in the tops of rotting wooden fence posts.

The regrowth of forest on old farmlands since about 1940 is providing vast forests once again, but most of this woodland is still too young to produce an abundance of old snags.

Removal of dead trees and snags is an unfortunate forestry practice. It is based on the assumption that dead trees may harbor tree diseases and that removal will make room for healthy trees. Fortunately, there is growing understanding that snags provide vital nest sites for woodpeckers and other cavity-nesting birds, most of which are insect-eaters.

Clear cutting, the removal of an entire block of forest, a widely practiced forestry harvest method, prevents the growth of large snags and thus contributes to a shortage of tree cavities. Although such cutting is usually followed by replanting, this practice leads to even-age growth with few snags. In contrast, selective cutting removes only choice lumber trees, leaving dead snags along with younger trees. Since the presence of insect-eating birds helps to keep forest insect populations in check, selective cutting is both good forestry and good wildlife management.

Many cavity nesters, such as woodpeckers, require more than one cavity for each nesting pair. If all conditions are ideal, a pair of woodpeckers uses only one cavity for nesting, but predators and such nest competitors as starlings may cause a cavity to become unsuitable and the pair may have to look for another nest site. In addition to the nesting cavity, a pair of woodpeckers also requires two additional roosting cavities where they spend the night (woodpeckers do not usually sleep together), and some have the habit of regularly changing their sleeping place—a behavior that probably reduces vulnerability to nocturnal predators. After leaving their nest, young woodpeckers require additional roosting cavities. In total then, a pair of woodpeckers requires *at least* four cavities during the year, one for nesting, two for adult roosts, and one more for roosting fledglings.

Tree cavities may occur when limbs break off and heartrot fungus invades the tree interior. More frequently, however, woodpeckers create tree cavities as they excavate insects and tunnel their nesting and roosting cavities. Preserving or creating ideal snags for woodpeckers is the best way to create nesting cavities for other birds, as woodpeckers are the principal developers of most nest cavities in trees.

Most woodpeckers do not usually use the same tree cavity for nesting more than once. This habit provides vacant nest sites for cavity nesters, such as bluebirds, nuthatches, screech owls, and many other secondary-cavity occupants that are not capable of excavating their own cavities. Such birds are dependent for homes on primary excavators, such as woodpeckers. Chickadees serve the useful function of enlarging woodpecker feeding holes into cavities large enough for their own use. Such small cavities may be enlarged later by titmice, wrens, swallows, flickers, and others until they become suitable for larger nesting birds. Mammals such as white-footed mice, flying squirrel, gray squirrel, and raccoon also help to enlarge tree cavities.

The numbers and variety of cavity-nesting birds are usually limited by the availability of suitable nesting and roosting sites in snags. When snags are removed from a forest, the number of cavity-nesting birds will soon decline. Since most cavity-nesting birds are insect-eaters, declines in such birds as woodpeckers, nuthatches, chickadees, and swallows can set the stage for outbreaks of destructive insects. Many foresters now recognize the value of cavity-nesting birds in suppressing population explosions of forest insects, and detailed studies are beginning to describe the nesting requirements of these birds.

In the northcentral and northeastern hardwood forests, the U.S. Forest Service recommends for each 20-acre woodlot preserving 4 to 5 snags over 18 inches dbh[1], 30 to 40 snags over 14 inches dbh, and 50 to 60 snags over 6 inches dbh.

To optimize the number of tree cavities in your woodlot, provide woodpeckers with an abundant supply of quality snags. The following table describes the characteristics of preferred nesting trees for nine eastern woodpeckers.

Generally, the bigger the snag the better for attracting cavity-nesting birds. Large snags, particularly those with large dbh, have more surface for excavation and hence can support a greater number and variety of cavity-nesting birds. Crowding may result when birds nest in small-diameter trees, and this may lead to reduced clutch size (number of eggs) and production of young.

Suitable trees for cavity excavation should have decayed heartwood (interior wood) at the appropriate height for a nest cavity. Trees with rotten heartwood are especially preferred by woodpeckers because of the ease of channeling out the soft wood. For woodpecker excavation a live tree that has rotten heartwood surrounded by a firm layer of living sapwood is ideal. Rotten heartwood makes such trees easy to excavate, and the tough sapwood provides excellent defense from predators such as raccoons that cannot usually enlarge such nest openings.

While many birds will nest in completely dead trees, these nests are especially vulnerable to predators. Least desirable for cavity nesters are trees that have only sapwood rot without heartwood rot. In such hard-cored trees, small woodpeckers such as downies must dig shallow, thin-walled nest cavities, thus exposing eggs and nestlings to both predators and temperature extremes.

Creating Tree Cavities and Snags

The most direct way to create tree cavities is to drill 2-inch-diameter holes into the heartwood. This makes an excellent beginning for a cavity excavator, such as a chickadee, especially if the heartwood is already rotten. You should drill entrance holes about 3 inches below stout limbs on leaning trees so that openings point about 10 degrees below horizontal and the downward position of the opening provides some protection from rain. This position may also be less conspicuous to predators.

[1]The trunk diameter at breast height measured 4.5 feet above soil surface.

CHARACTERISTICS OF PREFERRED NESTING TREES OF NINE EASTERN WOODPECKERS

Species	When using territory	Territory size (acres)	Minimum no. of snags used/pair	Average dbh of nest trees (in.)	Average height of nest trees (ft.)	Maximum pairs per 100 acres	Snags needed per 100 acres to maintain 100% of cavity nesters
Downy woodpecker	All year	10	4	8	20	10	400
Hairy woodpecker	All year	20	4	12	30	5	200
Pileated woodpecker	All year	175	4	22	60	0.6	24
Common flicker	Breeding	40	2	15	30	2.5	150
Red-bellied woodpecker	All year	15	4	18	40	6.7	270
Red-headed woodpecker	Breeding	10	2	20	40	10	200
Black-backed three-toed woodpecker	All year	75	4	15	30	1.3	52
Northern three-toed woodpecker	All year	75	4	14	30	1.3	52
Yellow-bellied sapsucker	Breeding	10	1	12	30	10	100

Adapted from K.E. Evans and R.N. Connor. "Snag Management." In Workshop Proceedings of Management of North Central and Northeastern Forests for Non-game Birds, U.S. Department of Agriculture, Forest Service publication GTR NC-51, 1979.

3-4"

CUT LIMB
ABOUT 6"
FROM TRUNK

3+"

6"

SAME SNAG
SEVERAL
YEARS LATER

A

B

DRILLED HOLES SHOULD
POINT 10° BELOW THE
HORIZONTAL. TO SPEED
CAVITY FORMATION,
INOCULATE WITH ROTTING
WOOD.

10°

C

Three techniques for creating artificial tree cavities: (A) Girdle the tree by cutting a 3–4-inch wide belt around the tree through the living tissue; (B) cut off a limb at least 3 inches in diameter, creating a stub 6 inches long; and (C) drill holes.

You can also start cavities in trees by selecting a limb at least 3 inches in diameter and cutting it off about 6 inches from the trunk. As the cut limb rots, the
tree will heal around the edges, but it will probably not close over the hole.

To create additional snags, select trees with at least a 12-inch dbh with minimum wildlife value and proceed to girdle enough trees to bring the snags per
acre up to the minimum for your forest type (see plant-selection tables for your
region to avoid important wildlife-attracting trees). To girdle a tree, simply use
an axe to remove a 3- to 4-inch band of bark around the entire circumference of
the tree. To kill the tree, the cut should go at least one inch below the bark. This
interrupts the flow of food and water between the roots and leaves. The tree will
die soon, but it will bring new life to the forest by increasing the population of
cavity-nesting birds and mammals.

Restoring Native Grasslands

Most of our natural grasslands have been replaced by cultivated fields and pastures. However, these once productive native grasslands can be locally restored
by planting the proper mix of grasses either as buffer strips edging shelterbelts
or as larger plantings. Grasslands are greatly improved by mixing in legume seed,
such as alfalfa and clover, to provide additional wildlife food and nitrogen for the
grasses. Some native prairie legumes and wildflowers are available commercially,
and these greatly enhance the already aesthetic value of native grasslands.

Little is known about the exact location of the former North American grasslands. Judging from annual rainfall, the principal factor limiting grass communities, and remnant habitats, the tallgrass prairies dominated roughly the eastern
third of the grasslands region. They graded into medium-height grasses and then
into the semiarid shortgrass plains that extended to the base of the Rocky Mountains. With these rough distributions in mind, select the height of grass mix that
is best adapted for your region. In the eastern prairie region, where rainfall is
more abundant, a mix of tall-, medium-, and shortgrass habitats can be established to provide more varied wildlife cover. Prescribed burning (every 5 to 10
years) and/or a planned grazing system is necessary to maintain the vigor of
seeded prairies and other grasslands.[2]

The following mixture of perennial grass and legume provides excellent cover
and food for ring-necked pheasant, short-eared owl, bobolink, meadowlark, and
other grassland birds. Based on your soil moisture, use the number of pounds of
all species above the double line for a *minimum* mixture. Any of the species listed

[2]For detailed techniques about establishing and maintaining prairie grasslands, see H. F.
Deubert, E. T. Jacobson, K. F. Higgins, and E. B. Podoll, "Establishment of Seeded Grasslands for Wildlife Habitat in the Prairie Pothole Region." Special Scientific Report—Wildlife No. 234. U.S. Fish and Wildlife Service, Washington, D.C., 1981. (Available from
Superintendent of Documents, U.S. Government Printing Office, Washington, DC
20402.)

below the double line can be added in the amounts shown to the minimum mixture.

PERENNIAL GRASS AND LEGUME MIX FOR EASTERN STATES AND PROVINCES

Species: Grasses and Legumes	Dry Soils (lb./a.)	Wet Soils (lb./a.)	Moist Soils (lb./a.)
Creeping red fescue	10		
Perennial ryegrass	4	4	
Reed canary grass		6	
Smooth bromegrass			4
Timothy			2
Alfalfa	4		8
Bird's-foot trefoil		5	5*
Red clover			4
Crown vetch			5‡
Sweet clover			12

*Substitute for alfalfa if desired.
‡Substitute for alfalfa if desired and if the soil pH is above 6.5 or if lime is being added.
Adapted from "Developing Odd Areas for Wildlife." U.S. Soil Conservation Service Publication J.S. 814, 1981.

RECOMMENDED MIXES OF NATIVE PERENNIAL GRASSES AND LEGUMES*

Tall Mixtures (3–6 ft.): grow best in eastern prairie states. They provide important roosting, loafing, and predator-escape cover for many grassland birds

Indian grass
Big bluestem
Sand bluestem
(sandy soils)
Prairie sand reed
(sandy soils)
Switch grass
Hairy vetch
Alfalfa
Sweet clover

Medium–height Mixtures (2–3 ft.): provide important nesting places for ring-necked pheasant, sharp-tailed grouse, and prairie chicken

Intermediate wheatgrass
Western wheatgrass
Little bluestem
Side oats grama
Alfalfa
Bird's-foot trefoil
Red clover

RECOMMENDED MIXES OF NATIVE PERENNIAL GRASSES AND LEGUMES* *(cont.)*

Short Mixtures (1–2 ft.): grow in both eastern prairie states and western plains states where water limits the growth of taller grasses. Shortgrass mixtures provide important cover and nest sites for such birds as meadow lark, quail, lark bunting, longspurs, and grassland sparrows	Wet Mixtures (3–6 ft.): will tolerate occasional flooding or sites that have wet soils (not frequent standing water). These grasses provide excellent cover at all seasons.
Blue gama	Reed canary grass
Buffalo grass	Indian grass
Kentucky bluegrass	Big bluestem
Red clover	Switch grass
White clover	Western wheatgrass
	Tall wheatgrass (alkaline soils)
	Red clover
	Alsike clover

*Contact your local office of the Cooperative Extension Service, Soil Conservation Service, or state/provincial wildlife department for details concerning the suitability of planting these grasses and legumes in your vicinity.

Brush Piles

Brush piles should be more than a heap of brush. Attention to building a useful foundation will greatly improve the value and life of the brush pile for both birds and mammals. Several approaches are commonly used to build brushpile foundations, but all rest on the need for animals to have a labyrinth of tunnels in which to hide from predators and gain shelter from weather extremes. You can create such tunnels by laying four 6-foot-long logs (4–8 inches in diameter) directly on the ground and then laying another four logs of similar length and diameter perpendicular to the first set. With branch stems pointing toward the ground, pile cut shrubs and pruned branches on top of the long foundation to make a peaked mound.

Another approach to building a foundation is to make three rock piles in a V formation or construct a brush pile over ceramic drainage tiles. Mound up large branches first and add smaller branches to the top of the pile.

Living shelters can be constructed from a conifer such as spruce or pine with well-formed lower branches. Construct a teepeelike shelter by slicing the underside of lower branches so that they fall to the ground, surrounding the tree trunk. Such shelters provide excellent cover for game birds such as grouse and quail. In

BASES FOR BRUSH PILES

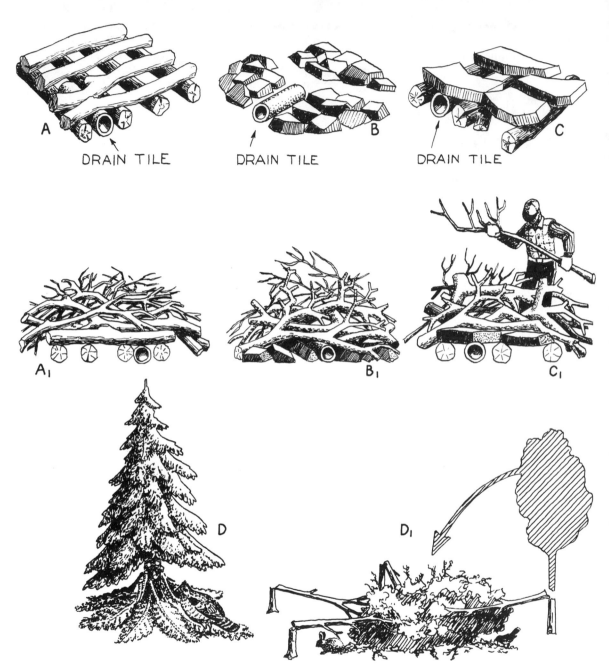

DRAIN TILE

DRAIN TILE

DRAIN TILE

A
B
C

A₁
B₁
C₁

D
D₁

A brush pile foundation should offer shelter to birds and other animals (A–C). On top of these foundations pile branches (A1–C1). A living shelter is formed by slicing off underside branches of a conifer (D) or felling trees (D1).

winter they also may serve as useful places to install supplemental grain feeding stations. If sufficient connecting bark is left intact, the branches may live in their new position for several years.

Windbreaks for Wildlife

In the windy prairie states and provinces, windbreaks (also called shelterbelts) are well recognized as an important technique for protecting crops, soils, buildings, and livestock from the impact of wind. The use of windbreaks, along with other soil conservation techniques, has greatly reduced losses to wind erosion since the dust bowls of the 1930s. By considering wildlife needs when constructing windbreaks, plantings can double as wind protection and useful wildlife habitat.

Although a two- or three-row windbreak will provide adequate shelter for crops and buildings, wildlife windbreaks should contain at least six rows. Where possible, they consist of up to eleven rows. Wide shelterbelts, with trees and shrubs of varying heights, can offer excellent cover and food for both birds and mammals on landscapes that otherwise could not support wildlife.

A six-row windbreak is approximately 60 feet wide and would cover 1.4 acres if it were 1000 feet long. An 11-row windbreak would be approximately 200 feet wide and would cover 4.6 acres if it were 1000 feet long. Such large amounts of agricultural land committed to wildlife windbreaks obviously means taking land from crop production, but the value of shelterbelts is so great that they usually more than pay for themselves. For example, a 1976 study in Nebraska found that agricultural lands adjacent to windbreaks produced an average of 55 bushels per acre, while unprotected cropland produced only 10 bushels per acre. The difference results from less water loss in the protected field and therefore greater water availability for crops. Windbreaks can also be money-makers by planting valuable hardwoods such as black walnut or adding a row of Christmas trees to the planting.

The ideal wildlife shelterbelt should contain a central row of tall conifers edged by deciduous trees, with both tall and small shrubs at the edges. The conifers provide seed crops and shelter from the extremes of both summer and winter weather, the deciduous trees provide food and nesting cavities, and the shrubs provide additional nest sites and often abundant fruit crops. Establishment of a row of herbaceous cover on the outside edges of the windbreak provides additional feeding and nesting habitat for pheasant, quail, and ground-feeding birds such as sparrows.

To establish a wildlife windbreak, plant large trees 10 feet apart, small trees 8 feet apart, and shrubs 6 feet apart. You should keep the following considerations in mind as you select and plant the trees and shrubs for your windbreak:

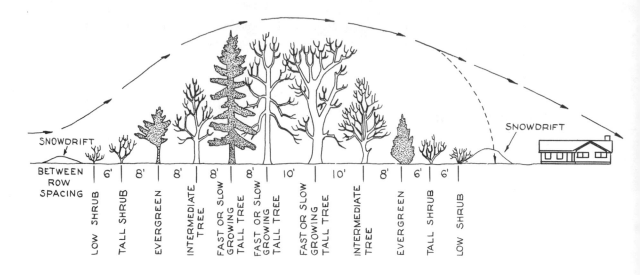

EVERGREEN TREE

DECIDUOUS (LEAFY) TREE

TALL SHRUB

SMALL SHRUB

LEGUMES AND GRASSES

1. Plant the tallest trees in the center and lowest shrubs on the outside.
2. Within each row, vary the kinds of trees and shrubs.
3. Select trees and shrubs that fruit at different times of the year.
4. Plant the conifers in a weaving row to give a more natural appearance and to avoid an open parklike appearance under the conifers.

5. Mix fast-growing and slow-growing trees and shrubs in the shelterbelt to provide cover in both the near and distant future.
6. Plant a 10–15-foot-wide buffer strip of perennial cover (grass, alfalfa, and clover) on the outside edge of the shelterbelt.
7. The length of windbreaks is even more important than width. Sacrifice some width to increase length if space is a limiting factor.
8. Erect fencing to exclude cattle and other livestock until windbreak plantings become well established.

In eastern states and provinces, damage from wind may not be as great a problem, but shelterbelts are still a valuable addition to agricultural land. In more protected areas, shrubby fencerows may provide adequate cover for wildlife and offer great benefit to cropland by increasing the number of insectivorous birds and predacious insects. These help reduce agricultural pests. A comparative study in Ohio found 32 times as many songbirds in brushy fencerows as in open cropland, and 60 times as many aphid-eating ladybird beetles as in sodded fencelines. To provide useful cover, brushy fencerows should be at least 10 feet wide and 150 feet long.

SOME BIRD-ATTRACTING WINDBREAK PLANTINGS FOR NORTHERN STATES AND PROVINCES*
(SOUTH DAKOTA AND POINTS NORTH)

Trees	Height (ft.)	Shrubs	Height (ft.)
Colorado blue spruce	80–100	Russian olive	10–20
White spruce	80–100	Chokecherry	6–20
Austrian pine	70–90	Siberian peashrub (*Caragana*)	8–12
Bur oak	70–80	Saskatoon serviceberry	6–12
Scotch pine	60–75	Scarlet	2–12
Green ash	30–50	Red-osier dogwood	4–8
Common hackberry	30–50	Silverberry	3–8
Black willow	30–40	Silver buffalo berry	3–7
Downy hawthorn	15–25	Snowberry	3–6
Amur maple	10–20	Common juniper	1–4

*See growth characteristics for prairie and plains trees and shrubs in Chapter II.

SOME BIRD-ATTRACTING WINDBREAK PLANTINGS FOR CENTRAL PRAIRIE AND PLAINS STATES* (FROM NEBRASKA SOUTH TO NORTHERN TEXAS)

Trees	Height (ft.)	Shrubs	Height (ft.)
Ponderosa pine	150–180	Russian olive	10–20
Black walnut	70–90	American cranberry viburnum	6–15
Bur oak	70–80	Tatarian honeysuckle	6–14
Eastern red cedar	40–50	Cardinal autumn olive	6–12
White mulberry	30–60	Skunkbush sumac	6–12
Common hackberry	30–50	Red-osier dogwood	4–8
Flowering crabapples	15–30	Silver buffalo berry	3–7
Hawthorns	15–25	Coralberry	2–5
Osage orange	10–50	Common juniper	1–4
Chokecherry	6–20	Prairie rose	1–2

*See growth characteristics for prairie and plains trees and shrubs in Chapter II.

No-till Cornfields

Fall plowing of cornfields is an agricultural trend intended to control infestations of corn borers and to eliminate the need for cultivating wet, spring soils. Following this technique, farmers plow under corn stubble in the fall to promote decomposition and recycling of nutrients in the stubble. However, fall plowing also dries out the soil and increases soil losses to wind erosion. The principal detriment to wildlife is that fall plowing turns under remnant corn and protective cover. Recent studies by the Indiana Natural History Survey found 448 more birds per square mile in cornstalk fields than in fall-plowed fields. Twenty-nine kinds of birds feed on discarded corn including eastern bluebird, cardinal, American robin, bobwhite quail, mourning dove, tufted titmouse, and ring-necked pheasant. In contrast, only nine species inhabited fall-plowed fields. Fall plowing also affects wintering hawk populations, as the number of meadow mice declines because of lack of food and cover.

Developing Unused Areas for Wildlife

Creative landscaping can turn unused areas in the backyard or back forty into productive wildlife habitat. In urban backyards options may be limited to secluded corners, but rural properties and farmland have many possibilities for

Corn stubble left standing over the winter provides vital cover and food for wildlife.

wildlife improvement, such a gullies, quarries, rock piles, corners of farm fields, pond margins, and abandoned roads. The first step in improving such areas is to select and establish wildlife-attracting vegetation (plant-characteristic tables for your region will help) and to plant this in clumped formation. Clumps of the same tree or shrub (five or more) are useful for several reasons. Plants of the same species are likely to fruit at the same time, thus making larger food supplies available and more conspicuous. Such plants as mulberry and American holly have both male and female plants, necessitating a close supply of pollen to ensure successful fruit sets. Also, planting at least five of each species provides some insurance that if one or two die, there will still be a few survivors. As space permits, plant unused areas with several different clumps of shrubs or trees selected to provide food at different seasons. Ideally, planting should provide food and cover throughout the year, which means including both evergreen and deciduous selections.

A circular clumped planting for an open area is illustrated here. Such plantings might surround a rock outcrop, eroded gully, or sinkhole. Position tall trees and shrubs in the middle of the circle and surround them with a border of low shrubs. A wildlife planting scheme using native wildlife plants for areas between pivot irrigators in prairie states and provinces is also shown.

Field border strips adapt the odd-area principle by planting useful strips of perennial grasses and legumes in such areas as woodland borders adjacent to cropland, borders of drainage ditches, margins between crop fields, and along pipelines and powerlines through woodlands. Using this technique, the farmer establishes a 15–30-foot-wide strip of grass and legume. Perennial grasses and legumes provide excellent cover and food in these otherwise unproductive areas. Rather than just strips of eroded soil or spindly crops, these odd areas can support meadowlark, song sparrow, pheasant, and quail, to name only a few.

WILDLIFE PLANTING FOR
AN OPEN AREA

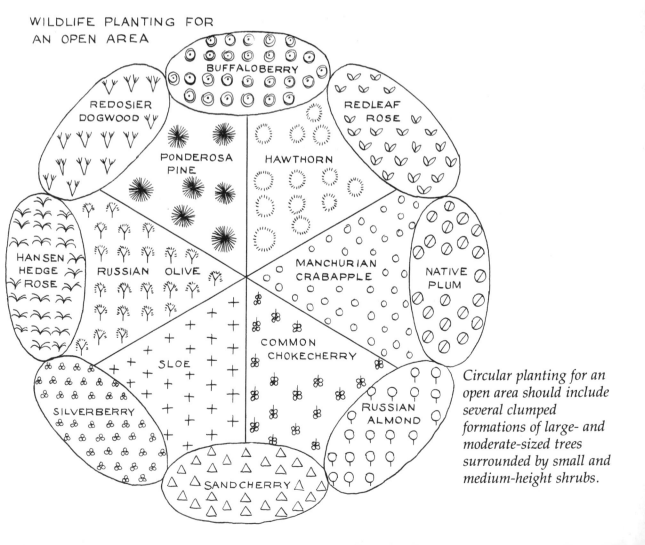

Circular planting for an open area should include several clumped formations of large- and moderate-sized trees surrounded by small and medium-height shrubs.

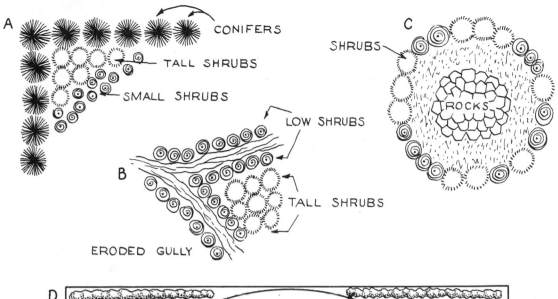

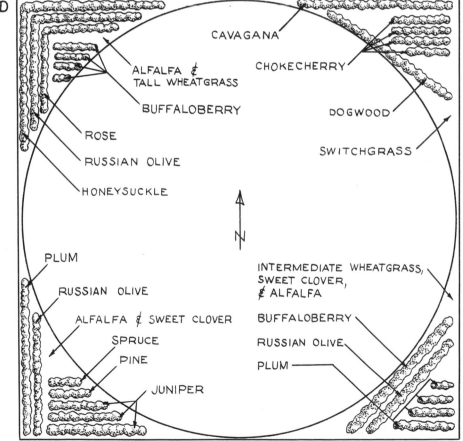

Odd areas, such as corners of fields (A), gullies (B), rock piles (C), and corners around pivot irrigators (D), can provide useful food and cover.

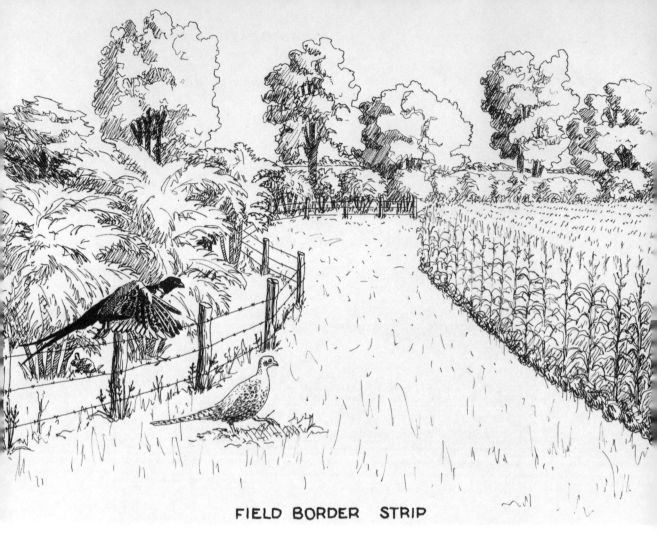

FIELD BORDER STRIP

The edges of an agricultural field can be a productive wildlife area when planted with grass and legumes.

Reviving Neglected Apple Trees

Throughout the northeast and Pacific coast regions, neglected apple trees are reminders of abandoned farmsteads and orchards. Long after they were abandoned, such apple trees continue to provide useful wildlife food crops, but shading from larger trees and competition from crowding shrubs greatly reduces the value of these useful bird-attracting trees. The fruit, seeds, and buds of apple trees are eaten by at least 28 different bird species and by almost as many kinds of mammals. Crabapples, hawthorns, and other fruit and nut trees are also important bird foods. As with the domestic apple, neglected, overgrown trees will usually benefit by the following techniques for improving fruit production and tree health.[3]

Step 1: Carefully examine the apple tree. Look for dead branches, diseased wood in the trunk, and the presence of more than one stem. If there is more than one stem, select the largest and most vigorous and remove the smaller competing stems by cutting them off as near the ground as possible. If the largest stem is badly diseased or broken, remove it and select the next largest, most vigorous stem for improvement.

Step 2: Remove all other shrubs and trees back to the drip line of the apple tree. If the tree is shaded by large overtopping trees, remove these on at least three sides, especially toward the south. Remove all the dead branches from the apple tree. Cut the branches off with pruning saw or pruning shears as close to the living branches as possible.

Step 3: Remove approximately one-third of the remaining live growth to open up thick clusters of branches. Clip off 1 to 2 feet from the ends of vigorous side branches of vertical sucker shoots. Do not remove the short spur branches that grow on the sides of larger branches because they bear fruit. If the tree is a young sapling with few side branches, the top may be cut off to encourage branching.

Step 4: Fertilize the tree by spreading a 10–10–10 fertilizer uniformly over the area covered by the tree. Apply 1 pound per inch of trunk diameter up to a maximum of 10 pounds per tree.

PLANTING TREES AND SHRUBS

You can buy bird-attracting trees and shrubs for your property from local retail nurseries or mail-order nurseries. You can also dig them up from nearby woods or fields where it is legal to do so. The most important factors are careful selection of plants that are likely to tolerate your climate and soil, careful preparation of the planting site, and care after planting. It is sometimes suggested that if you have only $20 for planting a tree, it is best to spend $1 for the tree and put the rest into preparing the site and maintaining it afterward, while the tree adjusts

[3]Adapted from "Care of Wild Apple Trees." New Hampshire Cooperative Extension Service, Folder 70.

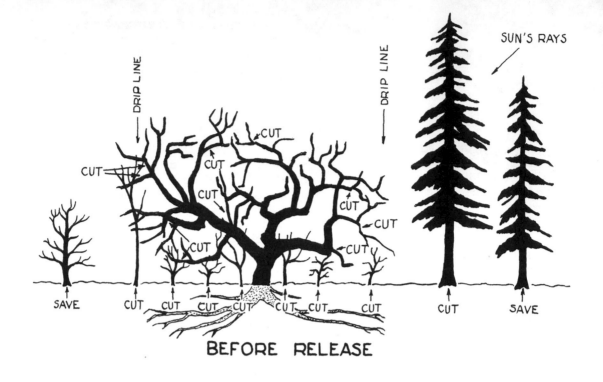

BEFORE RELEASE

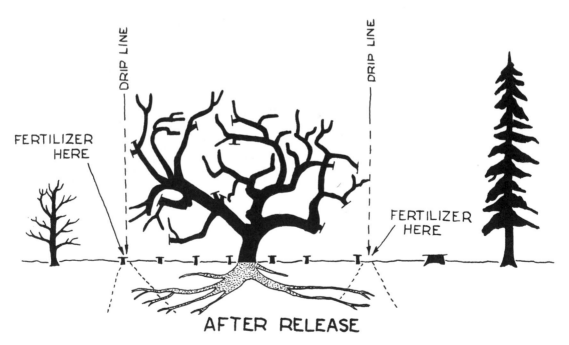

AFTER RELEASE

A neglected apple tree before (above) and after release from competition with nearby vegetation.

to its new location. This example may overstate the case, but it does emphasize the need for testing soil before planting, the need for great care in planting, and most important, the need for strict maintenance.

Transplanting Wild Trees and Shrubs

Wild trees and shrubs from nearby woods and thickets have the advantages of being inexpensive and hardy to your local climate. Wild plant stock may also be more resistant to insects and disease and well adapted to local soil conditions.

If done properly, moving wild trees and shrubs is not as simple as it might seem. First, you must get permission from a willing landowner; then the search begins for a suitable candidate for the transplant. Avoid overcollecting and re-moving rare plants that may be protected. It may take a long search to find a suitable tree or shrub for transplanting because many, if not most, wild plants have their roots and branches tangled with their neighbors'. Also, the main roots of wild plants may be few and widespread, making it difficult to transplant enough roots. To minimize these problems and give wild transplants the best chances for a long future, follow these five steps:

1. Make your selections for transplanting in early spring and plan to move the plants either the next winter or early the following spring. Select isolated trees (with no more than a 2-inch dbh) and shrubs. If a tree has a 2-inch dbh or a large shrub is involved, use a sharp spade to make an 8-inch-deep incision circling the tree approximately 2 feet from the trunk. If the tree has a 1-inch dbh or the shrub is small, the encircling cut should be only 1 foot from the trunk. This root-prune should be done in early spring so that roots will branch during the coming growing season, forming a less extensive but more compact and fibrous root system closer to the tree trunk or shrub crown. For larger plants, root pruning on one side in early spring and the other side later in the summer or the following spring will reduce the chances of shocking the plant. Do not disturb the tree after root pruning, and remove the branches from neighboring trees that may shade the tree or shrub.

2. Late in the following winter or early next spring, dig up the root-pruned plant by making a new trench about 6 inches farther from the trunk than your initial incision. Dig up as much soil as possible with the roots and wrap the root mass in burlap to protect the roots from desiccation. This is especially important for ever-greens.

3. As soon as possible after excavation, place the transplanted shrub at its new site. The depth of the prepared hole for the planting

should approximate the height of the root system and be twice as wide as the root span. Before placing the tree in the hole, check for adequate drainage by filling the excavation with water. If water remains in the hole 24 hours later, the soil is poorly drained and your transplant is likely to die unless it is a water-tolerant species (see plant characteristics tables). Sometimes the site can be improved by digging it at least another foot deeper and filling the bottom of the hole with gravel over a drain tile which allows removal of excess water from the site.

When you set the plant in the hole, take care to spread the roots in a natural way without bending or cramping. Position the plant so the roots are approximately at the same depth as they were at the site from which they were removed. Incorporate leaf mold or peat moss (1 part to 3 parts soil) into the soil used as backfill. You can also mix bone meal or one of the specialty, controlled-release fertilizers that are prepared for such use. Controlled-release fertilizers slowly release nutrients over an extended period of time, thus reducing the chances of fertilizer "hot pockets" that could damage new roots. Follow the directions for use of these products carefully.

Fill the hole three-fourths full with soil mixture and water thoroughly to eliminate pockets of air. Then fill the remainder of the hole with loose, unpacked soil. With extra soil or strips of sod, build a shallow rim around the excavation to help retain water. Water once a week thereafter if rainfall is not sufficient. You can

Two implements used for conserving water in arid habitats. The soaker hose (left) and water lance (right) both apply water directly to the tree's roots.

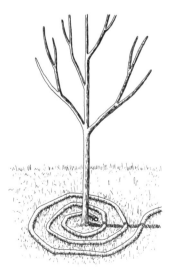 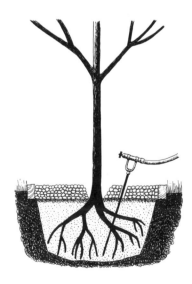

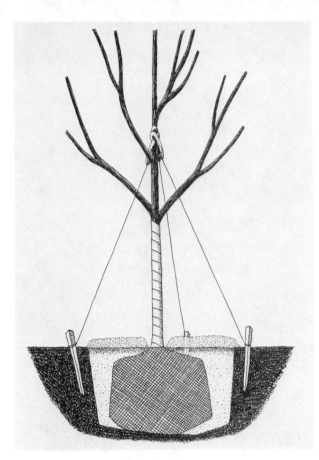

A staked wire support braces a newly transplanted tree against the threat of wind damage when planted in an exposed site. A guy protects the tree from improper settling and tilted posture by buttressing it against vibrating winds.

conserve water by using a canvas soaker hose or water lance that applies water directly to the roots and by spreading mulch over the planting hole.

4. After the transplant, remove approximately one-third of the branches by cutting with a sharp shears near the trunk or main branches. This pruning should be done so as not to destroy the natural shape of the plant. On fruiting trees, trim vertical branches, favoring a more spreading contour. When vertical branches are eliminated, sunlight can better reach the lower limbs, favoring production of abundant fruit crops.

   The main purpose of such pruning is to reduce the amount of leaves and stems and to bring this part of the plant in balance with the reduced root system. Without sufficient stem pruning, the reduced root system might not provide enough water for a full canopy of leaves during the transplant year and the plant may die of desiccation. Although pruning reduces the size of your transplant, it's good insurance for a healthy start and rapid growth the next year.

"Heeling in," or temporary planting in a shallow trench, protects bare-root trees before final planting.

5. The final step for protecting your transplants is to cover the base of the tree and watering basin with 3 or 4 inches of leaf mulch or straw. Mulches help to prevent desiccation during the summer and reduce competition from the weeds that will grow in the soil around your transplants and reduce available water and soil nutrients. Be sure to pull this mulch away during the winter to prevent mice from nesting near tree trunks and later gnawing the tender bark. Another useful precaution for newly transplanted trees is wrapping trunks with strips of heavy paper or burlap from one inch below the soil to the first branches. This will prevent sunscald bark damage—a common problem for many young and recently transplanted trees. If a new tree is in an exposed site, you can secure it against wind damage by guying it to a post or three nearby stakes. Guying also reduces wind vibration that disturbs the recently planted roots. Use sections of rubber hose to keep the guy wires from damaging the tree bark.

Competition from nearby tall grasses and herbaceous plants is a common problem for many young trees and shrubs. When planted in a spring meadow or thicket, competing vegetation may not seem a problem, but a month later, goldenrod and other annual growth may tower over small woody seedlings, seriously depleting light and water. To reduce such competition, cut away nearby vegetation several times during the growing season. Scalping—using a shovel to remove sod from a 2-foot-diameter circle around the planting hole—is another technique for minimizing competition from grass and weeds. Cover the scalped area with mulch.

Planting Bare-root Nursery Stock

Mail-order nurseries, state tree nurseries, and many local plant nurseries sell bare-root trees and shrubs that have usually been root-pruned and are often stem-pruned before shipping. Such plants are obviously easier to ship through the mails and are much less expensive than potted plants of the same size. Early spring is the best season to plant bare-root deciduous trees and shrubs. Summer is a stress period for many plants due to high evaporation, and in the fall there is not enough time for bare-root plantings to develop adequate winter root systems.

The chances for a successful transplant are high *if roots do not dry out*. Although most nurseries pack bare-root stock in wet peat moss before shipping, you must keep the roots moist until planting. Order plants from nearby nurseries whenever possible to increase your chances of receiving plant stock hardy to your local climate. When nursery stock arrives, check the roots carefully. If the roots appear dry, immediately soak them in water for several hours before planting. If it is too cold to plant when your order arrives, unpack the plants, sprinkle the tops and roots with water, and cover the roots with damp peat moss and a layer of burlap or canvas. Keep your plants in a cool but frost-free place until you can plant them. If the weather is warm, and you are not ready to plant, dig a shallow trench in a cool, moist area for a temporary planting called "heeling-in." Cut all strings and spread the plants out along the trench, taking care to bury all roots. Water thoroughly and tamp the soil firmly to reduce air pockets near the roots. Then be sure to keep the soil moist until you plant.

When planting, be certain to keep the roots moist. When placing bare-root trees and shrubs in their planting holes, spread the roots to avoid any kinking or twisting. This will minimize the risk of "girdling" roots later in the life of the tree. Follow steps 3 to 5 under "transplanting wild trees and shrubs" for planting bare-root plants where appropriate.

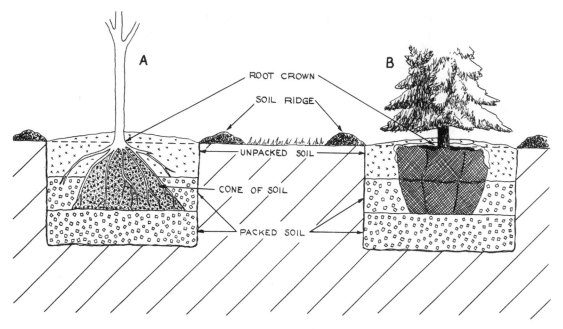

Soil profiles of bare-root tree (A) and balled and burlapped tree (B).

Planting Potted and Balled and Burlapped Trees and Shrubs

Local nurseries often have a good supply of trees and shrubs already potted or with root systems encased in soil secured with burlap. Such nursery-grown plants are usually more expensive than collected or bare-root plants, but they have been transplanted and root-pruned several times before they reach the local nursery. These plants usually develop excellent root systems near the trunk, a feature that gives a very high chance of surviving the rigors of the transplant process in either spring or fall plantings. To plant balled and burlapped plants, loosen the burlap at the trunk, but leave the burlap in place as you settle the plant into its hole. The burlap will soon rot away. If plastic burlap has been used to secure the ball, it should be removed carefully. Likewise, any synthetic cord used to secure the root ball should also be removed to prevent girdling.

Remove potted plants from their containers, and take care to cut through any roots that have wrapped themselves around the root mass. Encircling roots should be removed, and the soil around the roots should be disturbed to spread the roots. After placing the plants in their new holes, follow the same steps that were used to transplant wild trees and shrubs.

To determine whether mineral deficiencies exist in the soil, contact your local Cooperative Extension office or nursery to arrange for a soil test. Test results can be a useful guide for establishing a program for fertilization. Most local Cooperative Extension offices are prepared to provide fertilizer recommendations for use after plants are established.

Protecting Plantings from Rabbits, Mice, and Deer

In winter, when tender twigs, seeds, and other favorite foods are already eaten or buried under snow, mice, rabbits, and deer often turn to the tender bark of young trees and shrubs. To reduce the chances of mouse damage, pull straw mulch away from the trunks of new plantings in late fall. Where mice and rabbits are a known problem, wrap quarter-inch hardware cloth around the trunk at least 2 feet higher than the average winter snow line. Some nurseries also sell a heavy plastic that can be wrapped around young trees and shrubs for this purpose.

Deer are more difficult to keep away from plantings, because they become very bold at night, often browsing on expensive plantings in the suburbs. One technique for discouraging deer from eating foundation plantings is to spread dried blood, available from garden centers, and hair clippings from the barber around favorite plants. Apparently deer are cautious when they pick up the smell of other mammals and often avoid such areas. With this in mind, William, Mary, and Michael Deem of Bernardsville, New Jersey, have successfully discouraged deer from browsing their plantings by using beef suet streaked with red meat. They tie chunks of suet wrapped in cheesecloth to the top of stakes and place these in front of and behind shrubs that were previously damaged by deer. Their suet deer repellents also double as bird feeders.

Those who are really desperate from deer browsing may want to try the Tomko Timer-Clapper. This alarm makes a startling "clap" at variable intervals that scatters deer, starlings, and pigeons. For details write Tomko Enterprises, Inc., Route 58, RD#2, Box 937A, Riverhead, NY 11901.

CHAPTER II

SELECTING PLANTS FOR ATTRACTING BIRDS

Most of our knowledge of wild bird food habits comes from painstaking studies of stomach contents, studies conducted by the U.S. Fish and Wildlife Service and its predecessor, the U.S. Biological Survey. Not surprisingly, there is much more known about the food habits of ring-necked pheasant, bobwhite quail, and ruffed grouse than any other species, since the research of both federal and state wildlife agencies has historically been interested primarily in game species. Relatively little is known about the food habits of nongame birds and this is especially true for insect-eating birds such as warblers and flycatchers. There is even a question about whether purple martins really favor a diet of mosquitoes, since there has been no actual documentation. Certainly, there is much yet to learn about wild bird food preferences, and anyone with a pair of binoculars and a keen eye can make useful observations.

The tables that appear later in this chapter list plants that are well known or show promise as important food and cover for wild birds. They are included for the following reasons: to assist with inventories of existing vegetation to identify bird-attracting plants that should be protected or enhanced, and to provide lists of bird-attracting plants that could be planted to improve habitat quality for wild birds. For the purpose of this list, North America is divided into five major plant/animal regions: northeast, southeast, prairies and plains, mountains and deserts, and Pacific Coast. Each regional list is subdivided into three categories: preferred plants (those that show the greatest value for attracting birds); a repeat list of preferred plants that were described for another region; and other good choices (recommended plants with somewhat less or promising value).

Plant Names.   Common and Latin names follow *Hortus Third*, compiled by Liberty Hyde Bailey and Ethel Zoe Bailey, revised and expanded by the staff of the Liberty Hyde Bailey Hortorium (Macmillan, New York, 1976), or *Checklist of North American Plants for Wildlife Biologists*, by Thomas G. Scott and Clinton H. Wasser (The Wildlife Society, Washington, D.C., 1980).

Native vs. Alien.   Most of the recommended plants listed are native to North America. There are several good reasons for favoring natives when selecting plantings, the most important of which is that they have demonstrated their ability to survive in our climate and as such are already known to native birds. Alien (not native to North America) plants may be more susceptible to disease and could become pests if they escape cultivation (they inevitably will). Oriental bittersweet, Japanese honeysuckle, kudzu, and multiflora rose are all vivid examples of introduced species that have spread out of control in eastern North America. In the lists that follow, the recommended alien plants, such as Russian olive and white mulberry, have been cultivated successfully in North America for at least several decades without problems and have well-demonstrated value for attracting birds.

Height.   The heights given for recommended plants are either ranges of mature specimens or maximum height. However, even mature height can vary greatly depending upon such factors as available water, fertility, and exposure to wind. Plants growing in the northern plains, mountains, and deserts are especially influenced by these factors.

Zone.   Within each region, plant-hardiness zones suggest the northern distribution or limit to plant growth. The zone system used here follows the plant-hardiness zones established by the U.S. National Arboretum, Agricultural Service, U.S. Department of Agriculture, and the American Horticultural Society. The zones are based on 51 years of weather data used to chart average annual low temperatures. To identify appropriate bird plantings for your property, find your plant-hardiness zone and look for recommended plants within your home region. Remember that these zones are only estimates and that microclimate differences can account for as much as one or even two zone differences, even though the microclimates may be only a few miles or even feet apart. For example, it has been estimated that the north- and south-facing sides of the same home receive sunlight that may be the equivalent in microclimate of areas at least 300 miles apart. The south side of a home receives considerably more light than

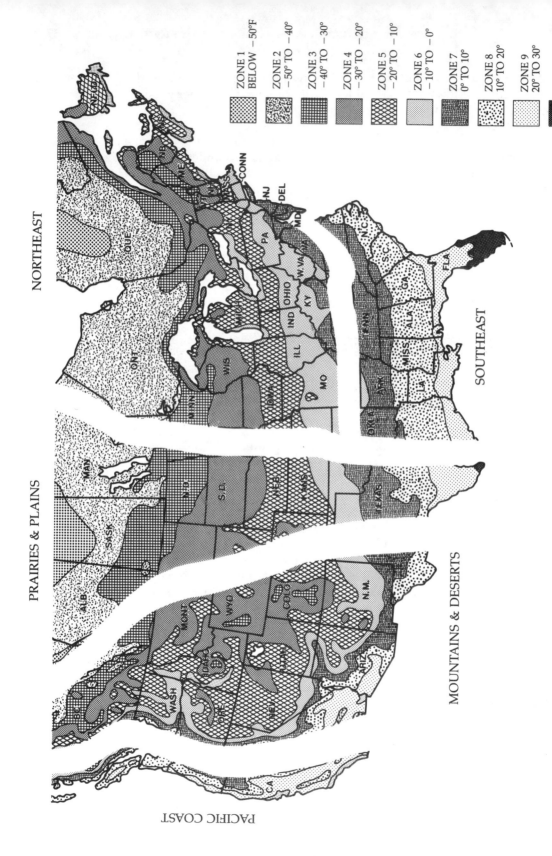

Vegetation regions and U.S. Department of Agriculture plant-hardiness zones.
Zones indicate approximate range of average annual minimum temperatures.

ZONE 1 BELOW −50°F
ZONE 2 −50° TO −40°
ZONE 3 −40° TO −30°
ZONE 4 −30° TO −20°
ZONE 5 −20° TO −10°
ZONE 6 −10° TO −0°
ZONE 7 0° TO 10°
ZONE 8 10° TO 20°
ZONE 9 20° TO 30°
ZONE 10 30° TO 40°

the north side and this is the best place to locate plants with more southern distributions. Likewise, low valleys and gorges serve as frost pockets and should be planted with vegetation that is suited to a more northern climate. Plant zones follow *Hortus Third*.

Soil.   Consider your soil type and available soil moisture when selecting plants. This is especially important for dry climates. Just as grass lawns are inappropriate and a waste of precious water in arid areas, many shrubs and trees with high moisture requirements make poor choices where water is scarce. The lists in the tables contain many excellent choices for native bird plantings in arid regions.

Light.   Light requirements vary greatly from one plant to the next. Consider your intended planting site before making selections.

Fruit Period.   Because seasons vary dramatically in length and timing from north to south, the fruiting periods are listed by season rather than month. When selecting plantings, choose a mix of fruiting periods so that some fruit is available from summer through winter.

There are various types of fruit, as illustrated here.

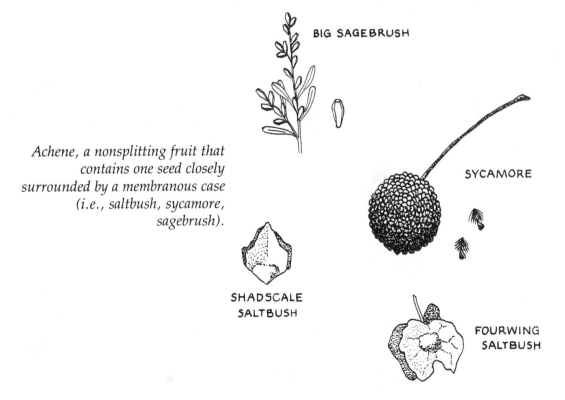

Achene, a nonsplitting fruit that contains one seed closely surrounded by a membranous case (i.e., saltbush, sycamore, sagebrush).

BIG SAGEBRUSH

SYCAMORE

SHADSCALE SALTBUSH

FOURWING SALTBUSH

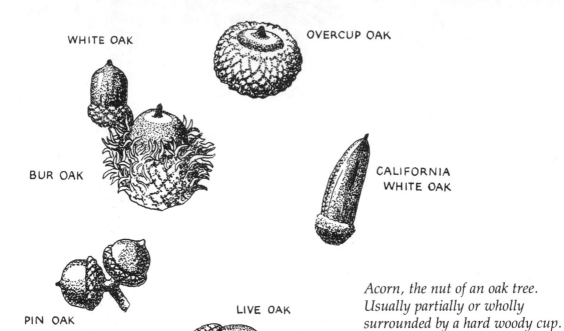

WHITE OAK

OVERCUP OAK

BUR OAK

CALIFORNIA
WHITE OAK

PIN OAK

LIVE OAK

*Acorn, the nut of an oak tree.
Usually partially or wholly
surrounded by a hard woody cup.*

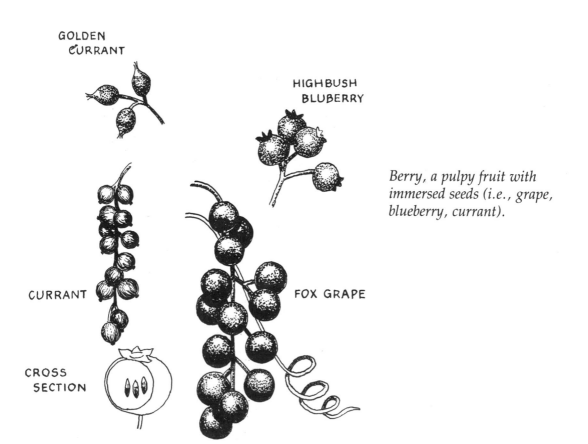

GOLDEN
CURRANT

HIGHBUSH
BLUBERRY

*Berry, a pulpy fruit with
immersed seeds (i.e., grape,
blueberry, currant).*

CURRANT

FOX GRAPE

CROSS
SECTION

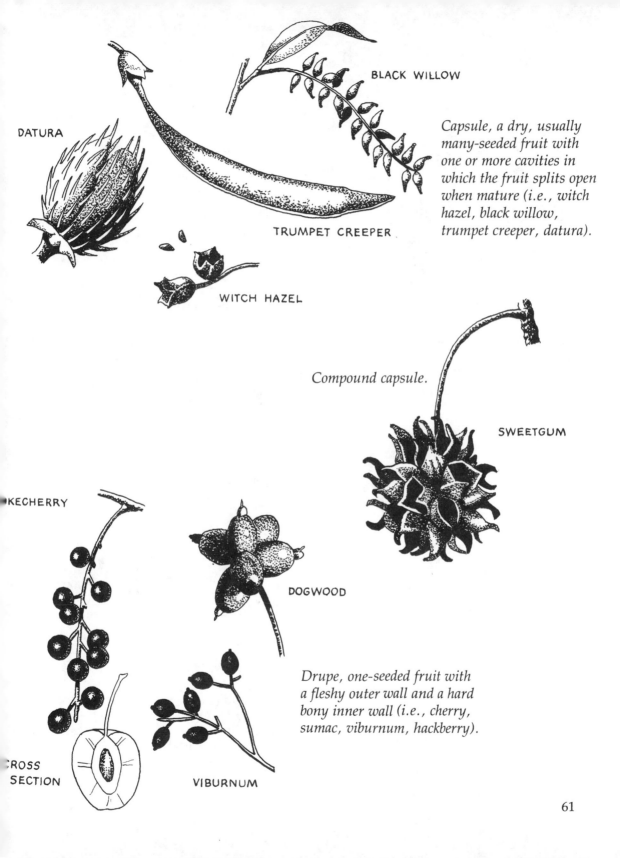

BLACK WILLOW

DATURA

Capsule, a dry, usually many-seeded fruit with one or more cavities in which the fruit splits open when mature (i.e., witch hazel, black willow, trumpet creeper, datura).

TRUMPET CREEPER

WITCH HAZEL

Compound capsule.

SWEETGUM

KECHERRY

DOGWOOD

Drupe, one-seeded fruit with a fleshy outer wall and a hard bony inner wall (i.e., cherry, sumac, viburnum, hackberry).

CROSS SECTION

VIBURNUM

61

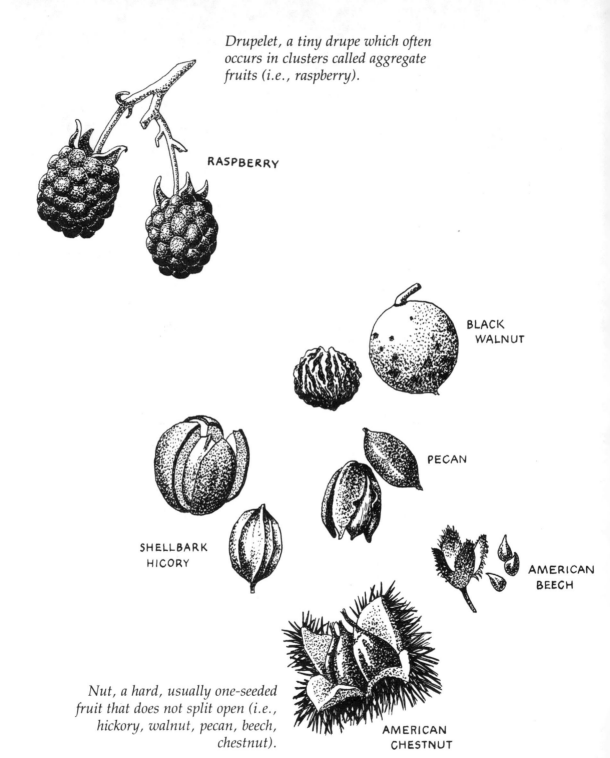

Drupelet, a tiny drupe which often occurs in clusters called aggregate fruits (i.e., raspberry).

RASPBERRY

BLACK WALNUT

PECAN

SHELLBARK HICORY

AMERICAN BEECH

Nut, a hard, usually one-seeded fruit that does not split open (i.e., hickory, walnut, pecan, beech, chestnut).

AMERICAN CHESTNUT

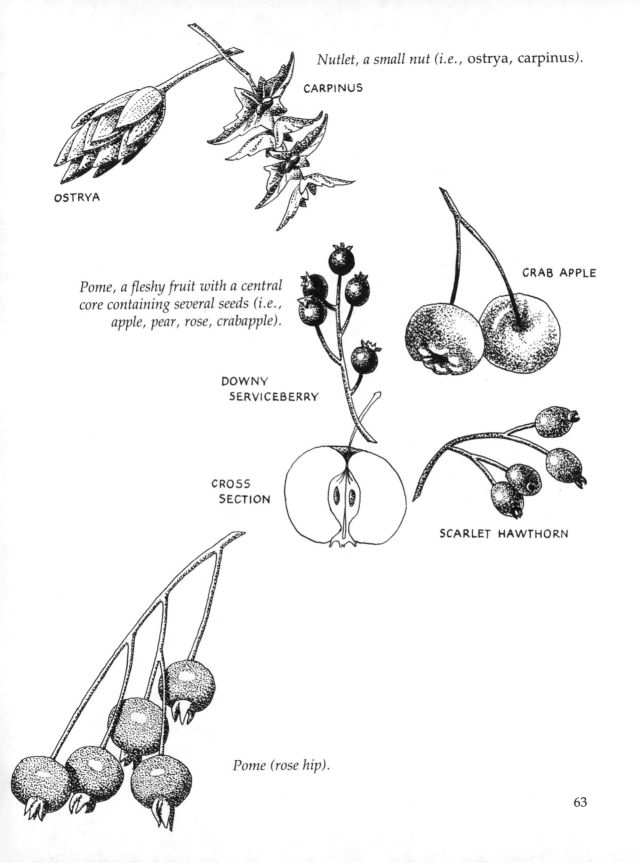

Nutlet, a small nut (i.e., ostrya, carpinus).

CARPINUS

OSTRYA

Pome, a fleshy fruit with a central core containing several seeds (i.e., apple, pear, rose, crabapple).

CRAB APPLE

DOWNY SERVICEBERRY

CROSS SECTION

SCARLET HAWTHORN

Pome (rose hip).

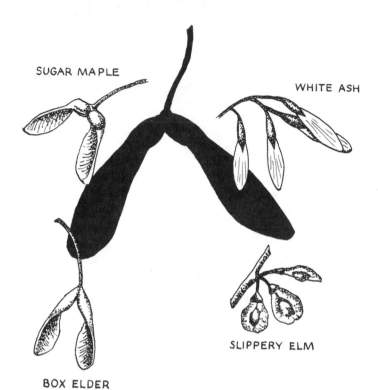

SUGAR MAPLE

WHITE ASH

Samara, a nonsplitting winged fruit (i.e., maple, ash, elm, bay elder).

SLIPPERY ELM

BOX ELDER

Syncarp, a fleshy aggregate fruit (i.e., osage orange).

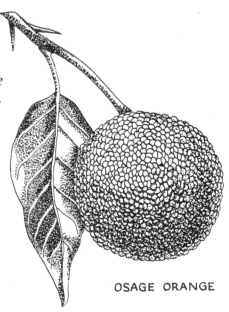

OSAGE ORANGE

BRAMBLES
Rubus spp.[1]

HIGHBUSH BLUEBERRY
Vaccinium corymbosum

This dense deciduous shrub provides food and useful nest sites for many birds. Highbush blueberry grows from 6–15 feet tall, and is native along the Atlantic coast from eastern Maine to northern Florida. It is found west through northern Ohio, southern Wisconsin, and southern Ontario, and may be cultivated as far north as zone 4. Temperatures below −20°F (−29°C) can kill small plants. Highbush blueberry prefers soils that are slightly acidic, sunlit, and well drained. It is ideal for planting in clumps in meadows or for creating hedges. Since it is shade intolerant, it should not be planted near larger trees. Most plants bear fruit when 8–10 years old, although under ideal conditions some plants fruit when only 3 years old. Its dense growth form provides excellent cover, and it is a favorite nest site for the gray catbird. Blueberries are a preferred food for American robin, eastern bluebird, orchard oriole, and at least 34 other species.

Brambles is the collective name for blackberries, raspberries, dewberries, and thimbleberries which comprise this complex of hundreds of closely related plants. Brambles vary greatly in height and tendency to form spiny dense tangles, but all produce fruit that is readily consumed by birds. At least 49 bird species eat bramble fruit. They are highly preferred by wild turkey, ruffed grouse, northern bobwhite, blue jay, gray catbird, veery, cedar waxwing, orioles, yellow-breasted chat, and many others. Brambles also provide dense cover and excellent nest sites safe from predators. Brambles are available at most nurseries or they can be transplanted easily from the field. For maximum fruiting and branching, they should be pruned and fertilized. Most bramble species native to the north-

[1]Abbreviation means that several species are available.

east are hardy as far north as zone 4. Bramble patches planted at the edges of woodlands or corners of small properties are one of the best ways to increase the numbers and variety of thicket-nesting birds on your property.

EASTERN RED CEDAR
Juniperus virginiana

BLACK CHERRY
Prunus serotina

Eastern red cedar is an excellent choice for providing food, cover, and nest sites for songbirds. This hardy native tree thrives as far north as zone 2 and occurs naturally as far south as Georgia and west to Minnesota and Texas. Only female plants produce the blue, berrylike cones, so it is best to plant several trees to improve the chances of good fruit crops. The fruit ripens in September and stays on the tree through the winter. Eastern red cedar usually grows to about 50 feet tall, but some trees are much taller. Plant red cedar in open, sunlit sites. It prefers limestone-derived soils, but it will grow in a variety of sites and frequently thrives in poor, overgrazed, and eroded soils. The dense, prickly branches provide excellent nest sites for northern mockingbird, brown thrasher, gray catbird, chipping sparrow, and many others. As their name suggests, cedar waxwings frequent this useful tree. They not only consume fruit, but also nest and roost in its dense cover. At least 54 species are known to eat red cedar fruit.

Few trees attract as many birds as our native black cherry. This rapidly maturing deciduous tree grows to about 50 feet tall and may live anywhere from 150 to 700 years. In early spring it has many drooping flower spikes. Equally abundant small, dark purple fruit become available from June to October. Most black cherries have heavy fruit crops every 3 or 4 years. Black cherry grows wild in open fields and thickets throughout most of eastern North America, from Quebec and North Dakota, and south to Texas and Florida. It is hardy as far north as zone 2 and grows in a variety of soils, ranging from rich and moist to light and sandy. Care should be taken not to plant black cherry trees in places where falling fruit collects on driveways, sidewalks, and patios. Although this cherry offers few suitable nest sites and sparse cover, at least 47 species readily consume the fruit, including ruffed grouse, common flicker, red-headed woodpecker, northern mockingbird, rose-breasted grosbeak, and white-throated sparrow.

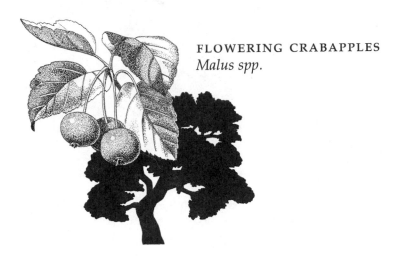

FLOWERING CRABAPPLES
Malus spp.

Flowering crabapples are highly decorative, small deciduous trees. One species, sweet flowering crabapple, *Malus coronaria,* is native from southern Ontario to Tennessee, but most of the 80 or more cultivated varieties (cultivars) available in northeastern North America are hybrids from crossing several alien species. Crabapples are usually hardy only as far north as zone 4, but that still leaves many varieties that are useful for planting even in northern Maine and southern Canada. Crabapples vary in height from 8 to 50 feet. Some, like Sargent crabapple (*M. sargentii*), are twice as broad as they are tall. They all require open, sunlit sites, but tolerate a variety of soils. For attracting the greatest variety of birds, it is best to select trees that have small fruits, because these are most readily plucked and swallowed. You should also try to choose crabapples that hold their fruits into winter when food supplies from other trees become scarce. Some of the types best known for these characteristics are Arnold, Bob White, Donald Wyman, Japanese, Dorothea, Hillieri, Jackie, Mary, Potter, Sargent, Siberian, Snowbank, Toringo, Drifter, and Tea.

VIRGINIA CREEPER
Parthenocissus quinquefolia

FLOWERING DOGWOOD
Cornus florida

This native deciduous vine produces small blue berries that are a favorite food for at least 35 bird species. In addition to thrushes and woodpeckers, several species of vireo and warblers also eat the fruits. Virginia creeper will climb the tallest trees and although it sometimes smothers small shrubs, you should try to tolerate and control it because it is an important food for birds. In the fall Virginia creeper is easy to identify even at great distances because it is the only vine that turns a brilliant crimson color. It is hardy north through zone 4 and has a wide distribution from Quebec to Florida and west to Mexico. Virginia creeper readily climbs trellises and stone walls. It enhances woodlands or even isolated trees with its brilliant fall color and with its fruit, which is available from August through the winter.

Flowering dogwood is one of the most important and widely distributed wildlife trees in the eastern United States. Showy white flower clusters and brilliant red fruits enhance this dogwood's graceful form. Flowering dogwood is hardy in zone 5 and occurs as a common understory tree in eastern deciduous forests from Maine to Kansas and south to Florida and Texas. Fruits are first available in August and most are usually consumed by November. Flowering dogwood's fall foliage varies from russet to deep red. Since these attractive native trees usually grow only to 10–30 feet, they are an excellent choice for small properties. They are also one of the best selections for enhancing deciduous woodlands, borders, and larger residential properties. Flowering dogwood grows in a wide variety of sites, including thoroughly drained uplands and moist stream banks. It prefers a soil pH range of 5–7. Among the 36 species that eat its fruit are six species of thrush, common flicker, pileated woodpecker, summer tanager, evening grosbeak, and pine grosbeak.

RED-OSIER DOGWOOD
Cornus stolonifera

AMERICAN ELDER
Sambucus canadensis

Red-osier dogwood is a low deciduous shrub that reaches a maximum height of only 4–8 feet with a spread of 10 feet or more. It is an important shrub for songbirds because it provides dense cover during the summer and produces a large crop of small white drupes that are about a quarter inch in diameter. The fruits are first available in July, but most are consumed by birds or have fallen from the shrubs by October. As its specific name suggests, red-osier spreads by creeping stolons that grow through the soil and rise nearby to produce new shrubs. Red-osier is a hardy northern plant, found as far north as the tree line in Canada. Warm temperatures seem to limit its southern distribution, as it is not found south of Washington, D.C. It is hardy in zone 2 and occurs west to California and Alaska. Red-osier fruits are readily eaten by at least 18 bird species, including wild turkey, ruffed grouse, American robin, gray catbird, and purple finch. It grows in a great variety of soils, but is especially useful in moist sites or as a streamside planting to reduce soil erosion.

American elder is an excellent choice for providing late-summer food and nesting cover in moist areas. This 3- to 10-foot-tall deciduous shrub produces abundant annual crops of tiny dark-purple fruits that are readily consumed by at least 33 species of birds. American elder forms dense thickets along sunny pond and stream edges and other moist habitats. It has large white flower clusters from late June to August and its fruits ripen from late July to September. American elder is hardy north to zone 4 and grows naturally from Nova Scotia west to Manitoba and south to Georgia and Louisiana. It is best propagated from rooted cuttings or seeds. Young plants will grow only a few inches their first year, but individual canes may grow as much as 15 feet in subsequent years. Annual pruning will greatly improve fruit production. For this purpose, leave five or six 1-year canes and one or two older canes for each shrub. If space permits, leave some plants unpruned to provide dense nesting cover. For shady areas, scarlet elder (*Sambucus pubens*) is a good choice. Mixtures of both elders offer varied colors and a greater seasonal availability of fruit, as the red-berried scarlet elder fruits from June through August, a full month earlier than American elder.

WILD GRAPES
Vitis spp.

There are at least 20 different species and varieties of wild grapes in the northeast. These climbing deciduous vines provide very attractive fruit and nest sites. At least 52 bird species eat wild grapes. Grape tangles are common nest sites for eastern kingbird, northern mockingbird, gray catbird, and brown thrasher. The loose, peeling bark is a favorite nest-building material for more than 16 species, including veery, cedar waxwing, rufous-sided towhee, and eight species of warbler. The best nest sites are created when grape vines smother large shrubs, creating dense thickets. Most grapes, such as fox grape (*Vitis labrusca*), grow best in open sunny areas where they find moist soils, but others, such as summer grape (*V. aestivalis*), grow in upland woods. Riverbank grape (*V. riparia*) is one of the hardiest and most widespread wild grapes, growing along streams north through zone 3 to Quebec, south to Tennessee, and west to Manitoba and New Mexico.

HAWTHORNS
Crataegus spp.

These small round-topped deciduous trees make up a widespread group of similar species. With the exception of a few distinctive types, hawthorn identifications baffle even the most astute botanists. Hawthorns grow best in open, sunlit habitats. In the spring hawthorns are covered with white and pink flowers, followed by an abundant crop of small orange or red pome fruits. As a group, hawthorns are easily recognized by their single large unbranched spines that grow from leaf axils. They are an excellent choice for yards and property borders, but you must take care not to let them become shaded by competing vegetation. Hawthorn fruits are readily consumed by at least 18 bird species, especially cedar waxwings. Their dense, forked branches provide choice nesting places for robins, cardinals, blue jays, and others. Cockspur hawthorn (*Crataegus crus-galli*) and Washington hawthorn (*C. phaenopyrum*) are two native species that are especially useful for attracting birds. Both bear prolifically, and are hardy as far north as zone 5.

AMERICAN HOLLY
Ilex opaca

The evergreen foliage of American holly makes it a useful cover tree for birds throughout the year. Large specimens grow to 50 feet and may spread up to 20 feet. The brilliant red drupe fruits are produced only on female trees, so when selecting plants it's best to choose specimens with fruit if possible. However, because holly flowers are pollinated by insects rather than wind, it is important to plant at least one male tree nearby. For maximum benefit to birds, trees should be planted in clumps or in a hedge. American holly thrives in partial shade and a variety of soils ranging from rich and moist to sandy. It is hardy only as far north as zone 6, naturally occurring from Massachusetts to Florida and west to southern Illinois and Indiana. At least 12 species of birds eat American holly fruit. It is especially preferred by northern mockingbird, eastern bluebird, and cedar waxwings. American holly is slow growing, but it can live for over 200 years.

A native of Korea and northern China, Amur honeysuckle is a prolific fruiting shrub that shows great promise as a wildlife planting in the northeast. Rem Red Amur honeysuckle is recommended by the U.S. Soil Conservation Service for its value in controlling erosion and providing food and cover for wildlife. Amur honeysuckle makes an excellent addition to a wildlife hedge containing other favor-

AMUR HONEYSUCKLE
Lonicera maackii

TATARIAN HONEYSUCKLE
Lonicera tatarica

ites, such as Cardinal autumn olive and Tatarian honeysuckle. While these favorite shrubs produce berries that are quickly consumed by songbirds, the fruit of Amur honeysuckle is not readily eaten in the fall and will persist on the shrubs into winter. The juicy red berries of Amur honeysuckle dry to brown, raisinlike fruits in the winter, which is when they are eaten by songbirds. Amur honeysuckle grows 8 to 12 feet tall, and fares best in deep, well-drained soils. It will tolerate up to 50 percent shade, but fruit production is greatest where it receives full sunlight. Space plants 6–8 feet apart when planting in rows. Amur honeysuckle is hardy north to zone 5, tolerating temperatures as low as −20°F (−29°C), and it will grow as far south as North Carolina and Tennessee.

Tatarian honeysuckle was introduced to North America from Turkey and southern Russia in 1752 as a decorative garden plant for its pink or white flowers and fruits. It has been used since as a popular cultivated shrub, but it has spread freely to neighboring thickets and woodlands and is now common from Ontario to Quebec and south to Kentucky and Iowa. Tatarian honeysuckle's dense growth habits and abundant red or yellow fruits qualify it as one of the best shrubs for attracting birds. Depending upon growing conditions, it grows to heights of 6 to 14 feet. It grows best in well-drained, sunny habitats and competes well with other shrubs. The easiest way to establish Tatarian honeysuckle is with 1- or 2-year-old seedlings. At least 20 bird species are known to eat the fruits of this and other honeysuckles.

American mountain ash is a moderate-sized deciduous tree or large shrub that reaches a maximum of 40 feet. It has blue-green foliage that turns a brilliant orange-red in the fall. Its large, showy white spring flowers and clusters of red pome fruits make this an attractive choice for both small city-yards and larger

AMERICAN MOUNTAIN ASH
Sorbus americana

properties. It is hardy through zone 2, occurring in northern Quebec and south into the Appalachians of Georgia. It grows best in sunlit, moist soil, but also does well in thin mountain soils and light shade. American mountain ash prefers slightly acidic soils, ranging from a pH of 4.7 to 6.0. Warm temperatures limit its southern distribution. Fruits are usually available in August or September and continue through the winter, but they are such a common source of food for cedar waxwings, eastern bluebirds, gray catbirds, and at least 13 other species that they seldom last past early fall.

RED MULBERRY
Morus rubra

Few trees are as attractive to songbirds as the red mulberry. At least 44 bird species consume the red fruits of this native deciduous tree. The fruits ripen from June to August and are usually consumed as soon as they become available. The inconspicuous green male and female flowers usually grow on different trees. Although pollen is spread by the wind, a male and female tree may be necessary for a good fruit crop. Red mulberry grows from 25 to 40 feet tall and thrives in a

73

variety of habitats including open forest and thickets. Red mulberry is hardy as far north as zone 6, occurring from Massachusetts to southern Florida and west to southern Michigan and central Texas. It grows naturally in rich flood-plain soils with a pH range from 6.0 to 7.5. Red mulberry is an excellent choice for a central backyard bird tree, but take care not to locate it near sidewalks or other areas where the accumulation of fallen fruit will be a problem.

WHITE OAK
Quercus alba

This magnificent tree may grow 100 feet tall, with massive trunks 4 feet in diameter. White oaks that grow in open areas may develop massive canopy spreads of up to 165 feet across, but such trees will not grow as tall as forest oaks. Where there is ample sun and water, white oaks will grow relatively fast, and under optimal conditions they may live for 500 years or more. This is certainly not a tree for a small urban yard, but where space permits few trees are as grand as this fine native giant. Unlike most oaks, the white oak produces an annual acorn crop. The acorns are a very important food for both mammals and birds. Turkeys, mallards, and wood ducks swallow the acorns whole, but smaller birds, such as common flickers, red-headed woodpeckers and blue jays must peck open the acorns. At least 28 species consume acorns. Several, including turkey, ruffed grouse, and northern bobwhite, also consume tender leaf buds. White oak is hardy north through zone 6 and occurs from southern Maine to southeastern Minnesota and south to eastern Texas and Florida.

Autumn olive is a spreading deciduous shrub native to China, Korea, and Japan. It is not related to the familiar olives found in tossed salads. It grows about 12 feet tall and thrives in a variety of habitats, such as gravel pits, roadbanks, clay soils, and other sites that are inhospitable to most shrubs. Autumn olive is covered with tiny, fragrant yellow flowers in early spring. The variety Cardinal was

"CARDINAL" AUTUMN OLIVE
Elaeagnus umbellata

RUSSIAN OLIVE
Elaeagnus angustifolia

developed by the Soil Conservation Service, and is notable for its especially profuse annual crop of small red fruits that ripen in the fall and last into winter. It can be established by planting 1- or 2-year-old seedlings in the fall or spring. The plants will produce fruit in 3 to 4 years, and will mature in 5 to 7 years. Autumn olive is hardy north to zone 4, and is now well established throughout the northeast from Maine to Pennsylvania. At least 26 bird species eat its fruit, especially tree swallow, northern mockingbird, American robin, eastern bluebird, and cardinal.

Russian olive is native to central Asia and southern Europe. It is frequently planted as a hardy windbreak on dry, arid soils, as it can withstand temperatures as low as $-40°F$ ($-40°C$), and will grow in even the most infertile soils. It is taller than its close relative, autumn olive (*Elaeagnus umbellata*), growing up to 20 feet in only two years. Russian olive has a silvery green foliage, fragrant yellow flowers, and abundant greenish-yellow fruits flecked with silvery scales. The olivelike fruit ripens from August to October and persists until spring. In some areas Russian olive is sensitive to trunk canker and wilt diseases, but where this is not a problem, it is one of the hardiest bird-attracting plants. It can be planted successfully as far north as zone 2. At least 25 bird species are known to eat Russian olive fruit and it is especially preferred by American robin, cedar waxwing, and evening grosbeak.

Eastern white pine's importance as a lumber tree is legendary, but its significance to wildlife is often overlooked. Within its large cones, there is an abundant crop of highly nutritious seed that is readily consumed by at least 38 bird species.

EASTERN WHITE PINE
Pinus strobus

DOWNY SERVICEBERRY
Amelanchier arborea

Some birds, such as red crossbill, favor white pine over all other foods. Birds that cannot actively shred cones will pick the seed from the ground. Cones usually appear when the trees are about 10 years old. White pine will often grow 100 feet tall, which ranks it as the largest conifer in the northeast. Its usefulness to birds does not stop with its seed crops, as its billowy foliage and branch structure provide abundant nest sites. Mourning doves favor white pine for nesting, and many cavity nesters, such as chickadees, nuthatches, and woodpeckers, excavate cavities in its soft wood. White pine is hardy north to zone 4 and occurs naturally from Newfoundland to Minnesota and southward in the Appalachians to Georgia.

Serviceberries are the small trees and shrubs that give the first color to the spring woods. Their white flowers decorate spring woodlands from March to June, usually weeks before the canopy closes. By June, small purple pome fruits begin to appear. Downy serviceberry is one of the most common and widely distributed members of this important native group. It is hardy as far north as zone 3, and ranges from Quebec south to Florida and west to eastern Minnesota and eastern Texas. It is a forest understory tree that grows 20–40 feet tall and can develop a trunk 16 inches in diameter. The serviceberry is an excellent choice for shady yards or as an additional planting in northeastern woodlands. Commercial stock is available from nurseries, but where it is abundant it can be easily propagated by transplanting root cuttings that are approximately 3–6 inches long. Downy serviceberry is an important food for at least 19 species of woodland birds, including ruffed grouse, hairy woodpecker, wood thrush, red-eyed vireo, scarlet tanager, and rose-breasted grosbeak. Closely related members of this genus, such as shadblow serviceberry (*Amelanchier canadensis*) and smooth serviceberry (*A. laevis*), are equally useful for attracting woodland birds.

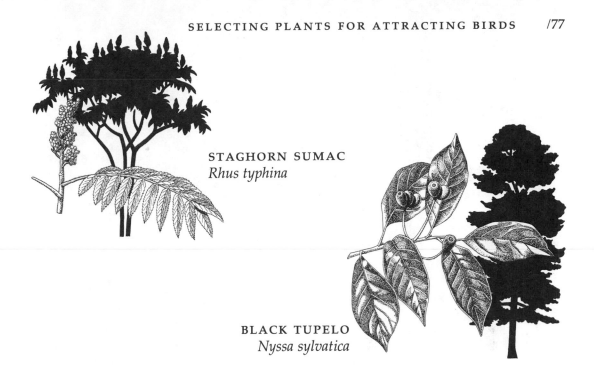

STAGHORN SUMAC
Rhus typhina

BLACK TUPELO
Nyssa sylvatica

Staghorn sumac shrubs form brilliant scarlet clumps on the fall landscape and their winter-persistent fruits are consumed by at least 21 bird species. This native deciduous shrub spreads from the original central plant at a rate of about 3 feet a year, eventually creating a large circular clone that may be 12 feet tall. Sumac clones begin to lose their vigor after about 15 years, but they can be rejuvenated by cutting stems back to the soil. The open nature of the stems and general absence of suitable forked branches create few good nest sites but some ground-nesting birds find shelter under the sumac's shade. Staghorn sumac is hardy as far north as zone 4 and occurs on eroded and disturbed soils from Nova Scotia and the Gaspé Peninsula of Quebec south to North Carolina and west to Iowa. The closely related and equally important smooth sumac (*Rhus glabra*) occurs from southwestern Quebec to southern British Columbia and in all contiguous 48 states.

Black tupelo usually grows in moist woodlands, but it is also an excellent tree for backyards or for landscaping pond banks. It usually grows to about 60 feet and is notable for its dark, glossy-green deciduous leaves that turn brilliant red in the fall. The branches are usually heavy with small, dark blue drupes by late August or October. These are consumed by wood thrush, common flicker, rose-breasted grosbeak, cedar waxwings, starlings, and many others. Black tupelo is hardy as far north as zone 5 and occurs from Maine to Missouri and south to Texas and Florida.

BIRD PLANTINGS FOR THE NORTHEAST
OTHER GOOD CHOICES

Evergreen Trees

Name	Zone	Native(N)/Alien(A)	Height (ft)	Light	Preferred Soil	Fruit Period	Type	Remarks
ARBORVITAE, EASTERN (*Thuja occidentalis*)	4	N	20–40	Sun/half sun	Moist	Early fall/fall	Cone	Forms dense hedges; used as nest site by grackles, robin, and house finch; seeds are a preferred food for pine siskin
FIR, BALSAM (*Abies balsamea*)	4	N	40–60	Sun/shade	Moist	Late spring/early summer	Cone	A favorite nesting tree for robins and mourning doves; sensitive to smoke; not good for large cities; seeds eaten by at least 13 species, including evening grosbeak, purple finch, and pine grosbeak
HEMLOCK EASTERN (*Tsuga canadensis*)	3	N	50–80	Variety	Moist loam	Early fall/fall	Cone	Very shade tolerant; preferred nest site for robin, blue jay, wood thrush; also important food tree for chickadees; forms hedges when trimmed; intolerant of air pollution
PINE, PITCH (*Pinus rigida*)	5	N	40–60	Sun	Dry/moist	Late fall/summer	Cone	Best pine for poor, sandy, or even gravelly locations
PINE, RED (*Pinus resinosa*)	2	N	to 80	Sun/half sun	Dry/drained	Late summer/fall	Cone	Heavy seed crops occur every 3–7 years; very hardy; will grow in even poor soil; at least 48 bird species eat the seeds of this and other pines
PINE, SCOTCH (*Pinus sylvestris*)	3	A	60–75	Sun/half sun	Drained/variety	Early fall/fall	Cone	Easy to grow in a variety of situations; produces good seed crops every 2–5 years
SPRUCE, COLORADO BLUE (*Picea pungens*)	3	N	80–100	Sun/half sun	Drained	Early fall/winter	Cone	
SPRUCE, RED (*Picea rubens*)	2	N	60–70	Sun/shade	Moist/drained	Early fall/fall	Cone	Important nesting and winter cover; at least 19 species eat seeds from these and other spruce; preferred food for crossbills, evening grosbeak, and red-breasted nuthatch
SPRUCE, WHITE (*Picea glauca*)	2	N	80–100	Sun/half sun	Late summer/late fall		Cone	

Large Deciduous Trees

Name	Zone	Native(N) Alien(A)	Height (ft)	Light	Preferred Soil	Period	Fruit Type	Remarks
ASH, BLACK (*Fraxinus nigra*)	2	N	40–70	Sun	Moist/ drained	Early summer/ early fall	Samara	Moderate value to wildlife; cardinals and pine grosbeaks are attracted to the seeds
ASH, GREEN (*Fraxinus pennsylvanica*)	2	N	30–50	Sun/ half sun	Moist/ dry/ drained	Early fall	Samara	Tolerant of city conditions; a good landscaping species; seeds are a preferred food of wood duck, bobwhite, evening grosbeak, purple finch, and pine grosbeak
ASH WHITE (*Fraxinus americana*)	4	N	70–100	Sun/ half sun	Dry/ rich/ moist	Early– late fall	Samara	Winged seed is preferred food for evening grosbeaks, purple finch, and others; hardy, disease resistant, and attractive for lawns
ASPEN, BIGTOOTH (*Populus grandidentata*)	4	N	30–70	Sun/ half sun	Dry/ moist/ drained	Late spring/ early summer	Capsule	Buds and catkins are a preferred food of ruffed grouse, and buds are readily eaten by evening grosbeak and purple finch; buds and catkins eaten by at least 8 bird species; especially important for ruffed grouse
ASPEN, QUAKING (*Populus tremuloides*)	1	N	40–60	Sun/ half sun	Dry/ moist	Late spring/ early summer	Capsule	
BEECH, AMERICAN (*Fagus grandifolia*)	4	N	40–70	Sun/ shade	Moist/ drained	Early– late fall	Nut	Nut crop provides excellent food for many birds and mammals; excludes grass beneath it, but forms imposing appearance with spreading crown; at least 25 bird species eat its fruit
BIRCH, GRAY (*Betula populifolia*)	5	N	20–30	Sun	Waste- lands/ moist/ dry	Fall	Samara	

Large Deciduous Trees (cont.)

Name	Zone	Native(N) Alien(A)	Height (ft)	Light	Preferred Soil	Period	Fruit Type	Remarks
BIRCH, PAPER (Betula papyrifera)	2	N	50–80	Sun/ half sun	Moist/ drained	Late summer/ early fall	Samara	Good seed crops every 1 to 2 years; seeds eaten by at least 12 species, including wood duck, ruffed grouse, goldfinch, juncos, pine siskin, and chickadees
BIRCH, SWEET (Betula lenta)	4	N	50–60	Sun/ shade	Moist/ fertile/ rocky	Late summer/ late fall	Samara	
BIRCH, YELLOW (Betula alleghaniensis)	4	N	60–70	Sun/ half sun	Cool/ moist/ drained	Late summer/ fall	Samara	
BUTTERNUT (Juglans cinerea)	4	N	40–60	Sun	Moist/ dry/ drained	Early– late fall	Nut	Nuts are favorite of Carolina wren, chickadees, nuthatches, and red-bellied woodpeckers; fast growing
COTTONWOOD, EASTERN (Populus deltoides)	2	N	80–100	Sun/ half sun	Moist	Spring/ early summer	Capsule	Soft wood excavated for nest sites by woodpeckers; prefers flood plains and riverbanks
HACKBERRY, COMMON (Celtis occidentalis)	5	N	30–50	Sun/ shade	Dry	Early fall/ late winter	Red or purple drupe	Especially useful to birds because fruits often persist into winter. At least 25 species eat the fruit; often used as windbreak or street planting
HICKORY, MOCKERNUT (Carya tomentosa)	5	N	40–50	Sun/ shade	Drained	Fall	Nut	At least 18 bird species eat hickory nuts—frequently cleaning up after squirrels, which break open the nuts; among the birds eating hickory nuts are cardinal, white-breasted nuthatch, rufous-sided towhee, red-bellied woodpecker, bobwhite, ring-necked pheasant, and wild turkey
HICKORY, PIGNUT (Carya glabra)	5	N	50–70	Sun/ shade	Drained	Fall	Nut	
HICKORY, SHAGBARK (Carya ovata)	5	N	70–80	Sun/ half sun	Dry/ light drained	Early fall	Nut	
LARCH, EASTERN (Larix laricina)	1	N	40–80	Sun	Moist	Late summer/ early fall	Cone	Frequent nest tree and an important seed tree for crossbills and purple finches

80

Name	Zone	Native(N) Alien(A)	Height (ft)	Light	Preferred Soil	Fruit Period	Fruit Type	Remarks
MAPLE, BOX ELDER (Acer negundo)	2	N	50–75	Sun/shade	Moist/tolerates poor soil	Late summer/fall	Brown samara	Preferred winter food of evening grosbeak and purple finch; very hardy, fast growing, but short-lived; used in shelterbelt plantings
MAPLE, NORWAY (Acer platanoides)	4	A	40–70	Sun/half sun	Dry/moist	Early–late fall	Yellow samara	An excellent shade tree that tolerates city air; 13 bird species eat the seeds of maples. Should not be planted where native maples will grow
MAPLE, RED (Acer rubrum)	4	N	50–70	Sun/half sun	Moist	Early summer/summer	Red samara	Spectacular red fall color; very hardy and may live 150 years
MAPLE, SILVER (Acer saccharinum)	4	N	60–80	Sun/half sun	Moist/dry	Early summer	Green or red samara	Grows fast, but relatively short lived; buds favored by evening grosbeaks; city tolerant
MAPLE, SUGAR (Acer saccharum)	4	N	60–100	Sun/shade	Fertile/moist/drained	Early summer/fall	Samara	Intolerant of city conditions; source of maple syrup; orange-yellow fall foliage; good nest tree for robins and vireos
MULBERRY, WHITE (RUSSIAN MULBERRY) (Morus alba)	5	A	30–60	Sun/half sun	Dry/moist	Late summer	White compound drupe	Abundant fruits are a preferred food for many birds; trees should be planted away from patios or sidewalks, as fruits can create a nuisance
OAK, BLACK (Quercus velutina)	5	N	80–150	Sun/half sun	Rich/moist/drained	Early–late fall	Acorn	Popular shade tree that may live for 200 years; acorn crops about every third year; preferred food for turkey, bobwhite, blue jay, and rufous-sided towhee
OAK, BUR (Quercus macrocarpa)	4	N	80–150	Sun	Dry/drained	Fall	Acorn	Tolerates city conditions; poor soils; a favorite food of the wood duck
OAK, PIN (Quercus palustris)	5	N	60–75	Sun/half sun	Moist	Early–late fall	Acorn	Useful ornamental in yards, along streets for unusually broad crown; at least 29 bird species eat the acorns of this and other oaks

Large Deciduous Trees (cont.)

Name	Zone	Native(N) Alien(A)	Height (ft)	Light	Preferred Soil	Fruit Period	Fruit Type	Remarks
OAK, NORTHERN RED (*Quercus rubra*)	4	N	60–80	Sun/half sun	Moist/rich/drained	Early–late fall	Acorn	Tolerates city conditions; acorns eaten by many birds; preferred by turkey, grouse, grackles; excellent shade tree; 3–5 years between acorn crops
OAK, SCARLET (*Quercus coccinea*)	5	N	70–80	Sun/half sun	Dry/sandy	Fall	Acorn	Preferred food for grackle, blue jay, turkey; ornamental use for red fall color. Biennial acorn crop
ORANGE, OSAGE (*Maclura pomifera*)	5	N	to 60	Sun	Dry/drained	Late summer/fall	Green syncarp	Useful primarily for dense hedge-rows; squirrels tear open large, grapefruit-sized fruit, and occasionally seeds are eaten by bobwhite and American goldfinch
PERSIMMON, COMMON (*Diospyros virginiana*)	5	N	30–50	Sun	Dry/moist/drained	Early–late fall	Orange-yellow berry	Fruit preferred by mockingbird, gray catbirds, and cedar waxwings; disease resistant
POPLAR, BALSAM (*Populus balsamifera*)	2	N	60–80	Sun	Dry/drained	Early summer	Capsule	A hardy northern tree; buds are a favorite food for ruffed grouse
SASSAFRAS, COMMON (*Sassafras albidum*)	5	N	10–50	Sun	Dry/moist	Late summer/fall	Blue drupe	At least 22 bird species eat this fruit; it is preferred by pileated woodpecker, eastern kingbird, gray catbird, eastern bluebird, and red-eyed vireo; colorful orange leaves in fall
SWEETGUM, AMERICAN (*Liquidambar styraciflua*)	6	N	50–120	Sun/half sun	Dry/moist/drained	Fall	Compound capsule	Seeds favored by finches, sparrows, turkey, mourning dove, and bobwhite; heavy seed crop every 3 years; highly disease resistant
TULIP TREE, NORTH AMERICAN (*Liriodendron tulipifera*)	6	N	60–150	Sun	Moist/drained	Fall	Samara	A beautiful ornamental; flower nectar is used by ruby-throated hummingbirds; hardy; a good street tree
WALNUT, BLACK (*Juglans nigra*)	5	N	70–120	Sun/half sun	Rich bottom-land/drained	Early–late fall	Nut	Edible nuts and very valuable wood. Excellent specimen tree. Nuts preferred by many birds and mammals; roots release toxic material that may kill some plants; should be isolated

Name	Zone	Native(N) Alien(A)	Height (ft)	Light	Preferred Soil	Fruit Period	Fruit Type	Remarks
WILLOW, BLACK (*Salix nigra*)	5	N	to 50	Sun	Moist/ wet	Spring/ summer	Capsule	Useful to birds as a nest site; good naturalizer for low, wet ground; problems include invasive roots; keep distant from dwellings; buds are preferred food of ruffed grouse and pine siskin

Small Deciduous Trees

Name	Zone	Native(N) Alien(A)	Height (ft)	Light	Preferred Soil	Fruit Period	Fruit Type	Remarks
APPLE, COMMON (*Malus pumila*)	4	A	20–30	Sun	Clay/ loam/ variety	Fall	Green-red pome	Used for nest site by eastern bluebird, red-eyed vireo, great crested flycatcher, and American robin; fruits eaten by many birds; fragrant spring blossoms
CHERRY, PIN (*Prunus pennsylvanica*)	2	N	10–30	Sun	Dry	Summer/ early fall	Red drupe	Grows best in disturbed or waste places. Eastern bluebird attracted to fruits, which are edible; best planted in clumps away from walks and patios; very valuable wildlife food
CHOKECHERRY, COMMON (*Prunus virginiana*)	2	N	6–20	Sun	Rich/ drained	Summer/ fall	Red/ black drupe	A pioneer species in old fields, along streams, and pastures. Good boundary planting along fences, and so on; at least 43 bird species eat its fruit; wilted leaves of all cherries are poisonous to livestock
DOGWOOD, ALTERNATE-LEAF (*Cornus alternifolia*)	4	N	20–30	Sun/ shade	Moist/ rich/ dry/ drained	Summer/ early fall	Blue-black drupe	An attractive small tree or shrub; makes excellent hedge, or plant in forest; at least 34 bird species eat the fruit, and it is a preferred food for downy woodpecker, brown thrasher, wood thrush, eastern bluebird, and cedar waxwing
HAWTHORN, COCKSPUR (*Crataegus crus-galli*)	5	N	20–30	Sun	Well drained	Late summer/ late winter	Red pome	White flowers in May; fruits persist through winter

Small Deciduous Trees (cont.)

Name	Zone	Native(N) Alien(A)	Height (ft)	Light	Preferred Soil	Fruit Period	Fruit Type	Remarks
HOP HORNBEAM, AMERICAN (*Ostrya virginiana*)	5	N	20–45	Sun/ half sun	Dry/ drained	Late summer/ fall	Brown nutlet	Fruits highly preferred by ruffed grouse; useful understory tree with its tolerance to shade; known for strong wood
HORNBEAM, AMERICAN (Musclewood) (*Carpinus caroliniana*)	2	N	20–40	Sun/ shade	Dry/ moist	Late summer/ fall	Brown nutlet	Seed preferred by ruffed grouse; attractive trunk
MOUNTAIN ASH, EUROPEAN (*Sorbus aucuparia*)	2	A	30–45	Sun	Dry/ moist/ drained	Fall/ late fall	Yellow-scarlet pome	Similar to American mountain ash; many cultivated varieties; a readily available and useful tree
MOUNTAIN ASH, NORTHERN (*Sorbus decora*)	2	N	to 15	Sun	Dry/ moist/ drained	Early fall/ winter	Orange pome	Sometimes grows as a shrub. Most northern distribution of our native species

Evergreen Shrubs

Name	Zone	Native(N) Alien(A)	Height (ft)	Light	Preferred Soil	Fruit Period	Fruit Type	Remarks
HOLLY, INKBERRY (*Ilex glabra*)	4	N	6–10	Sun/ shade	Dry/ moist/ sandy/ drained	Fall/ spring	Black berry	At least 15 bird species eat the berries of this shrub, including mockingbird, hermit thrush, bobwhite, and wild turkey
HUCKLEBERRY, BOX (*Gaylussacia brachycera*)	6	N	to 2	Sun	Dry/acid/ drained	Summer/ late summer	Black berry	51 bird species are known to eat the fruit of huckleberries; these low shrubs are frequent nest sites; berries eaten by ruffed grouse, flicker, blue jay, and red-headed woodpecker
JUNIPER, CHINESE (*Juniperus chinensis*)	5	A	2–12	Sun/ half sun	Dry/ moist/ drained	Per-sistent	Blue-green berry	At least 19 cultivated varieties are known; fruits appear only on female plants
Cultivars of Chinese juniper: Hetzii juniper	5	A	10–12	Sun/ half sun	Dry/ moist/ drained	Per-sistent	Blue-green berry	Rapid growth, spreads to 12 to 15 feet, with blue-green foliage
Pfitzerana juniper	5	A	to 6	Sun	Dry/ moist/ drained	Per-sistent	Blue-green berry	Vase-shaped form with spreading branches; the most prolific fruiter

Name	Zone	Native(N)/Alien(A)	Height (ft)	Light	Preferred Soil	Fruit Period	Fruit Type	Remarks
Sargentii juniper	5	A	to 2	Sun	Dry/moist/drained	Persistent	Blue-green berry	Spreads to over 6 feet wide
JUNIPER, COMMON (*Juniperus communis*)	2	N	1–4	Sun	Sterile	Early–late fall	Blue-black berry	Only female plant has berries; cultivated variety *depressa* (Canadian) juniper is vase-shaped, 3–4 feet tall; seven cultivated varieties; excellent cover for sandy, barren land
YEW, CANADA (*Taxus canadensis*)	2	N	to 3	Shade	Moist/drained/rich humus	Summer/early fall	Red drupe-like	Most useful as cover and nest site; sparse fruiting with only 7 bird species known to eat the fruit

Tall Deciduous Shrubs

Name	Zone	Native(N)/Alien(A)	Height (ft)	Light	Preferred Soil	Fruit Period	Fruit Type	Remarks
ALDER, HAZEL (*Alnus serrulata*)	5	N	6–12	Sun	Moist/swampy	Late summer/fall	Cone	Useful naturalizer for ponds, stream borders; reproduces quickly in full sun; seeds important food for goldfinches, pine siskins, and redpolls; fruit persists into winter
ALDER, SPECKLED (*Alnus rugosa*)	5	N	15–25	Sun	Moist/swampy	Late summer/fall	Cone	
BAYBERRY, NORTHERN (*Myrica pennsylvanica*)	2	N	3–8	Sun/half sun	Dry/sandy	Early summer/summer	Gray waxy berries	Hardy plant that grows well in swamp soils or sand dunes; berries attract at least 26 bird species; red-winged blackbirds commonly use it for nesting; aromatic; much fruit; coastal
BUCKTHORN, COMMON (*Rhamnus cathartica*)	2	A	10–20	Sun/shade	Dry/moist	Early summer/fall	Black drupe	Excellent background or hedge shrub; tolerates city conditions; fruits of these and other
BUCKTHORN, GLOSSY (*Rhamnus frangula*)	2	A	8–12	Shade/half sun	Dry/moist/peaty	Summer/fall	Black drupe	buckthorns eaten by at least 15 bird species, and are preferred foods of pileated woodpecker, mockingbird, and brown thrasher

Tall Deciduous Shrubs (cont.)

Name	Zone	Native(N) Alien(A)	Height (ft)	Light	Preferred Soil	Fruit Period	Fruit Type	Remarks
BUTTONBUSH, COMMON (*Cephalanthus occidentalis*)	5	N	3–12	Sun/shade	Wet	Early fall/early winter	Brown nutlike capsule	May form dense stands providing nesting sites for wetland birds; 7 types of waterfowl eat these seeds; ruby-throated hummingbirds readily feed at its flowers; often grows in standing water
CHOKEBERRY, BLACK (*Aronia melanocarpa*)	5	N	to 10	Sun/half sun	Moist/dry	Late summer/late fall	Black berry	Fruits eaten by at least 12 bird species, and preferred by cedar waxwing and brown thrasher; berries persist into the winter; also notable for brilliant fall foliage
CHOKEBERRY, RED (*Aronia arbutifolia*)	5	N	2–8	Sun/half sun	Wet/dry	Late summer/late fall	Red berry	
CRABAPPLE, SARGENT (*Malus sargentii*)	5	A	5–8	Sun	Well-drained	Late summer/early winter	Red pome	May grow twice as wide as tall; pruned, it forms a hedge; profuse white blooms in May
CRABAPPLE, TORINGO (*Malus sieboldii*)	5	A	3–10	Sun	Well-drained	Fall/late winter	Red-yellow pome	White flowers; sometimes grows as small tree; winter-persistent fruits
ELDER, SCARLET (*Sambucus pubens*)	5	N	2–12	Sun	Dry/rocky/drained	Early summer/early fall	Red berry	At least 23 bird species eat these colorful fruits; it is a preferred food of red-bellied woodpecker, American robin, veery, and rose-breasted grosbeak; highly decorative with abundant red berries. European *S. racemosa* is similar
EUONYMUS, WINGED (*Euonymus alata*)	4	A	8–15	Sun/half sun	Moist/drained	Fall	Purple capsule	Bright red foliage in fall; food for eastern bluebird, mockingbird, fox sparrow, and yellow-rumped warbler
FIRE THORN, SCARLET (*Pyracantha coccinea*)	7	N	to 8	Sun	Drained	Late summer	Red-orange berry	Fall foliage makes this one of the most attractive ornamental evergreens for the southern part of this region; useful along walls and as formal hedges; at least 17 bird species eat the berries

Name	Zone	Native(N) Alien(A)	Height (ft)	Light	Preferred Soil	Fruit Period	Fruit Type	Remarks
HAWTHORN, ONE-FLOWER (*Crataegus uniflora*)	7	N	3-8	Sun/half sun	Dry/sandy	Fall	Yellow/red pome	At least 36 bird species eat hawthorn fruit; this shrubby species provides good nest sites for birds, such as willow flycatcher
HAZEL AMERICAN (*Corylus americana*)	5	N	to 10	Sun	Dry/moist	Summer/fall	Brown nut	Nuts preferred by ruffed grouse, ring-necked pheasant, blue jay, and hairy woodpecker; nuts survive into winter; also good cover
HONEYSUCKLE, MORROW (*Lonicera morrovii*)	5	A	6-8	Sun	Dry/moist/drained	Early–late summer	Red/yellow berry	At least 20 bird species eat honeysuckle fruits; flowers are a favorite nectar source for ruby-throated hummingbird.
HONEYSUCKLE, STANDISH (*Lonicera standishii*)	5	A	5-6	Sun/half sun	Sandy	Early–late summer	Red berry	Excellent vegetation screens, and provide abundant food and cover. These species have greater ornamental value than native honeysuckles, with attractive flowers, foliage, and fruit
LESPEDEZA, JAPANESE (*Lespedeza japonica*)	5	A	6-10	Sun	Dry/moist/drained	Fall	Purple legume	Important food and cover for bobwhite quail
LESPEDEZA, KOREAN (*Lespedeza stipulacea*)	6	A	6-10	Sun	Dry/moist/drained	Fall	Purple legume	
OLIVE, RUSSIAN (*Elaeagnus angustifolia*)	2	A	to 20	Sun/shade	Dry/sandy/loam/clay	Late summer/fall	Silvery yellow drupes	Fruits attract at least 25 bird species; tolerant of salt and drought conditions; an excellent planting for city or country plantings (see illustration on p. 103).
ROSE, PASTURE (*Rosa carolina*)	5	N	5-7	Sun	Dry	Summer/early fall Persistent	Scarlet hip	Dense thickets provide excellent nest sites; rose hips are eaten by at least 20 bird species, and are preferred by mockingbird, Swainson's thrush, and cedar waxwing

Tall Deciduous Shrubs (cont.)

Name	Zone	Native(N) Alien(A)	Height (ft)	Light	Preferred Soil	Period	Type	Remarks
ROSE, SWAMP (*Rosa palustris*)	5	N	to 8	Sun	Damp	Late summer/ early fall	Scarlet hip	At least 36 bird species are known to eat serviceberries; these two shrub forms offer abundant summer foods
SERVICEBERRY, ALLEGHENY (*Amelanchier laevis*)	4	N	20–25	Sun/ half sun	Moist to wet	June– August	Purple-black	
SERVICEBERRY, SHADBLOW (*Amelanchier canadensis*)	5	N	20–25	Sun/ half sun	Swamps	Early– late summer	Purple pome	
SUMAC, DWARFLEAF (*Rhus copallina*)	5	N	4–10	Sun	Dry/ rocky	Fall	Red drupe	31 bird species are known to eat the fruits of sumac, especially catbird, wood thrush, eastern bluebird, and starling. Sumac fruits remain on branches into late winter and thus serve as "emergency" food
SUMAC, SMOOTH (*Rhus glabra*)	2	N	10–15	Sun	Variety/ tolerates poor soils	Late summer/ fall	Red drupe	
VIBURNUM, AMERICAN HIGHBUSH CRANBERRY (*Viburnum trilobum*)	2	N	6–15	Sun	Moist/ dry/ drained	Fall/ spring	Red drupe	A very hardy shrub useful for borders and hedges. The fruit survives the winter and thus offers a late-winter emergency food. It is preferred by only ruffed grouse, brown thrasher, and cedar waxwing, but an additional 29 bird species occasionally eat the fruit
VIBURNUM, ARROWWOOD (*Viburnum dentatum*)	2	N	to 15	Sun/ half sun	Moist	Late summer/ late fall	Blue drupe	Excellent cover and nesting sites; forms dense thickets; tolerates city pollution; useful planting for pond and stream edges
VIBURNUM, BLACKHAW (*Viburnum prunifolium*)	3	N	8–15	Sun/ shade	Dry/ moist/ drained	Fall/ spring	Blue-black drupe	Reddish fall color and attractive white spring flowers; at least 8 bird species eat these winter-persistent fruits
VIBURNUM, HOBBLEBUSH (*Viburnum alnifolium*)	4	N	to 10	Shade	Moist	Summer/ fall	Purple drupe	Useful understory planting in woodland; fruits eaten by at least 6 bird species
VIBURNUM, MAPLELEAF (*Viburnum acerifolium*)	4	N	3–6	Sun/ shade	Dry/ drained	Summer/ winter	Purple drupe	Highly tolerant of different soil and light conditions; at least 10 bird species are known to eat

Name	Zone	Native(N) Alien(A)	Height (ft)	Light	Preferred Soil	Period	Fruit Type	Remarks
VIBURNUM, NANNYBERRY (*Viburnum lentago*)	2	N	8–25	Sun/ shade	Dry/ moist/ drained	Late summer/ fall	Blue- black drupe	Forms dense clumps and can be pruned to form hedges; very hardy plant with wide range; at least 11 bird species eat these winter-persistent blue-black drupes
VIBURNUM, WITHEROD (*Viburnum cassinoides*)	2	N	6–12	Sun/ shade	Moist	Early fall/ winter	Blue- black drupe	Salt tolerant; good coastal planting; ornamental flowers and fruits; at least 9 types of bird eat this fruit
WILLOW, PURPLE OSIER (*Salix purpurea*)	5	A	10–20	Sun/ shade	Dry/ moist/ drained	Spring/ late spring	Whitish capsule	Rapid growth is useful in stabilizing banks; provides dense cover along streams and wet areas; 8 bird species eat catkins and buds
WILLOW, PUSSY (*Salix discolor*)	2	N	10–20	Sun	Low/ moist	Spring/ late spring	Capsule	Buds eaten by ruffed grouse; favorite nest site for American goldfinch
WINTERBERRY, COMMON (*Ilex verticillata*)	4	N	5–15	Sun/ half sun	Wet/ rich/ slightly acidic	Late summer/ fall	Red berry	Attractive fruits in fall, survive in winter; many birds attracted by berries, including mockingbird, catbird, brown thrasher, and hermit thrush
WINTERBERRY, SMOOTH (*Ilex laevigata*)	5	N	10–20	Sun/ shade	Dry/ moist	Early fall/ winter	Red berry	

Small Deciduous Shrubs

Name	Zone	Native(N) Alien(A)	Height (ft)	Light	Preferred Soil	Period	Fruit Type	Remarks
BARBERRY, JAPANESE (*Berberis thunbergii*)	5	A	to 5	Sun/ half sun	Dry/ drained	Summer/ winter	Red berry	Useful hedge planting; very ornamental in all seasons; not susceptible to black stem rust; prolific fruiting; variable palatability to birds
BLACKBERRY, ALLEGHENY (*Rubus alleghaniensis*)	4	N	3–8	Sun	Drained	Summer/ early fall	Black drupelets	Like other members of the raspberry genus, this is a very important late-summer bird food; at least 40 bird species eat raspberry/blackberry fruit in the northeast

Small Deciduous Shrubs (cont.)

Name	Zone	Native(N) Alien(A)	Height (ft)	Light	Preferred Soil	Fruit Period	Fruit Type	Remarks
BLUEBERRY, LOWBUSH (*Vaccinium angustifolium*)	3	N	to 2	Sun	Acid/ drained	Early summer/ fall	Blue berry	Blueberries are very important wildlife food; no fewer than 37 bird species are known to eat blueberries, and they are preferred food for 24 of these
BUCKTHORN, ALDERLEAF (*Rhamnus alnifolia*)	5	N	2–3	Shade	Damp	Late summer/ fall	Black drupe	Dark fruits and leaves; highly ornamental; dense foliage makes this plant good in border plantings; 15 bird species eat the berries, including mockingbird, pileated woodpecker, and brown thrasher
CORALBERRY (*Symphoricarpos orbiculatus*)	2	N	2–5	Sun/ shade	Dry/ drained/ moist	Early fall/ early winter	Purple/ red berry	Hummingbirds attracted to flowers; this hardy shrub forms dense thickets and is useful in erosion control; at least 14 bird species eat the colorful berries
COTONEASTER, ROCKSPRAY (*Cotoneaster horizontalis*)	6	A	2–3	Sun/ half sun	Drained	Fall	Red pome	Spreads to 15 feet; excellent in rock gardens or as ground cover; semievergreen in southeast
CURRANT, AMERICAN BLACK (*Ribes americanum*)	5	N	to 5	Sun/ half sun	Dry/ moist/ drained	Early summer/ early fall	Black berry	Attractive spreading shrub, but an alternate host for white-pine blister-rust disease; choice food for many birds, but plant away from white pine
DANGLEBERRY (*Gaylussacia frondosa*)	5	N	3–6	Sun	Acid/ drained	Early summer/ early fall	Dark blue berry	Attractive when used in borders and clumps. Berries eaten by ruffed grouse, mourning dove, mockingbird, and scarlet tanager, among others
DEWBERRY, NORTHERN (*Rubus flagellaris*)	4	N	1–2	Full sun	Dry/ drained	Summer	Black drupelets	As with other members of the raspberry family, this shrub provides both important summer food and nest sites. At least 49 northern bird species eat raspberry fruit and 12 species nest in its shelter

Name	Zone	Native(N) Alien(A)	Height (ft)	Light	Preferred Soil	Fruit Period	Fruit Type	Remarks
GOOSEBERRY, PASTURE (*Ribes cynosbati*)	5	N	3–4	Sun/ shade	Dry/ moist/ poor/ drained	Summer/ early fall	Purple berry	Excellent shrub for halting soil erosion in open pastures; gooseberry does well in barren soil and thrives in garden soil; good nest site; at least 16 bird species eat these berries
HONEYSUCKLE, AMERICAN FLY (*Lonicera canadensis*)	4	N	3–5	Shade	Moist	Early– late summer	Red berry	Provides food and shelter for at least 20 bird species, including catbird, robin, and goldfinch
HONEYSUCKLE, MISTLETOE (*Lonicera quinquelocularis*)	5	A	to 5	Sun/ half sun	Moist	Early winter	White trans- lucent berry	
HONEYSUCKLE, SWAMP FLY (*Lonicera oblongifolia*)	4	N	2–5	Sun/ half sun	Moist	Summer/ early fall	Red berry	
HUCKLEBERRY, BLACK (*Gaylussacia baccata*)	2	N	to 3	Sun/ half sun	Dry/ rocky/ sandy	Summer/ early fall	Black berry	Attractive ornamental with edible sweet fruits; forms low shrub with crown to 4 feet; at least 24 bird species eat huckleberry fruit
HUCKLEBERRY, DWARF (*Gaylussacia dumosa*)	5	N	1–2	Sun	Wet	Early summer/ fall	Black berry	Useful ground cover in wet meadows and boggy areas
MEADOWSWEET, NARROWLEAF (*Spiraea alba*)	4	N	1–4	Sun	Neutral damp	Summer/ fall	Incon- spicuous follicle	Important to wildlife as cover or nest site; forms thickets
RASPBERRY, BLACK (*Rubus occidentalis*)	4	N	3–6	Sun	Rocky/ rich	Summer	Black drupelets	At least 40 bird species eat raspberry fruits in the northeast; these thicket-forming shrubs grow in a wide variety of soils, but require full sun; at least 12 bird species nest in the protection of their prickly arching stems
RASPBERRY, RED (*Rubus idaeus*)	4	N	3–6	Sun	Drained/ poor	Summer	Red drupelets	

Small Deciduous Shrubs (cont.)

Name	Native(N) Alien(A)	Zone	Height (ft)	Light	Preferred Soil	Period	Fruit Type	Remarks
ROSE, MEADOW (*Rosa blanda*)	N	2	1–4	Sun/half sun	Dry/moist/rocky	Summer/early fall	Scarlet hip	Persistent fruits and dense thicket growth provides important food and cover for wildlife; natural hedges; frequent nest site for many birds; valuable as food for at least 20 bird species.
ROSE, RUGOSA (*Rosa rugosa*)	A	2	to 6	Sun/half/sun	Drained	Early summer/early fall	Scarlet hip	
ROSE, VIRGINIA (*Rosa virginiana*)	N	4	to 6	Sun	Dry/moist/drained/sandy	Summer	Scarlet hip	
SERVICEBERRY, BARTRAM (*Amelanchier bartramiana*)	N	3	2–4	Sun/half sun	Rich/peaty/variety	Early summer/early fall	Purple-black pome	Flower and fruits later than other serviceberries; berries are a preferred fruit for cedar waxwing, eastern bluebird, and many others; at least 40 northeast bird species eat serviceberry fruit
SERVICEBERRY, RUNNING (*Amelanchier stolonifera*)	N	5	1–3	Sun	Dry/moist/drained	Summer	Black pome	Low, dense shrub that grows in sand and gravel; as with other serviceberries, this is an important summer food for many songbirds
SNOWBERRY, COMMON (*Symphoricarpos albus*)	N	4	3–4	Sun/shade	Dry/drained/moist/limestone/clay	Late summer/late spring	White berry	Late fall and winter fruiting makes this a valuable wildlife plant. It tolerates city conditions and does well planted as a lawn border or in the forest understory; at least 8 bird species eat the berries
SPICEBUSH, COMMON (*Lindera benzoin*)	N	5	2–8	Sun/shade	Fertile/moist/drained	Summer/fall	Red drupe	A forest understory tree; fruits eaten by at least 15 bird species; preferred food of wood thrush and veery
ST. JOHN'S-WORT, SHRUBBY (*Hypericum spathulatum*)	N	5	1–4	Half sun/shade	Rocky/sandy	Late summer/winter	Reddish brown achene	Wide crown makes it highly ornamental; especially attractive blooms; good as mixed border species; fruits eaten by 5 bird species, including ring-necked pheasant, bobwhite, and junco

Ground Covers (Less than 12 inches tall)

Name	Zone	Native(N) Alien(A)	Evergreen (E) Deciduous (D)	Light	Preferred Soil	Period	Fruit Type	Remarks
BEARBERRY (*Arctostaphylos uva-ursi*)	2	N	E	Sun/ half sun	Drained/ acid	Summer/ fall	Red berry	Fruit persistent to spring; can grow in very poor soil; forms large mats; 34 bird species are known to eat its fruit
BILBERRY, BOG (*Vaccinium uliginosum*)	1	N	E	Sun	Dry/ drained	Late summer/ fall	Blue berry	Alpine and bog habitats in northeastern United States; good for rock gardens and other shallow soils; at least 87 bird species are known to eat its blueberry fruits
BUGLEWEED (*Ajuga reptans*)	4	A	Semi-E	Sun/ shade	Moist	Not important		Spreads rapidly; blue flowers in May are sometimes used by hummingbirds
BUNCHBERRY (*Cornus canadensis*)	2	N	D	Shade	Cool/ moist/ acid	Late summer	Red drupe	Large white bracts look like flowers; preferred food for Philadelphia vireo, warbling vireo, and veery
COTONEASTER, CREEPING (*Cotoneaster adpressa*)	5	A	D	Sun/ half sun	Moist	Late summer/ fall	Red pome	Grows 1 to 2 feet tall and up to 8 feet across
COWBERRY (*Vaccinium vitis-idaea*)	1	N	E	Sun	Dry/ drained	Fall	Red berry	An arctic ground cover mat; occurs south to northern Maine and Minnesota; larger berries at lower elevations
CROWBERRY, BLACK (*Empetrum nigrum*)	4	N	E	Sun to half sun	Cool/ moist/ acid	Summer/ late summer	Black berry	Grows best over rock and gravel; at least 40 bird species are known to eat these berries, including many ducks and shore birds
JUNIPER, CREEPING (*Juniperus horizontalis*)	3	N	E	Sun	Drained	Late summer/ winter	Blue-green berry	Grows best over gravel or shallow soil
Cultivars of Creeping Juniper: Bar Harbor juniper	3	N	E	Sun	Shallow	Late summer/ winter	Blue-green berry	6–12 inches tall and forms a mat 7 feet wide
Andorra juniper or plumosa	3	N	E	Sun	Shallow	Late summer/	Blue-green	18 inches tall and forms a mat 7 feet wide

Ground Covers (Less than 12 inches tall) (cont.)

Name	Zone	Native(N) Alien(A)	Evergreen (E) Deciduous (D)	Light	Preferred Soil	Fruit		Remarks
						Period	Type	
						winter	berry	
Blue rug juniper	3	N	E	Sun	Shallow	Late summer/ winter	Blue-green berry	3–6 inches tall and forms a dense mat 10 feet wide
JUNIPER, SARGENT (*Juniperus chinensis* var. *sargentii*)	3	A	E	Sun	Drained	Late summer/ winter	Blue-green berry	Forms large mats 12 inches tall and up to 10 feet across; most useful as cover; plant male and female bush for a berry crop
PARTRIDGEBERRY (*Mitchella repens*)	3	N	E	Shade	Moist/ acid	Summer/ late summer	Red berry	Creeping mat; berries eaten by grouse and at least 8 other bird species
STRAWBERRY, CULTIVATED (*Fragaria chiloensis*)	5	N	E	Sun/ half sun	Drained	Spring/ summer	Red berry	Cultivated strawberries provide cover and food for at least 29 bird species
STRAWBERRY, WILD (*Fragaria virginiana*)	4	N	E	Sun/ half sun	Drained	Spring/ summer	Red berry	Wild strawberry of east; smaller fruits than above
WINTERCREEPER (*Euonymus fortunei*) Colorata	5	A	E	Sun/ half sun	Moist/ drained	Fall/ winter	Pink capsule	Adaptable to a variety of soil and lighting conditions; Colorata is a groundcover form
WINTERGREEN, CHECKERBERRY (*Gaultheria procumbens*)	4	N	E	Half sun/ shade	Cool/ moist	Late summer/ early fall	Red berry	Slow growing, trailing plant for shady areas; at least 10 bird species eat these red berries

Vines

Name	Zone	Native(N) Alien(A)	Evergreen (E) Deciduous (D)	Light	Preferred Soil	Fruit		Remarks
						Period	Type	
AMPELOPSIS, HEARTLEAF (*Ampelopsis cordata*)	5	N	D	Shade	Moist/ drained/ fertile woods	Late summer/ late fall	Blue berry	May be cultivated on trellis; good cover for walls and fences; at least 10 bird species eat its fruit, including flicker, wood thrush, and brown thrasher
BITTERSWEET, AMERICAN (*Celastrus scandens*)	2	N	D	Sun	Dry/ drained	Late summer/ early winter	Red and yellow pod	Climbs to 60 feet; attractive yellow fall color; excellent ornamental; plant male and female plants nearby; at least 15 bird species eat its fruit

Name	Zone	Native(N)/Alien(A)	Evergreen (E)/Deciduous (D)	Light	Preferred Soil	Fruit Period	Fruit Type	Remarks
GRAPE, NEW ENGLAND (*Vitis novae-angliae*)	5	N	D	Sun	Fertile/drained	Early fall	Black berry	Grapes attract many birds, especially cardinals and catbirds; easily cultivated on arbors; at least 52 bird species eat grapes; they are preferred food for 24 species; many insect-eating birds, such as vireos, warblers, flycatchers, and cuckoos, are known to nest among grape vines or use grape bark in their nests
GRAPE, FOX (*Vitis labrusca*)	6	N	D	Sun/shade/variety	Dry/moist/drained	Late summer/fall	Black-amber berry	
GRAPE, FROST (*Vitis vulpina*)	6	N	D	Sun	Rich soils/bottom-land/drained	Fall	Black berry	
GRAPE, RIVERBANK (*Vitis riparia*)	3	N	D	Sun	Moist	Late summer/early fall	Blue-black berry	
GRAPE, SUMMER (*Vitis aestivalis*)	4	N	D	Sun	Dry	Fall	Black berry	
GREENBRIER, CAT (*Smilax glauca*)	6	N	D	Sun/variety	Swampy to drier woodland edges	Fall	Blue-black berry	Forms impenetrable tangle that offers excellent cover, food, and nest sites for at least 19 bird species; berries are preferred food for mockingbird, catbird, and Swainson's thrush
GREENBRIER, COMMON (*Smilax rotundifolia*)	5	N	D	Sun	Moist/drained	Early fall	Blue-black berry	Similar to above, but has strong thorns; fruits survive through winter; at least 20 bird species eat this fruit
IVY, ENGLISH (*Hedera helix*)	5	A	E	Sun to shade	Moist/drained	Fall	Black berry	Excellent cover on walls, trees, or ground; fruit used only rarely
MOONSEED, COMMON (*Menispermum canadense*)	6	N	D	Sun/shade/variety	Moist/drained	Late summer/fall	Black drupe	Ivylike foliage climbs to 12 feet; useful ground cover; dies back in winter; 5 bird species known to eat this fruit
TRUMPET CREEPER, COMMON (*Campsis radicans*)	5	N	D	Sun	Dry/moist/drained	Late summer/fall	Capsule	Forms shrubby vine to 30 feet; decorative orange flowers attract hummingbirds
WINTERCREEPER (*Euonymus fortunei*) Vegata	5	A	E	Sun/open shade	Moist/well drained	Fall/winter	Orange capsule	Dense foliage; holds fruits into winter; rapid growth; this cultivated form grows as a climbing vine

AMERICAN BEAUTYBERRY
Callicarpa americana

This native deciduous shrub of southern forests is an excellent choice for light-shade habitats. Small bluish flowers appear in leaf axils from March to June, and these form large clusters of lustrous pink-purple fruit by August. The fruit stays on the plants until midwinter and since the berries contain about 80 percent water, they are an excellent moisture source for birds during dry fall and winter seasons. At least 12 bird species consume the fruit, which are especially favored by northern bobwhite during the winter. American beautyberry produces the most fruit when it grows in sunny, well-drained soils, but it also thrives in partial-shade habitats, such as open pine forests. This 3- to 6-foot-tall shrub is hardy as far north as zone 7, occurring north to Maryland and Tennessee and south to eastern Texas and central Florida.

SCARLET FIRETHORN
Pyracantha coccinea

This European shrub has escaped from gardens throughout most of the southeastern United States, where it was first introduced, and is now hardy as far north as zone 6, and has naturalized along roadbanks and open habitats from Pennsylvania south to Florida and west to Louisiana. In the northern part of its range it is deciduous, but to the south it retains its dark, waxy green leaves through the winter. This and several closely related species range in height from 6 to 12 feet and are characterized by their dense clusters of orange or red fruits. Scarlet fire thorn has abundant small white flowers in May and June, followed by fruit that ripens in September and persists through the winter. It is an adaptable plant, capable of thriving in many soil types. Pruning gives it a denser form and increases its fruiting potential. Scarlet firethorn makes an excellent hedge-foundation planting, or choice for difficult rocky soils. The fruit is readily eaten by gray catbird, brown thrasher, purple finch, cedar waxwing, and at least 13 other species of bird.

COMMON GREENBRIER
Smilax rotundifolia

This stout woody vine climbs to 30 feet, creating dense tangles that are very attractive to birds. It has inconspicuous green flowers from April to August and small, blue-black berries that ripen by September. These are among the favorite fruits of wild turkey, ruffed grouse, northern mockingbird, Swainson's thrush, and at least 16 other bird species. In addition to the importance of the fruit, deer relish the leaves and several birds nest in greenbrier thickets. In areas where it does not occur, it can be established by transplanting rootstocks. These usually produce vigorous new canes 2 years later. Common greenbrier is hardy north to zone 5, and occurs from Nova Scotia to Florida and west to Texas and Michigan. Some no doubt regard this thorny vine as a weed, but its fruit and dense cover make it a valuable planting for many songbirds.

SUGAR HACKBERRY
Celtis laevigata

The small orange-to-black fruits of sugar hackberry are among the favorite foods of the cedar waxwing, yellow-bellied sapsucker, northern mockingbird, and at least 23 other types of bird. This deciduous native tree usually grows in moist woodlands, but it will also grow in drier areas and thus makes an excellent choice for a backyard bird-attracting tree. In forest habitats, sugar hackberry grows to 100 feet, self-pruning its lower branches to create a straight trunk. In sunny habitats, it retains more lower branches and is not as tall. The fruits ripen in late summer and stay on the trees through the winter. Sugar hackberry produces the most fruit when it is 30–70 years old. It is hardy as far north as zone 7, and occurs from Virginia and southern Indiana south to eastern Texas and central Florida.

SHAGBARK HICKORY
Carya ovata

This distinctive hickory usually has abundant nut crops every other year. It grows in well-drained soils and prefers an open, sunny habitat, but it will also grow in semishade, frequently occurring on dry hillsides in mixed forests of hickory and oak. It is slow growing and usually does not produce large fruit crops until it is about 40 years old. Shagbark hickories are certainly long-term investments for wildlife, as they may live to be 300 years old. Hickory fruits are eaten by wild turkey, mallard, wood duck, and many smaller birds that pick at nut scraps after they have been cracked open and discarded by squirrels. A few of the smaller birds that eat hickory nuts are Carolina chickadee, white-breasted nuthatch, pine warbler, and rufous-sided towhee. Shagbark hickory has an extensive distribution throughout southeastern Canada and United States. It is hardy north to zone 5, and occurs from southern Quebec and Nebraska south to northeastern Texas and northcentral Florida. It does not occur along the Atlantic or Gulf coastal plains.

A beautiful symbol of the deep south, the live oak is also a very important tree for wildlife. As with all oaks, the meaty nuts are important to both birds and mammals. In the southeast, acorns are preferred foods for wild turkey, wood duck, northern bobwhite, common grackle, scrub jay, brown thrasher, and many others. Live oak grows in a wide variety of soils, but does best in coastal sandy soils. It occurs commonly in coastal locations from Virginia south through Florida and west to eastern Texas. Its tolerance to salinity makes it an excellent selection in coastal habitats. Live oak has dark green, evergreen leaves and usually grows to about 50 feet. Acorns ripen in September and are usually available until December.

LIVE OAK
Quercus virginiana

CABBAGE PALMETTO
Sabal palmetto

Cabbage palmetto grows in sandy soils along the Atlantic coast from North Carolina to Florida, where it is the state tree. It grows in prairies, marshes, pinelands, and disturbed soils. This branchless tree grows up to 80 feet tall and produces large clusters of small black drupelike fruits. The fruit is frequently eaten by many kinds of bird, including northern bobwhite, cardinal, eastern phoebe, and red-bellied woodpecker. Since cabbage palmetto grows in disturbed soils, it readily colonizes roadsides and old fields. Such new habitats are permitting this useful native tree to become increasingly common. Its tolerance of various soil and water conditions, plus its value as a bird-attracting plant, make it an excellent choice for landscaping.

COMMON PERSIMMON
Diospyros virginiana

The fruit of common persimmon is a favorite of American robin, northern bobwhite, eastern bluebird, eastern phoebe, cedar waxwings, and at least six other species of eastern bird. The fleshy 1$\frac{1}{2}$-inch-diameter yellow fruits ripen from September to November. This 30–50-foot tree usually grows in moist soils or in old fields and roadsides, and first fruits when it is about 6 feet tall. Common persimmon is hardy as far north as zone 5, occurring from southern Connecticut south to Florida and west to Texas and Kansas. It usually grows in sunny habitats and does best in light soils.

LOBLOLLY PINE
Pinus taeda

This fast-growing pine grows to 100 feet tall and thrives on a variety of sunlit soils from poorly drained coastal plains to better drained hill country. Sometimes it grows in pure stands, but frequently mixes with shortleaf pine (*Pinus echinata*). Loblolly and other southern pines produce abundant seed crops that are an important food for many birds of the southeast pinelands. Southern pines are an important food source for Carolina chickadee, brown-headed nuthatch, rufous-sided towhee, and many others. Loblolly pine is an excellent choice for providing cover and food in the southeast. It occurs as far north as North Carolina and is found west to eastern Texas and south through most of Florida.

YAUPON HOLLY
Ilex vomitoria

Depending on growing conditions, the Yaupon holly can grow to 25 feet tall. Yaupon fruits best in open sunlight, but it also grows well in partial shade. It prefers moist, sandy soils with good drainage. Yaupon makes an excellent wild-life hedge, providing abundant nest sites and fruit. The plentiful red drupe fruits are about one-half inch in diameter, they ripen by October, and stay on the branch through the winter. As with most hollies, fruits usually appear only on female plants, but occasionally both male and female flowers grow on the same shrub. Yaupon fruits are readily eaten by gray catbird, northern mockingbird, brown thrasher, northern bobwhite, and many other songbirds. It is hardy as far north as zone 7 and occurs from West Virginia south to the Gulf coast and northern Florida.

MORE RECOMMENDED PLANTINGS
FOR ATTRACTING BIRDS IN THE SOUTHEAST

Evergreen Trees
CEDAR, EASTERN RED (*Juniperus virginiana*)
HEMLOCK, EASTERN (*Tsuga canadensis*)
HOLLY, AMERICAN (*Ilex opaca*)

Large Deciduous Trees
HACKBERRY, COMMON (*Celtis occidentalis*)
MAPLE, NORWAY (*Acer platanoides*)
MAPLE, RED (*Acer rubrum*)
MAPLE, SUGAR (*Acer saccharum*)
MULBERRY, RED (*Morus rubra*)
OAK, BLACK (*Quercus velutina*)
OAK, NORTHERN RED (*Quercus rubra*)
OAK, PIN (*Quercus palustris*)
OAK, SCARLET (*Quercus coccinea*)

Small Deciduous Trees
CRABAPPLES, FLOWERING (*Malus spp.*)
DOGWOOD, ALTERNATE-LEAF (*Cornus alternifolia*)
DOGWOOD, FLOWERING (*Cornus florida*)
HOP HORNBEAM, AMERICAN (*Ostrya virginia*)
MOUNTAIN ASH, AMERICAN (*Sorbus americana*)
MOUNTAIN ASH, EUROPEAN (*Sorbus aucuparia*)
SASSAFRAS (*Sassafras albidum*)

Evergreen Shrubs
COTONEASTER, ROCKSPRAY (*Cotoneaster horizontalis*)
HOLLY, INKBERRY (*Ilex glabra*)

HUCKLEBERRY, BOX (*Gaylussacia brachycera*)
JUNIPER, COMMON (*Juniperus communis*)
JUNIPER, CHINESE (*Juniperus chinensis*)
YEW, CANADA (*Taxus canadensis*)

Deciduous Shrubs
DOGWOOD, RED-OSIER (*Cornus stolonifera*)
DOGWOOD, SILKY (*Cornus amomum*)
ELDER, AMERICAN (*Sambucus canadensis*)
EUONYMUS, WINGED (*Euonymus alata*)
FIRE THORN, SCARLET (*Pyracantha coccinea*)
HUCKLEBERRY, DWARF (*Gaylussacia dumosa*)
OLIVE, CARDINAL AUTUMN (*Elaeagnus angustifolia*)
ROSE, PASTURE (*Rosa carolina*)
ROSE, RUGOSA (*Rosa rugosa*)
ROSE, SWAMP (*Rosa palustris*)
SPICEBUSH (*Lindera benzoin*)
SUMAC, SMOOTH (*Rhus glabra*)
SUMAC, STAGHORN (*Rhus typhina*)
VIBURNUM, HOBBLEBUSH (*Viburnum alnifolium*)
VIBURNUM, MAPLELEAF (*Viburnum acerifolium*)
VIBURNUM, NORTHERN ARROWWOOD (*Viburnum recognitum*)
VIBURNUM, SOUTHERN ARROWWOOD (*Viburnum dentatum*)

MORE RECOMMENDED PLANTINGS
FOR ATTRACTING BIRDS IN THE SOUTHEAST *(cont.)*

Ground Covers
BEARBERRY (*Arctostaphylos uva-ursi*)
BUGLEWEED (*Ajuga reptans*)
BUNCHBERRY (*Cornus canadensis*)
COTONEASTER, BEARBERRY (*Cotoneaster dammeri*)
COTONEASTER, CREEPING (*Cotoneaster adpressa*)
CROWBERRY, BLACK (*Empetrum nigrum*)
JUNIPER, CREEPING (*Juniperus horizontalis*)
JUNIPER, SARGENT (*Juniperus chinensis sargentii*)

Deciduous Shrubs
ALDER, SPECKLED (*Alnus rugosa*)
BARBERRY, JAPANESE (*Berberis thunbergii*)
BAYBERRY (*Myrica pensylvanica*)
BLACKBERRIES (*Rubus spp.*)
BLUEBERRY, HIGHBUSH (*Vaccinium corymbosum*)
BUTTONBUSH (*Cephalanthus occidentalis*)

DANGLEBERRY, BLACK (*Gaylussacia frondosa*)
PARTRIDGEBERRY (*Mitchella repens*)
STRAWBERRY, CULTIVATED (*Fragaria chiloensis*)
STRAWBERRY, WILD (*Fragaria virginiana*)
WINTERCREEPER (*Euonymus fortunei*) "colorata"
WINTERGREEN, CHECKERBERRY (*Gaultheria procumbens*)

Vines
AMPELOPSIS, HEARTLEAF (*Ampelopsis cordata*)
CREEPER, VIRGINIA (*Parthenocissus quinquefolia*)
GRAPE, FOX (*Vitis labrusca*)
GRAPE, FROST (*Vitis vulpina*)
GRAPE, SUMMER (*Vitis aestivalis*)
GREENBRIER, CAT (*Smilax glauca*)
IVY, ENGLISH (*Hedera helix*)
WINTERCREEPER (*Euonymus fortunei*) "vegata"

BIRD PLANTINGS FOR THE SOUTHEAST
OTHER GOOD CHOICES

Evergreen Trees

Name	Zone	Native(N) Alien(A)	Height (ft)	Light	Preferred Soil	Fruit Period	Fruit Type	Remarks
BLACKHAW, RUSTY (*Viburnum rufidulum*)	6	N	16–18	Sun	Sandy/ loam	Summer/ fall	Blue-black drupe	Choice food of eastern bluebird and cedar waxwing; semievergreen
DAHOON (*Ilex cassine*)	7b	N	to 40	Sun/ shade	Moist/ drained	Fall/ winter	Red/ yellow berry	Provides many birds with a good food source through the winter
FARKLEBERRY (*Vaccinium arboreum*)	6	N	to 30	Sun/ shade	Dry/ drained	Early fall	Black berry	Fruits eaten by many kinds of bird, especially favored by mockingbird
MAGNOLIA, SOUTHERN (*Magnolia grandiflora*)	7b	N	to 50	Sun	Moist/ drained	Summer/ fall	Rose drupe	At least 19 bird species eat this fruit, including catbird, fish crow, northern flicker, eastern kingbird, mockingbird, and wood thrush
MAGNOLIA, SWEETBAY (*Magnolia virginiana*)	5b	N	to 35	Sun	Moist/ drained	Fall	Red drupe	Choice food of eastern kingbird, mockingbird, robin, wood thrush, and red-eyed vireo
PINE, LONGLEAF (*Pinus palustris*)	7	N	to 125	Sun	Sandy	Fall	Cone	Grows very well near the sea; often a nest site; choice food for cardinal, brown-headed nuthatch, and tufted titmouse
PINE, SAND (*Pinus clausa*)	10	N	to 60	Sun	Sandy/ infertile	Persis-tent	Cone	Nest site of scrub jay; occurs in coastal Florida
PINE, SHORTLEAF (*Pinus echinata*)	6	N	to 100	Sun	Sandy/ loam	Fall	Cone	Frequent nest site; many species eat the seeds
PINE, SLASH (*Pinus elliottii*)	9	N	to 100	Sun	Sandy/ moist	Fall	Cone	One of the most rapid-growing, early-maturing eastern trees
PINE, VIRGINIA (*Pinus virginiana*)	5	N	to 40	Sun	Dry/ drained	Fall	Cone	Often a nest site; the seed is a choice food for bobwhite, cardinal, Carolina chickadee, brown-headed nuthatch, and song sparrow
REDBAY (*Persea borbonia*)	8	N	to 70	Sun	Moist	Late summer/ fall	Blue or purple drupe	Choice food of eastern bluebird, robin, and bobwhite; grows in swamps and along streams

Tall Deciduous Trees

Name	Zone	Native(N) Alien(A)	Height (ft)	Light	Preferred Soil	Fruit Period	Fruit Type	Remarks
HAWTHORN, BLUEBERRY (*Crataegus brachyacantha*)	8	N	to 40	Sun/ half sun	Sandy loam	Summer/ fall	Bright blue- black pome	Frequent nest site; thorny shrubs provide safe cover; at least 36 bird species eat the fruit of hawthorns
HICKORY, WATER (*Carya aquatica*)	7	N	to 100	Sun	Moist	Fall	Nut	Fair food for wood duck and mallard
OAK, BLACKJACK (*Quercus marilandica*)	6	N	to 30	Sun/ half sun	Dry/ sandy/ sterile	Fall 1 yr*	Acorn	Frequent nest sites for hawks and many other kinds of bird; choice food for bobwhite, wood duck, common grackle, brown thrasher, blue jay, red-headed woodpecker, and wild turkey
OAK, CHESTNUT (*Quercus prinus*)	6	N	60–80	Sun/ half sun	Dry/ sandy/ gravelly	Fall 2–3 yr*	Acorn	
OAK, LAUREL (*Quercus laurifolia*)	8	N	60–70	Varied	Moist	Fall 1 yr*	Acorn	
OAK, POST (*Quercus stellata*)	5	N	40–50	Sun/ half sun	Dry/ sterile	Fall 2–3 yr*	Acorn	
OAK, SPANISH RED (*Quercus falcata*)	7	N	to 80	Sun/ half sun	Dry/ sandy/ clay	Fall 1–2 yr*	Acorn	
OAK, SWAMP CHESTNUT (*Quercus michauxii*)	6	N	60–80	Sun/ half sun	Moist	Fall 3–5 yr*	Acorn	
OAK, WATER (*Quercus nigra*)	6	N	60–70	Sun/ half sun	Moist	Fall 1–2 yr*	Acorn	
OAK, WILLOW (*Quercus phellos*)	6	N	60–80	Sun/ half sun	Drained	Fall 1 yr*	Acorn	
PECAN (*Carva illinoensis*)	6	N	to 150	Sun	Dry/ moist/ drained	Early fall	Nut	A favorite of wood duck and eaten by at least 9 other bird species. Largest of all hickories

*Intervals between acorn crops.

Small Deciduous Trees

Name	Zone	Native(N) Alien(A)	Height (ft)	Light	Preferred Soil	Fruit Period	Fruit Type	Remarks
BUCKTHORN, CAROLINA (*Rhamnus caroliniana*)	6	N	25–35	Sun/shade	Moist/drained	Fall	Red/black drupe	Berries eaten by many songbirds, especially catbird
FRINGE TREE, CHINESE (*Chionanthus retusus*)	6	A	20–25	Sun/shade	Rich/acid	Fall	Dark blue drupe	Datelike seeds are eaten by many kinds of bird
FRINGE TREE, WHITE (*Chionanthus virginicus*)	5	N	20–25	Sun/half sun	Moist/drained	Fall	Dark blue drupe	Fruit eaten by many kinds of bird; often eaten by pileated woodpeckers; tolerates city conditions
HAWTHORN, PARSLEY (*Crataegus marshallii*)	6	N	15–25	Sun	Swampy	Late summer/winter	Bright red pome	The thorny thickets make good cover, providing brood-rearing areas for ruffed grouse
MYRTLE, WAX (*Myrica cerifera*)	7	N	to 40	Sun	Moist/sand	Fall/winter	Blue-gray nutlet	A good winter food source for many songbirds
OAK, BLUEJACK (*Quercus incana*)	8	N	to 20	Sun/half sun	Dry/sandy	Fall	Acorn	Very productive acorn producer; choice food of northern bobwhite and rufous-sided towhee
OAK, CHAPMAN (*Quercus chapmanii*)	9	N	to 25	Sun	Well drained	Matures in first season	Acorn	Covers wide areas with shrubby growth, giving much cover and food to many birds. Annual acorn crop
PLUM, AMERICAN (*Prunus americana*)	6	N	20–30	Sun/shade	Dry/moist/drained	Summer/fall	Red drupe	Occasional nest site; fruit eaten by many kinds of bird, including bobwhite, robin, ring-necked pheasant, and red-headed woodpecker
POSSUM HAW (*Ilex decidua*)	6	N	10–20	Sun/half sun	Dry/moist/drained	Fall/winter	Red berry	Good winter food for eastern bluebird, robin, cedar waxwings, purple finch, red-bellied woodpecker, and many others
VIBURNUM, POSSUM HAW (*Viburnum nudum*)	7	N	20	Sun	Swampy/sandy/acid	Fall	Pink to blue drupe	Good protection for birds in wet areas; food for bobwhite

Evergreen Shrubs

Name	Zone	Native(N) Alien(A)	Height (ft)	Light	Preferred Soil	Fruit Period	Fruit Type	Remarks
BLUEBERRY, GROUND (Vaccinium myrsinites)	7	N	to 3	Sun	Drained/sandy	May	Purple/black berry	Among the most important summer and early-fall foods for grouse
CHERRY LAUREL, CAROLINA (Prunus caroliniana)	7	N	to 18	Varied	Varied	Persistent	Black	Choice food of bluebird, mockingbird, robin, and cedar waxwings
COTONEASTER, BEARBERRY (Cotoneaster dammeri)	6	A	to 1	Sun/half sun	Drained	Fall/winter	Red pome	Provides good ground shelter; fruit eaten by many types of songbird
COTONEASTER, FRANCHET (Cotoneaster franchettii)	7	A	to 7	Sun/half sun	Drained	Fall	Red pome	
DAHOON, MYRTLE (Ilex myrtifolia)	7b	N	to 23	Varied	Sandy/acid	Fall/winter	Red/orange berry	Male and female plants needed for fruit set; berries readily eaten by mockingbird, cedar waxwings, robin, and eastern bluebird; occasional nest site for mockingbird, brown thrasher, and rufous-sided towhee
GALLBERRY, LARGE (Ilex coriacea)	7	N	to 8	Varied	Sandy/acid	Fall	Black berry	
HOLLY, CHINESE (Ilex cornuta)	7	A	to 7	Sun/half sun	Acid/drained	Summer/winter	Red berry	
HOLLY, JAPANESE (Ilex crenata)	6b	A	to 10	Sun/half sun	Drained/rich	Summer/winter	Black berry	
JUNIPER, JAPANESE GARDEN (Juniperus chinensis var. procumbens)	4	A	to 1	Sun/half sun	Drained	Late spring/summer	Blue berry	Provides good ground shelter; plant male and female for fruit.
JUNIPER, SHORE (Juniperus conferta)	5–6	A	to 1	Sun/half sun	Moist/drained	Late spring/summer	Blue berry	Shore juniper is very salt tolerant
OAK, DWARF LIVE (Quercus minima)	10	N	to 3	Varied	Sandy/clay	August/November	Acorn	Acorns are favored turkey food
PALMETTO, DWARF (Sabal minor)	8–9	N	to 8	Sun	Varied	Year round	Black	Good songbird food; good nest site for ground-nesting birds, such as the warbler

Deciduous Shrubs

Name	Zone	Native(N) Alien(A)	Height (ft)	Light	Preferred Soil	Fruit Period	Fruit Type	Remarks
DEERBERRY, COMMON (*Vaccinium stamineum*)	5	N	6	Sun/shade	Dry/drained	Late summer	Green to purple berry	Important food of ruffed grouse, bobwhite, and other ground-feeding birds
HONEYSUCKLE, WINTER (*Lonicera fragrantissima*)	6	A	6–8	Sun	Drained	Fall/winter	Red berry	Excellent nest site; very fragrant; choice food of catbird and mockingbird
LESPEDEZA, SHRUB (*Lespedeza japonica*) (*L. bicolor*)	5	A	4–8	Sun	Drained	Fall	Pod	Plant *L. japonica* in northern part of region; plant *L. bicolor* to the south. Mainly quail foods
OAK, RUNNING (*Quercus pumila*)	7	N	6	Sun/shade	Dry/drained	Summer/fall	Acorn	Acorns eaten by wild turkeys and ruffed grouse

Vines

Name	Zone	Native(N) Alien(A)	Evergreen Deciduous	Light	Preferred Soil	Fruit Period	Fruit Type	Remarks
GRAPE, WINTER SWEET (*Vitis cinerea*)	5	N	D	Sun/shade	Moist/drained	Fall	Black/purple berry	Grape vines overtopping other plants provide nest sites for such birds as cardinals, catbirds, and brown thrasher; these also use grape bark in their nests
GREENBRIER, LAUREL (*Smilax laurifolia*)	7	N	E	Sun/half sun	Moist	Late summer/persistent	Black berry	Provides excellent cover, food, and nest sites for many birds, including flicker, pileated woodpecker, ruffed grouse, and red-bellied woodpecker
HONEYSUCKLE, TRUMPET (*Lonicera sempervirens*)	4	N	Semi to E	Sun	Drained	Late summer/fall	Red berry	Hardiest of all the honeysuckle vines; excellent for hummingbirds
SNAILSEED, CAROLINA (*Cocculus carolinus*)	7	N	D to semi-E	Sun	Moist/dry/drained	Late summer/persistent	Red drupe	Pea-size fruit; often persists through winter; only female plant bears fruit; eaten by brown thrasher, mockingbird, and eastern phoebe
SUPPLEJACK, ALABAMA (*Berchemia scandens*)	6	N	D	Sun	Moist/rich	Summer/fall	Blue/black drupe	Climbs to 15–20 feet; at least 14 bird species eat its fruit

THE PRAIRIES AND PLAINS

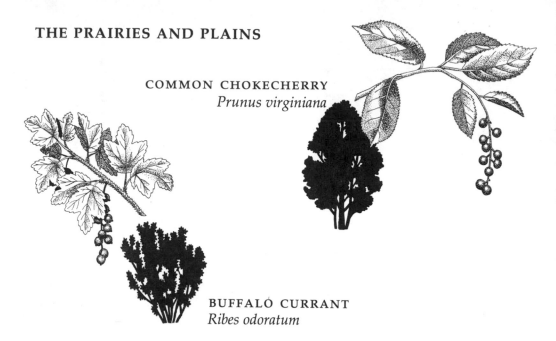

COMMON CHOKECHERRY
Prunus virginiana

BUFFALO CURRANT
Ribes odoratum

This common shrub or small tree of fencerows and thickets produces abundant fruits that range in color from red to black. The fruits are tart-tasting and readily consumed by at least 43 bird species—they are especially favored by the eastern bluebird. Common chokecherry grows from 6 to 30 feet tall and sometimes forms extensive thickets. It has also been used with some success for erosion control, since it thrives in a great variety of soils, including sand. Chokecherry is hardy north through zone 2 and has a widespread distribution from Newfoundland to British Columbia and south to Georgia and California.

Buffalo (clove) currant is a spine-forming shrub that grows to a maximum height of about 6 feet. It is a popular cultivated plant sometimes used in jams and jellies. Buffalo currant has fragrant, bright yellow flowers from April to May and blackish purple smooth berries that ripen from June to September. The fruits are eaten by many types of songbird as soon as they ripen. Buffalo currant grows along woodland borders, cliffs, rocky hillsides, and other open habitats. It prefers well-drained soil and is a common plant on open, sandy habitats from Minnesota and South Dakota south to Louisiana and east Texas. Buffalo currant adapts well to cultivation and is an excellent bird-attracting addition to property borders, fencerows, and other open habitats.

Common hackberry grows on rocky hillsides, open pastures, and moist stream banks, from the middle Atlantic states west to Manitoba, North Dakota, Nebraska, and Kansas. Since it is a drought-resistant native tree, it makes an excel-

COMMON HACKBERRY
Celtis occidentalis

lent choice for a shelterbelt planting. It is adaptable to a great variety of sites, but appears to thrive best on sunlit, alkaline soils. Common hackberry grows to 30–50 feet and produces an annual crop of quarter-inch red or purple drupe fruits that may survive through the winter if they are not quickly consumed by birds. At least 24 bird species eat common hackberry fruit—it is especially favored by wild turkey, common flicker, northern mockingbird, Swainson's thrush, and cardinal.

AMUR MAPLE
Acer ginnala

A native of the windswept plains of Siberia, the Amur maple is an excellent choice for providing cover and food in the very northern plains region north to Alberta and Saskatchewan. Named after the Amur River, which separates Manchuria and Siberia, this hardy little tree grows only about 20 feet tall, but it has a very graceful form and is a colorful addition to the fall landscape as its foliage turns from dark green to scarlet. Maple fruits are one of the favorite foods of evening grosbeak and are regularly eaten by sharp-tailed grouse, purple finch, pine grosbeak, and rose-breasted grosbeaks.

WHITE MULBERRY
Morus alba

White mulberry is one of the most widespread deciduous trees in the world. It is probably a native of China, although its original range is little known, since it has long been cultivated and spread around the world as the principal food of the silkworm. White mulberry grows to 40 feet and may develop a trunk diameter of 3 feet. As with the native red mulberry (*Morus rubra*), the male and female flowers may grow on the same tree or on neighboring trees. The fruit is usually white (though sometimes red or black) and matures from June to August. At least 44 bird species readily consume the fruit. White mulberry grows best in rich, moist soils, but since it is such a hardy tree it even does well in clay and sand. It is much more tolerant of wind than native mulberries and thus has a wider distribution in the prairie states where it makes an effective windbreak. White mulberry is naturalized in Texas, Oklahoma, Arizona, Arkansas, and Louisiana. It also occurs north through the eastern prairie states to Minnesota and east to Maine.

The burr oak is a hardy native western tree, capable of withstanding the wind and droughts that eliminate most trees from this region. Large burr oaks may grow 150 feet tall and live for 350–400 years. Its flowers appear from April to May and the distinctive large acorns ripen from August to September. This grand oak usually produces good nut crops every 2 to 3 years. Acorns are eaten by wood duck, jays, greater prairie chicken, northern bobwhite, and wild turkey. Burr oak grows on well-drained land in eastern Texas, Oklahoma, Arkansas, and Louisiana east to Georgia and north to Nova Scotia. It grows along rivers west to the Dakotas and Manitoba. Burr oak can withstand temperatures as low as $-40°F$ ($-40°$ C), which makes it hardy enough to survive the coldest regions of the northeastern and northcentral United States.

The Ponderosa pine is a huge tree that is native to the west—it may grow to a towering 150 feet and develop a trunk diameter of 5–8 feet. It usually grows in large single-species stands, but it can be effectively planted in shelterbelts to provide cover through the year for birds and serve as an effective windbreak. Pon-

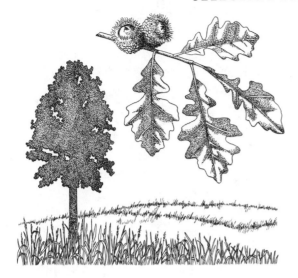

BURR OAK
Quercus macrocarpa

PONDEROSA PINE
Pinus ponderosa

derosa pine is rather drought- and fire-resistant, but not very resistant to insects. This impressive tree tolerates many types of soils and grows at elevations ranging from 2000 to 10,000 feet. It first produces seed when it is about 20 years old and doesn't reach maximum production until 150 years old. Good seed crops occur every 2 to 5 years. The tiny, abundant seeds (12,000 to a pound) are important food for blue grouse, band-tailed pigeon, Lewis' woodpecker, and many others. Ponderosa pine and its many varieties grow on dry, rocky hillsides from South Dakota and western Nebraska south to western Texas and west along the Pacific coast from California to British Columbia.

Saskatoon serviceberry varies in growth form, depending on soil and water availability. In rich, moist soils it forms dense thickets or grows 6–12 feet tall as a small tree. In hard, dry soils it often grows prostrate or takes on a stunted appearance. Saskatoon serviceberry has fragrant white flowers in May, and sweet and juicy purple-black pome fruits each July and August. This hardy serviceberry grows in open woods, thickets, stream banks, and canyons from South Dakota and Colorado to western Canada and north to Alaska. It also occurs through Cal-

SASKATOON SERVICEBERRY
Amelanchier alnifolia

ifornia to New Mexico. Its fruit is eaten by many kinds of bird, including blue grouse, mountain quail, black-billed magpie, common crow, American robin, and Swainson's thrush.

SNOWBERRY
Symphoricarpos albus

The snowberry is a thicket-forming deciduous shrub that will grow on rocky hillsides, gravel banks, and other sites that are too difficult for most other shrubs. Common snowberry grows up to 6 feet tall in good soil, but plants in poor sites are usually much smaller. It lives in both sunny and shady habitats—plants in the sun produce more of the white berries that give the plant its name. The berries mature in August and September and usually stay on the shrub through the winter, making snowberry an important source of winter food for many birds, including ruffed grouse, ring-necked pheasant, American robin, cedar waxwings, and pine grosbeak. The snowberry is an attractive native shrub and an excellent bird planting for waste areas, hedges, and property borders. It is hardy as far north as zone 4, and occurs from Nova Scotia south to Pennsylvania and west to Colorado.

SKUNKBUSH SUMAC
Rhus aromatica var. *flabelliformis*

This drought-resistant, deep-rooted shrub makes an excellent shelterbelt planting for the plains and prairies. Skunkbush sumac is a hardy, deciduous shrub that grows about 12 feet tall and earns its name from the offensive smell that results from crushing its leaves. It can be propagated from root cuttings. Red fruit ripen in August and September and are eaten by at least 25 bird species, including ruffed grouse, evening grosbeak, American robin, northern bobwhite, and greater prairie chicken. It grows best in open, sunny habitats on limestone soils, but can live in a great variety of sites. Skunkbush sumac occurs from the Dakotas south into northern Mexico and west to California.

MORE RECOMMENDED PLANTINGS
FOR ATTRACTING BIRDS IN THE PRAIRIES AND PLAINS

Evergreen Trees
ARBORVITAE, EASTERN (*Thuga occidentalis*)
CEDAR, EASTERN RED (*Juniperus virginiana*)
PINE, SCOTCH (*Pinus sylvestris*)
SPRUCE, COLORADO BLUE (*Picea pungens*)

Large Deciduous Trees
ASH, GREEN (*Fraxinus pennsylvanica*)
ASPEN, QUAKING (*Populus tremuloides*)
BIRCH, PAPER (*Betula papyrifera*)
CHERRY, BLACK (*Prunus serotina*)
CHERRY, PIN (*Prunus pennsylvanica*)
COTTONWOOD, EASTERN (*Populus deltoides*)

HACKBERRY, SUGAR (*Celtis laevigata*)
MAPLE, BOX ELDER (*Acer negundo*)
OAK, POST (*Quercus stellata*)
OSAGE ORANGE (*Maclura pomifera*)
PECAN (*Carya illinoiensis*)
WALNUT, BLACK (*Juglans nigra*)
WILLOW, BLACK (*Salix nigra*)

Small Deciduous Trees
APPLE, COMMON (*Malus pumila*)
CRABAPPLE, FLOWERING (*Malus spp.*)
HAWTHORN, WASHINGTON (*Crataegus spp.*)
MOUNTAIN ASH, AMERICAN (*Sorbus americana*)
MOUNTAIN ASH, EUROPEAN (*Sorbus aucuparia*)

MORE RECOMMENDED PLANTINGS
FOR ATTRACTING BIRDS IN THE PRAIRIES AND PLAINS

MOUNTAIN ASH, NORTHERN
(*Sorbus decora*)
PLUM, AMERICAN (*Prunus americana*)
POSSUM HAW (*Ilex decidua*)

Evergreen Shrubs

JUNIPER, CHINESE (*Juniperus chinensis*)
JUNIPER, COMMON (*Juniperus communis*)
JUNIPER CREEPING (*Juniperus horizontalis*)

Deciduous Shrubs

BUCKTHORN, COMMON
(*Rhamnus cathartica*)
BUCKTHORN, GLOSSY (*Rhamnus frangula*)
BUTTONBUSH (*Cephalanthus occidentalis*)
CORALBERRY (*Symphoricarpos orbiculatus*)

COTONEASTER, ROCKSPRAY
(*Cotoneaster horizontalis*)
CURRANT, AMERICAN BLACK
(*Ribes americanum*)
DOGWOOD, RED-OSIER (*Cornus stolonifera*)
ELDER, AMERICAN (*Sambucus canadensis*)
ELDER, SCARLET (*Sambucus pubens*)
EUONYMUS, WINGED (*Euonymus alata*)
HONEYSUCKLE, AMUR (*Lonicera maackii*)
HONEYSUCKLE, MORROW
(*Lonicera morrowii*)

HONEYSUCKLE, TATARIAN
(*Lonicera tatarica*) esp. var.
Cascade and Zabel's
OLIVE, CARDINAL AUTUMN
(*Elaeagnus umbellata*)
OLIVE, RUSSIAN (*Elaeagnus angustifolia*)
RASPBERRY, BLACK (*Rubus occidentalis*)
RASPBERRY, RED (*Rubus idaeus*)
SUMAC, SMOOTH (*Rhus glabra*)
VIBURNUM, AMERICAN
CRANBERRY (*Viburnum trilobum*)

Ground Cover

BEARBERRY (*Arctostaphylos uva-ursi*)
BUNCHBERRY (*Cornus canadensis*)
COTONEASTER, CREEPING
(*Cotoneaster adpressa*)
JUNIPER, CREEPING (*Juniperus horizontalis*)
STRAWBERRY (*Fragaria spp.*)

Vines

AMPELOPSIS, HEARTLEAF
(*Ampelopsis cordata*)
BITTERSWEET, AMERICAN
(*Celastrus scandens*)
CREEPER, VIRGINIA
(*Parthenocissus quinquefolia*)
GRAPE, FOX (*Vitis labrusca*)
GRAPE, RIVERBANK (*Vitis riparia*)
GREENBRIER, COMMON (*Smilax rotundifolia*)
HONEYSUCKLE, TRUMPET
(*Lonicera sempervirens*)
MOONSEED, COMMON
(*Menispermum canadense*)
TRUMPET CREEPER, COMMON
(*Campsis radicans*)

BIRD PLANTINGS FOR THE PRAIRIES AND PLAINS
OTHER GOOD CHOICES

Deciduous Trees

Name	Zone	Native(N) Alien(A)	Height (ft)	Light	Preferred Soil	Period	Fruit Type	Remarks
BIRCH, ALASKAN PAPER (Betula papyrifera var. humilis)	1	N	to 30	Sun	Dry/moist	Late summer/early fall	Samara	This Alaskan variety is hardier and shorter than eastern forms; seeds and buds are a favorite food of ruffed grouse, pine siskin, and American goldfinch
COTTONWOOD, PLAINS (Populus sargentii)	2	N	60–90	Sun	Moist	Spring/summer	Capsule	Frequent along streams in western plains; buds eaten by grouse
ELM, SLIPPERY (Ulmus rubra)	4	N	to 60	Sun	Dry/moist/rich/drained	Spring	Samara	Buds are eaten by birds; fruit is a favorite food of purple finch and American goldfinch
HACKBERRY, NETLEAF (Celtis reticulata)	6	N	to 21	Sun	Dry/rocky/sandy	Late summer	Red-brown drupe	Berries rich in calcium; food for northern (Bullock's) oriole, robin, roadrunner, and northern flicker
HAWTHORN, DOWNY (Crataegus mollis)	4	N	15–25	Sun	Dry	August/October/November	Red pome	These hardy hawthorns can survive the harsh conditions of the northern plains. As a group, hawthorns are known to attract at least 36 kinds of fruit-eating birds
HAWTHORN, FIREBERRY (Crataegus chrysocarpa)	3	N	to 13	Sun	Dry/moist/rocky	Early fall	Red pome	
HAWTHORN, FLESHY (Crataegus succulenta)	3	N	to 20	Sun	Dry/moist/rocky	Early fall	Red pome	
MULBERRY, TEXAS (Morus microphylla)	7	N	10–20	Sun	Moist/drained	Spring	Black compound drupe	A thicket-forming tree that does best in limestone soils; plant male and female trees nearby to produce fruit. A favorite of Gambel's and harlequin quail and many kinds of songbird
WILLOW, DIAMOND (Salix rigida)	4	N	15–24	Sun	Moist/sand or gravel	Early summer	Capsule	Plant willows to reduce streambank erosion and provide excellent cover. At least 23 bird species are known to eat buds and tender twigs; these include ruffed, blue, spruce, and sharp-tailed grouse. Willows should not be planted near underground plumbing as roots may clog pipes
WILLOW, PEACH-LEAVED (Salix amygdaloides)	5	N	40–60	Sun	Moist	Spring	Capsule	
WILLOW, SANDBAR (Salix interior)	2	N	to 30	Sun	Moist/alluvial	Spring	Capsule	
WILLOW, WHITE (Salix alba)	2	A	to 75	Sun	Moist	Early summer	Capsule	

Evergreen Trees

Name	Zone	Native(N) Alien(A)	Height (ft)	Light	Preferred Soil	Period	Fruit Type	Remarks
JUNIPER, ASHE (*Juniperus ashei*)	7	N	6–20	Sun	Dry/ sandy/ gravel	Fall/ year round	Blue berry	Copious seed production; important food for robins; central to southwest Texas. Forms dense thickets between 600 and 2000 feet
JUNIPER, ROCKY MOUNTAIN (*Juniperus scopulorum*)	4	N	30–40	Sun	Alkaline/ dry/ sandy	Fall/ year round	Blue berry	Drought-resistant; similar in appearance to eastern red cedar; not recommended for eastern part of this region
JUNIPER, ONE-SEED (*Juniperus monosperma*)	5	N	20–30	Sun	Dry/ rocky	Fall/ year round	Blue	Rapid growing for junipers; excellent nesting cover; as with all junipers only the female bears fruit; important food for Gambel's quail and several kinds of songbird
PINE, AUSTRIAN (*Pinus nigra*)	4	A	70–90	Sun to part shade	Varied/ sandy/ poor	Fall/ winter	Cone	Excellent cover and abundant seed production; use only where protected from direct wind; northern plains
SPRUCE, BLACK HILLS (*Picea glauca var. densata*)	3	N	to 70	Sun to half shade	Moist	Fall	Cone	More resistant to winter desiccation than Colorado blue spruce; northern plains

Deciduous Shrubs

Name	Zone	Native(N) Alien(A)	Height (ft)	Light	Preferred Soil	Period	Fruit Type	Remarks
BLACKBERRY, HIGHBUSH (*Rubus ostryifolius*)	6	N	3–8	Sun/ half sun	Dry/ moist/ drained	Summer	Black berry	At least 63 bird species are known to eat the fruit of blackberries and raspberries; also excellent cover
BUFFALO BERRY, SILVER (*Shepherdia argentea*)	2	N	3–7	Sun/ shade	Dry/ drained	Summer	Red berry	Can be grown in areas too dry, salty, or alkaline for other shrubs; at least 12 bird species eat its fruit, including robin and sharp-tailed grouse
CARAGANA, PIGMY (*Caragana pygmalea*)	1	A	3–4	Sun	Dry	Summer	Brown pod	Yellow flowers attract hummingbirds
CHERRY, BESSEY (*Prunus besseyi*)	3	N	to 2	Sun	Dry	Summer/ early fall	Black drupe	A prostrate shrub; fruit eaten by ring-necked pheasant and other birds; dense form provides excellent nesting cover

Name	Zone	Native(N) Alien(A)	Height (ft)	Light	Preferred Soil	Fruit Period	Type	Remarks
CHERRY, DWARF SAND (*Prunus pumila*)	4	N	3-5	Sun	Dry/ moist/ drained	Summer	Black drupe	A prostrate shrub that thrives in sandy soil; provides good nesting cover and food
CHERRY, KOREAN (*Prunus japonica*)	4	A	3-4	Sun	Varied	Summer	Red drupe	Abundant white flowers; cold-hardy
COTONEASTER, EUROPEAN (*Cotoneaster integerrimo*)	6	A	to 5	Sun	Dry	Early August	Red pome	Good hedge shrubs provide excellent cover and fruit
COTONEASTER, HEDGE (*Cotoneaster lucida*)	5	A	6-8	Sun	Dry	Early fall	Black pome	
COTONEASTER, SUNGARI ROCKSPRAY (*Cotoneaster racemiflora soongorica*)	4	A	to 8	Sun	Dry	Late summer/ fall	Pink pome	
CURRANT, WAX (*Ribes cereum*)	5	N	2-4	Sun	Dry	Summer	Red berry	Wild currants and gooseberries provide excellent cover and food for many song- and game birds. At least 33 bird species eat *Ribes* berries. This species of currant thrives in dry, rocky soils and prairies
GOOSEBERRY, MISSOURI (*Ribes missouriense*)	5	N	5-6	Sun/ shade	Dry/ moist/ drained	Summer/ early fall	Purple-black berry	Prickly stems; large, abundant fruit; excellent cover
JUNEBERRY, ROUNDLEAF (*Amelanchier sanguinea*)	5	N	8-12	Sun/ shade	Well-drained	Summer	Purple-black pome	Serviceberries (*Amelanchier*) are eaten by at least 36 bird species; this hardy shrub has great potential for wildlife plantings
OAK, SHIN (*Quercus mohriana*)	7	N	to 20	Sun	Dry	Fall	Annual acorn	Sometimes grows to a small tree
PEA SHRUB, SIBERIAN (*Caragana arborescens*)	3	A	8-12	Sun/ half sun	Dry/ poor	Fall	Brown pod	Use for windbreaks or open areas; does not tolerate wet soils; likes alkaline soil and drought
PLUM, SANDHILL (*Prunus angustifolia*)	6	N	to 20	Sun/ varied	Dry/ drained/ sandy/ light	July/ August	Red/ yellow drupe	Forms dense thickets; fruit eaten by several types of bird

Deciduous Shrubs (cont.)

Name	Zone	Native(N) Alien(A)	Light	Preferred Soil	Fruit Period	Fruit Type	Remarks
ROSE, PRAIRIE WILD (*Rosa arkansana*)	5	N	Sun to light shade	Drained	Summer	Purple pome	At least 38 bird species eat wild roses. This native prairie rose offers good shelter and food for prairie chicken, sharp-tailed grouse, and ring-necked pheasant
SILVERBERRY (*Eleagnus commutata*)	2	N	Sun/ shade	Varied	Summer/ fall	Silvery drupe	Very silver foliage; livestock won't eat leaves; forms thickets; eaten by ring-necked pheasant and prairie chicken. A very hardy shrub of the northern plains

Vines

Name	Zone	Native(N) Alien(A)	Light	Preferred Soil	Fruit Period	Fruit Type	Remarks
GRAPE, BUSH (*Vitis acerifolia*)	6	N	Sun	Dry/ drained/ sand	Summer	Purple-black	Forms dense thickets; good nest sites for many kinds of bird, especially cardinals and catbirds; Missouri south
GRAPE, MUSTANG (*Vitis mustangensis*)	5	N	Sun/ shade	Moist/ drained	Summer	Purple-black	Very vigorous grape that can survive great drought and heat. Fruit often persists into winter
WOODBINE (*Parthenocissus vitacea*)	4	N	Sun/ shade	Moist/ drained	Summer/ fall	Blue	Fruits eaten by many bird species; will cling to brick or stone; rapid growing, drought-resistant

THE MOUNTAINS AND DESERTS

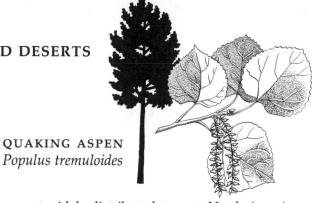

QUAKING ASPEN
Populus tremuloides

Quaking aspen is one of the most widely distributed trees in North America. It occurs from sea level to 10,000 feet, from New England to California and south to the mountains of Mexico. Within this wide range, it thrives best in the Rockies and coastal ranges where vast aspen forests grow. Most quaking aspen reach a height of 20–40 feet, but occasionally a tree can grow up to 100 feet. It is a fast-growing, hardy tree that thrives on sunlit, poor rocky soils that often result from logging and burning. It also grows near pond edges, stream banks, and other moist habitats. Leaf buds are the aspen's principal attraction for birds. Winter buds are one of the most important foods for ruffed grouse and a surprising variety of other birds, including northern shrike, northern oriole, rose-breasted grosbeak, and pine grosbeak. Several cavity-nesting birds, including yellow-bellied sapsucker, downy woodpecker, and black-capped chickadee, frequently excavate in this aspen's soft wood.

CASCARA BUCKTHORN
Rhamnus purshiana

Cascara buckthorn is a small deciduous shrub or tree, 20–40 feet tall. It is best known for the medicinal qualities of its bark, which are processed into a commercial laxative. The wildlife value of the plant is its black berries that ripen in late summer, are about one-half inch in diameter, and are sweet and juicy. Cascara buckthorn fruits are readily consumed by evening grosbeak, purple finch, pileated woodpecker, ruffed grouse, band-tailed pigeon, Steller's jay, American robin, western tanager, and many others. This important wildlife tree often grows in fencerows with hawthorn, crabapple, and serviceberry, but it is also moderately shade tolerant, and occurs in coniferous forests as an understory tree. Cascara buckthorn grows on rich bottomland and dry hillsides from British Columbia to California and east to the Rocky Mountains of Idaho and Montana.

GOLDEN CURRANT
Ribes aureum

Golden currant is a native spineless shrub that usually grows about 3–8 feet tall. It is commonly cultivated for its juicy fruit, and it makes an excellent wildlife planting for food and cover. Golden currant is named for its bright yellow flowers, which appear from March to June. The flowers are followed by quarter-inch fruits that vary in color from red or yellow to black. The shrub grows naturally in shady ravines and stream edges, where its fruit is frequently eaten by grouse and quail. At least 33 bird species are known to eat *Ribes* fruit. Golden currant has a wide distribution in the western mountains. It occurs from 3500 to 8000 feet in New Mexico and Arizona, and west in the mountains to California and north to Washington and neighboring Canada.

Blueberry elder is a broad, spreading shrub that sometimes grows as a 30- to 40-foot-tall tree. As with other members of the elderberry group, blueberry elder is one of the best choices for attracting a great variety of songbirds. Blueberry elder has yellowish white flowers from April to August, and produces abundant, sweet, and juicy fruits from August to September and sometimes as late as December. It grows best in low, moist areas in elevations from 2000 to 8000 feet, from western Texas and New Mexico west to southern California and north in the coastal ranges to British Columbia. The abundant fruits are consumed by many kinds of quail, flickers, and woodpeckers. They are also eaten by western kingbird, black phoebe, black-headed grosbeak, Swainson's thrush, phainopepla, band-tailed pigeon, and many others. This important wildlife planting is an excellent choice for landscaping pond and stream edges and other moist habitats.

BLUEBERRY ELDER
Sambucus caerulea

CANYON GRAPE
Vitis arizonica

The canyon grape is a vigorous climbing vine well adapted for dry habitats. It endures drought and cold, but cannot withstand excess moisture. Canyon grape occasionally develops a stem diameter of 1 foot—plants with 6-inch diameters are common. It sometimes overtops small shrubs and trees, creating an ideal nesting habitat for many kinds of songbird. Its sweet, black fruit ripens from July to August and is eagerly consumed by both bird watchers and birds. Canyon grapes are highly prized for jellies and preserves, and are readily consumed by several species of quail and of songbird, including common flicker, northern mockingbird, western bluebird, and western kingbird. This hardy grape occurs in ravines and gulches between 2000 and 7500 feet in most of New Mexico, Arizona, and Colorado.

GROUSEBERRY
Vaccinium scoparium

A low deciduous shrub, grouseberry is usually only 4–12 inches tall, but under ideal conditions it can grow up to 6 feet. It produces a crop of sweet, red or wine-colored fruits that mature by July through September. As with most members of the huckleberry-blueberry group, the fruit is a favorite bird food. The grouseberry's fruits are eaten by many bird species, including ring-necked pheasant, pine grosbeak, hermit thrush, and Swainson's thrush. Grouseberry grows at from 6000 to 11,500 feet in shaded forests of spruce, yellow pine, or aspen. It is usually found in moist, well-drained soils, and is naturally distributed from northern New Mexico west to the mountains of California and north to British Columbia and Alberta.

DOUGLAS HAWTHORN
Crataegus douglasii

Douglas hawthorn is widely distributed through the northwestern states and adjacent Canada. It grows in a variety of sunny habitats, including stream edges, abandoned fields, and open rangeland. This hawthorn often takes the form of a 5- to 10-foot-tall, many-branched shrub or a small tree that may grow 15–30 feet tall. Its glossy green leaves and abundant white blossoms make it an attractive plant in the wild or in cultivated areas. Its flowers appear from May to July and its half-inch black, juicy fruit ripens from July to September. Although this hardy native is not commercially available, it is a common shrub or tree from the Pacific coast across the plains to Michigan. With property owners' permission, specimens can be located for transplanting, but be careful to transplant small hawthorns to avoid damage to the deep taproot. This adaptable tree is a good food source for many types of fruit-eating bird, including Townsend's solitaire, American robin, ruffed grouse, cedar waxwings, pine grosbeak, and hermit thrush.

Mesquite is a common tree or shrub of the southwestern United States. It grows best on moist stream banks and canyons, but it also spreads to upland sites and sometimes creates serious problems to cattlemen, as it shades out grasses on overgrazed pastures. Mesquite grows up to 30 feet tall, though it is a much lower shrub in most of its range, and it is so rugged that it can live in areas occupied by few other shrubs or trees. Mesquite owes its tenacity to its long taproot system that may reach as much as 60 feet down to groundwater. Its principal value to

MESQUITE
Prosopis juliflora

birds is its thorny branches and foliage, which provide excellent cover and nest sites. Mesquite seeds are especially important to Gambel's quail, and they are also eaten by scaled quail, white-winged dove, and ravens. Because of its value as a cover plant, mesquite should be protected for wildlife cover in rocky soils, streamside habitats, and other property "corners" where few other woody plants will grow.

GREEN MOUNTAIN ASH
Sorbus scopulina

Green mountain ash is a native shrub that occurs in rocky soils from 6000 to 10,000 feet in western mountains from New Mexico north to Alberta and British Columbia. It is a stout shrub that grows from 3 to 15 feet tall. It has abundant white flowers in June, and orange pome fruits that mature from July to December. Although green mountain ash is rarely cultivated, its tolerance of dry mountain soils and wide range suggest that this species shows promise as a wildlife planting. Mountain ash fruit is eaten by many kinds of western woodpeckers, thrush, and grouse.

PRICKLY PEAR CACTUS
Opuntia spp.

Members of this highly diverse cactus group are especially adapted to the arid habitats of the western United States, especially the southwest. In overgrazed lands, *Opuntia* may be the dominant vegetation, and its well-armed prickly shelter gives abundant cover to many small animals. *Opuntia's* principal benefit to birds is its abundant crop of juicy fruits and seeds. These are often eaten by white-winged dove, Gambel's quail, scaled quail, curve-billed thrasher, golden-fronted woodpecker, cactus wren, and many others. Some botanists have described more than 100 *Opuntia* species in the United States. These vary greatly in size from low, creeping forms that are only a few inches tall to some, such as the sonora jumping cholla (*O. fulgida*), that may grow up to 12 feet tall.

COLORADO BLUE SPRUCE
Picea pungens

The stately Colorado blue spruce may grow up to 150 feet tall and develop a trunk diameter 3 feet wide. It is native along hillside streams and canyons at heights of from 6500 to 11,000 feet, in New Mexico, Arizona, Colorado, Utah, Idaho, and Wyoming. Many horticultural varieties are planted in diverse habitats throughout the northern states and most of southern Canada. Spruce needles are important food for blue and spruce grouse, and the seeds are eaten by many types of northern landbird, including crossbills, chickadees, pine grosbeak, red-breasted nuthatch, pine siskin, and cedar waxwings. Good seed crops usually occur every 2–3 years. Colorado blue spruce creates excellent nesting sites and protected roosting cover during the extremes of summer and winter.

WESTERN THIMBLEBERRY
Rubus parviflorus

As with most members of the bramble group, western thimbleberry is an important wild bird food. This is an especially prolific, spineless, fruiting species. It is adaptable to a variety of light conditions, occurring in woodlands, borders, and open habitats in the mountains of New Mexico north to British Columbia and Alaska. Fragrant white flowers appear during June and July, and are followed by red fruits that ripen during August and September. The fruits are consumed by many types of landbird, including western kingbird, cedar waxwings, common flicker, gray catbird, northern bobwhite, Swainson's thrush, red-headed woodpecker, and pine grosbeak. This attractive shrub is available through commercial suppliers.

MORE RECOMMENDED PLANTINGS FOR
ATTRACTING BIRDS IN THE MOUNTAINS AND DESERTS

Evergreen Trees
CEDAR, EASTERN RED (*Juniperus virginiana*)
JUNIPER, ONE-SEED (*Juniperus monosperma*)
JUNIPER, ROCKY MOUNTAIN (*Juniperis scopulorum*)
PINE, AUSTRIAN (*Pinus nigra*)
PINE, PONDEROSA (*Pinus ponderosa*)
PINE, SCOTCH (*Pinus sylvestris*)
SPRUCE, WHITE (*Picea glauca*)

Deciduous Trees
CHERRY, BLACK (*Prunus serotina*)
CHOKECHERRY, COMMON (*Prunus virginiana*)

MAPLE, BOX ELDER (*Acer negundo*)
POPLAR, BALSAM (*Populus balsamifera*)

Deciduous Shrubs
BUCKTHORN, ALDERLEAF (*Rhamnus alnifolia*)
BUFFALO BERRY, SILVER (*Shepherdia argentea*)
CURRANT, WAX (*Ribes cereum*)
DOGWOOD, RED-OSIER (*Cornus stolonifera*)
ELDER, SCARLET (*Sambucus pubens*)
FIRE THORN, SCARLET (*Pyracantha coccinea*)

MORE RECOMMENDED PLANTINGS FOR
ATTRACTING BIRDS IN THE MOUNTAINS AND DESERTS *(cont.)*

Deciduous Shrubs

HONEYSUCKLE, TATARIAN
(*Lonicera tatarica*)
OLIVE, RUSSIAN (*Elaeagnus
angustifolia*)
PEA SHRUB, SIBERIAN (*Caragana
arborescens*)
RASPBERRIES (*Rubus spp.*)
ROSE, MULTIFLORA (*Rosa
multiflora*)
ROSE, WOODS (*Rosa woodsii*)
SERVICEBERRY, SASKATOON
(*Amelanchier alnifolia*)
SILVERBERRY (*Elaeagnus
commutata*)

SNOWBERRY, COMMON
(*Symphoricarpos albus*)
SUMAC, SKUNKBUSH (*Rhus
aromatica*)
SUMAC, SMOOTH (*Rhus glabra*)

Vines

CREEPER, VIRGINIA
(*Parthenocissus quinquefolia*)
HONEYSUCKLE, TRUMPET
(*Lonicera sempervirens*)
WOODBINE (*Parthenocissus vitacea*)

BIRD PLANTINGS FOR THE MOUNTAINS AND DESERTS
OTHER GOOD CHOICES

Evergreen Trees

Name	Zone	Native(N) Alien(A)	Height (ft)	Light	Preferred Soil	Period	Fruit Type	Remarks
ASH, VELVET (*Fraxinus velutina*)	6	N	20–30	Sun	Moist/ drained	Fall	Samara	A variable, semievergreen tree; very alkali and drought-resistant; ash seeds are eaten by at least 9 bird species, including evening and pine grosbeaks
FIR, DOUGLAS (*Pseudotsuga menziesii*)	4	N	75–100	Sun	Dry/ moist/ drained	Fall	Cone	Thrives best on northern exposures; needles are important winter food of blue grouse, but there are few other records of bird use
FIR, GRAND (*Abies grandis*)	6	N	to 120	Sun/ part sun	Moist/ drained	Fall	Cone	At least 10 species of birds feed on the needles and seeds of
FIR, SUBALPINE (*Abies lasiocarpa*)	3	N	60–100	Sun/ shade	Cool/ moist/ deep	Fall	Cone	these large evergreens; as with Douglas fir, they are most useful as food for grouse, but when
FIR, WHITE (*Abies concolor*)	4	N	80–100	Sun/ shade	Dry/ moist/ drained	Fall	Cone	planted in yards, they provide important nest sites and cover
HEMLOCK, MOUNTAIN (*Tsuga mertensiana*)	6	N	75–100	Sun/ shade	Cool/ deep/ moist/ drained	Fall	Cone	Excellent choice for hedges or shady habitat. Preferred foods of chickadees and pine siskin;
HEMLOCK, WESTERN (*Tsuga heterophylla*)	7	N	125– 175	Sun/ shade	Dry/ moist/ drained	Fall	Cone	abundant seed crops every 2 to 3 years
JUNIPER, ALLIGATOR (*Juniperus deppeana*)	7	N	30–50	Sun	Dry/ rocky/ sterile	Fall	Blue-green berry	These drought-resistant junipers provide excellent cover and
JUNIPER, UTAH (*Juniperus osteosperma*)	5	N	to 20	Sun	Dry/ rocky/ sandy	Fall	Blue-green berry	food; at least 26 bird species are known to eat juniper berries; plant male and female to provide
JUNIPER, WESTERN (*Juniperus occidentalis*)	6	N	15–30	Sun	Dry/ rocky	Fall	Blue-green berry	a fruit crop; pinyon jay and Townsend's solitaire eat these berries

Evergreen Trees (cont.)

Name	Zone	Native(N) Alien(A)	Height (ft)	Light	Preferred Soil	Period	Fruit Type	Remarks
OAK, GAMBEL (*Quercus gambellii*)	7	N	15–30	Sun	Dry/ drained	Late summer	Annual acorn	Varies in form from large tree to small shrub, depending on available water; grows in sand or loam soils, sometimes creating dense ground covers; acorns eaten by acorn woodpecker, and scaled and Montezuma quail
OAK, CANYON LIVE (*Quercus chrysolepis*)	7	N	60–80	Sun	Dry/ drained	Fall	Biennial acorn	
PINE, LIMBER (*Pinus flexilis*)	6	N	25–50	Sun	Dry/ drained	Fall	Cone	Adaptable to many soil types and shows tolerance to wind; named for the flexible nature of young branches
PINE, LODGEPOLE (*Pinus contorta* var. *latifolia*)	4	N	70–80	Sun	Dry/ moist/ drained/ sandy	Late summer/ fall	Cone	Intolerant of pollution; tall trees often fall in strong winds
PINE, PINYON (*Pinus edulis*)	5	N	10–40	Sun	Dry/ drained	Fall	Cone	Slow growing and drought-resistant; seeds eaten by at least 9 bird species, including Montezuma quail and wild turkey
PINE, SUGAR (*Pinus lambertiana*)	6	N	175–200	Sun	Moist/ drained	Fall	Cone	Tallest pine, with enormous cones (26 inches); seeds are especially important to quail and grouse, but also eaten by many kinds of songbird
PINE, WESTERN WHITE (*Pinus monticola*)	6	N	90–150	Sun	Rich/ moist/ drained	Fall/ winter	Cone	At least 54 bird species eat pine seeds, and western white pine is one of the most important seed providers in this region; shade tolerant when young; requires full sun when mature
PINE, WHITEBARK (*Pinus albicaulis*)	4	N	10–40	Sun	Dry/ drained	Late summer/ fall	Cone	Very resistant to wind; sometimes taking a prostrate or shrub form when under stress from strong, persistent wind
SPRUCE, ENGELMANN (*Picea engelmannii*)	3	N	60–120	Sun/ shade	Rich/ moist/ drained	Fall	Cone	Important food for blue and spruce grouse, which eat the needles; seeds usually produced every third year
YEW, PACIFIC (*Taxus brevifolia*)	6	N	20–50	Sun/ shade	Moist/ deep	Fall	Red berry	Most shade-tolerant forest tree in the northwest; berries eaten by ruffed grouse

Deciduous Trees

Name	Zone	Native(N) Alien(A)	Height (ft)	Light	Preferred Soil	Fruit Period	Fruit Type	Remarks
ALDER, ARIZONA (*Alnus oblongifolia*)	7	N	20–30	Sun	Moist/ drained	Fall	Nutlet in cone	Useful plantings along streams, ponds and other moist-soil habitats; alders provide excellent cover and nest sites for songbirds; seeds are important food for goldfinch, siskins, and redpolls
ALDER, SITKA (*Alnus sinuata*)	1	N	5–30	Sun	Moist	Fall	Nutlet in cone	
ALDER, THINLEAF (*Alnus tenuifolia*)	2	N	6–25	Sun	Moist/ drained	Fall	Nutlet in cone	
ALDER, WHITE (*Alnus rhombifolia*)	5	N	40–100	Shade	Moist	Fall/ spring	Nutlet in cone	
BIRCH, WATER (*Betula occidentalis*)	4	N	20–25	Sun	Moist/ mineral	Fall	Samara	Catkins and buds are important food for grouse; birch seeds are favorite foods for redpoll and pine siskin
CHERRY, BITTER (*Prunus emarginata*)	7	N	35–40	Sun	Dry/ moist/ drained	Spring/ fall	Drupe	Large tree to shrub; forms dense thickets; eaten by at least 9 bird species, including Townsend's solitaire, bluebird, and band-tailed pigeon
COTTONWOOD, BLACK (*Populus trichocarpa*)	5	N	to 100	Sun	Moist/ sandy/ gravelly	Spring	Capsule	Ten bird species are known to eat cottonwood buds; especially important to ruffed grouse, greater prairie chicken, and sharp-tailed grouse; also eaten by evening grosbeak and purple finch; fairly salt tolerant, especially Fremont cottonwood
COTTONWOOD, FREMONT (*Populus fremontii*)	7	N	to 100	Sun	Dry/ drained	Spring	Capsule	
COTTONWOOD, NARROWLEAF (*Populus angustifolia*)	3	N	50–70	Sun	Moist/ drained	Spring	Capsule	
DOGWOOD, PACIFIC (*Cornus nuttallii*)	9	N	10–40	Sun/ shade	Drained	Late summer/ fall	White drupe	Fruit readily eaten by grouse, quail, flicker, bluebird, purple finch, and Swainson's thrush
HAWTHORNS (*Crataegus spp.*)	3–7	N	20–35	Sun/ half sun	Drained/ rich	Fall	Black pome	At least 36 bird species eat these fruits; occurs along banks of mountain streams or rich bottomlands; often forms thickets; sometimes grows as a shrub North: C. *erythropoda*, C. *columbiana* and C. *succulenta* Central: C. *chrysocarpa*, C. *rivularis* and C. *succulenta* South: C. *tracyi*, C. and *wootoniana*

129

Deciduous Trees (cont.)

Name	Zone	Native(N) Alien(A)	Height (ft)	Light	Preferred Soil	Fruit Period	Fruit Type	Remarks
MAPLE, BIGTOOTH (*Acer grandidentatum*)	6	N	30–40	Sun	Drained	Fall	Samara	Large trees to shrubs; tolerates poor soils; buds eaten by evening and pine grosbeaks
MAPLE, ROCKY MOUNTAIN (*Acer glabrum*)	5	N	20–30	Sun	Dry/drained	Late fall	Samara	
MESQUITE, SCREWBEAN (*Prosopis pubescens*)	7	N	15–30	Sun	Dry/moist	Summer/fall	Legume	Grows in river bottoms and canyons; varies from large tree to small shrub, depending on conditions; spiny, forms thickets; grows in wide variety of soils including gravel; eaten by bobwhite, roadrunner, and Gambel's quail
OAK, ARIZONA WHITE (*Quercus arizonica*)	7	N	to 40	Sun	Dry/drained	Fall	Annual acorn	Sometimes grows as a shrub; resists heavy grazing and is drought tolerant; oaks are very important wildlife food; at least 63 bird species are known to eat acorns
OAK, GAMBEL (*Quercus gambelii*)	6	N	25–35	Sun	Dry/drained	Fall	Annual acorn	
SYCAMORE, ARIZONA (*Plantanus wrightii*)	7	N	60–80	Sun	Moist/drained	Fall	Achene	A favorite food of goldfinch; also eaten by band-tailed pigeon
WILLOW, COYOTE (*Salix exigua*)	4	N	to 15	Sun	Moist/drained	Early summer	Capsule	Stabilizes stream banks; provides excellent cover and nest sites for many kinds of songbird; buds eaten by grouse
WILLOW, PACIFIC (*Salix lasiandra*)	1	N	to 30	Sun	Moist/drained	Early summer	Capsule	

Evergreen Shrubs

Name	Zone	Native(N) Alien(A)	Height (ft)	Light	Preferred Soil	Fruit Period	Fruit Type	Remarks
ACACIA, CATCLAW (*Acacia greggii*)	6	N	to 30	Sun	Dry	Summer/spring	Legume	A preferred food of quail and doves; thorny, excellent cover; sometimes grows as a small tree
ELDER, MEXICAN (*Sambucus mexicana*)	7	N	to 30	Sun	Moist	Year round	Black berry	This semievergreen shrub of the southwest can grow to a small tree with up to an 18-inch-diameter trunk; occurs in low, moist habitats, such as ditches, stream borders, and moist grasslands; at least 12 bird species eat the fruit

Name	Zone	Native(N) Alien(A)	Height (ft)	Light	Preferred Soil	Fruit Period	Fruit Type	Remarks
HACKBERRY, SPINY (*Celtis pallida*)	7	N	10–20	Sun	Dry	Summer/ fall	Yellow drupe	A valuable bird food and cover; plant in the southern part of this region; fruits are eaten by cactus wren, cardinal, pyrrhuloxia, scaled quail, and green jay
MANZANITA, GREEN-LEAF (*Arctostaphylos patula*)	7	N	1–10	Sun	Dry/ drained	Year round	Brown berry	Creeping mat or shrub of southwest mountains; occurs in dry, gravelly soils, often in association with ponderosa pine; fruit is eaten by grouse and quail
MANZANITA, POINT-LEAF (*Arctostaphylos pungens*)	7	N	1–10	Sun	Dry/ drained	Summer/ spring	Brown/ dark red berry	
OAK, PALMER (*Quercus palmeri*)	7	N	to 25	Sun	Dry/ drained/ sandy	Summer	Biennial acorn	Large, dense shrub, sometimes grows as a tree; grasslands and canyons of the southwest
OREGON-GRAPE (*Mahonia nervosa*)	5	N	to 26	Sun/ shade	Dry/ drained	Fall	Berry	Dense foliage offers excellent cover; several cultured varieties available; berries eaten by ruffed and blue grouse
SALTBUSH, DESERT HOLLY (*Atriplex hymenelytra*)	6	N	2–5	Sun	Dry	Early fall	Achene	Decorative and good cover for arid habitats; native to southwest; 29 bird species are known to eat saltbush fruit
SALTBUSH, BIG (*Atriplex lentiformis*)	6	N	6–10	Sun	Dry	Fall/ winter	Achene	Growing in dense patches, it provides excellent cover for quail and other desert wildlife; when pruned it forms excellent hedges for arid climate cities of the southwest and California. Deciduous in dry areas

Deciduous Shrubs

Name	Zone	Native(N) Alien(A)	Height (ft)	Light	Preferred Soil	Period	Fruit Type	Remarks
ACACIA, MESCAT (Acacia constricta)	7	N	6–18	Sun	Dry/ sandy	Summer	4-in. black pods/ legume	A common, spiny shrub of harsh soils in the extreme southern part of this region; seeds eaten by scaled quail and white-winged dove
BLUEBERRY, WESTERN BOG (Vaccinium occidentale)	5	N	to 4	Sun	Moist/ drained	Late summer	Blue berry	Blueberries and huckleberries are very important wildlife foods, with at least 87 bird species known to eat the fruits
CEANOTHUS, FENDLER (Ceanothus fendleri)	5	N	to 3	Sun/ shade	Dry/ drained	Late summer/ early fall	Red/ brown capsule	Useful for quail food and cover, and as a nest site for many kinds of songbird
CHERRY, BITTER (Prunus emarginata)	7	N	3–12	Sun/ shade	Dry/ moist/ drained	Spring/ early fall	Black drupe	Large shrub to small tree; forms dense thickets providing good nest cover and food for at least 6 bird species
CONDALIA, LOTEWOOD (Condalia obtusifolia)	7	N	to 10	Sun	Dry	Early summer	Black drupe	Very thorny, rounded shrubs of deserts and dry foothills in the southwest; ideal nest sites for songbirds; important food for scaled quail
CONDALIA, KNIFE-LEAF (Condalia spathulata)	7	N	to 10	Sun	Dry	Early summer	Black drupe	
CONDALIA, LOTEBUSH (Condalia lycioides)	7	N	to 10	Sun	Dry/ drained	Early summer	Purple drupe	
CURRANT, STICKY (Ribes viscosissimum)	4	N	1–4	Sun/ shade	Drained	Late summer/ early fall	Black berry	Thornless shrub with roots up to 4 feet deep; at least 33 bird species eat fruits of the currants and gooseberries
CURRANT, WAX (Ribes cereum)	4	N	2–4	Sun	Dry	Summer	Red berry	At least 33 bird species eat currants and gooseberry; wax currant is a very important bird food and cover plant throughout this region; it grows in green sunny fields or forest openings; an important food for grouse
DEWBERRY, ARIZONA (Rubus arizonensis)	6	N	2–3	Sun	Dry/ moist/ drained	Summer	Red drupelets	Trailing and very prickly; excellent cover for songbirds; fruit eaten by cardinals, house finch, Steller's jay, bluebirds, and many other songbirds

Deciduous Shrubs

Name								Description
DOGWOOD, BROWN (*Cornus glabrata*)	8	N	to 10	Sun	Moist	Late summer/fall	Drupe	Large shrub or small tree that, along with other western dogwoods, provides important food for grouse, quail, woodpeckers, and bluebirds; brown dogwood forms dense thickets along mountain streams
DOGWOOD, MINER'S (*Cornus sessilis*)	5	N	to 10	Sun	Moist	Late summer/early fall	Drupe	
ELDER, BLACK-BEAD (*Sambucus melanocarpa*)	6	N	3–12	Sun/shade	Moist	Late summer	Blue berry	At least 111 bird species are known to eat elderberry fruits; bunchberry elder is a small shrub that occurs on the eastern slopes of the Rocky Mountains; the larger black-bead elder grows along mountain streams and canyons in the conifer belt from New Mexico to southern Alaska
ELDER, BUNCHBERRY (*Sambucus microbotrys*)	3	N	to 5	Sun/shade	Moist/drained	Late summer	Red berry	
HACKBERRY, WESTERN (*Celtis douglasii*)	6	N	to 20	Sun/shade	Dry/moist/drained	Summer/winter	Brown drupe	Grows in dry, gravelly soils; fruits eaten by band-tailed pigeon, evening grosbeak, roadrunner, and many others; hackberry fruits are eaten by at least 20 bird species
HONEYSUCKLE, BEARBERRY (*Lonicera involucrata*)	4	N	to 10	Sun/shade	Moist/drained/calcerous	Late summer	Black berry	Grows in lime soils in woods and meadows to 10,500 feet; fruit eaten by at least 6 bird species, including cedar waxwings, pine grosbeak and Swainson's thrush; flowers are visited by blue-throated and magnificent hummingbirds
HONEYSUCKLE, UTAH (*Lonicera utahensis*)	6	N	to 5	Shade	Dry/drained	Summer/early fall	Yellow/red berry	An erect, clump-forming shrub; fruit eaten by hermit thrush, Townsend's solitaire, robin, and ring-necked pheasant
HONEYSUCKLE, HAIRY WHITE (*Lonicera albiflora*)	6	N	to 9	Sun	Moist/drained	Fall	Blue berry	A thicket-forming shrub or climbing vine of the southwest; occurs in thickets and banks of streams; eaten by bobwhite, catbird, robin, and hermit thrush

Deciduous Shrubs (cont.)

Name	Zone	Native(N) Alien(A)	Height (ft)	Light	Preferred Soil	Fruit Period	Fruit Type	Remarks
MOUNTAIN ASH, ALPINE (*Sorbus occidentalis*)	6	N	to 30	Sun	Moist/dry/drained	Late summer/winter	Red pome	At least 11 bird species readily eat mountain-ash fruit, including evening grosbeak, pine grosbeak, robin, blue grouse, and Clark's nutcracker; frequently forms dense thickets
MOUNTAIN ASH, GREENE (*Sorbus scopulina*)	6	N	to 15	Sun/shade	Moist/drained	Summer/winter	Red pome	
MOUNTAIN ASH, SITKA (*Sorbus sitchensis*)	5	N	to 15	Sun	Moist/dry/drained	Late summer/early winter	Red pome	
OLIVE, DESERT (*Forestiera pubescens*)	7	N	6–10	Sun	Dry/moist/drained	Early summer/early fall	Black drupe	Widely distributed spreading shrub of dry river bottoms in the southwest; principal food of scaled quail in Texas; also eaten by robins
RASPBERRY, BOULDER (*Rubus deliciosus*)	5	N	to 6	Sun	Dry/moist/drained	Summer/early fall	Red/purple	Plants of dry, rocky soils; offers excellent cover and nest sites for mockingbirds; at least 146 bird species are known to eat the fruits of these exceptionally important plants
RASPBERRY, WHITEBARK (*Rubus leucodermis*)	6	N	to 5	Sun	Dry/moist/drained	Summer/early fall	Dark purple	
ROSE, WOODS (*Rosa woodsii*)	6	N	to 3	Sun/half sun	Moist/drained	All year	Red hip	Widespread thicket-forming rose throughout the Rocky Mountains from 3500 to 10,000 feet; largest flowers of any wild western rose; fruits eaten by hermit thrush, Swainson's thrush, ruffed grouse, and other game birds
SAGEBRUSH, BIG (*Artemisia tridentata*)	4	N	2–10	Sun	Dry/drained	Fall	Achene	Occurs widely in the west, growing in dry and stony soils in deserts and up to timberline; principal food and cover for sage grouse; an indicator of alkaline-tree soils
SERVICEBERRY, UTAH (*Amelanchier utahensis*)	4	N	4–25	Sun	Dry/drained	Summer	Blue/black pome	Small-to-large shrub of rocky soil and dry hillsides; as with other serviceberries, this is an important food for songbirds

Deciduous Shrubs

Name	Zone		Height	Light	Moisture	Season	Fruit	Notes
SNOWBERRY, LONGFLOWER (*Symphoricarpos longiflorus*)	7	N	3-4	Sun	Dry	Summer	White berrylike drupe	Occurs in rocky foothills and canyons from 4000 to 8000 feet; the fruit of this and other snowberries is eaten by at least 26 bird species; special importance to grouse and other game birds
SNOWBERRY, MOUNTAIN (*Symphoricarpos oreophilus*)	6	N	to 4	Sun	Dry/moist/drained	Late summer	White berrylike drupe	Occurs in rocky soils of southwestern mountains from 5000 to 9000 feet; has ornamental value
SNOWBERRY, ROUNDLEAF (*Symphoricarpos rotundifolius*)	8	N	to 3	Sun	Dry/drained	Late summer/early fall	White berrylike drupe	Highly ornamental, slender plant; long cultivated; occurs in mountain canyons from 4000 to 10,000 feet
WOLFBERRY, ANDERSON (*Lycium andersonii*)	6	N	1-9	Sun	Dry/sandy	Spring	Red berry	Tolerant of alkaline soils; excellent cover; important food for verdin, gila woodpecker, and many other types of desert bird; flower nectar used by black-chinned hummingbird

Ground Covers (Less than 1 ft. Tall)

Name	Zone		Height	Light	Moisture	Season	Fruit	Notes
BLUEBERRY, DWARF (*Vaccinium caespitosum*)	4	N		Sun	Dry/drained	Summer/early fall	Blue berry	Creeping timberline shrubs that produce highly attractive berries; among the birds eating these fruits are cedar waxwings, ruffed grouse, flicker, hermit thrush, and pine grosbeak
WHORTLEBERRY, GROUSE (*Vaccinium scoparium*)	3	N		Sun/shade	Dry/moist	Summer	Blue berry	
WINTERGREEN (*Gaultheria humifusa*)	6	N		Sun/shade	Drained	Late summer	Berry	Small evergreen shrubs; form mats grow on sandy or other soils; at least 7 bird species are known to eat the fruits of wintergreens
WINTERGREEN, BUSH (*Gaultheria ovatifolia*)	6	N		Sun	Drained	Late summer	Berry	

Vines

Name	Zone		D/E	Light	Moisture	Season	Fruit	Notes
GRAPE, CANYON (*Vitis arizonica*)	7	N	D	Sun	Moist/drained	Summer/persists to fall	Blue-black berry	Grows best in moist, sandy soils; eaten by many types of bird, including Gambel's and scaled quail
HONEYSUCKLE, CHAPARRAL (*Lonicera interrupta*)	7	N	E	Sun	Dry	Summer/winter	Berry	Attractive fruits for Townsend's solitaire, thrashers, towhee, Swainson's thrush, and wren-tit; chaparral honeysuckle is an evergreen and sometimes grows as a shrub
HONEYSUCKLE, ORANGE (*Lonicera ciliosa*)	6	N	D	Sun/shade	Dry/drained	Summer/early fall	Red berry	

THE PACIFIC COAST

HOLLY-LEAVED BUCKTHORN
Rhamnus crocea

Buckthorn holly is a native evergreen shrub that usually grows only 2 or 3 feet tall. Rarely, it grows as a tree and it can reach a height of up to 25 feet. It produces red fruits in August and September that make an attractive contrast with the lustrous hollylike leaves. Holly-leaved buckthorn inhabits sunny, dry hillsides in Arizona and southern California. It is an excellent bird-attracting choice for this dry climate, as it provides excellent nesting places in its dense foliage. Its berries are eaten by many kinds of bird, including phainopepla, northern mockingbird, California thrasher, and Swainson's thrush. Plants transplanted from the country to moderately well-watered residential settings acquire a glossy foliage, the brown of lower leaf surfaces usually disappears, and the plants develop a less dense growth form, sometimes reaching a height of 5 feet. Since the male and female flowers are on different plants, it's necessary to transplant several for a good fruit crop.

HOLLY-LEAVED CHERRY
Prunus ilicifolia

Holly-leaved cherry, sometimes known by the Indian name, Islay, is an evergreen shrub or small tree, 6 to 25 feet tall. In its native habitat from San Francisco Bay south through the coast ranges of California to Baja California, holly-leaved cherry grows in many soil types, including sand, loam, and clay. It inhabits the dry chaparral, where it tolerates alkali soils and demonstrates its resistance to drought and fire. Yet when transplanted to more moderate climate, holly-leaved cherry makes a fine residential planting or pruned hedge. Holly-leaved cherry has small white flowers from March to May and sweet, dark red or purple fruits that often remain available into December. The fruit is eaten by many kinds of bird, including hairy woodpecker, scrub jay, phainopepla, and Swainson's thrush. Its dense foliage also provides excellent protection for bird nests.

PACIFIC DOGWOOD
Cornus nuttallii

A close relative of the spectacular flowering dogwood of the east, the Pacific dogwood has even larger flowers and leaves than its eastern relative. It inhabits the Pacific coastal mountains between 4000 and 6000 feet, from Vancouver Island, British Columbia, to the mountains of San Diego County. This attractive tree grows up to 60 feet tall, but usually it is much smaller. It has inconspicuous clusters of yellow-green flowers surrounded by 4–6 white bracts. This showy flower cluster measures up to 6 inches across. The fruit clusters ripen from October to November, and consist of 30–40 bright red berrylike drupes. The tree's fall color is as spectacular as its spring show, as the leaves turn a brilliant burgundy red. The fruits are one of the favorite foods of band-tailed pigeon and are also eaten by common flicker, hermit thrush, cedar waxwings, warbling vireo, purple finch, American robin, and pileated woodpecker. Pacific dogwood is a popular cultivated tree, and is available from several West Coast nurseries.

COMMON FIG
Ficus carica

Common fig is one of many tropical figs that are cultivated for human consumption in the southern United States. Commercial figs are grown in southern California, and the Gulf coasts of Texas and Louisiana. This species can be grown in more moderate climates as far north as zone 5. Common fig is a deciduous shrub or small tree that attains a height up to 30 feet. It has a low, wide, rounded crown that provides abundant shade. Common fig trees are self-fertile and most varieties produce two fruit crops each year. The fruits are readily eaten by many birds, so much so that bird damage to commercial crops is sometimes a problem. Among the birds that eat the fruit of common fig are western bluebird, house finch, black-headed grosbeak, yellow-billed magpie, northern oriole, Bullock's oriole, and yellow-rumped warbler.

TALL RED HUCKLEBERRY
Vaccinium parvifolium

Tall red huckleberry is a deciduous shrub that grows from 4 to 12 feet tall. It occurs mainly in the redwood region from California's Santa Cruz mountains, north in the humid coastal zone to Alaska. Tall red huckleberry has a spreading, cascading shape. It should be planted in acid soils under partial shade. The greenish or whitish flowers are often tinted with pink and appear in leaf axils in May and June. The clear, bright red fruits are about a quarter inch in diameter and ripen from June to September. The fruit is eaten by many kinds of song- and game birds, including several species of grouse, American robin, black-capped chickadee, wren-tit, Swainson's thrush, and common flicker.

This large native oak once dominated vast coastal regions from Santa Barbara to the Mexican border. Unfortunately, human population growth in this region has eliminated almost all of the great coastal oak groves, leaving only a few remnant reminders of their former grand stature. California live oaks may develop a trunk diameter of 12 feet and a remarkable spread of 130 feet, though even a tree this large will only grow about 75 feet tall. These adaptable evergreen oaks can live in many habitats, from windblown coastal sites to steep mountainsides, canyon walls, and open plains. Within these varied habitats, it prefers dry, well-drained soils, and can thrive in sand, loam, gravel, and other soil types. In very dry sites, it may grow no higher than a small shrub. California live oak produces an acorn crop each year, and this fruit is eaten by California quail, jays, woodpeckers, chestnut-backed chickadee, plain titmouse, and many others. This Cal-

CALIFORNIA LIVE OAK
Quercus agrifolia

ifornia native is adaptable to normal garden conditions. Young trees may be started from rooted nursery stock or acorns. Regular watering is not necessary, but it encourages rapid growth in young live oaks.

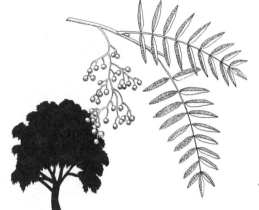

CALIFORNIA PEPPER TREE
Schinus molle

This pink-berried native of Peru is so commonly planted in coastal southern California that it has even become known as the California pepper tree. It is an attractive tree with wide-spreading branches and a round-topped crown that often grows to 50 feet, but is as often much smaller. The California pepper tree is frequently planted in lawns and roadsides, but causes some problems where it overhangs sidewalks, as the falling fruit and small branches can be a hazard underfoot. It also harbors black scale, a pest of citrus orchards. But if it is planted away from citrus trees and sidewalks, it will be a beautiful addition to the land-scape and an important food tree for birds. California pepper tree produces drooping clusters of white flowers that develop into abundant pink berries in the fall, which are eaten by many types of songbird, including western bluebird, common flicker, northern mockingbird, phainopepla, American robin, red-breasted sapsucker, hermit thrush, and cedar waxwing.

Shore pine is a native of the coastal region from northern California to Alaska. It usually grows to only 15 to 35 feet, and takes on a twisted and contorted form as its Latin name suggests. Away from the coast it becomes shrubby, and in more protected areas it takes on a straight-trunk form. At even higher and more pro-

SHORE PINE
Pinus contorta

tected altitudes, shore pine eventually grades into an important lumber tree, the lodgepole pine. Shore pine tolerates the rigors of the Pacific Coast zone so well that it may live to over 200 years. It is an excellent shelter planting for windy coastal areas and is one of the best choices for sandy or rocky soils. This is a popular residential tree in the Pacific Coast zone because in protected habitats it develops a pleasing pyramidal shape and its dense foliage serves as a good visual screen, offering excellent shelter for birds. Shore pine's cones are about 2 inches long and mature during August and September, providing tiny seeds that are eaten by many bird species.

FOUR-WING SALTBUSH
Atriplex canescens

This erect evergreen shrub will tolerate even the most arid western habitats. Four-wing saltbush is widely distributed in southern California to western Texas and Oklahoma and north to eastern Washington and Alberta. It thrives in a great variety of sunny, arid conditions, including grassy uplands, sandy deserts, or salt and alkali flatlands. Its principal value to birds is its ability to reduce soil erosion and provide shade and nesting cover in these harsh environments. It produces an annual crop of 1/4- to 3/4-inch-long winged seeds during August and September. The seeds are eaten by Gambel's quail, horned lark, and other ground-feeding birds. For these reasons four-wing saltbush is an excellent planting for conservation lands.

PACIFIC WAX MYRTLE
Myrica californica

Pacific wax myrtle is a large native evergreen shrub or small tree that grows 10 to 35 feet tall. Its dark green, glossy foliage and dense form make it a popular choice for cultivation in residential areas as a specimen tree or pruned hedge. Pacific wax myrtle occurs along the Pacific coast from Los Angeles to Washington, and is found most commonly in canyons and salt marshes. It develops purplish, waxy, nutlike fruits in July that persist over the winter until the following June. Like those of its close relative, eastern bayberry, these fruits are important food for many types of bird, including common flicker, tree swallow, chestnut-backed chickadee, towhees, wren-tit, and yellow-rumped warbler.

MORE RECOMMENDED PLANTINGS FOR ATTRACTING BIRDS ON THE PACIFIC COAST

Evergreen Trees
ARBORVITAE, EASTERN (*Thuja occidentalis*)
CEDAR, EASTERN RED (*Juniperus virginiana*)
FIR, DOUGLAS (*Pseudotsuga menziesii*)
FIR, SUBALPINE (*Abies lasiocarpa*)
FIR, WHITE (*Abies concolor*)
HEMLOCK, MOUNTAIN (*Tsuga mertensiana*)
HEMLOCK, WESTERN (*Tsuga heterophylla*)
JUNIPER, ROCKY MOUNTAIN (*Juniperis scopulorum*)
JUNIPER, WESTERN (*Juniperus occidentalis*)
PINE, LODGEPOLE (*Pinus contorta* var. *latifolia*)
PINE, PONDEROSA (*Pinus ponderosa*)
PINE, WESTERN WHITE (*Pinus monticola*)
YEW, PACIFIC (*Taxus brevifolia*)

Deciduous Trees
ALDER, SITKA (*Alnus sinuata*)
ALDER, THINLEAF (*Alnus tenuifolia*)
ALDER, WHITE (*Alnus rhombifolia*)
ASPEN, QUAKING (*Populus tremuloides*)
BIRCH, PAPER (*Betula papyrifera*)
BUTTONBUSH, COMMON (*Cephalanthus occidentalis*)
CHERRY, BITTER (*Prunus emarginata*)
COTTONWOOD, BLACK (*Populus trichocarpa*)
COTTONWOOD, FREMONT (*Populus fremontii*)
DOGWOOD, WESTERN (*Cornus occidentalis*)
HAWTHORN, COCKSPUR (*Crataegus crus-galli*)
HAWTHORN, DOUGLAS (*Crataegus douglasii*)

HAWTHORN, DOWNY (*Crataegus mollis*)
HAWTHORN, WASHINGTON (*Crataegus phaenopyrum*)
MAPLE, ROCKY MOUNTAIN (*Acer glabrum*)
MOUNTAIN ASH, AMERICAN (*Sorbus americana*)
MOUNTAIN ASH, EUROPEAN (*Sorbus aucuparia*)
MULBERRY, RED (*Morus rubra*)
MULBERRY, WHITE (*Morus alba*)
POPLAR, BALSAM (*Populus balsamifera*)

Evergreen Shrubs
ACACIA, CATCLAW (*Acacia greggii*)
CACTUS, PRICKLY PEAR (*Opuntia spp.*)
CURRANT, GOLDEN (*Ribes aureum*)
JUNIPER, CHINESE (*Juniperus chinensis*)
JUNIPER, COMMON (*Juniperus communis*)
SALTBUSH, DESERT HOLLY (*Atriplex hymenelytra*)
SNOWBERRY, COMMON (*Symphoricarpos albus*)
SNOWBERRY, MOUNTAIN (*Symphoricarpos oreophilus*)
SNOWBERRY, ROUNDLEAF (*Symphoricarpos rotundifolius*)
SUMAC, SKUNKBUSH (*Rhus aromatica*)
THIMBLEBERRY, WESTERN (*Rubus parviflorus*)
WOLFBERRY, ANDERSON (*Lycium andersonii*)

Deciduous Shrubs
BUCKTHORN, CASCARA (*Rhamnus purshiana*)
BUFFALO BERRY, SILVER (*Shepherdia argentea*)

DOGWOOD, BROWN (*Cornus glabrata*)
DOGWOOD, MINER'S (*Cornus sessilis*)
DOGWOOD, RED-OSIER (*Cornus stolonifera*)
ELDER, BLACK-BEAD (*Sambucus melanocarpa*)
ELDER, BLUEBERRY (*Sambucus caerulea*)
MOUNTAIN ASH, ALPINE (*Sorbus occidentalis*)
MOUNTAIN ASH, GREENE (*Sorbus scopulina*)
OLIVE, CARDINAL AUTUMN (*Elaeagnus umbellata*)
OLIVE, RUSSIAN (*Elaeagnus angustifolia*)
RASPBERRY, WHITEBARK (*Rubus leucodermis*)
ROSE, NOOTKA (*Rosa nutkana*)
ROSE, RUGOSA (*Rosa rugosa*)
SAGEBRUSH, BIG (*Artemisia tridentata*)
SALTBUSH, BIG (*Atiplex lentiformis*)
SERVICEBERRY, SASKATOON (*Amelanchier alnifolia*)

Ground Cover
BEARBERRY (*Arctostaphylos uva-ursi*)
BILBERRY, BOG (*Vaccinium uliginosum*)
BUNCHBERRY (*Cornus canadensis*)
JUNIPER, CREEPING (*Juniperus horizontalis*)
STRAWBERRY (*Fragaria spp.*)
WINTERGREEN (*Gaultheria humifusa*)

Vines
HONEYSUCKLE, ORANGE (*Lonicera ciliosa*)
HONEYSUCKLE, CHAPARRAL (*Lonicera interrupta*)

BIRD PLANTINGS FOR THE PACIFIC COAST
OTHER GOOD CHOICES

Evergreen Trees

Name	Zone	Native(N) Alien(A)	Height (ft)	Light	Preferred Soil	Fruit Period	Fruit Type	Remarks
CHERRY, CATALINA (*Prunus lyonii*)	8	N	15–35	Sun	Dry/drained	Late summer/early fall	Purple/black drupe	Native to several southern California islands; fruit is readily eaten by many kinds of songbird; often cultivated as an ornamental tree
FIR, NOBLE (*Abies procera*) (formerly *nobilis*)	6	N	60–225	Sun	Drained	Fall	Cone	Long lived and rapid growth; seeds are food for chickadee, jay, nuthatch, and many other species; native to Cascade Mountains of Oregon and Washington
FIR, SHASTA RED (*Abies magnifica*)	6	N	60–200	Sun	Drained	Early fall	Cone	Abundant seed crop every 2 to 3 years; choice food for blue grouse, pine grosbeak, and many other species; native to Oregon Cascades; good ornamental value
HOLLY, ENGLISH (*Ilex aquifolium*)	7	A	8–25	Sun/half sun	Moist/drained	Fall/winter	Red berry	Fruit persists on the tree through the winter; an ornamental native to Europe and Asia; holly berries are eaten by at least 32 bird species
JUNIPER, CALIFORNIA (*Juniperus californicus*)	8	N	10–30	Sun	Dry	All year	Blue-green berry	Berries eaten by at least 10 bird species, including mockingbird, Townsend's solitaire, varied thrush, and cedar waxwing; excellent cover for dry soils
LAUREL, CALIFORNIA (*Umbellularia californica*)	7	N	20–75	Sun/shade	Moist/drained	Fall	Drupe	Depending on growth conditions, a shrub, tree, or creeping ground cover; eaten by Steller's jay and Townsend's solitaire
OAK, BLUE (*Quercus douglasii*)	7	N	20–60	Sun	Dry/drained	All year	Annual acorn	Acorns are eaten by wild turkey, band-tailed pigeon, quail, jays, and many other species; both oaks occur in scattered groves along lower, dry mountain slopes
OAK, ENGELMANN (*Quercus engelmannii*)	7	N	20–50	Sun	Dry/drained	All year	Annual acorn	

Evergreen Trees (cont.)

Name	Zone	Native(N) Alien(A)	Height (ft)	Light	Preferred Soil	Fruit Period	Fruit Type	Remarks
PINE, DIGGER (*Pinus sabiniana*)	8	N	40–80	Sun	Dry/ moist/ drained	All year	Cone	Native to dry foothills of northern and central California
PINE, JEFFREY (*Pinus Jeffreyi*)	6	N	60–200	Sun	Drained	Fall	Cone	Occurs naturally high in the mountains; cones sometimes grow to 15 inches long
PINE, MONTEREY (*Pinus radiata*)	7	N	40–100	Sun	Drained	On exposure to heat	Cone	Cones occur every 3 to 5 years; commonly planted in gardens and yards in coastal zone near San Francisco
PINE, TORREY (*Pinus torreyana*)	7	N	20–40	Sun	Drained	All year	Cone	Native to coastal southern California; dense foliage and often twisted trunks give this tree interesting ornamental value as well as cover and food value for coastal landbirds

Deciduous Trees

Name	Zone	Native(N) Alien(A)	Height (ft)	Light	Preferred Soil	Fruit Period	Fruit Type	Remarks
ALDER, RED (*Alnus rubra*)	5	N	40–80	Sun/ shade	Moist/ drained	Fall/ winter	Nutlet in cone	Native along coastal stream banks and shore flats from Alaska south to southcentral Oregon; seeds eaten by goldfinch, pine siskin, bufflehead, green-winged teal, and American widgeon
ASH, OREGON (*Praxinus oregona*)	7	N	30–70	Sun	Moist/ drained	Fall	Samara	Native along stream banks and moist valley bottoms from British Columbia to southern California; fruit may persist on the tree for 12 months; plant male and female for seed crop; favorite of evening grosbeak

Deciduous Trees

Name								Notes
CRABAPPLE, OREGON (*Malus diversifolia*)	3	N	10–30	Sun	Moist/drained	Fall	Purple pome	Native on the Pacific coast from Alaska to northern California; sometimes occurs as a shrub; a favorite food of robin and ruffed grouse; many cultivated varieties are also available; some other flowering crabapple species and varieties hardy to Alaska include Japanese Hopa, Radiant, Pink Cascade, Sparkler, and Dolgo
MADRONE (*Arbutus menziesii*)	7	N	20–100	Sun	Dry/moist/drained	Summer/winter	Orange/red berry	Native in the foothills and lower mountain slopes of coastal ranges from British Columbia to southern California; fruit persists through early winter; at least 5 bird species eat its fruit, including band-tailed pigeon and wild turkey
MAPLE, CALIFORNIA BOX ELDER (*Acer negundo* var. *californicum*)	3	N	20–40	Sun/shade	Dry/moist	Summer/fall	Samara	Native to streams and valleys of coast ranges; extensively cultivated for street and park plantings; its seeds are eaten by at least 4 bird species, including evening grosbeak and ring-necked pheasant
OAK, OREGON WHITE (*Quercus garryana*)	7	N	35–60	Sun	Dry/drained	All year	Annual acorn	Acorns are important food for turkey, band-tailed pigeon, Lewis' woodpecker, and ring-necked pheasant; Oregon white oak often occurs as a shrub
OAK, VALLEY WHITE (*Quercus lobata*)	9	N	40–125	Sun/shade	Dry/drained	Fall	Annual acorn	
SYCAMORE, WESTERN (*Platanus racemosa*)	10	N	40–90	Sun	Drained/moist	Fall/winter	Achene	Grows along streams and adjacent floodplains in central and southern California; seeds are a favorite goldfinch food
WILLOW, SCOULER (*Salix scouleriana*)	5	N	4–30	Sun	Dry/moist/drained	Summer	Capsule	Very common tree of mountain and stream banks from southern Alaska to southern California; excellent for stabilizing stream banks; 23 bird species, especially grouse and quail, are known to eat the tender buds and twigs of willows

Evergreen Shrubs

Name	Zone	Native(N) Alien(A)	Height (ft)	Light	Preferred Soil	Fruit Period	Fruit Type	Remarks
BUCKTHORN, CALIFORNIA (COFFEE BERRY) (*Rhamnus californica*)	7	N	to 8	Sun	Dry	Early fall	Drupe	Eaten by at least 7 bird species, including band-tailed pigeon
BLADDERBUSH (*Isomeris arborea*)	9	N	to 7	Sun	Loamy	Summer/ fall	Capsule	Usually grows in alkaline soils; semievergreen; good cover year round; spreads to 6 feet
CHRISTMASBERRY (TOYON) (*Photinia arbutifolia*)	8	N	10–20	Sun/ shade	Dry/ drained	Late fall/ winter	Red pome	Occurs on lower mountain slopes from central to southern California; extensively cultivated for attractive dark green leaves and red fruit; fruits are eaten by at least 7 bird species, including band-tailed pigeon and California quail
GRAPE, OREGON (*Mahonia nervosa*)	7	N	to 2	Sun/ shade	Dry/ drained	Late summer	Berry	Forms dense, low thickets; resistant to black stem rust; excellent cover
HUCKLEBERRY, EVERGREEN (*Vaccinium ovatum*)	7	N	to 10	Sun/ shade	Moist/ drained	Late summer	Black berry	Important food for blue grouse and many types of songbird; at least 87 bird species are known to eat blueberry and huckleberry fruits
MANZANITA (*Arctostaphylos manzanita*) and (*A. diversifolia*)	7	N	12–15	Sun	Dry/ drained	Year round	Red berry	Occurs along California coast and in coastal mountains of southern California; fruit eaten by at least 8 bird species, including California jay, band-tailed pigeon, fox sparrow, wren-tit, and mockingbird
SALTBUSH, BREWER (*Atriplex brewerii*)	9	N	1–5	Sun	Dry	Early fall	Achene	Excellent cover for dry habitats; salt tolerant; makes good windbreaks and hedges (with pruning); semievergreen
SALTBUSH, DESERT (*Atriplex polycarpa*)	5	N	to 6	Sun	Dry	Fall	Achene	Male and female plants; semievergreen; spreads 6 feet

Name								Notes
SUMAC, LAUREL (*Rhus laurina*)	9	N	10–20	Sun	Dry/drained	Early fall/persistent	Red drupe	Thick evergreen leaves produce dense shade and endure salt, extreme heat, and drought; at least 6 bird species are known to eat fruit, including quail and wren-tit; occurs in coastal southern California
SUMAC, LEMONADE (*Rhus integrifolia*)	9	N	to 30	Sun	Dry/drained	Late summer	Red drupe	
SUMAC, SUGAR (*Rhus ovata*)	9	N	to 10	Sun	Dry/drained	Late summer/persistent	Red drupe	

Deciduous Shrubs

Name								Notes
BLACKBERRY, CALIFORNIA (*Rubus macropetalus*)	8	N	to 6	Sun	Dry/moist/drained	Late summer	Black drupelets	Climbing or shrublike; fruits readily consumed by at least 12 bird species
CHOKECHERRY, WESTERN (*Prunus virginiana* var. *demissa*)	2	N	10–20	Sun/shade	Dry/moist/drained	Summer/early fall	Red/purple drupe	Forms dense thickets and provides prolific fruit that are consumed by at least 6 bird species, including ring-necked pheasant and sharp-tailed grouse
ELDER, PACIFIC RED (*Sambucus callicarpa*)	8	N	to 20	Sun/half sun	Dry/moist/drained	Late summer/early winter	Red berry	Thrives in rich, moist soil; prolific fruits are readily eaten by at least 8 bird species, including California quail, robin, and Swainson's thrush
OSOBERRY (*Osmaronia cerasiformis*)	4	N	to 12	Shade	Well drained	Late summer	Purple-black drupe	Fruits readily eaten by many kinds of bird
ROSE, BALDHIP (*Rosa gymnocarpa*)	6	N	to 3	Sun	Dry/drained	Fall	Red hip	Pink flowers; excellent cover; food for at least the following: ruffed and blue grouse, Swainson's thrush, Townsend's solitaire, ring-necked pheasant, and bluebird
ROSE, CALIFORNIA (*Rosa californica*)	4	N	to 10	Sun	Dry/drained	Fall	Red hip	
SALMONBERRY (*Rubus spectabilis*)	6	N	to 6	Sun	Dry	Summer	Yellow/red druplet	Readily eaten by robin, blackbird, cedar waxwings, pine and black-headed grosbeak, and band-tailed pigeon
SERVICEBERRY, WESTERN (*Amelanchier florida*)	2	N	3–20	Sun	Dry/moist/drained	Late summer	Blue pome	An important food for at least 10 western bird species, including flicker, cedar waxwings, western tanager, evening grosbeak, and black-headed grosbeak

Vines

Name	Zone	Native(N) Alien(A)	Light	Preferred Soil	Fruit Period	Fruit Type	Remarks
GRAPE, CALIFORNIA (*Vitis californica*)	7	N	Sun	Moist/ drained	Summer/ fall	Purple berry	Tall climbing vine with fragrant flowers; fruits are favorites of many kinds of bird, including flicker, grouse, quail, mockingbird, wren-tit, western bluebird, and cedar waxwings
GREENBRIER, CALIFORNIA (*Smilax californica*)	7	N	Sun/ shade	Moist/ drained	Summer/ fall	Berry	Smooth or prickly vine that often spreads by rootstocks; fruits eaten by mockingbird, thrasher, robin, and Swainson's thrush
HONEYSUCKLE, PINK (*Lonicera hispidula*)	7	N	Sun	Dry/ drained	Summer/ persists through winter	Red berry	Evergreen vine that sometimes grows as a 12-foot shrub; white or purple flowers; fruits eaten by at least Townsend's solitaire, robin, towhee, and wren-tit

Ground Cover (1 ft. or less)

Name	Zone	Native(N) Alien(A)	Light	Preferred Soil	Fruit Period	Fruit Type	Remarks
GROUND, ROSE (*Rosa spithamea*)	7	N	Sun	Dry/ drained	All year	Red hip	Low bush provides good cover and fruit for ground-feeding birds
MANZANITA, PINE-MAT (*Arctostaphylos nevadensis*)	7	N	Sun	Dry/ drained	Summer/ early fall	Red berry	Creeping evergreen mat; white flower and persistent fruit; provides excellent food into winter for grouse, jays, and band-tailed pigeon
STRAWBERRY, CALIFORNIA (*Fragaria californicus*)	7	N	Sun	Dry/ moist/ drained	Spring/ early summer	Red berry	At least 7 bird species eat strawberry fruit, including California quail, mockingbird, brown towhee, robin, and black-headed grosbeak
STRAWBERRY, WOOD (*Fragaria bracteata*)	5	N	Sun/ half sun	Dry/ moist/ drained	Spring	Red berry	A perennial herb; occurs in prairies and open, dry woods; at least 9 bird species are known to eat this fruit, including cedar waxwings, ruffed grouse, song sparrow, pine grosbeak, robin, and black-headed grosbeak

IMPORTANT UPLAND WEEDS

Many of the most despised yard and garden weeds are extremely valuable producers of wild bird seed. The massive quantities of seed produced by these weeds far exceeds the comparatively meager supplies of commercial grain doled out at backyard bird feeders. Weeds are clearly the staple of life for most of our common seed-eating birds. A wider recognition of the value of weeds to wild birds might lead to a more tolerant view of these abundant, useful plants.

By definition, a weed is simply an unwanted plant. Most are nonshowy, tenacious, and prolific seeders and can adapt to trampling, pulling, and poisoning. Weeds are survivors. The very act of trying to displace them usually improves the soil for the next generation.

To understand the value of weeds for attracting birds, let a back corner of your yard grow to seed or till a small section of lawn, exposing bare soil. The natural supply of dormant seeds will soon produce a crop of seed-producing bristle grass, ragweed, lamb's-quarters, amaranth, and many more. On larger properties, the same technique can be applied to half-acre weed plots. Plant succession leading to goldenrod, aster, and perennial grasses will exclude the seed-producing weeds after 2 to 3 years, necessitating another tilling to maintain this rich, natural food supply.

Well named for their bristly seed heads, the bristle grasses are the most important upland "weeds" for wild birds. Closely related to the cultivated millet found in bird seed mixtures, bristle grasses are abundant and widespread

BRISTLE GRASS
Setaria spp.

throughout the United States and southern Canada. The two most important members of this genus are introduced annual grasses from Europe, yellow bristle grass (*Setaria lutescens*) and green bristle grass (*S. viridis*). They commonly grow between rows of cultivated crops and other disturbed soils. At least 66 different wild bird species feed on bristle grass seed, which comprises at least 10 percent of the diet for 28 of these species at certain times of the year. Bristle grass is an especially important source of food for mourning doves, bobwhite, red-winged blackbird, indigo bunting, brown-headed cowbird, dickcissel, horned lark, Lapland longspur, and pyrrhuloxia, as well as clay-colored, grasshopper, and tree sparrows.

DIGITARIA SANGUINALIS

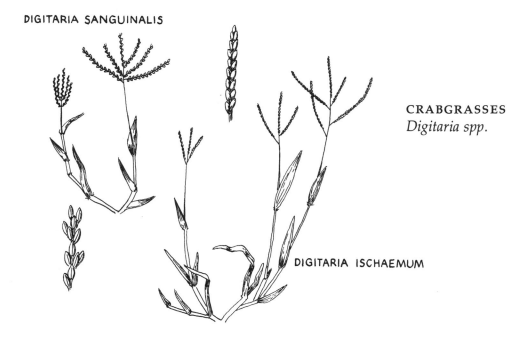

CRABGRASSES
Digitaria spp.

DIGITARIA ISCHAEMUM

Although there is a strong prejudice against crabgrass in lawns and gardens, these tenacious annual grasses are prolific seed producers and form an important part of the diet of many seed-eating songbirds. Two European introductions from this genus, hairy crabgrass (*Digitaria sanguinalis*) and smooth crabgrass (*D. ischaemum*), are especially widespread and abundant in disturbed soils and lawns across North America. These are important food plants for many seed-eating birds. Many songbirds would benefit if landowners would let even a small patch of crabgrass grow tall enough to seed. At least 21 bird species eat crabgrass seed, but it is especially important for mourning dove, dark-eyed junco, and Lapland longspur, as well as the chipping, clay-colored, field, Lincoln's, Savannah, and tree sparrows.

PANIC GRASS
Panicum spp.

At least 160 species of panic grass grow in North America. Most are annual native grasses of dry uplands that grow best in cultivated or disturbed soils. Like the bristle grasses, the widespread and abundant panic grasses are very important foods for ground-feeding birds. Common witchgrass (*Panicum capillare*) and fall panic grass (*P. dichotomiflorum*), are two of the most common and ubiquitous species. Panic grasses are most common in the southeastern United States, but many kinds also occur in the north and west. At least 61 bird species eat panic grass seed, most frequently bobwhite, wild turkey, red-winged blackbird, brown-headed cowbird, blue grosbeak, Smith's longspur, and pyrrhuloxia, as well as the lark, clay-colored, Lincoln's, Savannah, tree, song, swamp, and white-crowned sparrow.

DOVEWEEDS
Croton spp.

Doveweeds, sometimes called crotons, are important wild bird foods in the southern and prairie states. Their common name comes from their popularity as a preferred food for mourning, ground, and white-winged doves. Doveweed seed is also favored by prairie chicken, bobwhite, cardinal, pipits, pyrrhuloxia, and many other ground-feeding birds. Most doveweeds, as with wooly croton (*Croton capitatus*), are annual, but others, such as Gulf croton (*C. punctatus*), are perennial. Crotons are noted for their resistance to grazing by cattle.

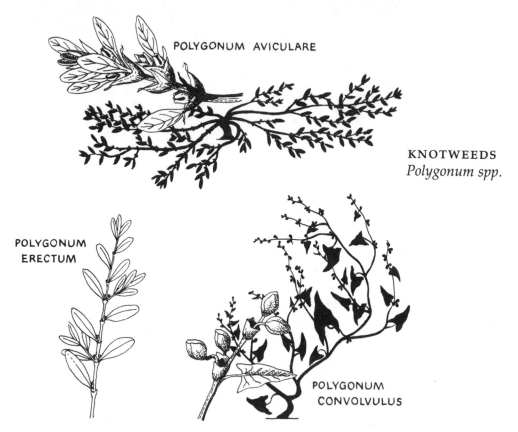

POLYGONUM AVICULARE

KNOTWEEDS
Polygonum spp.

POLYGONUM
ERECTUM

POLYGONUM
CONVOLVULUS

The knotweeds are a diverse group of mostly dry-habitat plants. Although they vary from low, creeping species, such as prostrate knotweed (*Polygonum aviculare*), to upright forms, such as erect knotweed (*P. erectum*) and black bindweed (*P. convolvulus*), a twining vine, all provide important seed supplies for wild birds. The large seeds of black bindweed are especially important to upland game birds, such as the greater prairie chicken and Hungarian partridge. At least 39 bird species eat knotweed seeds. They are especially favored by ground-feeding birds, including rosy finches, horned larks, and McCown's longspur, as well as the fox, grasshopper, Harris', lark, Savannah, song, and white-crowned sparrow.

Lamb's-quarters is an introduced annual herb from Eurasia that grows commonly in disturbed soils of gardens and roadsides throughout most of North America. An individual lamb's-quarters plant may produce 75,000 tiny seeds, which may be available from June to October. At least 32 bird species are known to eat lamb's-quarters seeds. They are most readily eaten by ground-feeding songbirds, such as snow bunting, dark-eyed junco, horned lark, McCown's longspur, common redpoll, and white-crowned sparrow.

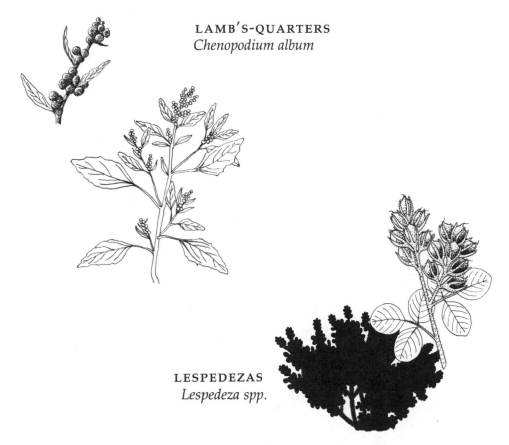

LAMB'S-QUARTERS
Chenopodium album

LESPEDEZAS
Lespedeza spp.

The lespedezas are woody shrubs or herbs in the pea family. Native lespedezas, such as hairy bush clover (*Lespedeza hirta*), are perennial, small shrubs up to 4 feet tall, but there are also several introduced species, such as common lespedeza (*L. striata*) and Korean lespedeza (*L. stipulacea*), that are annual herbs and grow only about 1 foot tall. Although several ground-feeding songbirds, such as dark-eyed junco, white-throated sparrow, and mourning dove feed on lespedeza seed, this varied group is best known as a very important food and cover for bobwhite quail. Common lespedeza is best adapted to the southeastern United States, while Korean lespedeza is a better choice north of Kentucky.

Pigweeds are annual native plants of disturbed soils, such as vacant lots and waste areas. Some sources suggest that pigweeds are especially common in areas where pigs have rooted up the soil—a theory that may explain their unlikely name. Members of the amaranth genus are prolific seed producers—single plants are known to produce over 100,000 tiny seeds. As with ragweed, the best way to encourage a crop of pigweed is to thoroughly till the soil. Pigweeds, ragweeds, and other plants of disturbed soils can maintain themselves for only 2 to 3 years

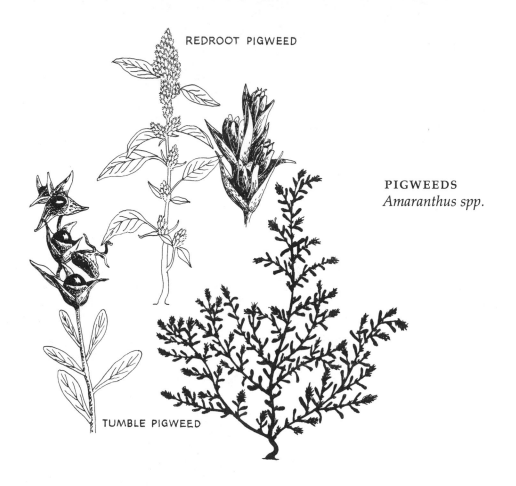

REDROOT PIGWEED

PIGWEEDS
Amaranthus spp.

TUMBLE PIGWEED

before they will be crowded out by such perennials as asters and goldenrod. At least 47 bird species eat pigweed seeds, which are especially important to mourning doves, snow bunting, and goldfinches, as well as the chipping, clay-colored, Lincoln's, Savannah, song, and white-crowned sparrow.

Pokeweed is a native smooth-stemmed plant found in moist, disturbed soils. The large, poisonous taproot may produce plants that grow up to 12 feet tall. Each fall, pokeweed dies back to the ground; however, new stems may grow from the same root for 10 or more consecutive years. As many as 1000 juicy, dark purple berries ripen annually from August to October and are readily consumed by at least 52 kinds of bird. Pokeweed fruit is especially preferred by mourning doves, catbirds, mockingbirds, thrushes, and cedar waxwings. Some birds may become intoxicated after eating pokeberry fruit. A pokeweed patch in a corner of the backyard will make an excellent addition to bird foods.

POKEWEED
Phytolacca americana

RAGWEEDS
Ambrosia spp.

Our native ragweeds are best known as nuisances to hay fever sufferers, but their reputations should also include their great importance as seed producers for wild birds. As such, they have few rivals. No fewer than 60 bird species readily eat ragweed seeds. Common ragweed (*Ambrosia artemisiifolia*) is the most important ragweed in the east, as is western ragweed (*A. psilostachya*) in western states and provinces. These ragweeds have abundant, oil-rich seeds, and frequently hold their tiny seeds into the winter, long after most other seeds are covered by snow. Since ragweed seeds can live in the soil for years and wait for favorable growing conditions, the best way to get a good ragweed crop is to simply disturb the soil by tilling. Ragweed seeds are especially important to snow bunting, American goldfinch, dark-eyed junco, horned lark, and common redpoll, as well as the fox, Harris', song, white-crowned, and white-throated sparrow.

SHEEP SORREL
Rumex acetosella

SUNFLOWERS
Helianthus spp.

Sheep sorrel is often one of the most common plants in open, short-grass meadows. This diminutive member of the dock family is naturalized from Europe. It spreads seeds by creeping perennial rootstock, and now grows throughout most of North America in acidic, low-fertility soils. Its seeds are its principal value to birds. At least 29 bird species are known to eat sheep-sorrel seed, including many game and songbirds. Sheep sorrel seed is also a food for ruffed grouse, red-winged blackbird, and hoary redpoll, as well as the grasshopper, Savannah, song, swamp, tree, and white-crowned sparrow.

Most sunflowers grow in open, sunny habitats. More species thrive in the prairie and plains states than any other region, but sunflowers occur throughout North America and some even grow in woodlands. Most, such as the Jerusalem artichoke (*Helianthus tuberosus*), are perennial and grow each year from hardy rootstock. Common sunflower (*H. annuus*) is an annual species with prolific seed production. Its cultivated varieties are among the most important wild bird foods. Some birds, such as chickadees, nuthatches, and titmice, prefer sunflowers over all other seeds and will feed exclusively on them if given the opportunity. At least 43 bird species eat sunflower seeds.

CHAPTER III

POOLS AND PONDS

In dry habitats of the southwestern states, water may be more attractive to birds than food. Even in the moist Pacific northwest and northeastern states, water may be locally scarce during the summer, and for most of the northern winter it becomes mostly inaccessible, locked in ice and snow.

Birds can get much of their water needs from their food, and some even eat snow, but all species require at least some water for drinking, and birds ranging in size from eagles to hummingbirds bathe in water at all seasons. Most waterfowl, wading birds, and shorebirds are, of course, totally dependent on very specific aquatic habitats. Providing clean water at the proper level in the correct habitat at the right time of year is difficult, yet when done properly, open water is one of the most useful management tools for attracting birds and improving wildlife habitat.

WATER PROJECTS

Birdbaths

A predator-safe birdbath that offers open water throughout the year will help to attract birds that seldom visit feeders, such as warblers and vireos.

Birdbaths are usually sold with raised pedestals or stands, but many species seem to prefer baths at ground level, the usual place that rain puddles appear in nature. The principal advantage of a raised birdbath is protection from such predators as house cats that might easily pounce on birds that are vulnerable while water-soaked and busy splashing around. Raised birdbaths are also more conspicuous and easier to maintain where there are deep winter snow accumulations.

A wide variety of birdbaths are available from commercial suppliers (see Appendix D), but water can be provided just as easily from homemade baths and pools. Garbage can lids are an ideal shape for a birdbath. They can be used on the ground, supported with bricks, or secured on top of a ceramic drain tile with a weight tied to the handle. Plastic lids are not as useful because the sides are very slick, thus making it difficult for birds to work their way into the bath and gain secure footing. This can be improved by spreading a thin layer of silicone bathtub caulk over the inside of the lid and then sprinkling sand into the still-wet caulk.

Make sure that your birdbath has a very gentle incline into the water and that the water in the bath is not more than 2 or 3 inches deep. Birds will not bathe in many manufactured baths because the sides are too steep.

The location of the birdbath often determines which types of bird it will attract. Bold species, such as robins and jays, will visit birdbaths in open areas or near shrubs, but warblers, wood thrush, and other secretive birds are more likely to visit baths that are tucked into shady, protected spots. The only problem with such sites is that birds there are more vulnerable to lurking house cats. If house cats prowl your property, keep your birdbaths in the open, at least 15 feet from shrubs and on a pedestal at least 3 feet off the ground.

Water supplies should be dependable. When water is available consistently, birds will visit the bath as part of their daily routines. Unpredictable water sources are visited rarely. Also, the water in birdbaths should be changed every few days and the surface scrubbed clean of algae that may thrive in the bird-fertilized water.

You can make your birdbath more attractive by creating motion on the water's surface. This attracts the attention of birds that might otherwise overlook the water. Dripping water is especially attractive to warblers. Burbling, gurgling, or dripping water attracts birds, but fast-moving, powerful sprays may startle and disperse them.

The most effective way to provide dripping is to install a specially designed water adapter called the Water Drip. In this system, a special Y valve attaches to your house water outlet, transferring water through a narrow-diameter hose that leads to a hook-shaped, narrow-diameter metal pipe that trickles water into the birdbath. The Fountain Mist is another specially designed attractant for birdbaths. This device brings water from the house outlet, creating a miniature fountain spray in the middle of the birdbath that varies in height.

A simpler method is to hang a bucket with a hole punched in its bottom over the bath. Experiment with the size of the hole, starting with a small nail hole, enlarging it until a regular pattern of water drips from the bucket (about 20 to 30 drops per minute). Keep the bucket covered to reduce evaporation and the chance of detritus clogging the drip hole.

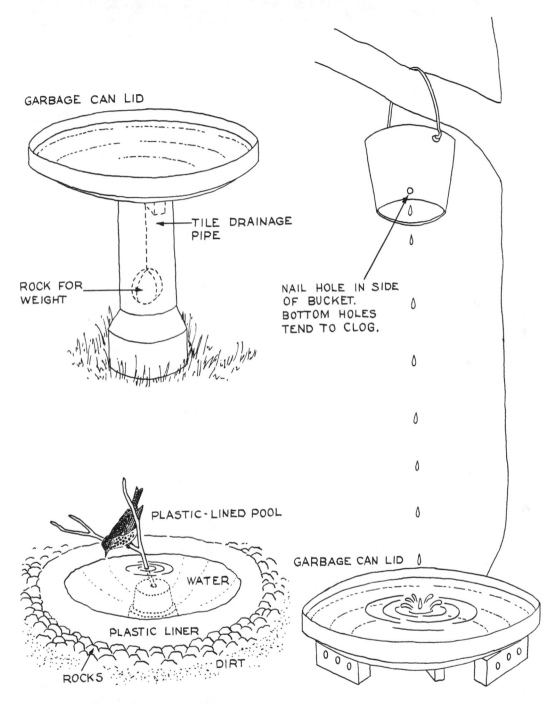

GARBAGE CAN LID

TILE DRAINAGE PIPE

ROCK FOR WEIGHT

NAIL HOLE IN SIDE OF BUCKET. BOTTOM HOLES TEND TO CLOG.

PLASTIC-LINED POOL

WATER

PLASTIC LINER

DIRT

ROCKS

GARBAGE CAN LID

Examples of birdbaths made from everyday materials, such as garbage can lids, metal buckets, and drainage pipes. Water dripping from a bucket into a bath creates surface motion attractive to small birds.

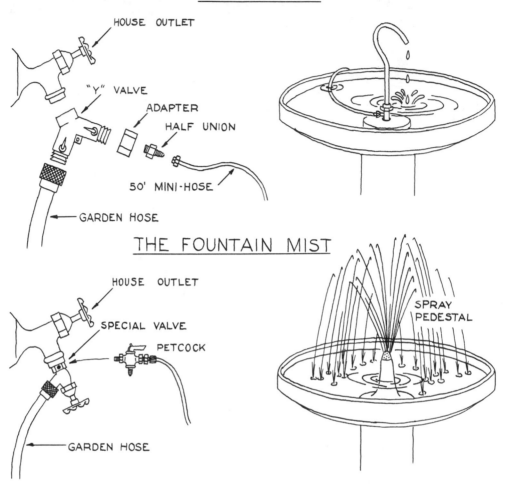

WATER DRIP

HOUSE OUTLET

"Y" VALVE

ADAPTER

HALF UNION

50' MINI-HOSE

GARDEN HOSE

THE FOUNTAIN MIST

HOUSE OUTLET

SPECIAL VALVE

PETCOCK

GARDEN HOSE

SPRAY PEDESTAL

Two types of commercial water attractants—the Water Drip and the Fountain Mist. Both are available from the Beverly Company, Box 101, New Harbor, ME 04554.

During northern winters you can keep birdbath water ice-free by using a water heater. The simplest, and least expensive, design consists of a light fixture mounted in the base of a flower pot. A shallow ceramic or plastic dish with thin walls rests on top of the flower pot. A heavy-gauge outdoor power cord, which leads to an outdoor power receptacle, fits through the drain hole in the bottom of the pot. For added safety, check with an electrician to be sure that the receptacle has a ground fault interruptor. The size of the light bulb will depend on how severe your winters are as well as the dimensions of the water supply. A 40-watt light bulb is usually adequate.

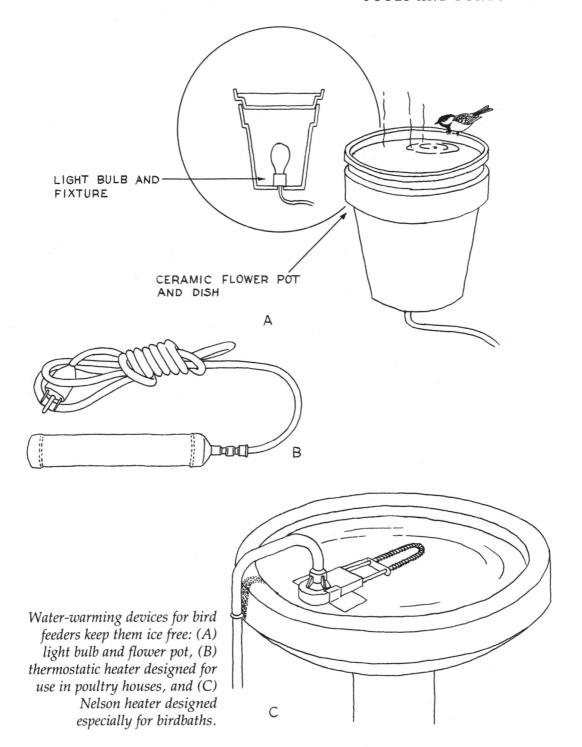

LIGHT BULB AND
FIXTURE

CERAMIC FLOWER POT
AND DISH

A

B

Water-warming devices for bird feeders keep them ice free: (A) light bulb and flower pot, (B) thermostatic heater designed for use in poultry houses, and (C) Nelson heater designed especially for birdbaths.

C

You can also insert a submersible water heater into the bath. Two kinds are available through suppliers (Appendix D). The first, a thermostat-controlled heater designed for use in poultry houses, warms water to about 50°F (9°C) and then turns off. Hold this heater in place with a brick or other heavy weight. The second, the Nelson heater, is specially designed for birdbaths, with a flat base and curved stem that mounts over the side of the bath. Its thermostat keeps water at 40°–50°F (5°–9°C).

When using submerged birdbath heaters, be sure to keep the heater covered with water. If all the water in the bath evaporates—and it will every few days—the heater will burn itself out and it may crack ceramic baths or melt plastic.

Backyard Pools

Where space permits, an in-ground pool designed expressly for birds will attract many species and add an interesting touch to your bird-feeding area, especially if it is creatively landscaped with ferns or other low rock-garden plants. Such pools are especially useful in arid or hot climates.

Place the pool far enough from bird feeders so that it is not always filling with seed hulls and discarded grain. Also pick a site within reach of your garden hose—cleaning the pool is very important.

Although a pool's shape is not important to birds, the pitch of its slope is of the utmost importance. The pool should grade gently from ½ inch of water to no more than 4 inches. It can contain several square feet of water, although smaller pools are also attractive. Such pools will provide bathing water for both smaller birds, such as warblers, and large birds, such as robins and jays.

A long length of rope is useful in laying out a pool. Move the rope on the ground until you find a pleasing shape, then use a shovel to excavate the hole to a depth of about 9 inches. Your completed pool will need a watertight liner. This is best constructed from concrete mix, which comes in small manageable bags that are ideal for this project.

First fill the hole and sides with several inches of sand, then cut a piece of welded wire (1 × 2 inch mesh) to fit the hole, pressing it down over the sand. Pour 3 inches of cement over the wire so that it is buried inside the concrete. The

In-ground backyard pools should have a shallow slope and occasional rocks placed in deeper water to serve as convenient island perches.

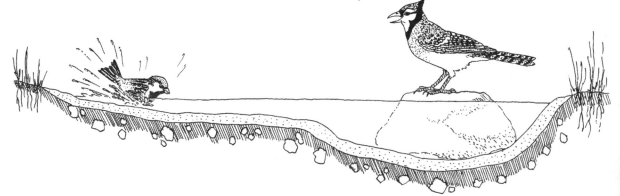

sand will lessen the chances of frost heaving under the pool in winter and the wire will give added strength to the concrete. The finished depression for the pool should be no more than 3 inches deep and should have gently sloping sides. More elaborate pools with water circulating between levels can be constructed following a similar design. Pumps for circulating water are available from Lily-pons Water Gardens, Brookshire, TX 77423-0188.

"Guzzlers" for Desert Birds

In semiarid habitats, rain from occasional downpours may be collected and stored for wildlife using a variety of catchment schemes, collectively known as "guzzlers." Guzzlers have been a spectacular success for increasing populations of desert quail and songbirds that were previously limited by scarce water supplies.

Although the forms vary considerably, the basic idea is similar to a cistern in which water coming off a roof is caught and tunneled into a secure tank for later use. Corrugated sheet metal forms an "apron" that catches rain and guides it into a steel, fiberglass, or concrete tank, which may hold up to 1000 or more gallons. To reduce evaporation, guzzlers should be located on a north-facing slope in areas that are not likely to be flooded. For this reason, avoid locating guzzlers in a wash or gully. Cover the holding tank with a removable lid to further reduce evaporation and the growth of algae and to facilitate annual cleaning. If you have a farm and want to protect guzzlers from wandering cattle, it is best to install a sturdy barbed-wire fence around the entire water-collection area.

To construct a smaller-scale water catcher, slant two pieces of corrugated metal to feed water into an eave gutter that delivers it into a small pool or pan. The amount of water that can be collected from flat surfaces in arid regions is truly amazing.

SIZES OF RAIN-COLLECTING APRONS

Minimum Annual Rainfall (inches)	Square Feet of Collecting Surface Required		
	600g.	700g.	900g.
1	965	1,127	1,453
2	482	563	726
3	322	376	485
4	242	282	365
5	192	225	290
6	162	189	243
7	138	161	208
8	121	141	182
9	107	125	161
10	97	113	146
11	87	102	132
12	80	94	121

Adapted from Stanford D. Schemnitz, ed., *Wildlife Management Techniques Manual*, 4th ed. Washington, D.C.: The Wildlife Society, 1980.

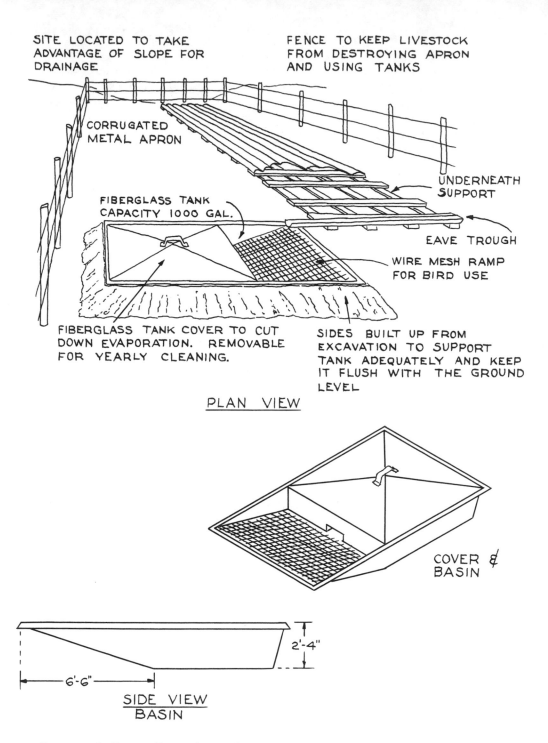

SITE LOCATED TO TAKE ADVANTAGE OF SLOPE FOR DRAINAGE

FENCE TO KEEP LIVESTOCK FROM DESTROYING APRON AND USING TANKS

CORRUGATED METAL APRON

UNDERNEATH SUPPORT

FIBERGLASS TANK CAPACITY 1000 GAL.

EAVE TROUGH

WIRE MESH RAMP FOR BIRD USE

FIBERGLASS TANK COVER TO CUT DOWN EVAPORATION. REMOVABLE FOR YEARLY CLEANING.

SIDES BUILT UP FROM EXCAVATION TO SUPPORT TANK ADEQUATELY AND KEEP IT FLUSH WITH THE GROUND LEVEL

PLAN VIEW

COVER & BASIN

2'-4"

6'-6"

SIDE VIEW
BASIN

Large-scale "apron" guzzler with detail of water holding tank (redrawn from J. Yoakum et al. "Habitat Improvement Techniques," in Stanford D. Schemnitz, ed., Wildlife Management Techniques Manual, *4th ed., Wildlife Society, Washington, DC, 1980).*

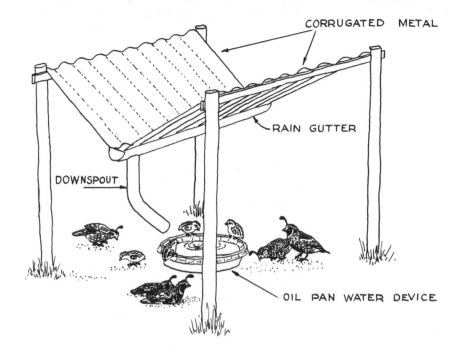

CORRUGATED METAL

RAIN GUTTER

DOWNSPOUT

OIL PAN WATER DEVICE

A small-scale guzzler feeds water into a gutter and is then filtered into a pan.

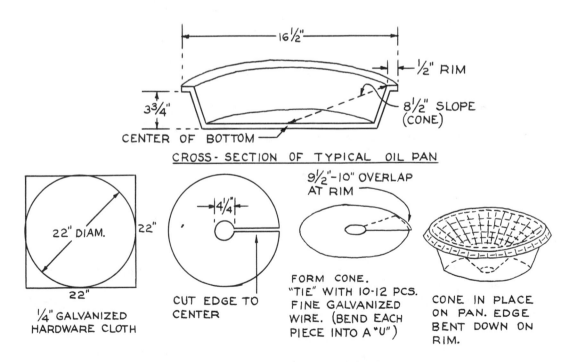

16½"

½" RIM

8½" SLOPE (CONE)

3¾"

CENTER OF BOTTOM

CROSS-SECTION OF TYPICAL OIL PAN

22" DIAM.

22"

22"

¼" GALVANIZED HARDWARE CLOTH

4¼"

CUT EDGE TO CENTER

9½"-10" OVERLAP AT RIM

FORM CONE. "TIE" WITH 10-12 PCS. FINE GALVANIZED WIRE. (BEND EACH PIECE INTO A "U")

CONE IN PLACE ON PAN. EDGE BENT DOWN ON RIM.

A water-collection pan with a wire cone prevents small birds from drowning.

Regardless of the size of the water-collecting tank, it is essential that it not have steep or slippery sides, which will be a sure deathtrap for birds. Larger tanks should have sloping ramps so that birds can walk to the water. To improve traction, tack small wooden slats or a piece of hardware-cloth wire to the ramp.

Theodore Nelson of Crockett, California, suggests a simple, safe water-collection device for quail and songbirds. He has found that a galvanized oil-collection pan equipped with a hardware-cloth cone will keep quail chicks from drowning in the pan. For a $16^{1/2}$-inch-diameter oil pan, he suggests cutting a 22-inch-diameter circle of hardware cloth. The circle of mesh is cut from the edge to the center and the interior is cut into an open circle before overlapping and forming a rim over the pan.

Designing Ponds and Marshes for Birds

Ponds and marshes can be constructed in almost any site with suitable soil and a freshwater source such as a natural spring or a flowing stream or an adequate-sized watershed that will permit enough water to fill the impoundment. Most ponds are designed for fishing, however, and this usually means they are not especially good for birds. Ideally, bird ponds should be shallow, with gently sloping shorelines and a scattering of small islands. They should also be equipped with a drawdown gate that will permit various levels of drainage.

Cattle should not be permitted to graze at the pond edge or wallow in the shallow water, as they will trample vegetation and muddy the water. If there are cattle near your pond, fence it to keep the cattle out. Provide water for cattle with a special valve-controlled pipe that brings water through the dike to a nearby watering tank. For attracting birds, there also should be at least 5 hours of direct sunlight each day to favor growth of aquatic plants and suitable adjacent vegetation for food and cover.

Dense brush adjacent to the pond on at least one side is attractive to many songbirds, and standing dead trees in the water or along the shoreline are frequently used as nest sites by woodpeckers and tree swallows and often double as perches for kingfishers, flycatchers, and herons.

Mud flats are also an important feature of a bird pond, as they are choice feeding areas for shorebirds and popular loafing areas for waterfowl. Ponds and marshes constructed with a variable-level drawdown are ideal for creating mud flats. For ponds without a drawdown gate, you can create a small mud flat by spreading a piece of heavy plastic along a section of the shore. Secure the plastic by burying the edges in soil and cover it with several inches of sand or soil. Occasional raking or grating will help keep plants from colonizing this small mud flat.

Shallow water is essential for encouraging submerged plants, tadpoles, small fish, and such aquatic insects as dragonfly and mayfly nymphs. These are important foods for ducks and marsh birds. Ponds can be constructed for both birds and fish, but it is necessary to pay careful attention to water depth. Large fish require at least 8 feet of water to survive the winter. By creating the pond with both deep and shallow waters, the fish will have room, and the shallows will benefit birds and fish by providing shelter for newborn fish and invertebrates, the foods for birds. The deep part of the pond should have a slope of 3:1, grading into a 6:1 slope to create a shallow water shoreline. Gently sloping shorelines provide slightly different microhabitats in the various vegetation belts that soon circle the pond. Variety in shoreline vegetation will lead to a greater diversity of birds.

When emergent vegetation completely dominates the water area, growing from one side to the distant shore, by definition the pond becomes a marsh. Marshes make excellent bird habitat, attracting such species as bitterns, rails, and marsh wrens that might not be drawn to pond margins because of insufficient emergent vegetation.

To improve the quality of marshes for water birds, try to keep a single vegetation species (particularly cattails), introduced species, such as purple loosestrife (*Lythrum salicaria*), or woody shrubs, from dominating the marsh or pond border. Manual cutting, dredging, burning, or artificial changes in water level are all useful tools to maintain some open water and a high diversity of useful aquatic plants. To protect water birds and other aquatic life in your pond or marsh, avoid using herbicides. For details on the best techniques for slowing this natural succession in your vicinity, contact your local office of the Soil Conservation Service or Cooperative Extension Service.

You can also improve the quality of a pond or marsh for birds by increasing the amount of shoreline. Shoreline, the junction of land and water, is an extremely rich habitat for a great variety of aquatic animals, such as insects, frogs, turtles, and crayfish. To increase the proportion of shoreline to surface area of a pond, construct the pond with an irregular shore, to create points and coves. This pattern also increases visual isolation and permits birds of the same species to

Cross-section of a pond suitable for fish and wading birds. A 3:1 shoreline gradient creates the preferred fish habitat; wading birds will gravitate toward the shallower shoreline gradient of 6:1.

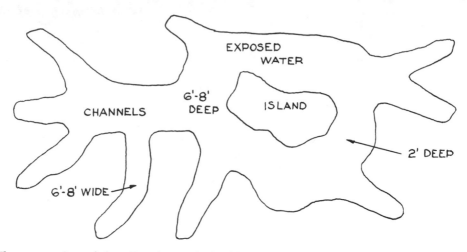

The proportion of shoreline is maximized by creating an amoeba-shaped pond with peninsulas which form numerous points and coves. Small islands provide excellent nesting and loafing areas for waterfowl.

nest in more secluded areas out of sight and sound of competitive neighbors. For example, in this way more than one pair of territorial mallards can occupy the same pond; there may also be feeding space for two or more great blue herons rather than just one.

Small islands not only add valuable shoreline, but they also serve as favorite roosting and nesting places for waterfowl. Loons and grebes most frequently build their floating raftlike nests in the emergent vegetation around small islands.

Because of their isolation on water, islands are usually safer nesting places than adjacent shorelines where such predators as fox and raccoon can sneak up on incubating birds with little warning. Perhaps for this reason, water birds usually prefer to nest on islands when they are available. Similarly, artificial loafing and nesting rafts are attractive to Canada geese, common terns, and common loons (see section on nesting platforms in Chapter IV). Large islands can accommodate more nesting birds, but even small islands of only 30 or more square feet are large enough to shelter at least one waterfowl nest.

Constructing Ponds and Marshes

Ponds and marshes can often be constructed in areas that are likely to attract waterfowl. Soil type is the most important characteristic of any potential pond site. Soils with heavy clay content will hold water and are necessary for building ponds. Ponds constructed over sandy or gravel soils will surely leak.

The first step is to dig a test pit with a backhoe. Usually several pits are best to sample the soil column throughout the proposed pond site. Even if your neighbor has a pond or marsh, it is best to thoroughly check the soil so that no surprises, such as layers of gravel or sand, turn up after pond construction begins. Even a thin layer of sand (known as a lens) can drain water out of a pond basin.

Coordinate the digging of test pits with a visit from your local Soil Conservation Service (SCS) agent. SCS agents are experienced advisers in pond construction and can tell by examining the soil from the test pit if your pond is likely to hold water.

If the soil is too sandy, you have a couple of choices aside from abandoning the project. The pond can be lined with bentonite, a heavy clay, or a plastic pool liner can be installed over the entire basin. Both are expensive, but proven options. If there *is* some gravel, but otherwise good clay, you'll have an opportunity to test your gambling instincts.

The SCS agent will survey your pond site to determine the boundaries of the pond and can offer names of local earth movers who are experienced at pond construction. He or she can also mark out the boundaries of the pond with colored surveyor flags. The size of the pond will probably be determined by property boundaries and the size of the surrounding watershed that will drain into the pond. If bentonite or pond liners are not necessary, a one-half-acre pond can be built for under $1500. The only major costs will be the fees for the bulldozer operator and the construction of a water-control device. With one bulldozer, run by a capable operator, the whole construction can be done in a couple of days.

Before construction begins, draw up a detailed map to scale, showing the size, shape, and slope of the pond. Then review the details of your plan with the bulldozer operator. This is the time to insist on shallow slopes for most of the shoreline, locations for islands, and other design details. This may be contrary to the experience of your bulldozer operator, who is probably more familiar with steep-sided ponds for fish.

The first step is to clear all trees, shrubs, and sod from the pond site. Some of these plantings should be saved for creating brush piles (see Chapter I). Then all topsoil is stripped and piled aside. The operator begins excavating the basin of the pond, using the heavy clay to build a dike on the downhill side. This is also the time to build up islands within the basin. The bulldozer compacts the soil in the bottom of the pond, and then for the final step, spreads the topsoil on top of the dike and onto the islands. Without replacement of topsoil, it would be nearly impossible to establish vegetation.

The dike and islands should be fertilized and planted with grass as soon as possible after construction to reduce erosion (check with the SCS for recommended seed mixtures for your vicinity). Wildlife shrubs (see plant selections, Chapter II) can be planted on the dike, but trees should not be permitted to grow on it. Strong winds may eventually blow them down, resulting in serious weakening of the dike.

Controlling Water Levels

The ability to control the water level is an important feature of a bird-attracting pond. In general, waterfowl impoundments should be drained every 5 years. Research by the Canadian Wildlife Service on Canadian duck impoundments has found that after 4 years the soil and water in artificial waterfowl ponds sharply decline in fertility.[1] At the same time, useful waterfowl vegetation is replaced by less abundant and less attractive foods.

To improve aging ponds for waterfowl, drain ponds in late winter or early spring and disk or rototill the pond bottom to mix decomposed organic matter with mineral soils. Burning will also help to release nutrients. These techniques provide a suitable soil for favorite duck foods such as smartweeds (*Polygonum spp.*). If smartweeds or other suitable plants do not appear (see the next section for desirable waterfowl plants), plant the pond bottom to buckwheat (*Fagopyrum spp.*) and Japanese millet (*Echinochloa crusgalli frumentacea*) at 25 pounds of seed an acre. Let these mature over the summer and then flood the pond again in the fall. In the provinces and northern U.S. states, waterfowl impoundments should remain filled during spring and summer for the next 4 years as duck-breeding habitat. Reduce water levels in the fall to create shorebird habitat and to promote growth of duck foods.

Green-tree Reservoirs

Green-tree reservoirs are bottomland forests flooded for waterfowl. Hardwood forests with oak, beech, sweetgum, and tupelos are ideal for this purpose. Suitable forests for this technique are located in valleys with a small stream. Here a low dam creates a temporary backwater, flooding the forest floor with 1 or 2 feet of water. The technique is useful in southern states where there is open water throughout the winter.

By flooding woodlands in late fall or early winter, acorn and other mast crops become available to wintering waterfowl that would not otherwise visit dry woodland habitats. If there are openings in the woodland and ample sunlight, food production for waterfowl can be further increased by planting Japanese millet, corn, or grain sorghum during the summer. Late fall flooding apparently benefits trees, and as long as the water is drained from the woodland when leaf buds swell in the spring, there will be no damage to the trees.

Stocking New Ponds for Water Birds

New ponds and water impoundments will naturally attract a surprising variety of aquatic plants and animals. The first animals to appear in new ponds are small but vitally important to water birds. A close examination of pond water will show it alive with tiny crustaceans and insects. These aquatic invertebrates provide basic food for waterfowl. Invertebrates are high in protein and play important

---

[1]W. R. Whitman. "Impoundments for Waterfowl." Occasional Paper No. 22. Canadian Wildlife Service, Ottawa, 1978, 22 pp.

STOP PLANK GATE

USE CEDAR
FOR PLANKS.
4' LONG

SLIDING GATE VALVE

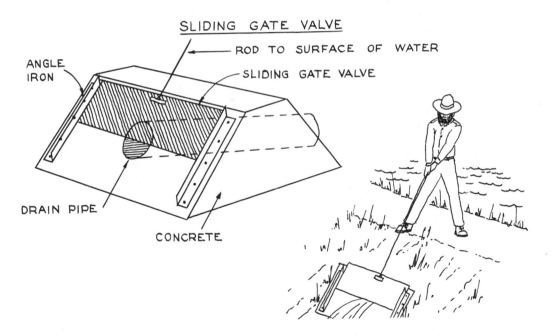

ROD TO SURFACE OF WATER

SLIDING GATE VALVE

ANGLE
IRON

DRAIN PIPE

CONCRETE

Water-control devices such as the stop plank gate and sliding gate valve will lower water levels when pond soil and water quality need rejuvenation.

roles in the diets of laying females and molting adults. They are especially important foods for rapidly growing young.

Tiny aquatic crustaceans find their way into impoundments from adjacent wetlands and on the feathers and feet of waterfowl. Some may also be windblown, while others can live for years as eggs in dry soil. Most aquatic insects, such as midges, mayflies, and dragonflies, have flying adult forms and these are quick to colonize new bodies of water. The number and kinds of invertebrates reach their greatest variety within the first 2 years and are constant by 4 or 5 years. When impoundments back water up over upland vegetation, there is a dramatic peak in the abundance of crustaceans and insects, as the flooding releases abundant nutrients through the decay of vegetation.

Aquatic plants usually find their way to new ponds by either wind or waterfowl. There is a rapid succession that begins with submerged and floating leaf plants and proceeds toward increasing amounts of emergents, such as cattails and bulrushes. The advanced stages of succession are less productive for most waterfowl, but they do favor marsh birds, such as rails and bitterns.

Frogs, toads, salamanders, and crayfish can hop, slide, and crawl miles to the nearest pond or marsh to reach a new habitat. Such travels are usually made on mild, raining nights. Once a few frogs or toads colonize a new pond, their calls will attract others, until they occupy all available shoreline. Population growth is very rapid for amphibians. For example, a female bullfrog (*Rana catesbeiana*) may lay 20,000 eggs each year. The abundance of tadpoles becomes a prime attractant for herons, kingfishers, and other predatory birds. Fish may naturally colonize new ponds from such connecting water sources as streams, or they may arrive as eggs clinging to the feathers of birds.

Natural colonization of ponds by aquatic plants and animals may proceed at a slower than desired rate where new ponds are isolated from well-established ponds or marshes. To speed up colonization of preferred species of fish, amphibians, crayfish, and vegetation, transplant amphibian eggs, small fish, or young plant specimens from nearby waters. Many of these species are also available from plant and animal dealers.

Minnows are the preferred fish for attracting herons, kingfishers, rails, mergansers, and many other freshwater birds. The best species for stocking will vary from one region to the next, so it is best to check with your local Cooperative Extension Office. Minnows are usually readily available at local fishing bait shops.

Many kinds of aquatic plants are also available. Those that can be purchased from plant dealers and nurseries are listed in the plant source directory in Appendix B. A review of some of the most important plants appears in the following section.

Green-tree reservoirs serve as a food supply, attracting waterfowl to areas, especially in the southern states, that might otherwise be too dry.

WINTER:
KEEP WATER UP.

SPRING:
DRAW DOWN BEFORE
BUDS OPEN.

SUMMER:
WOODS ARE DRY. ACORNS
GROW. WEEDS THRIVE
IN CLEARINGS.

FALL:
FLOOD AFTER LEAF FALL.
TREE SEEDS PROVIDE
DUCK FOOD.

IMPORTANT WETLAND AND AQUATIC PLANTS

Waterfowl and marsh birds, such as coots, rails, and gallinules, are intimately tied to various mixes of emergent, floating, and submerged vegetation. Most of the plants in this group are prolific seed-producers, an adaptation that increases a given plant's chances for its seed to find just the right new environment. Birds benefit by eating the seed, and sometimes spread it to new locations. Birds also feed on rootstocks, underground tubers, plant stems, and even leaves of certain marsh and aquatic plants.

Because most wetland and aquatic plants distribute their prolific seeds effectively, plant succession usually occurs rapidly without assistance from humans. However, obtaining a desirable mix of the proper aquatic plants for attracting birds is often a difficult task because succession quickly changes ponds into marshes and marshes into brushy fields. Wetland managers must frequently manipulate water levels by using dikes and levees, and sometimes must burn woody and dry grass off marshes to expose root systems for waterfowl. In other areas, dredging may be necessary to deepen water or remove such unproductive competitive plants as purple loosestrife (*Lythum salicaria*).

Some aquatic plants—among them arrowheads, chufa sedge, paspalum, smartweeds, wild rice, naiads, pondweeds, and water lilies—are available through commercial suppliers for stocking small ponds and marshes.

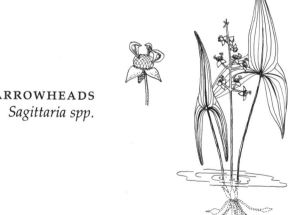

ARROWHEADS
Sagittaria spp.

Arrowheads occur along pond and lake edges throughout North America, but they are most abundant and important for wildlife in the eastern half of the continent. Both the seeds and tuberous roots of arrowheads are consumed by waterfowl, but the tubers are by far the more important and have even given the arrowheads another common name—duck potato. *Sagittaria* tubers are most readily available when the plants are growing partially submerged or in soft mud. The two most abundant and useful species are *S. latifolia* and *S. cuneata*, although the former species often has tubers that are too large or buried too deep for ducks. Arrowheads are especially important to canvasback, black duck, gadwall, wood duck, ring-necked duck, trumpeter and whistling swans, sandhill crane, and king rail. They are also occasionally eaten by at least another 10 kinds of dabbling and diving waterfowl.

SCIRPUS ACUTUS

BULRUSHES
Scirpus spp.

SCIRPUS AMERICANUS

Bulrushes are among the most important wetland plants for water and marsh birds. Bulrushes are tall perennial native sedges that often form dense stands or fringes along the shores of ponds and lakes. Of the more than 40 species found in North America, common three-square (*Scirpus americanus*) and hard-stem bulrush (*S. acutus*) are two of the most widespread and important kinds. Bulrushes not only produce abundant seed crops but the stems and rootstocks are important food for geese, swans, cranes, godwits, and rails. Bulrushes also provide important nesting cover for marsh wrens, blackbirds, waterfowl, bitterns, coots, and grebes. Bulrush seeds are important foods for at least 24 kinds of waterfowl.

Chufa, sometimes known as nut grass, is by far the most important member of the *Cyperus* sedges as a wildlife food. Introduced from Africa, chufa now grows in damp, sandy soils and mud flats throughout most of the United States and southern Canada. Both the edible tubers and seeds are readily eaten by waterfowl and songbirds. Sometimes it occurs as an unwelcome weed in cultivated fields

CHUFA SEDGE
Cyperus esculentus

and gardens, but here too its food value has been discovered by birds. At least 12 species of water birds, including American coot, sandhill crane, mallard, and green-winged teal readily eat chufa tubers.

CORDGRASSES
Spartina spp.

Two species of cordgrass dominate the salt marshes of the eastern and Gulf coasts. In brackish coastal waters from Newfoundland to Texas, marsh cordgrass (*Spartina alterniflora*) grows at the edge of the water, while the shorter, mat-forming salt hay (*S. patens*) grows at slightly higher levels. The seeds of these perennial grasses provide important food for black duck, clapper rail, Virginia rail, seaside sparrow, and sharp-tailed sparrow. The tender sprouts are a favorite food of brant, whooping crane, and Canada and snow geese.

The paspalum grasses are most abundant in the southeastern United States where 42 species are known. At least 6 kinds occur west to the Pacific coast. Most paspalum grasses are perennial natives, growing in a wide variety of habitats, from dry, upland sites to marshland. Field paspalum (*Paspalum laeve*) and fringe-leaf paspalum (*P. ciliatifolium*) are especially common in the eastern United States, occurring in fields and other dry habitats. Bull paspalum (*P. boscianum*)

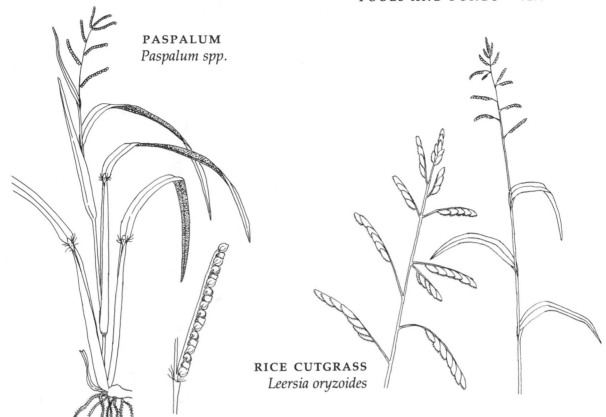

PASPALUM
Paspalum spp.

RICE CUTGRASS
Leersia oryzoides

grows in moist meadows, marshes, and roadside ditches. At least 16 bird species are known to eat paspalum seed. It is especially preferred by purple gallinule, sora rail, ground dove, wild turkey, mottled duck, and snow goose.

Rice cutgrass is a native perennial grass that often grows in the shallow water around ponds and lakes. It is common throughout the eastern United States and southern Canada and also occurs on the Pacific coast in freshwater wetlands. Named for the serrate edges to its leaves, it should not be confused with saw grass, a dominant sedge of southern swamps and marshes. At least 12 species of waterfowl readily eat the seeds and many also dig up and consume the roots. It is especially favored by black duck, common goldeneye, mallard, shoveler, and blue-winged teal.

Wild rice is a prolific seeding, annual grass. It grows in shallow water where there is deep, soft mud with enough circulation to prevent stagnation. Wild rice often fringes lakes and slow-moving rivers in the northern United States and southern Canadian provinces. It occurs along the Atlantic coast to Florida, but it is most abundant and has its greatest value to birds in the northern part of its

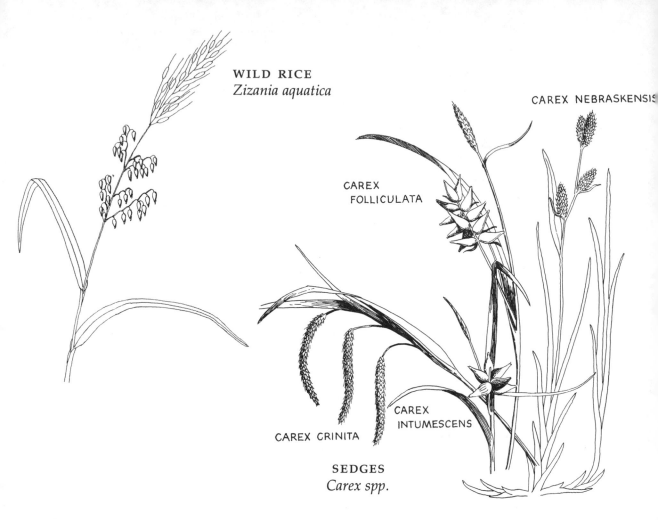

WILD RICE
Zizania aquatica

CAREX NEBRASKENSIS

CAREX
FOLLICULATA

CAREX
INTUMESCENS

CAREX CRINITA

SEDGES
Carex spp.

range. The large seeds of this plumelike grass are favorite foods for many water birds. In Minnesota, wild rice comprises between 25 and 50 percent of the food of mallards during late summer. It is also an important food for red-winged black-bird, bobolink, Virginia and sora rails, black duck, blue-winged teal, wood duck, redhead, ring-necked duck, and lesser scaup.

There are at least 500 species of *Carex* sedges in North America. Although they represent a nightmare for most plant taxonomists, they are a delight to at least 53 species of waterfowl, shorebirds, upland game birds, and songbirds that feed on their abundant seeds. *Carex* sedges occur most commonly in wet meadows and marshy habitats, but some kinds also grow in dry fields. Many kinds grow in dense clumps, a growth habitat that provides excellent nesting cover for wa-terfowl and many other types of ground-nesting bird. *Carex* seeds are especially favored by green-winged and cinnamon teal, sora and yellow rails, young ruffed grouse, snow bunting, Lapland longspur, and swamp sparrow.

CHARA
Chara spp.

NAIADS
Najas spp.

SOUTHERN NAIAD

Chara, sometimes known as muskgrass or stonewort, is a group of about 50 species of branching, lime-encrusted algae. The chara algae are found throughout most of North America in fresh, alkaline, or brackish water habitats, ranging from large lakes to farm ponds, roadside ditches, and coastal estuaries. This prolific alga sometimes forms large, floating mats, and is especially attractive to waterfowl when it is in its reproductive stage, bearing multitudes of microscopic oogonia. Chara algae are available to both dabbling and diving waterfowl, as the various species live in water ranging from a few inches to over 30 feet deep. Chara is an important food for American coot, pintail, redhead, ring-necked duck, greater scaup, green-winged teal, American widgeon, and ruddy duck. It is also commonly eaten by at least 15 other species of diving and dabbling waterfowl.

Naiads are annual freshwater herbs found mainly in eastern North America. They are identified by opposite or whorled leaves that have fine teeth on both edges. Naiads can tolerate less light than many other freshwater plants and sometimes occur in deep water, though they most commonly grow where water is only 1 to 4 feet deep. Of the 8 species of eastern North America, northern naiad (*Najas flexilis*) and southern naiad (*N. guadalupensis*), are the most abundant and important for wild birds. Southern naiad is somewhat tolerant of brackish water, but it and the northern species occur mainly in freshwater ponds and lakes. Waterfowl readily consume the abundant naiad seeds (nutlets) found in leaf axils as well as plant leaves and stem. Naiads are important foods for coot, American widgeon, lesser scaup, bufflehead, teal (both blue- and green-winged), canvasback, and Canada goose.

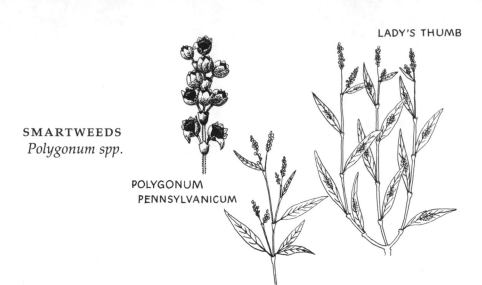

SMARTWEEDS
Polygonum spp.

POLYGONUM
PENNSYLVANICUM

LADY'S THUMB

Several wetland species in the *Polygonum* genus are especially important to waterfowl and landbirds. Collectively grouped under the common name smartweeds (also known as knotweeds), two of the most important are lady's thumb (*P. persicaria*), named for the purple "thumbprint" on the center of each leaf, and pink knotweed (*P. pennsylvanicum*). These and several other members of this group grow on mud flats at pond and marsh edges and sometimes in moist, cultivated fields. A useful management practice for attracting waterfowl is to drain ponds or lakes down a couple of feet during early spring, plant a crop of smartweed on the exposed mud, and then flood the mature plants in time for the fall waterfowl migration. Smartweed is best propagated in early spring by transplanting rootstocks or by burying one half of foot-long cuttings into the mud. At least 24 waterfowl species eat smartweed seed, but it is especially favored by black duck, mallard, pintail, and blue-winged teal. The seed is also readily eaten by 37 other bird species, including northern bobwhite, cardinal, and common redpoll, as well as fox, song, swamp, and white-throated sparrow.

SPIKE RUSHES
Eleocharis spp.

Spike rushes are leafless sedges that grow in shallow water and the muddy shorelines of freshwater ponds and marshes throughout North America. There are approximately 45 species, and these range from only a few inches to several feet in height. Some kinds are annual and others are perennial, but almost without exception, spike rushes are a favorite food readily consumed by at least 27 species of waterfowl and marsh bird, such as coots, rails, and snipe. Spike rushes are especially preferred by American widgeon, black duck, mallard, shoveler, green-winged teal, and Canada and snow geese. All spike rushes produce a compact seed head, and it is this food supply that attracts so much attention from water birds.

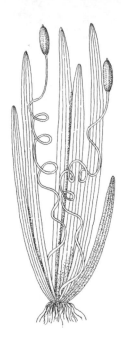

WILD CELERY
Vallisneria americana

WIDGEON GRASS
Ruppia maritima

Wild celery, sometimes known as freshwater eelgrass, is an aquatic submerged perennial of shallow ponds and lakes. It does not tolerate strong brackish waters. Wild celery spreads by creeping rootstocks, but also produces flowering stems that float on the surface. The leaves, rootstocks, and seeds are readily consumed by both diving and dabbling ducks. As its Latin name suggests, the canvasback (*Aythya valisineria*) has a special preference for wild celery. Where this plant is abundant, it may comprise between 25 and 50 percent of the canvasback's food. Wild celery is also an important food for American coot, black duck, ring-necked duck, ruddy duck, common goldeneye, redhead, lesser and greater scaup, and tundra swan.

Widgeon grass is one of the most important waterfowl foods in North America because of its preference for alkaline or saline waters. It thrives in brackish water along the Atlantic, Gulf, and Pacific coasts, and is the dominant aquatic plant in many alkaline lakes and marshes from the prairies to the west coast. This preference for saline and alkaline waters excludes it from most freshwater ponds and lakes of the eastern United States and Canada. Another merit of widgeon grass as a waterfowl food is that its roots, stems, leaves, and seeds are all edible. Within its range, it is a staple food for gadwall, shoveler, blue- and green-winged teal, redhead, greater and lesser scaup, oldsquaw, brant, and Canada goose. It is also eaten by mallard, pintail, mottled duck, canvasback, king eider, and purple gallinule.

DUCKWEEDS
Lemna spp.

Duckweeds (*Lemna spp.*) and the closely allied genera *Spirodela, Wolffia,* and *Wolffiella* are tiny green plants capable of totally covering small ponds, swamps, and marshes with their leaves. By far the most abundant and most important is common duckweed (*L. minor*). These tiny green plants are a staple in the diet of common coot and American widgeon. They are also eaten by at least 14 kinds of ducks, purple gallinule, and sora rail.

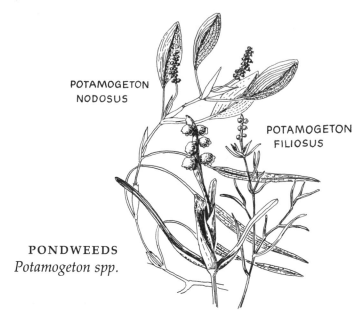

POTAMOGETON NODOSUS

POTAMOGETON FILIOSUS

PONDWEEDS
Potamogeton spp.

Pondweeds are the dominant aquatic vegetation in many ponds and lakes throughout North America. Their abundance in both quantity and variety of species is greatest in the northeastern United States, but throughout their wide range, pondweeds rank at the top of the list for submerged and floating plants as wild bird foods. Pondweeds are important not only for seed production, but the tender stems and leaves and edible tubers of certain varieties all contribute to their attractiveness to wetland birds. Sago pondweed (*Potamogeton pectinatus*), a narrow-leafed, submerged species, is especially important to waterfowl because of its edible tubers and seeds. In addition to coots, avocets, dowitchers, and godwits, 25 species of waterfowl rely on pondweeds for food.

The familiar water lilies of ponds, lake shores, and other shallow fresh waters are both an attractive addition to quiet waters and a useful wild bird food. Water lilies occur almost exclusively in eastern North America, and although there are at least 8 water-lily species found in this region, the seeds, stems, and rootstocks of the white-flowered American water lily (*Nymphaea odorata*) and the yellow-flowered banana water lily (*N. flava*) of Gulf coast waters, are the most frequently used members of this genus. Canvasbacks are known to feed extensively on the roots of the banana water lily. Ten other kinds of ducks are known to eat water-lily seeds and rootstocks. Water-lily stems, roots, and seeds are also a favorite food of sandhill cranes and gallinules. The familiar yellow-flowered cow lilies or yellow pond lilies (*Nuphar spp.*) are much less favored by waterfowl.

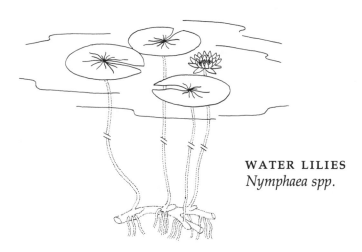

WATER LILIES
Nymphaea spp.

CHAPTER IV

NESTING STRUCTURES

Scarcity of suitable nest sites often prevents birds from occupying otherwise good habitat. When nest sites limit population growth, artificial nesting structures can sometimes lead to dramatic increases in bird numbers.

Frances Hammerstrom's American kestrel nest box program demonstrates such an increase. In a 20-year period before her nest box effort began in central Wisconsin, she found only three pairs of nesting kestrels using 8330 acres of open countryside. In the 5 years following placement of 50 kestrel nest boxes, she found 8–12 broods per year raised in her boxes. This amounts to a spectacular 1600 percent increase in kestrels. Equally dramatic results have also occurred where artificial nest boxes have helped to boost populations of bluebirds, wood ducks, tree swallows, and many of the other 86 species of North American cavity-nesting birds.

Artificial nest structures help increase all bird populations, not just cavity nesters. Imaginative projects have recently demonstrated that many types of bird that usually use treetop nests, such as osprey, eagles, double-crested cormorant, great horned owl, great gray owl, and long-eared owl, will accept artificial nesting platforms. Similarly, certain aquatic birds, such as terns, loons, ducks, and geese, which face a scarcity of predator-safe islands, will nest on artificial floating platforms. Even the endangered Everglade kite will nest in specially constructed metal baskets in preference to building its flimsy nest among swaying marsh vegetation.

Songbirds, such as sparrows, finches, and warblers, may be excluded from otherwise good habitat because they are unable to find adequate supports for woven nests. These species usually nest in shrub or tree crotches. Selective pruning to create such sites can be a useful way to increase populations of certain songbirds.

Sometimes artificial nest structures provide more secure nesting places than do natural nest sites, because artificial nesting structures can be constructed to resist predators, parasites, and destruction from the elements. Bluebird boxes, for example, may be made with entrance holes small enough to exclude starlings, and they can be equipped with a special raccoon guard on the mounting pole. Likewise, artificial nest platforms for osprey built on top of rigid platforms may be more secure than ageing treetop nests that could topple in strong winds.

Just as the number of suitable sites may limit population size, the availability of adequate roosting sites may also be a limiting factor. This is especially true in open windswept habitats where artificial roosting trees can serve a vital function for open-country birds, such as quail. Likewise, roosting boxes for forest birds, such as chickadees, may provide essential cover from the extremes of winter weather.

Yet artificial nesting sites are not always a benefit. For example, wrens and tree swallows will nest in milk cartons and tar-paper birdhouses, but the heat of long summer days on such thin-walled homes can overheat and kill the young. Aesthetics are also important. Artificial nests and roosts should be constructed from economical building supplies and designed with an eye to letting the structure become part of the habitat.

NEST BOXES

Where snags and tree cavities limit numbers of cavity-nesting birds, artificial nest boxes may increase populations and entice birds to occupy a new habitat. Sometimes birds that normally nest only in large trees (i.e., barred owl, screech owl, and flicker) can be lured to younger forests with artificial nest boxes that simulate large tree trunks with significant-sized cavities.

Recent interest in conservation of North American bluebird populations through the use of nest boxes has resulted in many useful nest box designs for small cavity-nesting birds. This interest has contributed to a wide range of management options for other cavity-nesting birds and useful information about common problems, such as parasite control and exclusion of nest predators and competitors.

Construction Materials

The best materials for building nest boxes are 3/4-inch white cedar, western cedar, or exterior-grade plywood. These woods are most weather tolerant, but such other woods as pine, spruce, and poplar are easy to work with and will last for many years. Rough-grade lumber is ideal for nest boxes as the rugged cuts give a natural look and aid birds in climbing out of the boxes. Avoid using unseasoned woods or interior-grade plywood, as these will warp or separate as they weather. Rough slabs covered with bark from sawmill waste are excellent building materials for birdhouses, as they have a natural appearance.

Birds will nest in boxes constructed from almost anything—milk cartons, coffee cans, plastic jugs, sheet metal, tar paper, PVC sewer pipe—but these materials usually offer more problems from overheating, chilling, leaking, and condensation than they are worth. Two exceptions are metal martin and wood duck house designs. Aluminum martin houses are considerably lighter, and therefore are less likely to topple, than wooden equivalents. Metal wood duck houses may also have higher occupancy and nesting success rates than wooden boxes because they are safer from raccoon predators.

When assembling wooden houses, hold parts together with clamps and join all connecting wood surfaces with a water-repellent, exterior-construction adhesive for best weatherproofing. Be sure to use galvanized nails; they will long outlast steel nails. Brass wood screws will give an even better grip than nails, but the cost of using brass will quickly mount if you are mass-producing boxes. For top-opening boxes, use brass or stainless steel hinges. Thick rawhide is a useful substitute for metal hinges.

Exterior Finishes

Nest boxes are most frequently used when they are brown, tan, or gray. After a single field season, most woods will weather to a pleasing light gray that approximates the color of tree bark. To darken and preserve new pine boxes, mix a little brown or green oil-based paint with linseed oil. Thomas McElroy, Jr., author of *The New Handbook of Attracting Birds*, has found that pine nest-boxes treated with a generous supply of this mixture have lasted for 20 years without any need to clean up flaking and peeling paint. Also, two cuprinol wood preservatives, clear (#20) and green (#10), are EPA approved for contact with plants and animals. The clear stain darkened with wood stain makes an excellent preserving mixture for new pine nest-boxes.

Avoid using lead-based alkyd paints or creosote. Although bright colors should generally be avoided, purple martin houses should be painted white to reduce temperatures in these comparatively thin-walled and exposed structures. The interior of boxes should not be painted or treated with preservatives.

Drainage

Natural tree cavities, such as woodpecker holes, usually have excellent drainage, as wood chips rest on absorbent, dry heartwood, creating a snug cavity with thick, insulating walls. Also, woodpecker holes are generally located on the underside of leaning trunks, a feature that further improves drainage. With the water-safe characteristics of natural cavities in mind, nest boxes should be constructed to keep adults, eggs, and young as dry as possible while they are in the nest. Bluebirds are one exception to this rule, as they can nest successfully in the rotted tops of fence posts and in broken-off snags.

To keep nest boxes from leaking when it rains, be sure to extend the roof at least 3 inches beyond the front of the box. Flat-roofed houses should have a $1/8$-inch-deep drip line cut parallel to the face of the box; this keeps water from draining back toward the front of the box. To provide drainage, cut the corners off the floor of the box or drill $3/8$-inch drainage holes in each corner of the bottom. Also, be sure not to mount houses on leaning trees that would angle boxes toward the sky.

Ventilation

Boxes constructed from $3/4$-inch wood generally have ample insulation to protect birds from excessive summer heat and unseasonal cold weather during the nesting season. Ventilation can be improved in well-sealed boxes by drilling several vent holes near the top of the sides or by dropping the front of the box down from the roof by a quarter inch. In addition to providing improved ventilation, these spaces provide a light source that may be useful to encourage birds to enter nest boxes early in the season when they are exploring for new cavities. Long ago, John Burroughs noted that when prospecting cavity nesters poke their heads into a tight-fitting entrance hole, they totally block all light from the cavity, as their body fills the entrance hole. The total blackness may spook inexperienced birds unaccustomed to the suddenly dark interior.

Wood Chips

Since most small cavity-nesting birds are dependent on woodpecker excavations for nest sites, we can do well to study a woodpecker cavity to determine preferred dimensions, height above the ground, and thickness of the walls for nest boxes. Since most woodpecker holes have a soft layer of wood chips in their bottom, many birds accustomed to this—wood ducks, American kestrel, screech owl, barred owl, and flicker, among others—will reject artificial nest boxes unless you put 3 to 4 inches of wood shavings or small wood chips in the bottom. Avoid using sawdust in nest boxes, as this soaks up and retains water.

Since chickadees are capable excavators, they prefer to make their own nesting cavities, so pack a nest box completely full of wood shavings and let the chickadees excavate a cavity of their preference. This technique may also prove useful for attracting downy and other small woodpeckers which normally shun artificial nest boxes.

Mounting Nest Boxes

Nest boxes for small cavity-nesting birds should usually be placed on special mounting poles or fence posts to reduce the chances of predation and to facilitate cleaning. Gas pipes with a ³/₄-inch internal diameter make excellent mounting poles. To set the poles easily and safely, use a post pounder rather than wielding a heavy sledge from the top of a ladder. Post pounders are often available from equipment rentals or they can be built at home. A post pounder is a heavy pipe with a cap that fits over the mounting pole. The pounder is lifted a couple of feet above the post and then dropped onto it, driving the post into the ground. A homemade pounder can be constructed from a 2¹/₂-foot length of 1¹/₂-inch-internal-diameter gas pipe with one threaded end onto which a heavy gas cap is tightened.

Mount nest boxes for forest species directly to trees at the recommended height as outlined on page 206, using nailless mounting devices (page 281) whenever possible.

Cleaning Nest Boxes

Nesting material left in birdhouses over the winter will probably attract mice, which will then fill the boxes completely with grass and other vegetation. Nest boxes packed with mouse and old bird nests are seldom occupied by birds, so cleaning is important. It can also help to control parasitic insects, mites, and lice.

Nest boxes with a swing-out side are easiest to clean. In this design, a single wood screw holds the bottom of the wall secure to the base of the box. Side-opening boxes are easier to clean than top-opening boxes, which must first be taken off their mounts. Front-opening nest boxes are not free to easily swing up because of the large raccoon/starling guard that binds against the roof.

Although top-opening boxes are more difficult to clean, they are the best choice for researchers. They have the advantage of permitting researchers to band young and check adults, for young birds are less likely to prematurely fledge and adults can be easily trapped on their nests. Young birds that do leave the nest early probably will not stay in the nest box even if they are returned, although they are not likely to survive outside.

Boxes that are under close inspection should be cleaned between broods to remove infertile eggs, dead nestlings, and nest parasites. Removing the first nest keeps the adults from building a new nest on top of it, a behavior that raises the nest contents dangerously near the entrance hole, where they are more vulnerable to predation by starlings and raccoons.

NEST BOX MOUNTING TECHNIQUES

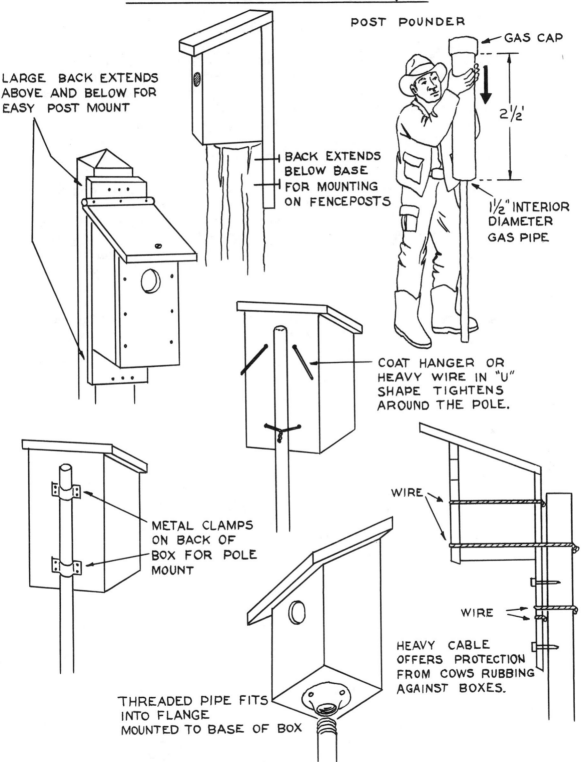

POST POUNDER

GAS CAP

2½'

1½" INTERIOR
DIAMETER
GAS PIPE

LARGE BACK EXTENDS
ABOVE AND BELOW FOR
EASY POST MOUNT

BACK EXTENDS
BELOW BASE
FOR MOUNTING
ON FENCEPOSTS

COAT HANGER OR
HEAVY WIRE IN "U"
SHAPE TIGHTENS
AROUND THE POLE.

METAL CLAMPS
ON BACK OF
BOX FOR POLE
MOUNT

WIRE

WIRE

HEAVY CABLE
OFFERS PROTECTION
FROM COWS RUBBING
AGAINST BOXES.

THREADED PIPE FITS
INTO FLANGE
MOUNTED TO BASE OF BOX

Various techniques for mounting nest boxes on fence posts and metal poles.

PARASITES

An active bird nest contains a community of many living creatures that find food in various ways from the nest. Some mites are harmless, scavenging on food scraps and feathers, but most invertebrates found in nests feed directly on nestling birds and their parents. In small numbers, the mites, lice, flies, and wasps which naturally occur in bird nests are not dangerous; larger numbers, however, may cause fatalities and necessitate limited control.

An important reason for the annual spring cleaning is to remove nesting material that may harbor the pupal cases (puparia) of blowflies. Species of the genus *Protocalliphora* (formerly *Apaulina*) have larvae that specialize in drinking blood from nestling birds. Several studies have found that over 80 percent of bluebird nest boxes contain blowfly larvae. This cycle starts when adult blowflies lay their eggs on newly hatched nestlings. The eggs hatch and the larval flies attach themselves to the young birds. The larvae feed on nestlings at night, a behavior that may permit them to avoid predation by adult birds that tend the young during the day. At night the larvae emerge from the nesting material, feed on the nestlings, and then disappear back into the nest bottom during daylight hours.

Normally, small numbers of blowfly larvae are not a problem for healthy young birds, but if numbers grow too high (over 150 larvae in a nest), they can kill the young. However, even smaller numbers can weaken young birds, making them more vulnerable to predators, rigorous weather, or poor food supplies. Blowflies are known to parasitize bluebirds, tree swallows, American robins, house wrens, barn swallows, cliff swallows, and many other small landbirds.

Parasitic blowfly larvae usually attach themselves to the soft parts of nestling birds, especially feet and facial areas.

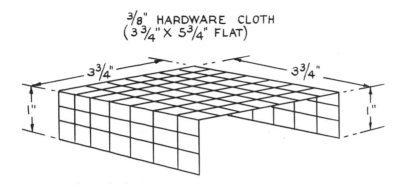

³/₈" HARDWARE CLOTH
(3 ³/₄" X 5³/₄" FLAT)

This simple blowfly trap, designed by Ira Campbell of Timberville, Virginia, is made of hardware cloth mesh. The mesh covers the bottom of the bluebird nest box and traps the blowfly larvae below as they fall through.

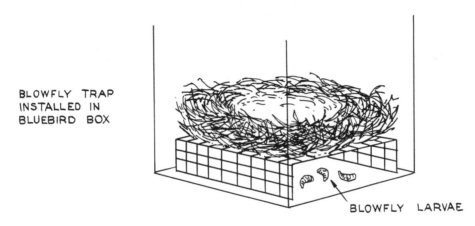

BLOWFLY TRAP
INSTALLED IN
BLUEBIRD BOX

BLOWFLY LARVAE

Recently, an innovative trap for blowfly larvae was designed and tested by Ira Campbell of Timberville, Virginia. His clever design is based on the habits of the legless blowfly larvae. Noting that the larvae hide at the bottom of the nest box during the day and then wiggle their way back through the nest material at night to feed on the nestlings, he designed an easy-to-build trap that consists of a piece of ³/₈-inch-square hardware cloth cut and bent so that it sits one inch off the bottom of the box and covers the entire floor of the nest box. In boxes equipped with these traps, blowfly larvae move to the bottom of the nest, but fall through the mesh and are trapped in the bottom. In recent controlled field tests, Campbell found that bluebirds accepted boxes fitted with the wire traps just as frequently as boxes without traps. He had no losses to blowfly parasitism in 53 boxes with the false bottoms, but 12 nestling bluebirds died in 47 control boxes without traps.

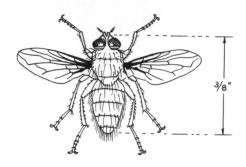

BLOWFLY
PROTOCALLIPHORA MARUYAMENSIS

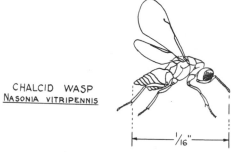

CHALCID WASP
NASONIA VITRIPENNIS

Adult blowfly, Protocalliphora maruyamensis, *and its much smaller predator, the chalcid wasp,* Nasonia vitripennis.

One of the natural population checks on blowflies is a small chalcid wasp (*Nasonia vitripennis*). This tiny wasp is only about ¹⁄₁₆ inch long, but it does a remarkably effective job in reducing blowfly populations. The chalcid wasps seek out the blowfly pupal cases in the nesting material and lay their eggs on the fly pupae within. When the eggs hatch, the wasp larvae consume the blowfly pupae.

Knowledge of the life cycles of the blowfly and the predatory chalcid wasp is essential, because while it is important to remove old bird nests with their overwintering blowfly pupae, the old nesting material is also the overwintering habitat for chalcid wasp larvae. If nesting material is cleaned from boxes in the fall and scattered on the ground or burned, the larvae of the useful chalcid wasps will be lost along with the blowflies. For this reason, John Terres, in *Songbirds in Your Garden*, recommends a mid-March cleaning of nest boxes. At this season the nest contents are collected and scattered on the ground away from the nest boxes. This spring cleaning is also a good time to remove mouse nests, open drainage holes, and repair broken boxes for the coming nesting season.

When you check or clean nest boxes, you sometimes discover lice and mites on nestlings and nesting material. Bird lice of the order *Mallophaga* are usually less than ¹⁄₈ inch long, but are among the most common bird ectoparasites. Most birds have at least a few of these tiny wingless insects. A few lice cause little harm to healthy birds, as they eat mainly feather fragments, with occasional blood meals from newly emerging feathers. Young birds, however, sometimes have

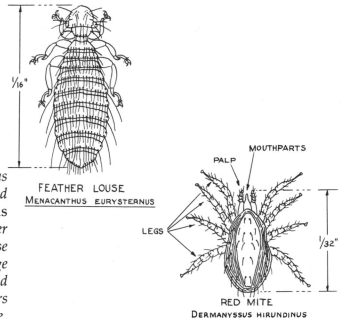

FEATHER LOUSE
MENACANTHUS EURYSTERNUS

MOUTHPARTS
PALP
LEGS
RED MITE
DERMANYSSUS HIRUNDINUS

Feather lice, such as Menacanthus eurysternus, *and red mites, such as* Dermanyssus hirunda, *feed mainly on feather fragments. Small numbers of these insects do little harm, but large populations require burning old nests and spraying box interiors with Pyrethrum insecticide.*

large infestations of lice and these may seriously weaken nestlings, reducing their chances for survival. Bird lice will not bite humans.

Mites are also common external parasites on wild birds. As with lice, small numbers of mites are common on most wild birds, but large populations of some kinds can prove fatal. The most easily seen mites are the tiny red ones that hide in bird nests and come out at night to suck blood from nestlings and adults. *Dermanyssus hirundinus* is one of the most common of these in bluebird, tree swallow, house wren, and purple martin nests, and it can be a serious health hazard to nestlings. These mites not only weaken nestlings by drinking blood, but they can also carry certain virus infections. A favorite hiding place for *Dermanyssus* mites is in the cracks and crevices in the bottoms of nest boxes. Most birds also carry feather mites of the family *Analgesidae*. These are the tiniest bird ectoparasites, most not exceeding 1/32 inch. Feather mites do not drink blood, but nibble on feathers and surface skin, doing little harm.

Small populations of lice and mites are normal and should not cause concern. When large populations (hundreds) occur, they should be destroyed by burning all nesting material and spraying the interior of nest boxes with pyrethrum insecticide containing 0.5 percent pyrethrin. Pyrethrum insecticides were originally made from the dried flower heads of certain old world chrysanthemums; now the same chemical is artificially synthesized. Pyrethrum is highly toxic to insects but will not harm birds. It is very short-lived, a characteristic that makes it safe for use in nature, but may necessitate more frequent applications. Pyrethrum dust or a 1 percent rotenone powder is useful for eliminating lice and mites from hand-held birds. Avoid getting these powders in bird eyes. Nest boxes with very high mite infestations should be thoroughly cleaned and scalded with boiling water or washed with a 5 percent solution of washing soda, paying special attention to all cracks and crevices. After washing, spray the box interior with gamma benzene hexachloride at 10-day intervals to remove the most persistent infestations.

NEST PREDATORS

Raccoons

Raccoons are probably the most common nest box predator. Their keen sense of smell and capable climbing skills permit them to find and raid bird nests in even the highest treetops. To these talents, add a quick mind and long, dexterous, strong legs, and it is easy to see why raccoons can be a serious threat to cavity-nesting birds. Look for claw marks on nest boxes or nest contents pulled out of box entrances as evidence of a raccoon raid.

The simplest protection from raccoons is to deepen the entrance hole by mounting a block of wood, 1¼ inches thick, over the entrance to the nest box. This helps to prevent raccoons from reaching deep into nest boxes (adult raccoons have front legs that are about 10–11 inches long).

Automobile chassis grease liberally applied to mounting poles is another useful raccoon deterrent. Beginning 12 inches under the nest box, coat at least one foot of the mounting pole with a cake-frosting-thick layer of grease. One heavy coating in February or March is usually enough to last through the breeding season. Another useful technique for deterring raccoons, cats, and snakes from climbing poles to bird feeders is a 2-foot length of 4-inch-diameter galvanized stovepipe, aluminum downspout, or PVC sewer pipe mounted under the nest box (see the section on feeding station precautions in Chapter V). Black PVC pipe is least obtrusive. To help deter climbing snakes and mice, plug the top of the guard with a wooden plug. Nest boxes that are attached to isolated trees may be protected from climbing cats and raccoons by strapping a 3-foot collar of galvanized metal around the tree. Paint metal tree guards brown to improve aesthetics. Where tree canopies adjoin, however, it is nearly impossible to keep raccoons from climbing down to boxes.

For wood duck boxes mounted on poles in standing water, the best protection from pole-climbing raccoons is a 2-foot length of 4-inch stovepipe hanging under the nest box or a cone baffle with a 36-inch diameter. A flat-type raccoon guard is a simplified version of the cone baffle. This can be constructed from a 40 × 40 inch piece of sheet metal and mounted on either metal or wood posts. Baffles constructed from garbage can lids, such as those described for defending feeders from squirrels, can also be effective if the diameter of the lid is at least 36 inches (see the section on precautions in Chapter V).

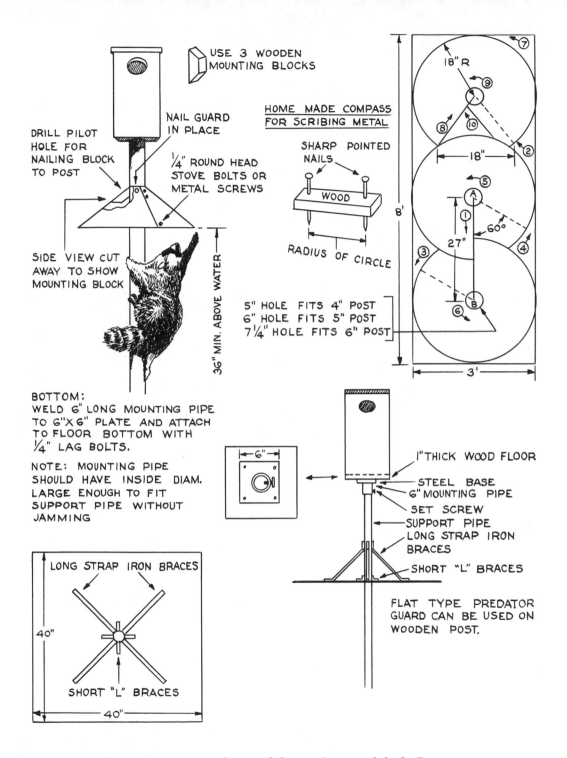

USE 3 WOODEN MOUNTING BLOCKS

NAIL GUARD IN PLACE

DRILL PILOT HOLE FOR NAILING BLOCK TO POST

¼" ROUND HEAD STOVE BOLTS OR METAL SCREWS

SIDE VIEW CUT AWAY TO SHOW MOUNTING BLOCK

36" MIN. ABOVE WATER

HOME MADE COMPASS FOR SCRIBING METAL

SHARP POINTED NAILS

WOOD

RADIUS OF CIRCLE

18"R

18"

8'

27"

60°

3'

5" HOLE FITS 4" POST
6" HOLE FITS 5" POST
7¼" HOLE FITS 6" POST

BOTTOM:
WELD 6" LONG MOUNTING PIPE TO 6"X 6" PLATE AND ATTACH TO FLOOR BOTTOM WITH ¼" LAG BOLTS.

NOTE: MOUNTING PIPE SHOULD HAVE INSIDE DIAM. LARGE ENOUGH TO FIT SUPPORT PIPE WITHOUT JAMMING

6"

1" THICK WOOD FLOOR
STEEL BASE
6" MOUNTING PIPE
SET SCREW
SUPPORT PIPE
LONG STRAP IRON BRACES
SHORT "L" BRACES

FLAT TYPE PREDATOR GUARD CAN BE USED ON WOODEN POST.

LONG STRAP IRON BRACES

40"

40"

SHORT "L" BRACES

Raccoons are the most serious predators of the nesting wood duck. Raccoons can swim, climb, and pry open even secure next boxes, and therefore all wood duck boxes should be protected with carefully constructed raccoon guards. These designs are redrawn from "Nest Boxes for Wood Ducks," 1976, U.S. Department of Interior, Wildlife Leaflet WL 510.

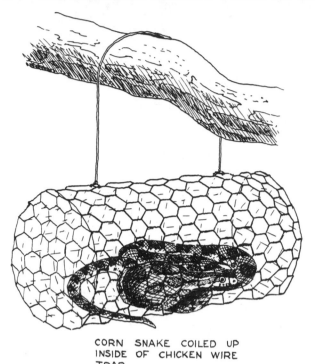

CORN SNAKE COILED UP
INSIDE OF CHICKEN WIRE
TRAP.

This snake trap, designed by Melissa Leonard of Smithville, Texas, baits egg-eating rat and corn snakes. The snake enters a closed cylinder of chicken wire, consumes a large chicken egg, and then cannot leave because of its additional girth.

Snakes

Snakes are rarely a threat to adult birds, but tree-climbing snakes, such as rat snakes (*Elaphe spp.*), can be a local predator on eggs and nestlings of small birds. While there should be room for snakes—in fact, all predators—in your wildlife plan, some management of snake populations may be useful, particularly in southern states where snakes may be especially common. Smooth 2-foot-long, 4-inch-diameter guards described for deterring raccoons should be ample defense for protecting bird nests from snakes, but if this does not work, an idea suggested by Melissa Leonard of Smithville, Texas, may be the solution for displacing especially persistent snakes. She has successfully moved snakes from her property to nearby gopher colonies by building a humane snake trap. To remove egg-eating snakes, she places a hard-boiled, medium-size chicken egg (rubbed in chicken droppings) in a closed cylinder of 1-inch chicken wire. Snakes enter the cylinder, swallow the egg, but with their new "waistline" they can't leave the wire cage.

Ants and Wasps

Paper wasps of the genus *Polistes* often establish their hanging colonies from the roof of nest boxes in early spring before birds begin to nest. Although wasps rarely kill birds in nest boxes, it is not surprising that few birds will attempt to nest in a box already claimed by a well-established paper wasp colony.

If you discover ant or wasp colonies when checking nest boxes in early spring before birds begin looking for nest sites, spray the interior of the box with a liberal dose of pyrethrum spray at night when most of the insects will be in the box. After spraying through the entrance hole, plug it with a rag. The spray will kill most of the insects by morning.

Fire ants (*Solenopsis invicta*) are a serious threat to cavity-nesting birds in the southeastern United States. This tenacious predatory ant is native to South America, but for the past 50 years it has spread through much of the southeast. It is nearly impossible to eradicate, but according to R. B. Layton of Jackson, Mississippi, it can be kept from climbing into nest boxes where it is known to eat nestling birds. Layton's technique for discouraging fire ants is to place a barrier covered with STP oil additive between the nest box and the base of the mounting pole. Ants that climb the pole cannot make it past this greasy barrier. He also recommends the dried seed ball of sweet gum (*Liquidambar styraciflua*) as an ideal barrier. Fire ants have been unable to cross sweet gum fruits or thread spools coated with this heavy grease. Another technique is to put a 1-inch wire band of Tanglefoot around the pole just above the vegetation line. Tanglefoot, available at garden centers, creates a sticky barrier for insects. It can also be a hazard to small birds, but if used minimally near the base, it should not be a problem.

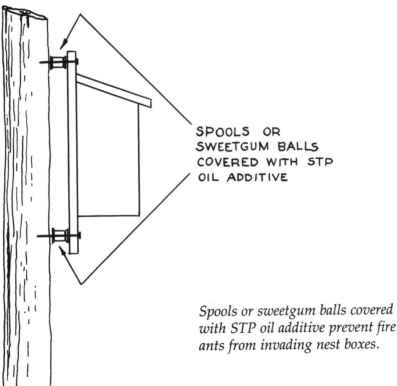

SPOOLS OR
SWEETGUM BALLS
COVERED WITH STP
OIL ADDITIVE

Spools or sweetgum balls covered with STP oil additive prevent fire ants from invading nest boxes.

Livestock

Cattle and horse pastures are excellent habitats for bluebirds and tree swallows, as there is usually abundant insect food and little competition from house wrens, which frequent brushy fencerows. Unfortunately, nest boxes attached to fence posts or positioned atop isolated poles within pastures are often used by cattle as rubbing posts, and one such encounter is enough to destroy a nest box and its contents.

Until recently, horses and cattle in need of a back scratch have been a serious problem for anyone hoping to attract cavity-nesting birds to this otherwise excellent habitat. Now a simple livestock guard designed by Richard Tuttle of Delaware, Ohio, offers a promising solution.

This guard consists of two 24-inch sections of angle iron secured perpendicular to each other 3 feet from the ground on a metal pole. The guard is completed by addition of a ring of barbed wire. Although horses and cattle will rub against unyielding barbed-wire fences, the livestock guard is different. When livestock lean against the guard, the pole will slightly bend, then snap back at the animal, striking it with the barbed wire—a second experience is seldom necessary.

Livestock guards should be painted a light color to reduce the chances of an animal stumbling over it at night. Guards mounted in horse pastures should also be marked to avoid collisions by frolicking horses. Two 3-inch-wide rings of white 4-inch-diameter PVC pipe dangling below the house will warn most horses during day and night.

The poles that support the livestock guard and nest box should be protected by 4-inch-diameter metal or PVC sheathing or greased with STP motor additive to keep raccoons from climbing them. Be sure to have the enthusiastic blessing of livestock owners before mounting nest boxes in pastures.

NEST COMPETITORS

Competition for quality nesting cavities is often very intense for native birds because of the introduction of two European species, the house sparrow and European starling. Since both species are resident in breeding habitats throughout the year, they usually have first pick of the best nest sites. Migratory birds, such as tree swallow, great-crested flycatcher, and bluebirds, often find themselves competing with these aggressive aliens when they return from winter migrations. Both house sparrow and starling are not only competitive when it comes to housing, but they will also prey on eggs and nestlings when they evict other, less aggressive species from nesting cavities. House sparrows are even known to kill adult male bluebirds as they fight for occupancy rights of a choice nest site. If the adult bluebird or large young are killed in a nest box, the house sparrows will build their nests on top of the carcasses. Starlings can be even more aggressive in fights over suitable nesting sites. Not infrequently they attack and kill

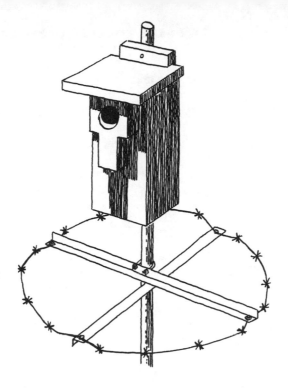

FIG. I. STEEL LIVESTOCK GUARD   FIG. 3. WOODEN LIVESTOCK GUARD

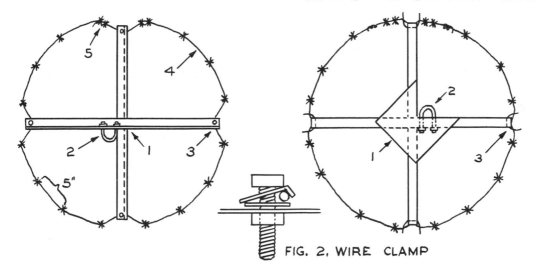

FIG. 2. WIRE CLAMP

Livestock guards painted a light color and placed around nest box mounting poles protect birds from cattle who find one brush with barbed wire sufficient. Redrawn from Richard M. Tuttle, "Livestock Guards Make Bossie, Black Beauty, and Bluebirds Compatible," Sialia, 1982, 4(2): 65–69.

downy woodpeckers, and will even take on the much larger flickers as they fight over nesting sites.

Both house sparrows and starlings are most abundant in open habitat near human housing. House sparrows are rarely found far from human habitation, but starlings sometimes live in mature forest where they occupy vacant woodpecker cavities.

Starlings can be excluded from nest boxes with $1\frac{1}{2}$-inch holes, a very useful distinction that will keep them out of nest boxes especially built for wrens, chickadees, titmice, bluebirds, and tree swallows. Although starlings can't squeeze into a $1\frac{1}{2}$-inch entrance hole, they can sometimes reach in and peck young or eggs. To provide even further protection for small cavity nesters, place a $\frac{3}{4}$-inch-thick block of wood over the entrance hole. This extra thickness is enough of a barrier to keep starlings from reaching in. The same guard doubles as a raccoon guard, as even the agile raccoon cannot reach around the angle created by a properly positioned starling/raccoon guard. So far, there is no way to exclude starlings from the larger nest boxes used to attract such birds as flickers, screech owls, and wood ducks.

Although house sparrows can be excluded from boxes that have up to a $1\frac{1}{8}$-inch entrance hole, most other species are very vulnerable to nest competition and predation by house sparrows, and to date no completely successful exclusion technique has been devised to keep them out of most nest boxes.

Where house sparrow populations are so high that other birds are not given a chance to nest, the property owner has the opportunity (responsibility) to tilt the nesting table in favor of native birds that may already be rare or crowded from your community by introduced birds.

When contemplating control of starlings and house sparrows, it should be kept in mind that there is nothing innately "evil" about these birds. It is true that they may crowd bluebirds out of your neighborhood, may attack and kill nestlings and adults of other species, and are generally brash and rowdy by human standards. But it is just this kind of comparison that should be avoided. House sparrows and starlings are intelligent, adaptable, successful birds and that is why they are so abundant. Destruction of some individuals may be necessary through trapping, especially with house sparrows since they cannot be excluded from most nest boxes, but it should always be done as expediently and humanely as possible.

At present, no one has yet devised a nest box that house sparrows will always avoid, but several features of the house sparrows' behavior can be used to reduce competition with other cavity-nesting birds. Placement of the nest box is probably the most important. House sparrows seldom occur far from human habitation, so they will less frequently use boxes posted far from houses and barns. Timing is also important. Since house sparrows are resident in their territories all winter, they have first selection of nest boxes come spring. By keeping nest entrances plugged or removing boxes from their mounting posts until preferred species arrive, the house sparrows will not be able to stake early claims. This technique is especially usful for purple martin houses.

If house sparrows are discovered using a nest box, their nest should be removed and the entrance covered for a few days. This may encourage the sparrow to go elsewhere, but if there is a high population of sparrows and a low number of suitable nest sites, the sparrow will likely attempt renesting in the same or a nearby nest box. Persistent removal of nests can succeed in discouraging house sparrows, but nests may have to be removed every few days for a week or more.

Where sparrow populations are high and they dominate most nest boxes, the only realistic way to lower populations will be trapping and removal. Several effective live traps are available for capturing large numbers of sparrows (write Woodstream Corp., Dept. HT, Box 327, Lititz, PA 17543, for a good selection of sparrow traps and check Appendix D). Trapping helps to lower local house sparrow populations and offers some temporary relief for nest competition. Once sparrows are trapped, they may be released elsewhere (Europe!) or humanely destroyed.

One Indiana resident conducted a sparrow-trapping program on his property for 10 years, recording the number of sparrows trapped each year. During the first year of the trapping effort, he captured 1200 house sparrows, but 10 years later, he was able to trap only 14. Trapping efforts have demonstrated that if a territorial male house sparrow is removed from a nest box, his mate will soon abandon the site. In contrast, however, if the female is removed, the male will quickly remate and stay on territory, actively defending the nest box from other prospecting birds.

Be sure to check sparrow traps hourly to release species other than house sparrows. Trap operators should be well-versed in sparrow identification to be sure that only house sparrows are detained. Because they are introduced species, house sparrows, starlings, and pigeons are not protected by wildlife laws, but all other birds (including their nests, eggs, and parts) are protected by both federal and state/provincial laws and cannot legally be captured or held without special permits.

Joseph Huber uses commercial sparrow traps throughout the year to lower house sparrow populations along his bluebird trail within the city limits of Heath, Ohio. To supplement the commercial traps, he developed a nest-box trap for removing house sparrows from nest boxes. By successfully trapping and removing male house sparrows in early spring, he has made his nest boxes available for wrens, chickadees, and bluebirds. Without trapping and removal, his city nest-box trail would likely have produced only house sparrows. The trap may be portable, attaching to the inside nest boxes, or it may be built in to all boxes and set as needed. The trap should be used in top-opening boxes, so that sparrows can be easily removed. It is essential to stand by and watch whenever a nest trap is used to humanely remove sparrows as soon as they are trapped and to release all birds other than house sparrows.

Detailed construction instructions follow:

1. Cut a piece of plywood (A) approximately 4 × 8½ inches (or to a size that fits your nest box).
2. Before drilling the 1¾-inch entrance hole (B), be sure that it will align with the hole in your nest box.
3. Cut the steel plate (C). Drill ⅛-inch hole in the steel plate for the pivot screw.
4. Bend a 10½-inch brass rod (³⁄₃₂-inch diameter) to the shape shown in Figure 1. Bend the lower part of the rod forward 90°, as shown in Figure 2. This is the trigger (D).
5. Install the trigger (D) on the plywood with two insulated electrical staples (E) that will serve as hinges.
6. Install the steel plate (C) with the pivot screw (G). The dotted lines show the steel plate in the closed position (C') after the trigger has been tripped.
7. Bend a brass rod or wire coat hanger into a U-shaped clip (H), and use this to wedge the plywood trap against the inside front of the nest box.

When to Use the Trap

Use the in-box trap only when house sparrows are actively building a nest or when they have eggs in the nest. Never set the trap if you have merely seen sparrows at the box. Learn to identify a house sparrow's nest. Generally, the more advanced the sparrows are in the nesting cycle, the more quickly you can catch them.

When you decide to set the trap, be sure the nesting material in the box does not interfere with its operation. It is best to test the mechanism several times to be sure the trap plate is not binding.

If you catch a female house sparrow first, remove her, reset the trap immediately, and try to catch the male. When you trap the male sparrow (which usually ends the problem), clean out the nest box so that it is ready for bluebirds and other native cavity-nesters. A box containing a nest signals other bird species that it is occupied. A note of caution: Use of this trap requires special attention. Careless use could result in the death of birds that are protected by law.

Positioning Nest Boxes

The location of a nest box is one of the most important considerations in not only attracting birds, but also in optimizing their chances for a successful nesting. Most birds select nest sites based on a mixture of genetic information and learned

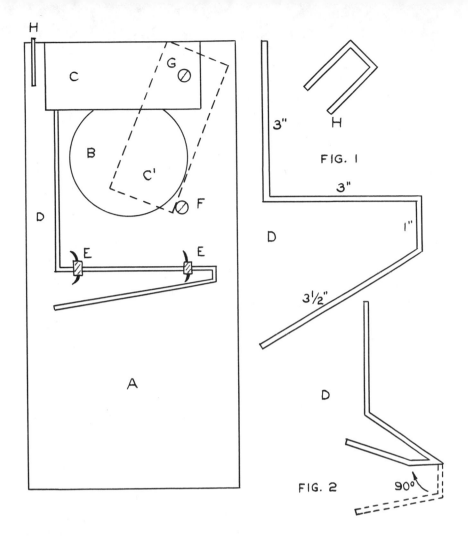

HOW TO CONSTRUCT A HUBER HOUSE SPARROW TRAP

Key to Plan

   4-in. × 8½-in. plywood (A)
   1¾-in. entrance hole (B)
   ⅛ in. × 1¼ in. × 3 in. steel plate (C)
   Brass rod (³⁄₃₂ in. diameter) for trigger (D)
   Insulated electrical staples for hinges (E)
   #6 × ½-in round-head wood screw for stop screw (F)
   #6 × ½-in. round-head wood screw for pivot screw (G)
   U-shaped clip (H)

The Huber House Sparrow Trap is an easy-to-build and effective solution to live-trapping house sparrows that take over other species' nest boxes. Construction details and trapping techniques are reprinted from Joseph Huber, "Huber House Sparrow Trap," Sialia, 1983, 5(3): 100–101.

experience. Wood ducks, for example, prefer to nest in tree cavities near quiet, shallow water, a preference that has obvious benefit for newly hatched broods. When offered a variety of artificial homes, they usually prefer wooden homes to metal ones, but after some experience with metal houses, they will nest just as readily and may actually prefer them in areas where raccoon predation is a serious problem. Wood ducks, therefore, have a genetic preference for nesting near wooded, quiet water, but within that habitat, they learn which nest sites are most likely to prove successful.

Preferences for specific nest site characteristics, such as habitats, height above the ground, distance to water, or proximity to feeding habitat, usually have adaptive value. Birds that deviate too far from normal nesting situations are likely to have unsuccessful nesting efforts. With this in mind, it becomes all the more important to place nest boxes not only within the right habitat, but to pay attention to microhabitat needs, such as height above the ground, distance to dense cover, and spacing between boxes. Such specific requirements vary from one species to the next and are unfortunately largely unknown for most birds. The following discussion of nest site characteristics describes some of the habitat needs of selected cavity-nesting birds.

NEST BOX DESIGNS

A standard wooden box for cavity-nesting birds can be modified for various species by changing the size of the floor, depth of the box, and size and shape of the entrance hole. The following table summarizes recommended box sizes for 32 species, with suggestions for positioning the box at various heights for different birds. The table also recommends preferred habitats for locating boxes. See page 206 for bluebird box designs that are easily adapted to other species.

Bluebirds

People have provided housing for bluebirds for at least 150 years, but only in the past 40 years have declines in bluebird populations sparked interest in using nest boxes to help increase their numbers. Lawrence Zeleny, founder of the North American Bluebird Society, holds that eastern bluebirds have declined by as much as 90 percent since 1940. The populations of western and mountain bluebirds have also declined, but less dramatically.

The decrease in bluebird numbers coincides with regrowth of expansive farmlands into forest, widespread use of persistent pesticides, and the introduction of two serious nest competitors, the house sparrow and European starling. Loss of nest cavities in old apple orchards and wooden fence posts, and removal of dead snags from forests are probably all contributing factors to the decrease.

To help reverse this decline, an army of volunteers has been nailing together bluebird houses for the past several decades. To facilitate monitoring, nest boxes are usually mounted along "trails" where nest contents are easily checked and the boxes can receive regular cleaning and maintenance. Some bluebird trails span impressive areas, crossing hundreds of miles in Canada and the United States. The longest trail stretches for over 2000 miles from the vicinity of Winnipeg, Manitoba, westward beyond Saskatoon, Saskatchewan. On this trail, bluebird boxes are mounted on fence posts about every 100 yards. Several thousand bluebirds fledge from these boxes each year.

Proper location of bluebird nest boxes is more important than subtleties of box design. Bluebirds rarely nest in urban or forested areas. They prefer open countryside, with a scattering of trees and low undergrowth. Large lawns, pastures, golf courses, parks, and other open areas are their preferred habitats. Bluebird nest boxes should be mounted 3 to 6 feet above the ground. Although bluebirds will nest lower, the chances of predation increase and it becomes too difficult to clean boxes mounted higher than about 5 feet. Because bluebirds are highly territorial, it is usually unproductive to mount nest boxes closer than 100 yards apart.

Bluebird boxes should face and be within 50 feet of a tree, fence, or other structure on which fledglings can perch after their first flight. This reduces the chances of the young birds landing on the ground where they are more vulnerable to cats and other predators.

Proper location of nest boxes can also help to minimize competition with nest competitors, such as house wrens and house sparrows. To reduce competition from house wrens, locate bluebird boxes away from brushy fencerows. House sparrows are much more difficult to discourage, but competition can sometimes be reduced by locating bluebird boxes far from human habitation.

While careful location of boxes may help to discourage wrens and house sparrows, preferred habitat for bluebirds is also the favorite habitat for tree and violet-green swallows. Both of these common swallows are aggressive nest competitors with bluebirds, and in areas where swallow populations are large and nest sites are scarce, the swallows may usurp nest boxes from bluebirds and sometimes even build their own nests on top of bluebird nests that contain eggs or living young.

Some recent studies of swallow territoriality offer a possible management option for reducing bluebird/swallow competition. The idea rests simply on the fact that birds of different species will generally tolerate overlapping territories, but two breeding pairs of the same species will aggressively fight to dominate an area around the nest.

By placing paired nest boxes a few feet apart, a territorial pair of swallows will chase other swallows from the vicinity of their nest, and in so doing they keep the other box available for bluebirds. In areas where both tree and violet-green swallows nest, boxes should be set out in threes, so that each species of swallow can use a box and there will still be one remaining for bluebirds.

NEST BOX DIMENSIONS FOR COMMON CAVITY-NESTING BIRDS

Species	Floor (in.)	Chips	Depth (in.)	Entrance above floor (in.)	Diameter of Entrance (in.)	Height (ft) Above Ground or Water (W)	Preferred Habitat Codes§
Wood duck	12×12	+	22	17	4	20-10,6W	3,5
Common goldeneye	12×12	+	24	20-22	4-5	4-20	3,5
Barrow's goldeneye	6-9×6-9	+	9-52	7-48	3-4	4-20	3,5
Bufflehead	7×7	+	16	13-14	$2^7/_8$	10-20	3,5
Hooded merganser	10×10	+	15-18	10-13	5	4-6	3,5
Common merganser	9-11×9-11	+	33-40	28-35	5	8-20	3,5
American kestrel	8×8	+	12-15	9-12	3	10-30	1,4
Barn owl	10×18	+	15-18	0-4	6	12-18	4
Barred owl	12×12	+	20-24	14	6×6	15-20	5
Screech owl	8×8	+	12-15	9-12	3	10-30	2
Boreal owl	6-7×6-7	+	9-18	7-15	$2^1/_2 \times 4^1/_2$-5	10-25	9
Saw-whet owl	6×6	+	10-12	8-10	$2^1/_2$	12-20	2
Red-headed woodpecker	6×6	+	12	9	2	10-20	2
Golden-fronted woodpecker	6×6	+	12	9	2	10-20	2
Downy woodpecker	4×4	+	9	7	$1^1/_4$	5-15	2
Hairy woodpecker	6×6	+	12-15	9-12	$1^5/_8$	12-20	2
Northern flicker	7×7	+	16-18	14-16	$2^1/_2$	6-30	1,2
Great crested flycatcher	6×6	+	8-10	6-8	$1^9/_{16}$*	8-20	1,2
Ash-throated flycatcher	6×6	+	8-10	6-8	$1^1/_2$*	8-20	1,6
Purple martin	6×6	–	6	1	$2^1/_4$	10-20	1
Tree swallow	5×5	–	6-8	4-6	$1^1/_2$*	4-15	1
Violet-green swallow	5×5	–	6-8	4-6	$1^1/_2$*	4-15	1
Chickadees	4×4	+	9	7	$1^1/_8$	4-15	2
Titmouse	4×4	+	9	7	$1^1/_4$	5-15	2
Nuthatches‡	4×4	+	9	7	$1^3/_8$	5-15	2
Carolina wren	4×4	–	6-8	4-6	$1^1/_2$*	5-10	2,7
Bewick's wren	4×4	–	6-8	4-6	$1^1/_4$	5-10	2,7
House wren	4×4	–	6-8	4-6	1-$1^1/_4$	4-10	2,7
Bluebirds (eastern & western)	4×4	–	8-12	6-10	$1^1/_2$*	3-6	1
Mountain bluebird	4×4	–	8-12	6-10	$1^9/_{16}$*	3-6	1
Prothonotary warbler	4×4	–	6	4	$1^3/_8$	4-12,3W	3,5

*Precise measurement required; if diameter is larger, starlings may usurp cavity.

‡Brown-headed and pygmy nuthatches (1⅛), red-breasted nuthatch (1¼), and white-breasted nuthatch (1⅜) will all use the same box. However, the smaller opening sizes where appropriate may discourage use by house sparrows.

+ Add 2–3 inches of wood chips.

§Preferred habitat codes:

1. Open areas in the sun (not shaded permanently by trees), pastures, fields, or golf courses.
2. Woodland clearings or the edge of woods.
3. Above water, or if on land, the entrance should face water.
4. On trunks of large trees, or high in little-frequented parts of barns, silos, water towers, or church steeples.
5. Moist forest bottomlands, flooded river valleys, swamps.
6. Semiarid country, deserts, dry open woods, and wood edge.
7. Backyards, near buildings.
8. Near water; under bridges, barns.
9. Mixed conifer–hardwood forests.

Adapted from Daniel D. Boone, *Homes for Birds*. Conservation Bulletin 14, 1979, 22 pp.; also Susan E. Quinlan, *Bird Houses for Alaska*, vol. 1, no. 3, Alaska Wildlife Watcher's Report, Alaska Department of Fish and Game, 1982, 8 pp.

House sparrows are the most serious nest competitor for bluebirds. Unlike starlings, which may be excluded by use of a 1½-inch entrance hole, house sparrows can easily use bluebird boxes and their persistence at renesting after egg destruction (at least eight times) is legendary.

Because house sparrows are far from fussy when selecting a cavity, certain features of nest boxes and mounting positions may offer promise in discouraging sparrows while encouraging other species. Some bluebird enthusiasts have noted that house sparrows do not like to nest lower than 3 feet above the ground, while bluebirds will sometimes use boxes mounted at this height. Others have noted that bluebirds will nest more readily in smaller boxes than will house sparrows. James Baxter of Girard, Pennsylvania, has observed that bluebirds will nest in boxes with internal dimensions of only 3½ × 4 inches and with a somewhat larger than usual entrance hole of 1¾ inches. He also notes that bluebirds will use a fairly shallow box with only 3½ inches from the entrance hole to the floor of the box. This puts the bluebird nearly at eye level with the entrance hole. The box combines three features that house sparrows *generally* dislike: (1) 3½ feet from the ground, (2) smaller than usual internal dimensions, and (3) shallower than usual depth.

All three of these characteristics *may* discourage house sparrows, but they also make the nest box more vulnerable to such predators as raccoons and starlings. Raccoon guards on mounting poles might help, but the trade-offs gained from discouraging house sparrows but increasing risk of predation are apparent. The appropriate box dimensions and designs no doubt vary from one region to the next, depending on the local conditions and the most pressing competitors and predators—house sparrows, starlings, snakes, or raccoons.

Dick Peterson of Brooklyn Center, Minnesota, has designed a unique nest box that is now widely distributed by the Bluebird Recovery Committee of the Audubon Chapter of Minneapolis. The special feature of this box is the steep sloping roof and front of the box, which results in a very small floor space. According to Peterson, the advantage of this box is that parent bluebirds expend less time carrying nesting material to build a suitable-sized nest and there is less space for blowfly larvae to hide. This box also has an elongated entrance hole, 1⅜ inches wide and 2¼ inches long. The hole keeps starlings out without a nest guard and permits the bluebirds to slip in with ease.

The illustration shows two nest boxes recommended for bluebirds. Both designs can be easily adapted for other species by following recommended box dimensions on page 206.

During winter nights, bluebirds conserve body heat by roosting together with as many as a dozen birds in the same tree cavity. Bluebirds use natural cavities more frequently than nest boxes for roosting, probably because such sites have fewer cold-air leaks. Recently, Richard Tuttle "winterized" some of his bluebird houses by plugging drainage holes with quarter-inch wooden dowels and securing felt weather-stripping to all ventilation slots, thus restricting drafts and

This small-bottomed box was designed by Dick Peterson of Brooklyn Center, Minnesota. The small floor space may be an advantage, for adult bluebirds will spend less time building their nests. The smaller nest bottom may also attract fewer blowfly larvae. Redrawn from original plan by Dick Peterson.

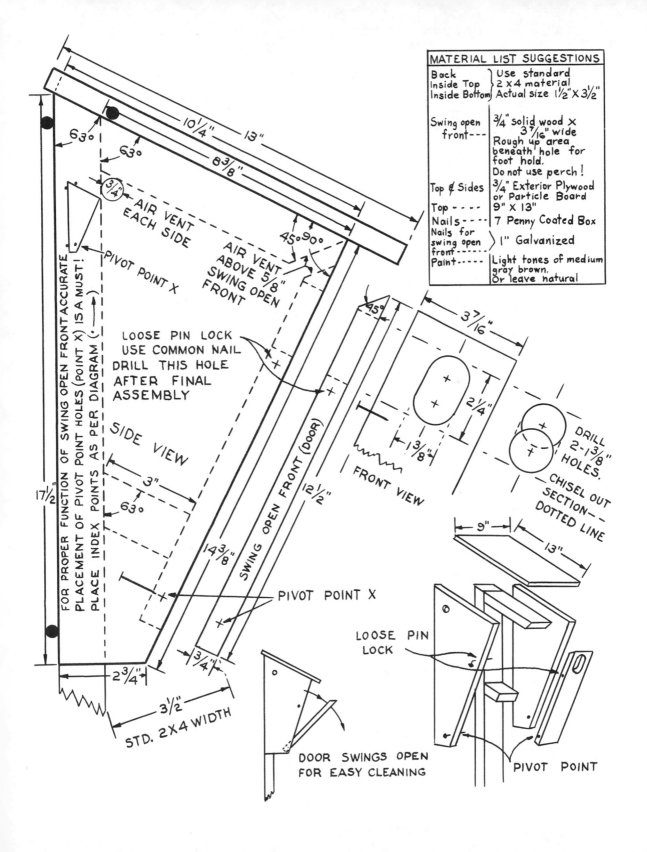

MATERIAL LIST SUGGESTIONS

Back, Inside Top, Inside Bottom	Use standard 2 x 4 material. Actual size 1½" X 3½"
Swing open front	¾" solid wood x 3 7/16" wide. Rough up area beneath hole for foot hold. Do not use perch!
Top & Sides	¾" Exterior Plywood or Particle Board
Top	9" X 13"
Nails	7 Penny Coated Box
Nails for swing open front	1" Galvanized
Paint	Light tones of medium gray brown. Or leave natural

10¼" — 13"

63° 63°

8 3/8"

¾

AIR VENT EACH SIDE

AIR VENT ABOVE 5/8" SWING OPEN FRONT

45° 90°

PIVOT POINT X

LOOSE PIN LOCK USE COMMON NAIL DRILL THIS HOLE AFTER FINAL ASSEMBLY

SIDE VIEW

3"

63°

17½"

FOR PROPER FUNCTION OF SWING OPEN FRONT ACCURATE PLACEMENT OF PIVOT POINT HOLES (POINT X) IS A MUST! PLACE INDEX POINTS AS PER DIAGRAM (·—·)

SWING OPEN FRONT (DOOR)

12½"

45°

3 7/16"

2¼"

1 3/8"

FRONT VIEW

DRILL 2-1 3/8" HOLES.

CHISEL OUT SECTION— DOTTED LINE

9"

13"

14 3/8"

PIVOT POINT X

¾"

2¾"

3½"

STD. 2X4 WIDTH

LOOSE PIN LOCK

PIVOT POINT

DOOR SWINGS OPEN FOR EASY CLEANING

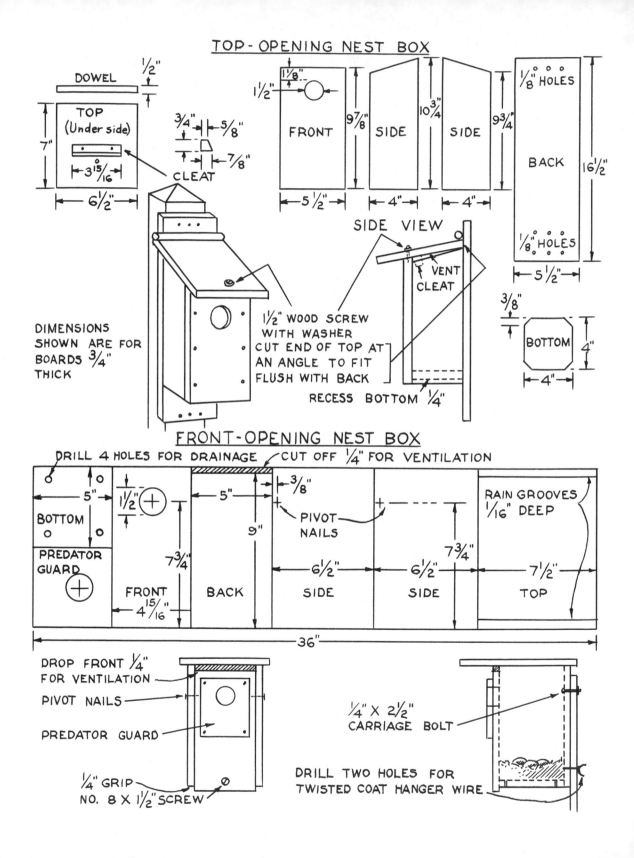

TOP-OPENING NEST BOX

DOWEL

1/2"

TOP
(Under side)

7"

3 15/16"

6 1/2"

CLEAT

3/4"   5/8"

7/8"

FRONT

1 1/8"

1 1/2"

9 7/8"

5 1/2"

SIDE

10 3/4"

4"

SIDE

9 3/4"

4"

BACK

1/8" HOLES

1/8" HOLES

16 1/2"

5 1/2"

3/8"

BOTTOM

4"

4"

SIDE VIEW

VENT
CLEAT

1 1/2" WOOD SCREW
WITH WASHER
CUT END OF TOP AT
AN ANGLE TO FIT
FLUSH WITH BACK

RECESS BOTTOM 1/4"

DIMENSIONS
SHOWN ARE FOR
BOARDS 3/4"
THICK

FRONT-OPENING NEST BOX

DRILL 4 HOLES FOR DRAINAGE   CUT OFF 1/4" FOR VENTILATION

BOTTOM

5"

PREDATOR
GUARD

FRONT

4 15/16"

1 1/2"

7 3/4"

5"

BACK

9"

3/8"

PIVOT
NAILS

SIDE

6 1/2"

SIDE

6 1/2"

7 3/4"

TOP

RAIN GROOVES
1/16" DEEP

7 1/2"

36"

DROP FRONT 1/4"
FOR VENTILATION

PIVOT NAILS

PREDATOR GUARD

1/4" GRIP
NO. 8 X 1 1/2" SCREW

1/4" X 2 1/2"
CARRIAGE BOLT

DRILL TWO HOLES FOR
TWISTED COAT HANGER WIRE

improving the boxes for roosting purposes. He found that bluebirds roosted more often in his winterized houses than those not sealed for winter. He also noted that early spring clutches are more likely to succeed in winterized boxes than those with usual drainage and ventilation holes. Winterizing materials are removed after spring weather stabilizes.

There are several bluebird recovery groups around the United States and Canada, the largest of which is the North American Bluebird Society, Box 6295, Silver Spring, MD 20906. This group publishes *Sialia,* a very useful journal that reports on various techniques for improving the status of bluebirds and other cavity-nesting birds.

Purple Martins

Today almost all purple martins nest in artificial nesting structures, but it was not always that way. Before Europeans colonized North America, purple martins nested in woodpecker-riddled snags and crevices in cliffs. They probably were rare in the vast eastern forests and were most abundant in open, grassy valleys along rivers, lakes, and seacoast marshes. The greatest populations in precolonial times were probably in partly forested central regions of North America, an area that remains the heart of the purple martin's current distribution.

Native Americans were the first to attract martins to artificial nesting structures. Their technique was to hang dried gourds from trees near villages so that martins would consume nuisance flies and mosquitoes. In the southeastern United States, martin gourds remain a popular way to house purple martins.

Thoroughly dry the gourds before cutting a 2½-inch entrance hole through the middle of the side. Then scrape out the gourd seeds and save them for a new crop. Drill ½-inch holes in the bottom of the gourd for drain holes and drill a ¼-inch hole through the top of the neck to attach a line. Replace used gourds each year.

As with all martin houses, gourds should be mounted atop a pole approximately 14 feet tall. Position mounting pole in an open field *at least* 15 feet from any overhanging limbs or buildings, as the martins like to circle around their colony and appear to shun homes that are vulnerable to climbing predators. A location near open water, such as a pond, river, or lake, is especially attractive to martins.

Gourd martin-houses and modern equivalents made from bleach bottles have several disadvantages. Because they are thin-walled, gourds offer little insulation from the sun on hot summer days, which presumably adds to the discomfort of growing nestlings, resulting in increased probability of premature fledging. If a young bird leaves the nest before it can fly, it will likely land on the ground where it is more vulnerable to predators such as cats and raccoons.

Because martins are highly social, they readily accept multiple housing units. As many as 200 pairs of martins have nested in the same house, with many of

◄ *Top-opening and front-opening nest boxes can be adapted to many different cavity-nesting birds (see page 30). This top-opening box is redrawn from Lawrence Zeleny,* The Bluebird *(Indiana University Press, Bloomington, 1976). The front-opening box is redrawn from* Blueprint for a Bluebird, *Publication 339, Ohio Division of Wildlife.*

the adults returning to the same colony year after year. Some of the young produced in a colony also return to the same house, but most join nearby colonies or start new colonies in the vicinity of their original home.

Multiple-unit martin houses offer several distinct advantages over gourds: thick, wooden walls provide protective insulation, and the houses may be constructed with a central chamber that conducts heat, as a chimney does, up to the roof where it disperses through ventilation holes. Another advantage of this kind of house is that a broad porch may prevent young birds from premature fledging.

Aluminum martin houses offer all the pluses of wooden houses, and have the added advantage of much lighter weight. Light weight reduces the chances of the house falling in strong winds and makes it easier to raise and lower.

Since purple martins spend 7 months of every year either going to, residing in, or returning from their South American wintering habitat, their nesting boxes are often usurped by resident house sparrows and starlings that become well established in the martins' absence.

A cluster of dried gourds is an inexpensive and time-proven artificial nesting structure for purple martins.

PLANS FOR A MARTIN HOUSE

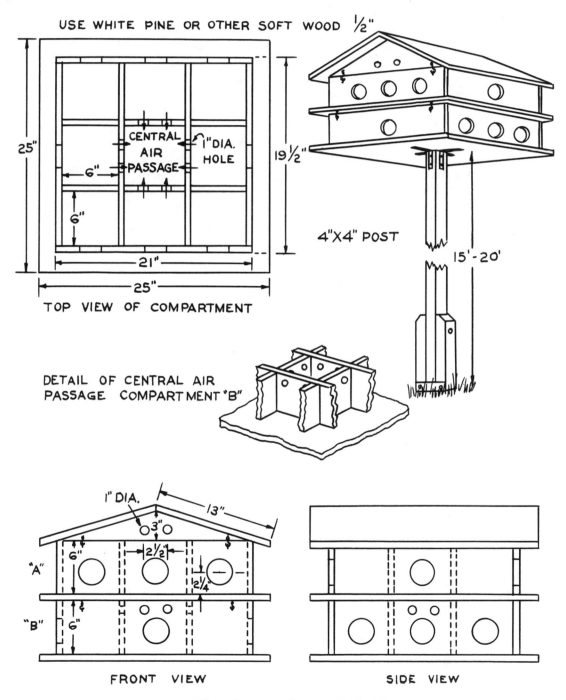

USE WHITE PINE OR OTHER SOFT WOOD ½"

25"

CENTRAL AIR PASSAGE

1" DIA. HOLE

6"

6"

19½"

21"

25"

TOP VIEW OF COMPARTMENT

4"X4" POST

15'-20'

DETAIL OF CENTRAL AIR PASSAGE COMPARTMENT "B"

1" DIA.

13"

3"

6"

2½"

"A"

2¼"

"B"

6"

FRONT VIEW

SIDE VIEW

Plans for a wooden martin house.

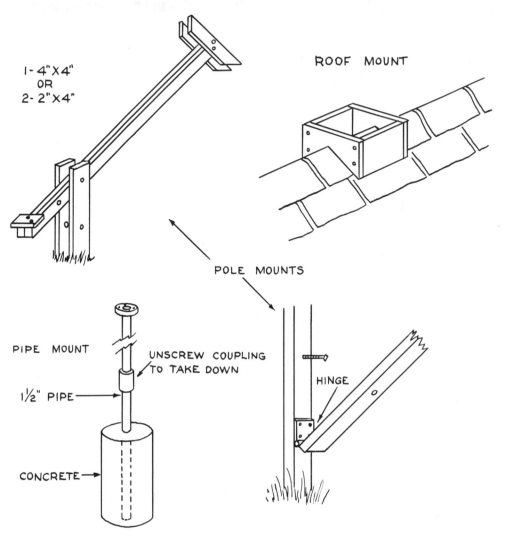

1 - 4"X4"
OR
2 - 2"X4"

ROOF MOUNT

POLE MOUNTS

PIPE MOUNT

UNSCREW COUPLING
TO TAKE DOWN

1/2" PIPE

HINGE

CONCRETE

Various techniques for mounting martin houses.

Since purple martins require a 2½-inch hole, both starlings and house sparrows can easily gain access to martin nest-boxes. Some observers suggest, however, that starlings do not like to nest in boxes with shiny white interiors, so painting the box interior white will not only keep martins cool but may discourage starlings.

House sparrows are much more difficult to discourage, as they thrive in a wide variety of nest sites and find martin houses ideal. The best way to discourage house sparrows is to lower martin houses in the fall, clean and paint them over the winter, and put them up again when the first martins return.

Martins generally appear within a week of their arrival from the previous year. In Louisiana they arrive in mid-February; in Illinois by mid-March; and not until mid-April in Nova Scotia and Washington State. Once martins become established, older, experienced birds can defend their nests from house sparrows, but young, first-nesting birds are easily discouraged by the aggressive sparrows. Unless martin houses are lowered in the winter, they are sure to become sparrow slums.

Because of the necessity of lowering and raising martin houses, the mounting pole design is an especially important part of the house. The figure illustrates several mounting devices.

Detailed plans for a homemade aluminum martin house are available from Nature Books Publishers, Box 12157, Jackson, MS 39211. Aluminum martin houses and mounting poles are available from Trio Manufacturing Co., Griggsville, IL 62340. Trio Manufacturing also publishes *Nature Society News—The Purple Martin Paper*, a popular monthly newsprint publication devoted to articles about martins and other cavity-nesting birds.

Wrens

For bluebird enthusiasts, the ambitious nest-building habits of house, Bewick's, and Carolina wrens are often unappreciated, as they often fill several nest boxes full of sticks and only rear their young in one box. Bluebird boxes are best placed far from brushy thickets to avoid wren competition, but where this is not possible, several boxes built especially for wrens may help to discourage wrens from using bluebird nesting boxes.

Although wrens will nest in larger boxes, the sizes recommended in the table on page 206 are large enough to meet their needs, as they must do more work gathering sticks if they nest in a larger box. An oblong entrance is best, as it is much easier for wrens to pull nesting sticks through such an opening. For house wrens, openings should be 7/8 inches high by 2½ inches long. Bewick's wrens require a somewhat larger, 1-inch-tall opening, and Carolina wrens must have a 1½-inch-tall opening. House sparrows will not be able to squeeze through entrances up to 1 inch high. A pile of thin sticks cut 3 to 4 inches long and placed near nesting boxes will facilitate nest building.

Wood Ducks

The wood duck's magnificent plumage and its cavity-nesting habits contributed to a serious decline in numbers earlier this century. The massive conversion of eastern forests to cropland, draining of swamplands, introduction of cavity-competing starlings, and market hunting all contributed to the decline.

Since the early 1930s, the U.S. Fish and Wildlife Service and many state game agencies have launched impressive wood duck restoration efforts through the use of artificial nest boxes. While it is impossible to separate the effects of nest boxes from those of the regrowth of woodlands since the 1940s, it is clear that at least locally, nest boxes have substantially increased wood duck populations.

Several features of wood duck behavior make them especially responsive to nest box programs. As with most ducks, female wood ducks usually return to the vicinity of their hatching place when they reach breeding age. Here they select a nest site similar to the one they remembered from their duckling days. Once a nest site is selected, they often reuse the box year after year. Also, wood ducks are surprisingly colonial in their nesting habits. It is not uncommon for females to occupy nest boxes positioned only inches apart or even several boxes nailed together, apartment fashion.

Although wood ducks are sometimes desperate for nest sites (even trapping themselves in chimneys), a good nest box positioned in poor habitat can be a hazard rather than a help. Quality wood duck habitat consists of shallow water with abundant shrubs and trees close by. Although it is important to protect nesting birds from excessive human disturbance, sizable wood duck "colonies" sometimes occur in even tiny urban wetlands. The water should have ample aquatic vegetation and food for ducklings, such as insect larvae and tiny crustaceans. Staff from your local state/provincial wildlife department can help to determine habitat quality.

It is also essential to protect wood duck nest boxes from predators. Without protection, attractive boxes may lure birds to nest in predator-vulnerable locations. For this reason, the best location for a wood duck box is on a separate pole, positioned about 6 feet above the water. One way to sink wood duck poles into a pond or marsh bottom is to cut a hole through the ice in the winter and then pound the sharpened post well into the bottom muck. Because wood ducks will nest in cluster housing and it is often more difficult to erect boxes than it is to build them, it makes sense to position more than one box on a good nest box support.

Boxes mounted on trees at the edges of ponds are more vulnerable to predators, as it is easier for raccoons and snakes to climb into nesting trees from adjacent vegetation. If boxes must be located on land, they should be mounted at least 10 to 20 feet high on trees at or near water. Although wood ducks will nest considerable distances from water, the young are very vulnerable to predators if they must perform a long overland trek to the nearest swamp or marsh.

Since wood ducks naturally nest in tree cavities with soft heartwood or on chips from a woodpecker excavation, they will not use artificial nest boxes unless there are several inches of sawdust or wood chips to cushion their eggs. To meet this need, add about 4 inches of fresh sawdust or wood chips each year to the bottom of wood duck houses. Another important feature of the box should be a strip of hardware cloth tacked to the inside of the box between the entrance hole and the bottom of the box.

An entrance hole 3 inches high and 4 inches wide will discourage some raccoons from reaching into nest boxes. A more successful entrance for eliminating raccoon predation is a 6-inch-square sleeve constructed from three-quarter-inch wood that fits over a 4-inch entrance hole (see illustration A). While this guard prevents raccoon predation, it may attract starlings, and is therefore not recommended where starlings are a problem. Starlings can totally fill wood duck nest boxes with sticks and other vegetation, even building their nests over complete wood duck clutches. Where competition with starlings is a problem, slowly replace standard boxes with horizontal nesting structures that permit more light to reach the nesting cavity (see illustration B). Similarly, some experimental boxes with clear Plexiglas roofs also discourage starlings.

Most wood ducks prefer to nest in wooden boxes. They will also use metal "boxes," and will even nest in specially modified plastic buckets (see illustration C). The illustrations show plans for a standard wood duck house constructed from one piece of 10-foot-long 1 × 12 inch rough-cut lumber and for a rocket-shaped metal house especially useful for discouraging raccoons, squirrels, and snakes (see illustration D).

Within their breeding ranges, hooded merganser, bufflehead, and common goldeneye also use artificial nest boxes. See the table on page 206 for recommended nest box dimensions. Position nest boxes as recommended for wood ducks.

RACCOON- AND STARLING-PROOF WOOD DUCK BOXES

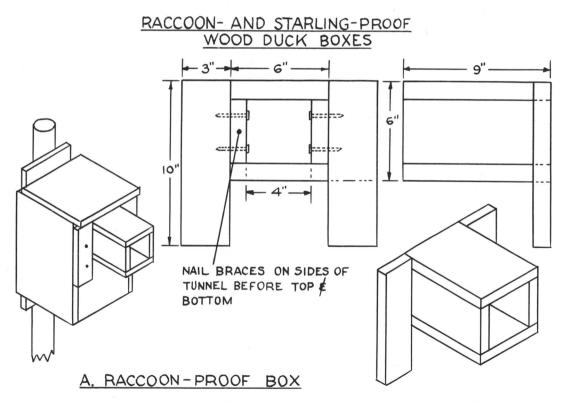

NAIL BRACES ON SIDES OF TUNNEL BEFORE TOP & BOTTOM

A. RACCOON-PROOF BOX

(A) The raccoon-proof wood duck box prevents raccoon predation by lengthening the box opening, thereby placing duck eggs out of their reach.

Barn Owls

Where nesting sites limit barn owl populations, nesting boxes or shelves can have dramatic effects. One of the best examples of this is the project of Carl Marti and Kathryn Denn of Weber State College, Ogden, Utah, and Phillip Wagner of the Utah Division of Wildlife Resources. They noted that barn owls regularly roosted in abandoned silos, but only one in 50 silos had a suitable surface on which the owls could nest. In 1977 and 1978 they placed a total of 30 boxes in silos and of these, 24 were used by barn owls. During this period, 154 young owls fledged from their nesting boxes.

However, such projects are not always a success. Recently, the Illinois Department of Conservation mounted 124 boxes similar to those used in Utah inside silos in 31 Illinois counties. Although it may be too early to determine the eventual outcome of this effort, so far none of the boxes has been used. Illinois barn owl populations may be too low to respond to a nest box program.

The actual dimensions of barn owl nesting boxes are probably not nearly as important as placement of nesting structures in suitable habitat near good feeding areas. In northwestern Connecticut, Arthur Gingert of the National Audubon Society's Miles Wildlife Sanctuary has successfully lured barn owls to breed on an open shelf placed high in abandoned silos. His nesting shelf has a 12-inch-tall rim to keep young owls from falling out of the nest prematurely and an 8-inch-high divider across the middle of the shelf to help separate young and reduce competition for food.

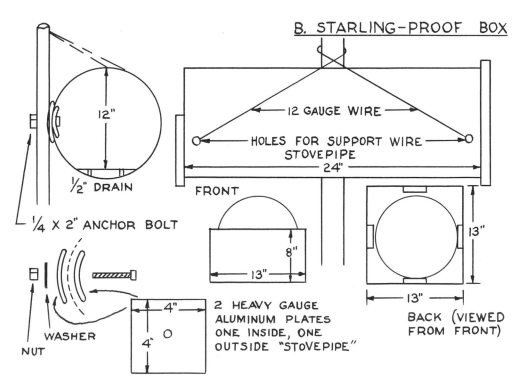

C. STANDARD WOODEN WOOD DUCK BOX

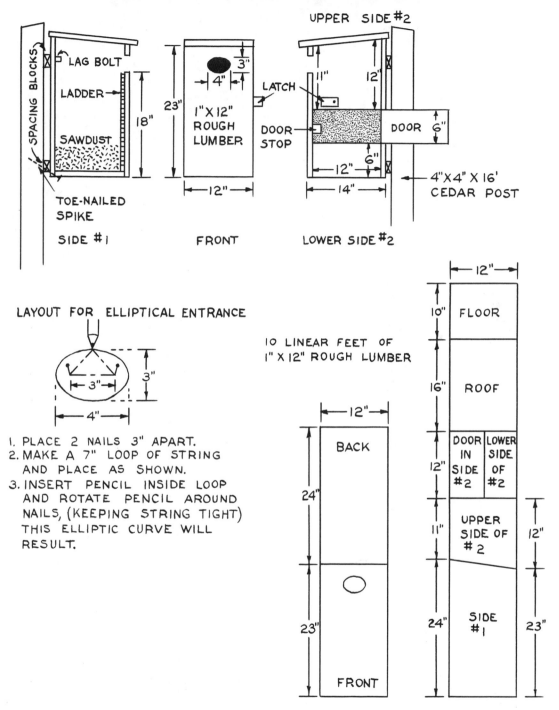

UPPER SIDE #2

SPACING BLOCKS

LAG BOLT

LADDER

SAWDUST

TOE-NAILED SPIKE

SIDE #1

23"

18"

3"

4"

1"X 12" ROUGH LUMBER

FRONT

12"

LATCH

DOOR STOP

DOOR

11"

12"

6"

12"

6"

14"

DOOR

4"X 4" X 16' CEDAR POST

LOWER SIDE #2

LAYOUT FOR ELLIPTICAL ENTRANCE

3"
3"
4"

1. PLACE 2 NAILS 3" APART.
2. MAKE A 7" LOOP OF STRING AND PLACE AS SHOWN.
3. INSERT PENCIL INSIDE LOOP AND ROTATE PENCIL AROUND NAILS, (KEEPING STRING TIGHT) THIS ELLIPTIC CURVE WILL RESULT.

10 LINEAR FEET OF 1" X 12" ROUGH LUMBER

BACK
12"
24"
23"
FRONT

12"
FLOOR   10"
ROOF   16"

DOOR IN SIDE #2 | LOWER SIDE OF #2   12"

UPPER SIDE OF #2   11"

SIDE #1   24"

12"
23"

(B) The interior of the starling-proof wood duck box is too brightly lit for most starlings. The starling-proof design is redrawn from "Nest Boxes for Wood Ducks," 1976, U.S. Department of Interior, Wildlife Leaflet WL 510.
(C) Standard design for a wooden wood duck box. Redrawn from "Nest Boxes for Wood Ducks." 1976, U.S. Department of Interior, Wildlife Leaflet WL 510.

D. ROCKET WOOD DUCK BOX

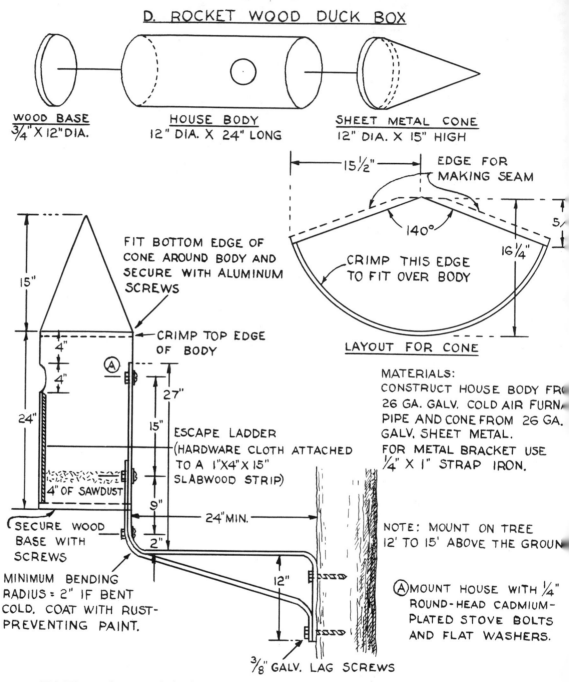

WOOD BASE
¾" X 12" DIA.

HOUSE BODY
12" DIA. X 24" LONG

SHEET METAL CONE
12" DIA. X 15" HIGH

15½"

EDGE FOR
MAKING SEAM

140°

5/

16¼"

CRIMP THIS EDGE
TO FIT OVER BODY

LAYOUT FOR CONE

15"

FIT BOTTOM EDGE OF
CONE AROUND BODY AND
SECURE WITH ALUMINUM
SCREWS

CRIMP TOP EDGE
OF BODY

24"

4"

4"

Ⓐ

27"

15"

ESCAPE LADDER
(HARDWARE CLOTH ATTACHED
TO A 1"X4"X 15"
SLABWOOD STRIP)

4" OF SAWDUST

9"

24" MIN.

SECURE WOOD
BASE WITH
SCREWS

2"

MINIMUM BENDING
RADIUS = 2" IF BENT
COLD. COAT WITH RUST-
PREVENTING PAINT.

12"

⅜" GALV. LAG SCREWS

MATERIALS:
CONSTRUCT HOUSE BODY FR(
26 GA. GALV. COLD AIR FURN
PIPE AND CONE FROM 26 GA.
GALV. SHEET METAL.
FOR METAL BRACKET USE
¼" X 1" STRAP IRON.

NOTE: MOUNT ON TREE
12' TO 15' ABOVE THE GROUN

ⒶMOUNT HOUSE WITH ¼"
ROUND-HEAD CADMIUM-
PLATED STOVE BOLTS
AND FLAT WASHERS.

(D) The rocket wood duck box is useful on trees or unshielded wood posts. The metal design protects nesting ducks from raccoons, squirrels, and snakes. Redrawn from "Wood Duck Nest Boxes," USDA Soil Conservation Service JS 234, 1975.

Where good feeding habitat exists but abandoned silos and barns are not available, an exterior barn-owl box may prove to be an alternative. The box illustrated here was designed by Larry McKeever of the Owl Rehabilitation Research Foundation, Vineland Station, Ontario. It has an extended roof that provides protection over a large landing platform in front of the box. Another unique feature of the box is the detachable base that facilitates cleaning. This is useful because barn owl nests require a thorough scrubbing at the end of the breeding season. Barn owl boxes and shelves should be filled with several inches of coarse wood shavings and pine needles. Nesting structures should be at least 10 feet off the ground and should be installed by late winter.

Barred Owls

Until recently, barred owls were not known to nest in artificial nest boxes. However, recent work by David Johnson of Park Rapids, Minnesota, has demonstrated that if boxes are constructed to the proper dimensions and placed in suitable habitat, barred owls will readily use nest boxes. Johnson has field tested 35 specially constructed barred owl boxes in various forest habitats in northcentral Minnesota and had 8 pair of barred owls nest in 35 boxes in 1983. These produced a total of 28 young. Bernard Forsythe of Wolfville, Nova Scotia, has had a similar success in luring barred owls to nest boxes in Nova Scotia. Both Johnson and Forsythe agree that barred owls need an entrance hole that is either 6 inches in diameter or 6 inches square. The boxes should be 20–24 inches tall and 12 inches square. Several inches of wood chips, dried leaves, or moss should be added to the bottom of the nest box.

Barred owl boxes should be mounted at least 17 feet up in a tree with a substantial trunk. The use of barred owl boxes in young forests, without suitably large nesting trees, demonstrates that as long as there is an ample food base, nest boxes can substitute for old-age natural cavities and permit barred owls to inhabit younger forests. Mount nest boxes in wet forests near a pond, stream, or swamp.

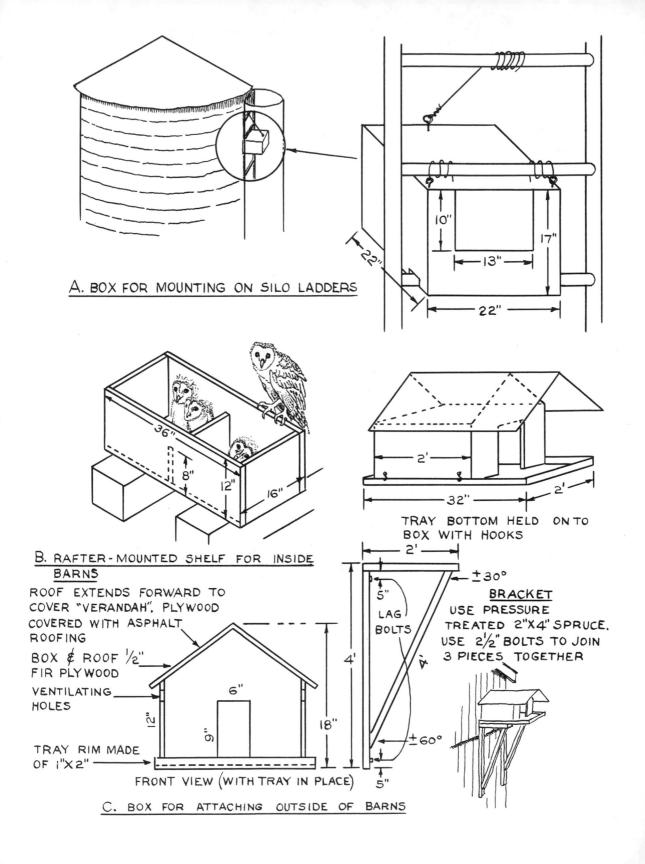

A. BOX FOR MOUNTING ON SILO LADDERS

10"
13"
17"
22"
22"

B. RAFTER-MOUNTED SHELF FOR INSIDE BARNS

36"
8"
12"
16"

TRAY BOTTOM HELD ON TO BOX WITH HOOKS

2'
32"
2'

ROOF EXTENDS FORWARD TO COVER "VERANDAH", PLYWOOD COVERED WITH ASPHALT ROOFING

BOX & ROOF ½" FIR PLYWOOD

VENTILATING HOLES

TRAY RIM MADE OF 1"X2"

6"
12"
9"
18"

FRONT VIEW (WITH TRAY IN PLACE)

C. BOX FOR ATTACHING OUTSIDE OF BARNS

2'
5"
LAG BOLTS
4'
4'
±30°
±60°
5"

BRACKET
USE PRESSURE TREATED 2"X4" SPRUCE. USE 2½" BOLTS TO JOIN 3 PIECES TOGETHER

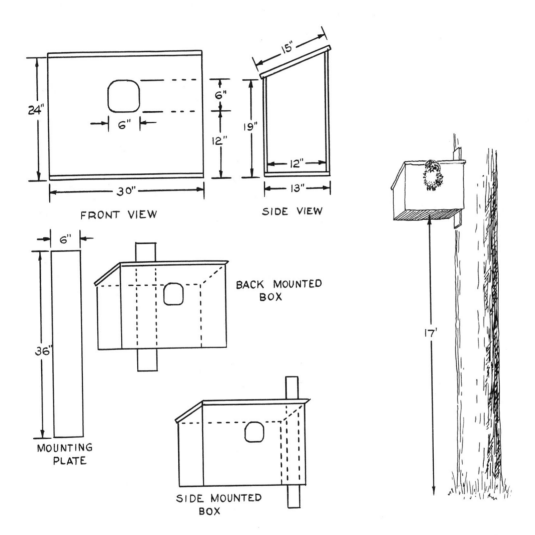

Above: the barred owl nest box, designed by David Johnson, attracts owls because of its 6-inch entrance hole and suitable dimensions. A wet forest environment is the proper habitat.

Left: designs for barn owl nest boxes: (A) for use in silos, (B) rafter mount for inside barns, and (C) on the exterior of barns and other large outbuildings.

NEST PLATFORMS AND SHELVES

A diverse assemblage of birds, including eagles, American robins, barn swallows, mourning doves, double-crested cormorant, osprey, and great horned owl, will nest on suitable platforms when faced with a scarcity of natural nest sites. Most species will not attempt breeding unless there is ample food, but where this exists, the presentation of a secure nesting platform in the right habitat may be all that is necessary to entice these birds to your property.

American Robin, Phoebes, and Barn Swallows

Robins build their mud-lined nests in a variety of places, including deciduous and evergreen trees and shrubs. One of their favorite places, however, is under building eaves where they find a flat supporting structure. Phoebes usually build their nests under bridges near moving water or in a natural rock crevice near a stream. As with robins, they also may build their nests under protected building eaves if they can find a secure base for support. Suitable nest sites may be so rare that they will attempt to nest immediately over busy entranceways.

To encourage robins and phoebes to nest on your home or outbuildings where you want them, construct a nesting shelf and attach it under a protective eave. For somewhat exposed areas, follow design A and for areas with protection use B. A few sprigs of evergreen needles, such as arborvitae, stapled to the face of robin nest shelves may increase acceptance of the nest shelf.

Barn swallows, as their name suggests, prefer to nest inside barns, but they will also nest under porches or any abandoned building to which they can gain entrance. A simple L-shaped platform, shown in C, is all that is necessary to support barn swallow nests. Sometimes cliff swallows or cave swallows (southwest Texas only) will nest on this platform when it is mounted under building eaves.

Mourning Doves

Mourning doves usually build a flimsy stick nest in a tree or shrub crotch, but strong winds and rain often destroy many of them. Nestling survival can be improved by building cone-shaped nesting platforms from quarter- or three-eighths-inch hardware cloth. These easy to build nesting structures should be positioned in forked branches from 6 to 16 feet high in trees with moderate shade. Good dove nest sites should have an excellent view of the ground and a clear flight path to and from the nest. Since mourning doves sometimes nest in loose colonies, several nesting cones can be positioned near each other in the same tree.

The wire nesting cones should be nailed securely to the tree using two nails on each side of the cone. After installation, carefully bend down the lip of the cone to give a smooth-lipped landing place. Best results in the Central Valley of Cal-

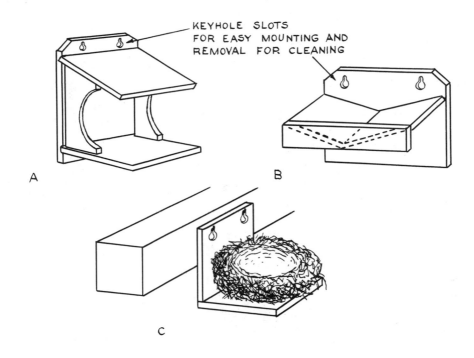

KEYHOLE SLOTS
FOR EASY MOUNTING AND
REMOVAL FOR CLEANING

A

B

C

	FLOOR DIMENSIONS INCHES	HEIGHT OFF GROUND FEET
PHOEBE	6X6	8 – 12
ROBIN	6X8(DEEP)	6 – 15
BARN SWALLOW	6X6	8 – 12

Nest platforms for phoebe, robin, and barn swallows. Design A is for somewhat exposed locations; B is best under eaves and other protected sites. A and B will attract both the phoebe and the robin. Design C's L-shaped platform is an appropriate nest structure for barn swallows.

ifornia were obtained by installing nest cones in late February, March, and April before most doves established their nesting territories. Clean old nests from the wire cones each spring.

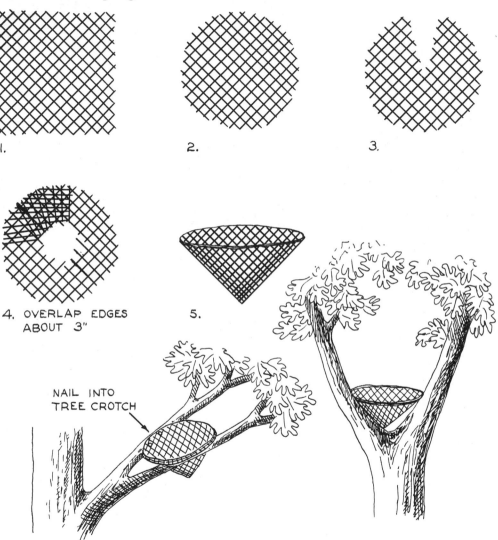

Nest cones for mourning doves. Cones are constructed from a 12-inch square of ¹/₄- or ³/₈-inch galvanized hardware cloth. The squares (1) are cut into a circle (2), notched (3), and overlapped into a cone (4–5). These are then secured to tree crotches with nails or wire. Redrawn from J. Cowan, " 'Pre-Fab' Wire Mesh Cone Gives Doves Better Nest Than They Can Build Themselves," Outdoor California, 20:1 1959, 10–11.

Great Horned, Long-eared and Great Gray Owls

Tree-nesting owls that rely on the vacant nests of crows and hawks frequently face a shortage of secure nesting sites. Great horned owls begin nesting in January or February throughout much of North America, long before other birds begin to nest. They sometimes take over favorite nesting sites of osprey and bald eagle, but more frequently, they must nest in weathered crow or hawk nests that often crumble before their young can fledge.

Bernard Forsythe of Wolfville, Nova Scotia, has successfully lured both great horned and long-eared owls to artificial nesting platforms constructed high in living coniferous trees. Climbing up a suitable tree, he nails a board or stout pole across two branches, forming a triangular support for a chicken-wire basket. The chicken wire is attached by tacks or staples to the trunk, branches, and pole, creating a shallow basket with a depth of 1 or 2 inches. Inside the basket, he builds a stick nest, tying a few branches to the mesh with string. The nest is lined with coniferous branches that are woven into the chicken wire. The nest is completed by a soft layer of twigs, leaves, and moss, with several inches of sphagnum moss laid on top. Care is taken to build the nest without open holes in which an egg could disappear and become chilled. Nest-building supplies are hoisted up the tree packed in a plastic bag.

The space around owl nests should be fairly open so that the adults can easily fly into the nest, yet the site should not be so exposed that it is easily discovered by crows, ravens, or other predators. For great horned owls, position the nest about 20 feet off the ground and cut away all branches within 2 feet over the nest (A). Long-eared owl nests can be 15 feet off the ground with a 15-inch clearance above the nest (B).

In the woods between Lac du Bonnet, Manitoba, and the boglands of northern Minnesota, Robert Nero, Ray Tuokko, and Herb Copland have built more than 140 artificial or reconstructed great gray owl nests. Like great horned and long-eared owls, the rare great gray owls are dependent primarily on old crow and hawk nests, many of which deteriorate before their young fledge. Of 45 recent nestings between 1974 and 1981, 26 nestings in this study area occurred in artificial nests.

Robert Nero and his associates build their nests 15 to 25 feet up in deformed American larch with a crown of upright limbs in which they can construct their nest. They attach the cradle of chicken wire and then build up a 2-foot-high nest using crushed tamarack twigs, bark, and moss to make a dense lining. The whole structure is about 18–24 inches across. Three or more nests are built in nearby trees to provide a choice of nest sites.

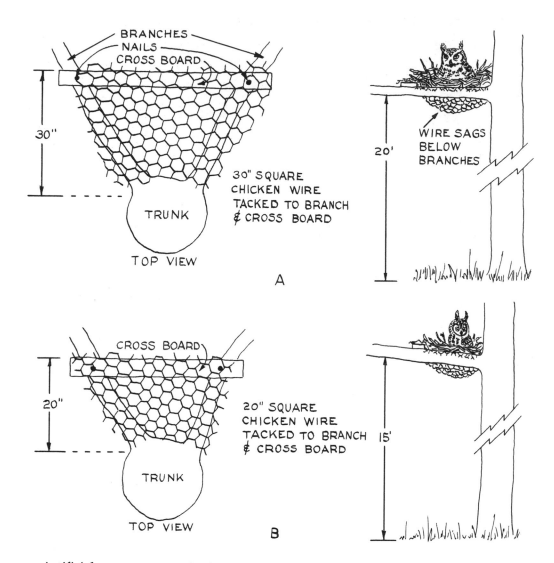

Artificial nest structures built in mature conifers for the great horned owl (A) and the long-eared owl (B). The basket is constructed from chicken wire and either a board or pole; inside rests a nest of branches. Designed by Bernard Forsythe of Wolfville, Nova Scotia.

Eagles, Ospreys, and Hawks

On treeless western rangelands and vast coastal salt marshes, nest sites for eagles, ospreys, and hawks are often very scarce. When natural nest sites are unavailable, these grand birds often resort to nesting on manmade structures, such as windmills, power company utility poles, and navigational markers. Sadly, many are electrocuted on power lines and their nests must be removed. To lure them away from such hazards, an increasing number of wildlife agencies, conservation groups, and concerned individuals are creating artificial nest sites.

Where possible, the best technique is to cut the top off a large, solitary tree and build a nest platform on top of the trunk. Where suitable trees are not available, artificial nesting poles and structures are usually readily accepted.

Ospreys are especially quick to use artificial nest platforms in both inland and coastal areas. Peter Ames and Paul Spitzer of Old Lyme, Connecticut, have designed an osprey nesting platform and mounting poles that have withstood the rigors of salt marsh habitats in Connecticut and Massachusetts for over 20 years. Their mounting posts and support structures are constructed from 16-foot 4 × 4 inch seasoned oak or white cedar. The mounting poles are buried at least 3 feet into a salt marsh and braced by four 6-foot strut braces built of seasoned oak. The braces are predrilled and are nailed together with galvanized nails.

The platform is constructed around a pine sheath that slips over the top of the mounting pole. Four 2 × 4 inch, 30-inch-long fir struts form a foundation for eight 1 × 2 inch fir strips that support a 3 × 3 foot piece of turkey wire tacked to the struts.

Artificial nesting platforms similar to the one described here have been successfully used by ospreys, bald and golden eagles, red-tailed and ferruginous hawks, great horned owls, and ravens. Nesting platforms constructed in sunny, arid habitats should have a wooden protective canopy the size of the nest platform to provide partial shade.

Ducks and Geese

Canada geese, mallards, black ducks, and many other kinds of waterfowl prefer to nest on small islands where they can keep an alert watch for predators. Even beaver and muskrat houses often serve as nesting sites. Artificial nest sites can be fashioned by building a floating 6 × 6 foot wooden raft over a Styrofoam core. Such rafts should be anchored to the bottom using bleach bottles filled with sand or instant concrete mix. Fill the raft with straw and paint the Styrofoam a dark brown color to help it blend with the environment. To help young birds find food and shelter, position the raft near emergent vegetation at the edge of a pond or lake.

A goose or duck nesting platform for use in marsh habitats can be constructed on 7-foot-long steel post legs set into the marsh soil. The platform consists of a 2 × 4 inch frame that supports 1 × 8 inch planks. A truck tire wired to the platform and filled with straw makes an excellent goose nest site.

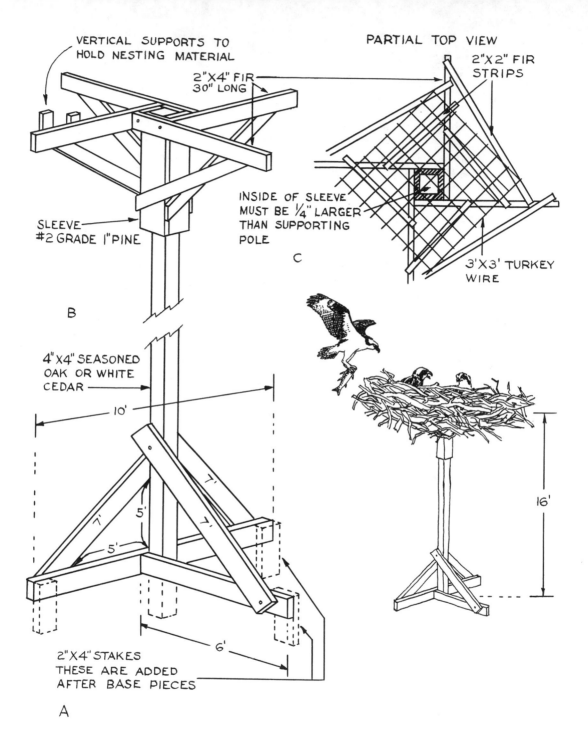

VERTICAL SUPPORTS TO
HOLD NESTING MATERIAL

PARTIAL TOP VIEW

2"X4" FIR
30" LONG

2"X2" FIR
STRIPS

SLEEVE
#2 GRADE 1" PINE

INSIDE OF SLEEVE
MUST BE 1/4" LARGER
THAN SUPPORTING
POLE

C

B

3'X3' TURKEY
WIRE

4"X4" SEASONED
OAK OR WHITE
CEDAR

10'

7'

7'

5'

5'

7'

16'

2"X4" STAKES
THESE ARE ADDED
AFTER BASE PIECES

6'

A

*Nesting platform for ospreys and other tree-top raptors. The post and supports
should be constructed out of seasoned oak or white cedar. Designed by Peter Ames
and Paul Spitzer of Old Lyme, Connecticut.*

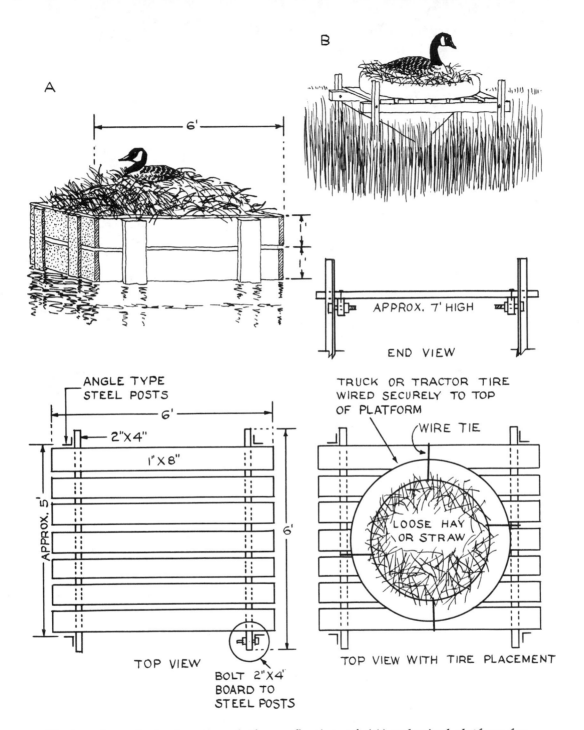

A

B

6'

APPROX. 7' HIGH

END VIEW

ANGLE TYPE
STEEL POSTS

6'

2"X4"

1"X8"

APPROX. 5'

6'

TOP VIEW

BOLT 2"X4'
BOARD TO
STEEL POSTS

TRUCK OR TRACTOR TIRE
WIRED SECURELY TO TOP
OF PLATFORM

WIRE TIE

LOOSE HAY
OR STRAW

TOP VIEW WITH TIRE PLACEMENT

Designs for waterfowl nesting platforms: floating raft (A) and raised platform for marshes (B). Redrawn from J. Yoakum et al., "Habitat Improvement Techniques," in Stanford D. Schemnitz, ed., Wildlife Management Techniques Manual, *4th ed. Wildlife Society, Washington, DC, 1980.*

Loons

Loon populations in the northern United States and southern Canada have declined seriously in recent years due to loss of wetlands, disturbance by careless boaters, loss of fish from acid precipitation, and predation by increasing numbers of raccoons. Recently, the use of artificial nesting rafts has helped increase loon production by providing safe nesting places.

Loon conservation groups in Maine, New Hampshire, and Wisconsin have experienced success with such artificial platforms. In 1982 the New Hampshire Loon Preservation Committee placed 50 nesting rafts and found loons nesting on 15 of these floating structures. These accounted for one-fifth of the loon chicks produced in New Hampshire in 1982.

The successful loon nesting structures used in New Hampshire are constructed from four 8-inch-diameter, 6-foot-long barkless cedar logs. These are notched to create a low profile and are held together with 8-inch-long galvanized spikes. A 5 × 5 foot piece of turkey wire (2 × 4 inch mesh) is then attached to the raft with 1½-inch galvanized fence staples to create a slightly sagging basket that holds a thick mat of sod, soil, and rotting wood. Marsh plants such as cattail, bulrush, and other emergent vegetation are then planted on the "island." The completed nesting surface of the raft measures 4 feet on a side. It is secured 30–50 yards from shore in 4 to 6 feet of water by two wire-cable anchor lines, each attached to an 8 × 8 × 16 inch cinder block.

Quiet ponds and lakes where loons are observed during the summer are the best sites for locating loon nesting-rafts. To coordinate your interest in loons with those already studying the species, and to find the nearest loon research group, write North American Loon Fund, Main Street, Humiston Building, Meredith, NH 03253.

Common and Forster's Terns

Terns may experience a shortage of nesting sites where vegetation has grown up too high or where nest site competitors, such as herring and great black-backed gulls, crowd terns onto marginal habitats.

Artificial nesting platforms may prove useful where vegetation management is not a solution to habitat needs. In such circumstances, the Royal Society for the Protection of Birds and the Wisconsin Department of Natural Resources have used artificial nesting platforms to assist, respectively, common and Forster's terns.

In Wisconsin, Forster's terns usually nest on floating phragmites mats in well-protected areas. The chances of storm damage to nests on such ephemeral nesting sites is so great that few nests produce chicks. When given a choice early in their nesting season of using emergent vegetation or 19 artificial platforms, a colony of about 200 terns on Lake Poygan abandoned natural sites in favor of the more secure platforms. All 19 platforms were used, producing at least 56 chicks.

CONSTRUCTION

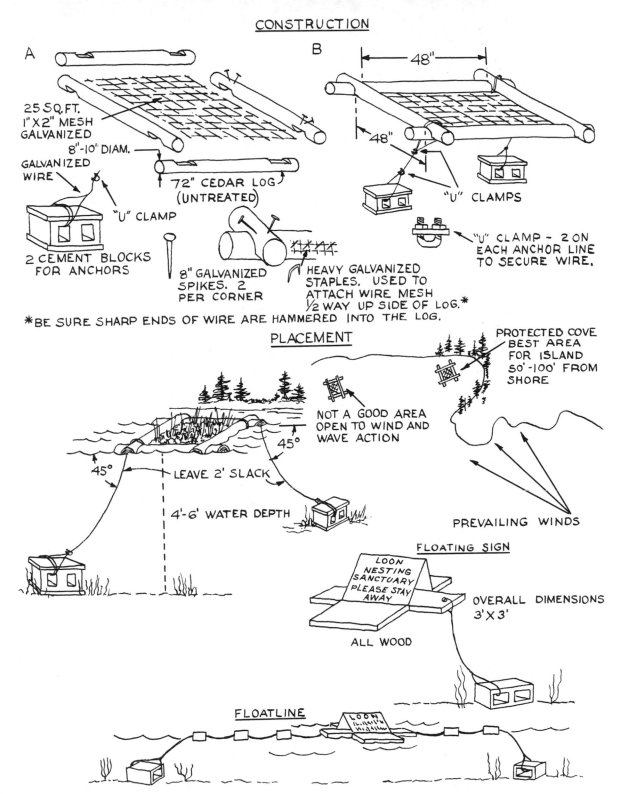

A

25 SQ. FT.
1" X 2" MESH
GALVANIZED

8"-10" DIAM.
GALVANIZED
WIRE

"U" CLAMP

2 CEMENT BLOCKS
FOR ANCHORS

72" CEDAR LOG
(UNTREATED)

8" GALVANIZED
SPIKES. 2
PER CORNER

HEAVY GALVANIZED
STAPLES. USED TO
ATTACH WIRE MESH
½ WAY UP SIDE OF LOG.*

B

48"

48"

"U" CLAMPS

"U" CLAMP – 2 ON
EACH ANCHOR LINE
TO SECURE WIRE.

*BE SURE SHARP ENDS OF WIRE ARE HAMMERED INTO THE LOG.

PLACEMENT

PROTECTED COVE
BEST AREA
FOR ISLAND
50'-100' FROM
SHORE

NOT A GOOD AREA
OPEN TO WIND AND
WAVE ACTION

45°

45°

LEAVE 2' SLACK

4'-6' WATER DEPTH

PREVAILING WINDS

FLOATING SIGN

LOON
NESTING
SANCTUARY
PLEASE STAY
AWAY

OVERALL DIMENSIONS
3' X 3'

ALL WOOD

FLOATLINE

LOON
NESTING
SANCTUARY

Construction and placement of loon nesting platforms. Redrawn from "An Artificial Island for Loons," North American Loon Fund, Meredith, N.H., undated.

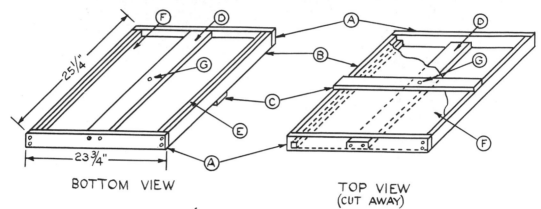

BOTTOM VIEW

TOP VIEW
(CUT AWAY)

FRAMES CUT FROM 1"X 4"X 8' NO. 3 PINE

(A) ENDS (2) ¾" x 1¾" X 23¾"
(B) SIDES (2) ¾" x 1¾" x 23¾"
(C) CENTER BRACE, TOP (1) 1¾"x ¾"x 23¾"
(D) CENTER BRACE, BOTTOM (1) ¾" x 1¾" x 23¾"
(E) STYROFOAM SUPPORT, BOTTOM (2) ¾" x ⅞" X 23¾"
(F) STYROFOAM FLOTATION PANEL (1) 1" X 22" X 23¾"
(G) ANCHOR ROPE HOLE ½" I.D.

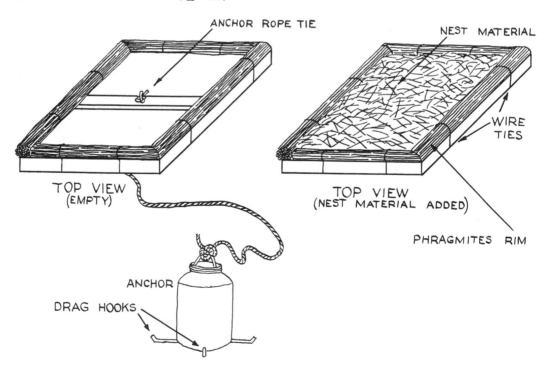

TOP VIEW
(EMPTY)

TOP VIEW
(NEST MATERIAL ADDED)

ANCHOR ROPE TIE

NEST MATERIAL

WIRE TIES

PHRAGMITES RIM

ANCHOR

DRAG HOOKS

Tern nesting platforms anchored in shallow water provide a suitable nesting habitat for the Forster's tern. Redrawn from Arlen F. Linde and Carl Gierke, "Forster's Tern Nesting Platform Study." Bureau of Research, Wisconsin Department of Natural Resources, 1980.

The platforms used in Wisconsin consisted of a frame built of $3/4 \times 13/4$ inch lumber over 1-inch-thick sheets of rugged blue waterproof Styrofoam. Bundles of phragmites wired every 6 inches to the frame formed a rim 4 inches high around the platform. The platform interiors were then filled with a layer of loose phragmites and cattail for a nesting substrate. The platforms were positioned near each other adjacent to phragmites habitat in shallow water. One-quarter-inch polypropylene cord attached each raft to an anchor made from concrete poured into used paint pails. The addition of drag hooks protruding from the base of the anchor is recommended to keep the rafts from drifting.

SOCIAL ATTRACTANTS

For colonial birds, such as terns, and many other species that nest in groups, new colonies are often slow to start, even when nest sites and food supplies are abundant. My research with terns, puffins, razorbills, and Leach's petrels on off-shore Maine islands points to the importance of somehow encouraging those first timid, pioneering colonial birds to begin nesting.

In our studies of colony formation, we have used decoys and tape recordings of breeding calls to entice birds to begin nesting on former colony sites. Using these devices, we attracted common, arctic, and roseate terns and have watched the colony grow from the 80 original pairs to over 1000 pairs in just 4 years. Likewise, we have started four colonies of Leach's petrel—robin-sized members of the albatross order—on former breeding sites on offshore Maine islands by broadcasting the underground mating calls of "established breeders" from artificial burrows. Petrels will not visit these burrow sites without recordings, but are readily attracted when they hear the loud call of established breeders.

An Arctic tern offers a small shrimp to a decoy in a courtship attempt. Decoys and tape recordings helped establish a new colonial breeding site on a former nesting island off the coast of Maine.

These studies suggest that other types of colonial birds, such as martins, barn swallows, herons, and burrowing owls, may start new colonies more readily if they are socially stimulated. Decoys and/or recorded vocalizations may help to advertise available nest sites and attract and stimulate enough birds to start new colonies.

ROOSTING SITES

At night and in extreme weather, birds must find suitable protective cover in various kinds of roosts. Cavity-nesting birds, such as woodpeckers, chickadees, and titmice, usually sleep in tree cavities. Some, such as chickadees and bluebirds, often huddle together with other members of their winter flock. Cavity-nesting birds will use nest boxes, especially if they have a minimum of cracks and other drafty openings. There is some evidence that nest boxes that are sealed by plugging drain holes and closing ventilation slots are more readily accepted as winter roosts by bluebirds than boxes that are not "winterized." Special weathertight roosting boxes designed with an entrance hole at the bottom to retain warm air and alternating perches to keep birds from "decorating" their neighbors at night may also be helpful in providing protection during extreme cold weather. Face roosting boxes toward the south to maximize direct sunlight, and position them in a location sheltered from the prevailing wind.

Birds of arid regions, such as songbirds and desert quail, are especially dependent on adequate roosts to moderate the extreme temperature changes from day to night. In such habitats, a scarcity of roost sites may severely limit bird populations, so artificial roosting trees will provide much needed protection.

In harsh climates roosting shelters may provide essential cover for birds. Weathertight roosting boxes are often used by small birds in cold northern climates (A); southern exposure should be maximized. Artificial tree roosts provide critical cover in arid regions (B). This plan for an artificial tree is redrawn from Yoakum et al., "Habitat Improvement Techniques," Wildlife Management Techniques Manual, *4th edition, 1980, S.D. Schemnitz, editor.*

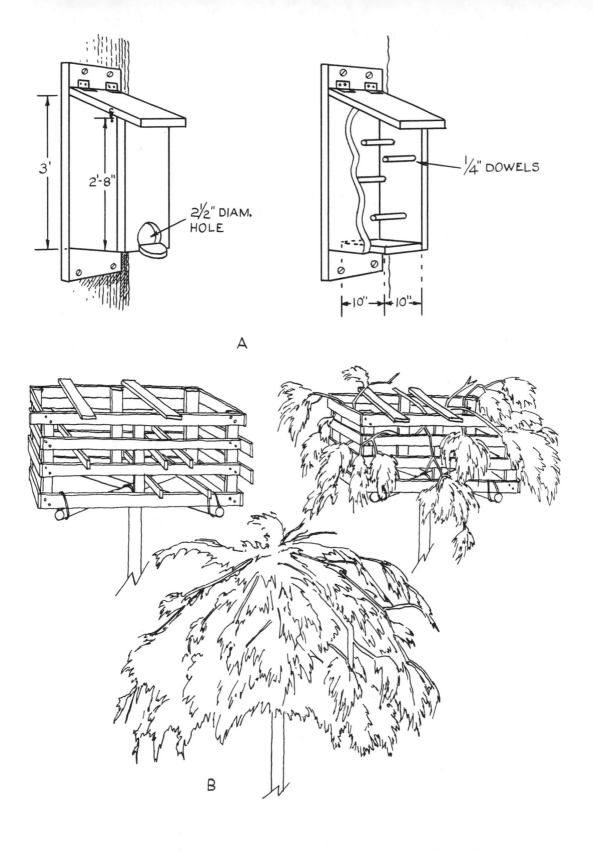

3'

2'-8"

2½" DIAM. HOLE

¼" DOWELS

10" 10"

A

B

CHAPTER V

SUPPLEMENTAL
FEEDING

A recent survey of the U.S. Fish and Wildlife Service estimates that one-third of U.S. households feed wild birds and of these, 43 percent maintain regular feeders.[1] A 1975 survey by DeGraaf and Payne estimated that most households that feed birds will use about 60 pounds of seed each year.[2] These impressive statistics account for over one-third million tons of seed dispensed annually from at least 12 million backyard feeders at an annual estimated cost of over a half billion dollars. Yet, even with such quantities of seed being fed to wild birds, the effects remain largely unknown.

Understanding the effects of feeding on bird behavior, health, population size, and other variables is usually difficult if not impossible because of the many changes that are happening at the same time. For the past several decades we have not only fed birds, but we have also seen landscapes changed by new farming practices that promote expansive plantings of single-species croplands. We have also seen pavement spread over millions of acres of prime bird habitat. Population changes must be measured by the decade, and this is seldom done.

[1]1980 National Survey of Fishing, Hunting, and Wildlife-Associated Recreation. U.S. Fish and Wildlife Service and U.S. Bureau of the Census, Washington, D.C., 154 pp.

[2]R. DeGraaf and B. Payne. "Economic Values of Non-game Birds and Some Urban Wildlife Research Needs." In *Trans. North American Wildlife and Natural Resources Conference*, vol. 40, 1975, pp. 281–287.

Within our dynamic, changing landscape, what can we say about the effects of feeding wild birds?

To put bird feeding into perspective, consider that even the most regular visitors at feeders will not feed exclusively on human handouts. Most birds are quick to use whatever foods they can find in their environment, and when they are away from feeders they continue to forage on weeds, seeds, fruits, insects, and whatever other foods they can find. Feeders provide a supplement to natural food supplies and only rarely do they comprise the bulk of a wild bird's diet. Clearly, birds have survived and thrived in North America long before the present enthusiasm for feeding birds, which dates only to the early 1950s. If all feeding were to stop overnight, there would probably be no species extinctions or even major population declines.

Plants, birds, and mammals have coadapted over thousands of years to disperse seeds and find food. Many surprising and often intricate interactions exist. For example, fruits of trees and shrubs, such as hawthorn and crabapple, attain their bright bird-attracting colors only when fruits are ripe and ready for dispersal by birds. Likewise, the same gray squirrels that may drive backyard bird watchers to distraction by consuming grain, also sometimes help wild birds by tunneling through several feet of snow to reveal and crack open otherwise unavailable bird foods, such as osage orange, walnuts, and acorns.

Wild birds depend on wild foods, which they find with remarkable efficiency. Their senses are finely tuned to recognize and consume foods as they become available. Such availability has probably been a major factor affecting the timing and direction of migration. Considering the many generations of birds that have adapted to finding the proper mixes of food, cover, and water, it seems unlikely that many wild bird populations could now be seriously dependent on the charity of bird feeders. Yet the question remains, where food is unusually concentrated in rich supplies, what effect does this have on migration, survival, and population growth?

Supplemental feeding presents certain hazards, and these should be recognized by anyone interested in feeding birds. Large feeding stations create unusually large winter flocks, and these often attract such efficient predators as hawks and cats. Also, feeders attract sick birds that can spread disease to healthy visitors at your feeders.

Supplemental feeding can also alter normal winter dispersals and detain birds from their usual migrations. Such was the case at the Horicon National Wildlife Refuge in southeastern Wisconsin where crops planted especially for Canada geese attracted increasingly large numbers until as many as 208,000 geese crowded onto the refuge rather than migrating down the Mississippi to their usual wintering grounds in Louisiana. Such numbers resulted in overcrowding and competition with other waterfowl for food and space. The crowding also created a setting for a potentially disastrous disease outbreak. After several generations of supplemental feeding, there was concern that the migratory habits of the geese would change and that the ancestral migration to Louisiana would be forgotten. Recent changes in supplemental feeding and habitat management have reduced Canada goose numbers at Horicon and encouraged them to resume their traditional migration route. Such wintering shifts may occur to small land-bird populations in response to food availability, but they are very difficult to detect.

It is likely that some species or populations benefit from supplemental feeding far more than others. For example, small birds, such as common redpolls, have body temperatures that may be over 105°F (41°C) on frigid winter nights. Even with an insulating covering of feathers, heat loss through the skin is a potentially serious problem for such small birds because of their comparatively high proportion of skin surface to small body mass. Such birds benefit from dependable supplies of high-energy food like sunflower and niger seeds.

Although heat loss may be a danger, studies of black-capped chickadees show how behavioral—both social and physiological—adaptations help them survive such conditions. When temperatures drop, chickadees respond by fluffing their well-insulated plumage and huddling together at night with flock members and mates in tree cavities or other sheltered places. Chickadees can also store food and remember places where they found a good meal at least 8 months later.

Chickadees have remarkable physiological adaptations for conserving body heat during long, winter nights. As temperatures drop to freezing, chickadees enter a torpid condition to which body temperatures may drop by 20°F (−7°C). Their breathing rate also slows as the temperature drops. When the air temperature is 88°F (31°C), chickadees breathe at a rate of approximately 95 times per minute, but when air temperature drops to −15°F (−27°C), they slow their breathing to just 65 times per minute.

Susan M. Budd, a Cornell University graduate student, found that black-capped chickadees living off a normal diet of insects and wild plant seeds put on enough fat during daylight hours to increase their body weight by an average of 7.5 percent before each long winter night. Usually this fat was depleted by morning. In contrast, chickadees that ate a diet of sunflower seeds put on an average of 11.8 percent fat. Young birds, sick birds, or others that are not as efficient at finding food are especially vulnerable to starvation.

The more we know about winter birds, the better we can appreciate how well-adapted most species are to their environments. Small birds, such as chickadees, have many adaptations for surviving the rigors of winter, but they have little in the way of reserve foods, and are usually quick to eat supplemental food supplies offered at feeders. For such species, supplemental feeding may make a life or death difference under prolonged, extremely cold weather conditions or during sudden ice storms.

Nonmigratory birds are, in general, more likely to benefit from supplemental feeding than are highly mobile species. The former comprise a second group that may find benefit from supplemental feeding program. A recent study by A. Starker Leopold and Mark F. Dedon of the University of California in Berkeley illustrates this point. While most North American mourning doves are migratory, apparently doves that live in Berkeley and several other areas in central and southern North America are not. The study reveals that in Berkeley, a developed community with no vacant lots for weed seeds and other natural foods, mourning doves are heavily dependent on bird feeders and probably could not exist in that community without supplemental feeding. In contrast to mourning doves, highly mobile, flocking species, such as evening grosbeak and American goldfinch, will quickly move on when foods run low. They can simply fly to a neighbor's feeder or leave the area entirely.

Food availability throughout the year is certainly a limiting factor for many kinds of birds. When food limits are removed, it is interesting to see how some birds respond. The extraordinary population growth of red-winged blackbirds in North America illustrates the link between food availability and population growth. Red-winged blackbirds were originally restricted to marshlands where food was scarce and competition with other birds was intense. However, the recent trend toward large farms that specialize in vast fields of corn, wheat, and other grains, along with mechanical harvesters that leave some grain behind, is likely one of the principal factors contributing to the growth of red-winged blackbird populations.

Similarly, populations of herring and great black-backed gulls in New England were also limited by scarce food at the sea edge, especially in winter. Since early this century, these gull populations have increased greatly due to the abundance and availability of newly found foods from garbage dumps, fish processing plants, and fishing boats. The response of these species to large supplemental food supplies suggests that the same effect would be working in favor of certain backyard feeder birds.

Perhaps the tons of grain consumed each year from North American feeders may temper population fluctuations resulting from poor local food supplies or harsh winters. Supplemental feeding may also help to explain the explosive range expansion of the house finch, a native of the western United States that was introduced in western Long Island, New York, in 1940. In the past 40 years, house finches have spread from New York City to the Mississippi, frequently inhabiting backyards with active feeding stations. Similarly, feeding could also help to explain the northward range extensions of southern seed-eating birds, such as cardinal, tufted titmouse, mourning dove, and red-bellied woodpecker. But the question remains, have these species leapfrogged their way north along a sunflower seed pipeline, or is their recent range expansion totally dependent on human handouts?

Range expansions following bird feeders would seem a clear-cut case, except that northern range extensions are not unique to seed-eating birds. Recently, northern mockingbird, blue-winged warbler, Louisiana water thrush, blue-gray gnatcatcher, and turkey vulture have also experienced northward range extensions.

Such expansions may result from regrowth of old fields into thickets and young forests. Another alternative explanation is that the climate of northern latitudes has slowly warmed for the past 120 years, resulting in less rigorous winters. This trend, known as the Greenhouse Effect, is likely a result of increased atmospheric carbon dioxide from burning coal and oil products. Between 1940 and 1970 there has been an average increase of 1.4°F (17°C). However, it is anyone's guess whether these are meaningful changes to bird populations. Also, warming temperatures do not help to explain why some northern birds, such as evening grosbeaks, American robin, and barn swallow, have expanded their breeding range south.

Range expansions and contractions probably result from varied causes, including changes in climate, land-use patterns, and changes in distribution of important cover or food plants. However, the recent growth of supplemental bird feeding warrants its inclusion as one of the several likely factors influencing population size and range expansion for certain, but probably not all, species that visit feeders.

Although the effects of supplemental feeding will long be a topic of debate, feeding birds is clearly a delight and an educational experience. While it is important to minimize the hazards associated with concentrating birds at feeders, we need not search too far for a rationale beyond recognizing that feeding birds is one of the best ways to introduce children and adults to the joys of watching birds. Without feeders, the elusive and highly mobile nature of wild birds makes it difficult to close the distance and glimpse their beauty.

FEEDINGS BIRDS THROUGH THE SEASONS

Spring

Early spring is an important season for feeding birds because most preferred natural foods are consumed over the winter. At this season, late snows and ice storms may bury remaining food supplies, creating conditions that can lead to starvation. Ample food and water supplies are especially attractive to migrating birds because of the great energy cost of migration; for this reason, supplemental feeding may provide important refueling stops for migrants. Resident birds that are already familiar with your feeders may help attract migrants.

It is likely that where other requirements exist, the availability of a constant supply of food and water will increase nesting populations or entice birds to breed on properties they might otherwise avoid. Where food is scarce, birds may not breed because ample food is a prerequisite for coming into the reproductive condition.

You can further increase your chances for attracting breeding birds by providing nesting materials, such as chicken feathers, hair, and short (3 to 4 inch) pieces of yarn and string. In dry seasons, muddy a patch of soil to provide nesting material for robins, swallows, and phoebes. Crushed eggshells or finely crushed oyster shells are good supplements to feed at this season, as the calcium requirements for females are very high just prior to egg laying. Early spring is also the season to position new nest boxes, clean out old ones, and plant bird-attracting trees, shrubs, and vines.

Nesting materials such as string, yarn, and chicken feathers are often used for nest building by northern orioles and similar birds. String and yarn should be only 3–4 inches long to prevent the birds from becoming accidentally entangled.

Summer

Summer is the season of greatest natural food abundance. Insect populations are at their highest and many tree, shrub, and vine fruits are available. But it is also the period of greatest food needs, as parent birds must provide food for themselves and their young. The rapid growth rates of young birds necessitate high-protein diets. For this reason, most birds (even seed-eating specialists) feed their growing young a diet consisting almost exclusively of insects.

In his excellent book, *Songbirds in Your Garden,* John K. Terres lists 33 species of insect- and seed-eating birds that readily consumed his mixture of peanut butter (one part), cornmeal (four parts), flour (one part), and vegetable shortening (one part). Using this mixture in the summer, he attracted a surprising variety of such birds as tanagers, thrushes, and warblers that usually eat insects. This is a better mixture to use in the summer than suet-based mixes or raw suet, as suet will turn rancid at summer temperatures and may mat facial and breast feathers, possibly resulting in infection of facial skin, poor insulation, and waterproofing. Such nonsuet mixtures are readily eaten by parent birds, which sometimes feed them to their young and later bring young to the feeders. Place the mixture in hanging food logs, cupcake baking trays, or suet feeders (see the section on feeder design later in this chapter).

Another way to attract insect-eating birds is to offer mealworm larvae. Mealworms are inch-long, hard-shelled larvae of darkling beetles. Mealworm larvae are readily eaten by cardinals, towhees, sparrows, and many kinds of insect-eating birds. Place the mealworm larvae in either a shallow glass or smooth, metal-walled container on a feeding table or offer the mealworms by hand. When mealworms are tossed onto the ground, wild birds will soon overcome their fear of humans and approach for a handout.

Insect-eating birds such as this rufous-sided towhee are attracted to mealworm larvae when offered in a shallow, smooth-walled tray.

Halved grapefruit and oranges conspicuously displayed are an excellent way to attract fruit-eating birds such as this red-crowned woodpecker.

Mealworms are easily cultured by placing breeding stock in an aquarium, shoebox, masonry jar, or other smooth-walled container. For mass production, use a 55-gallon steel drum. Fill the container half full of bran mixed with bread crumbs, cornmeal, farina, or crushed crackers. Then for moisture, place a few thin slices of apple on the surface and cover the grain and apple with several layers of newspaper. After several months, replenish the mixture by adding another layer of bran mixture, more apple slices, and newspaper. Be sure to cover the container with a tight-fitting but well-ventilated cover, such as window screening, to keep the flying adults and larvae in the container. Mealworms are available from Rainbow Mealworms, 126 E. Spruce St., P.O. Box 4907, Compton, CA 90224.

Summer feeding stations can attract fruit- and nectar-eating birds in addition to seed- and insect-eating species. Tanagers, orioles, and certain woodpeckers are sometimes attracted by an offering of fruit. Overripe citrus fruits and bananas are favorites. Cut fruit open to display the interiors and place them on feeding tables or on spikes.

Summer is also the season for feeding hummingbirds and other nectar-eating birds. As described earlier (see Chapter I), the best way to attract hummingbirds to your yard is to provide abundant orange and red tubular flowers from late spring to early fall. Hummingbirds not only feed on nectar from such blooms, but also eat insects and small spiders that they find in the flowers. Supplemental feeding of hummingbirds may be useful to hold birds in your yard until flowers bloom or as a lure to entice the hummers into better viewing areas.

Artificial sugar solutions are not complete diets, and care must be taken to keep hummingbird feeders clean of fungus that might grow in them. To avoid this problem, clean feeders every 2 or 3 days under hot running tap water, taking care to scrub carefully with a bottlebrush. Although honey is more nutritious than granular sugar, when it is mixed with water, it ferments faster in the sun than sugar water, and rapidly cultures mold that can kill hummingbirds. For this reason, honey/water mixtures are not recommended as hummingbird food.

Mixtures of water and granular white or brown sugar are the best food for hummingbirds, as they offer less risk from fermentation and mold. However, there is some danger that mixtures with more than 1 part sugar to 4 parts water can harm hummingbirds by enlarging their livers. Although sugar/water mixtures do not ferment as rapidly as honey/water mixes, feeders should be cleaned and refilled after several days. To prepare a sugar/water solution, mix sugar and water together in equal (1:1) proportion, and then boil the mixture to retard fermentation and dissolve all sugar. Then dilute to 1 part sugar and 4 parts water by adding cold water. Store the unused quantity in a refrigerator.

Use 1 part sugar to 4 parts water when first attracting hummingbirds, but decrease the proportion of sugar to 1 part sugar to 6 parts water after hummers learn the location of your feeders. This minimizes the dangers of liver damage and encourages the birds to feed more on natural foods. To help attract hummingbirds to new feeders, paint the feeding tube with red enamel or mount red plastic flowers over the feeder entrance. Although red-colored sugar water is not necessary to attract hummers, five drops of red food coloring added to each quart of sugar water will help you see the level of sugar water remaining in feeders from a distance.

Sometimes ants, bees, and wasps drink more sugar water than hummingbirds. When this happens, you can discourage ants by hanging feeders on thin monofilament fishing line. Larger bees and wasps may be deterred by coating the feeding portals with salad oil.

Worldwide, about 1600 species of birds (20 percent of all living birds) eat nectar. Most of these live in the tropics where flowers bloom year-round. In North America sugar water feeders will attract at least 53 bird species. The sugar solution described above is readily eaten by orioles, mockingbirds, grosbeaks, tanagers, and several warblers (see feeding tables later in this chapter). Feeders of various sizes, separated in different locations, will help to minimize competition. Many commercial hummingbird feeders are available (see Appendix D), but simple homemade feeders are easy to make. A mouse or hamster watering bottle, available at most pet stores, makes a good oriole feeder.

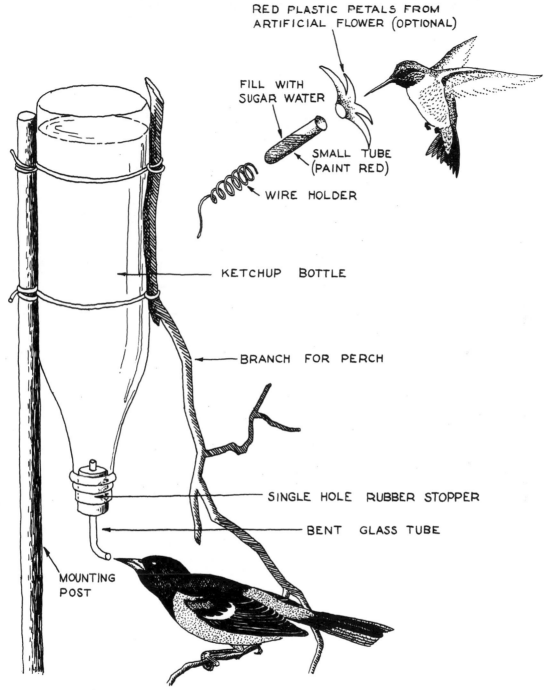

RED PLASTIC PETALS FROM
ARTIFICIAL FLOWER (OPTIONAL)

FILL WITH
SUGAR WATER

SMALL TUBE
(PAINT RED)

WIRE HOLDER

KETCHUP BOTTLE

BRANCH FOR PERCH

SINGLE HOLE RUBBER STOPPER

BENT GLASS TUBE

MOUNTING
POST

A homemade sugar water dispenser, here made out of a ketchup bottle, attracts hummingbirds and larger perching birds such as orioles. The proportion of sugar to water must be carefully measured and adequate cleaning measures maintained to ensure the health of feeding birds.

Fall

Although natural foods such as insects and fruit are especially abundant in the fall, this is also a season of great food demand, as bird populations are at their highest levels from the new crop of fledglings. There is also great need for migrants to put on enough fat for migration. Oil-rich seeds, such as sunflower and niger seeds, are readily eaten at this season as birds build up fat reserves in preparation for long migrations. Some migrants, such as white-crowned sparrow, increase their body weight by as much as 40 percent before starting their southern migration. En route to their winter habitat, they can rebuild such fat deposits in only 3 to 5 days if they stop over in an area with a rich food supply. Late summer and early fall are also seasons for replacing flight and body feathers. During this season, most birds replace all of their feathers (several thousand), and this requires great quantities of food.

Surviving the first year of life is a major accomplishment for most birds. In many species, it is normal for 80 percent of the young birds to die in their first year. This heavy toll comes from a variety of causes, including predation, accidents, weather, and poor navigation, but certainly high on the list must be the bird's success in finding food. The transition from dependence to independence happens in only a few days for most songbirds. Supplemental feeding in the fall could make a difference for some young birds that otherwise would not build up enough fat for migration.

By feeding birds in early fall, you are more likely to attract and hold fall migrants. In the northeast, for example, fall feeding (September to October) may entice short-distance migrants, such as white-throated sparrow and rufous-sided towhee, to spend winter in your yard rather than wintering farther south. Also, many species have a postbreeding dispersal in which adults and young scatter from their breeding areas. Frequently, such early-fall dispersals result in northward movements. Where southern seed-eating birds, such as cardinal and tufted titmouse, find abundant food supplies, they are likely to stay for the winter, acting as pioneers to further expand the species' range. If you wait until the first snows cover your feeders to begin your feeding effort, you'll likely miss these interesting additions to your backyard bird list.

Early fall is the best time of year to plant balled and burlapped or container-grown evergreens. It is also a good season to put up roosting boxes for wintering birds (see the final section in Chapter IV).

Winter

Winter, with its cold temperatures, sharp winds, lack of deciduous cover and long nights is by far the most difficult season for many birds of the northern latitudes. Such rigors probably help to define the distance and timing for the many migratory species that vacate northern climates in the winter. Natural foods decline in abundance from the onset of the first killing frost until the burst of spring growth.

In addition, already sparse food supplies may be completely unavailable under deep snows or layers of ice. These are the circumstances when supplemental feeding probably has its greatest value to wild birds. To be most useful, seed and suet supplies should be available at dawn and dusk, the two greatest periods of bird foraging. After a long night at subfreezing temperatures, bird activity at feeders is greatest in early morning, decreases greatly during midafternoon, and increases again from late afternoon until dusk.

Beef kidney suet provides a rich supply of fat and is readily eaten by at least 80 species of North American birds, including many insect-eating species, such as woodpeckers, chickadees, titmice, wrens, orioles, shrikes, thrushes, and warblers. It is difficult to explain exactly why suet has such broad appeal since it looks so unlike most foods eaten by these birds. Although chickadees and some other suet eaters are known to pick fat from deer carcasses and thus may have experience with this useful food, it seems more likely that the white, greasy, and stringy consistency of suet looks and may taste something like the fatty bodies of overwintering insect eggs and pupae. These are normally gleaned with great difficulty from tree bark and leaf litter. What a bonanza a chunk of suet must seem to a chickadee accustomed to tediously searching for tiny insect eggs.

Feed suet to birds whole or melt and resolidify it for a more workable form. Melt suet by first chopping it into small pieces, and then cook the pieces very slowly in a large pot or double boiler. The browned pieces can then be chopped to a fine mix in a food processor or blender, and then returned to the pot for melting. Melting suet does not change its nutritional value.

To increase the variety of birds that will feed on suet, mix it with such ingredients as cornmeal, shortening, bacon grease, and peanut butter until the mixture is the consistency of bread dough. Hang raw suet in mesh onion bags or offer it in hardware cloth feeders. Suet mixtures are best offered in hanging food sticks, pressed into the crevices of large pine cones, or in cupcake baking tins.

Mixing suet and seed is counterproductive because it attracts both seed and suet eaters to the same feeder, rather than offering the food separately at nearby locations to avoid competition and crowding. Seed-eating birds will peck through the mixture for preferred seeds, wasting most other ingredients. It is also likely that greasy seeds extracted from suet balls are harder to crack open than dry seed. See the final section of this chapter for suet feeder designs.

Winter is also a good time to put out food for fruit-eating songbirds, such as northern mockingbird and eastern bluebird. If you see these birds near your feeder, sprinkle a few raisins on a conspicuous surface such as a flat rock or on a table feeder. Dried or frozen fruits such as grapes and cherries are very useful for attracting winter birds, such as robins, mockingbirds, and waxwings, that would not otherwise visit your feeders.

If there is little shelter near bird feeders, you can provide good cover by tying several old Christmas trees together and securing this bundle close to the feeder. Empty birdhouses and special overnight roosting boxes (see final section of Chapter IV) can provide additional shelter from extremely low temperatures and also afford protection from such nocturnal predators as cats and raccoons that sometimes prey on sleeping songbirds.

In northern latitudes open water may be unavailable for several months. Most northern birds can survive by obtaining moisture from their food and from eating snow and ice, but even hardy northern species will drink and bathe in open water at birdbaths when it is available. See Chapter III for details on keeping water supplies open.

SETTING UP A FEEDING STATION

Variety is the most important consideration when setting up a new bird feeding station. Since bird species have different preferences, the best way to attract a variety is to offer as varied a choice as possible. Place several kinds of feeders at different heights above the ground, and different distances from human activity and the nearest cover. Provide millet and cracked corn on the ground for sparrows, doves, and quail; sunflower seeds, mixed grain, and fruit at tabletop level for cardinals, grosbeak, and finches; and suet feeders on tree trunks or hanging from tree limbs for woodpeckers and chickadees.

By providing different foods—suet, grain, dried fruit, and fresh fruit—from different feeders, you can also reduce the competition that occurs when food is offered only at one large feeder. Although chickadees and titmice are so fearless they will take seed from feeders mounted directly on windows (or, with patience, even from your hand), house sparrows will not usually come as close. Another value of multiple feeders is that you can specialize for more selective feeding. Feeders designed to exclude certain birds because of size or feeding behavior can help to make more expensive grains available only to preferred species.

Commercial seed mixtures are a wasteful way to feed birds. Mixtures containing sunflower seeds are often largely wasted, as the many birds with an appetite for sunflower seeds will pick and scratch through most other seeds, discarding them onto the ground where they will be lost or left to rot. Another reason for avoiding mixes is that birds that eat sunflower seeds generally prefer to eat from hanging feeders, while the species that prefer millet and cracked corn prefer to feed at table and ground feeders. Separate feeders for different kinds of grain will reduce competition at feeders and avoid unnecessary loss of grain.

Another good way to reduce congestion at feeders is to provide a convenience perch for birds that are waiting in line. This simply consists of a branch or sapling near a feeder. Birds will readily perch on exposed branches and fly to the feeder of their choice as space becomes available.

CONVENIENCE PERCH
ATTACHED TO SIDE
OF FEEDER.

A convenience perch attached to a feeder reduces congestion and provides a ready place for chickadees and titmice to crack open seeds.

When selecting the locations for your feeders, choose sites with good visibility from your house and, if possible, with southern exposure. This will keep strong northern winds from blowing grain from feeders and will provide a somewhat warmer, more protected area for birds to congregate. Also try to locate feeders within about 20 feet of nearby shrubs or thicket cover. This gives birds a ready place to escape if they are attacked by hawks or cats. But dense cover within a few feet of feeders is sometimes a hazard, as it gives cats a place to hide before pouncing on feeding birds.

Expectations

The speed with which your feeding station is discovered and visited by birds depends not only on the location and visibility of the feeder, but on the kinds of birds in your vicinity and the sizes of the populations. In general, forested habitats have fewer birds than shrubby edge habitats and, therefore, it may take longer for birds to discover feeders in wooded areas. Similarly, urban habitats may have fewer birds than suburban or rural habitats, but even feeders placed outside windows in tall apartment buildings have a chance of attracting sparrows and the occasional migrating goldfinch.

The variety of birds that will come to feeders also depends on ranges. The farther north you live, the fewer species nest and winter in your area. However, those birds that do winter in northern habitats are generalist feeders and are usually especially quick to visit feeders.

If you have chickadees in your neighborhood, they will probably be the first to discover new bird feeders, as these inquisitive, active birds are constantly searching for food. They are usually joined by a variety of other species, such as nuthatches, titmice, and woodpeckers, forming a mixed winter flock. Chickadees not only lead the way for other species, but banding studies have shown that they also remember feeder locations for months, if not years.

The numbers of birds and frequency with which they visit feeders are also related to the amount of feeding in your neighborhood. If you are the only one feeding, you are likely to have more birds at your feeders.

Thus you can see that it may take from a few minutes to several months before birds start visiting your feeders. To attract birds more quickly to new feeding stations, scatter grain on the ground or on top of roofed feeders. A simple table feeder set in an open site is the most conspicuous for displaying foods. After birds become accustomed to visiting a table feeder, replace it with a hopper feeder or other weatherproof feeder to reduce exposure of food to rain and snow.

Feeding Continuity

One of the most commonly repeated rules for operating a feeding station is, "Once you start, keep the food coming." This idea rests on the thought that birds become dependent on a feeding area in the winter and will starve to death if the food supply were to disappear in midwinter, when needs are greatest. This adage is probably valid at isolated locations where feeding stations are few and where feeders provide large amounts of food from early fall into the winter. These stations might detain migrants in the fall and concentrate them in unusually large numbers, making birds vulnerable to food shortages caused by heavy snows. In reality, however, this situation is probably rare.

More commonly, feeder birds do not depend on either single food supplies or solely on food that they find at feeders. Most birds feed in mixed-species flocks that forage over at least several acres in the winter. Within this area they have a pattern of feeding that may include many different backyards. Dan Gray, a Cornell University Ph.D. candidate, has followed winter flocks of color-banded black-capped chickadees from feeder to feeder, following what he calls a "trapline," regularly searching in places where they previously found food. If a feeder was empty, he observed that chickadees simply moved on to the next likely feeding site and that they could remember places up to 8 months later where they were successful. Other winter feeder birds may feed in similar ways.

Certainly, in nature there is no such thing as a cornucopia sunflower plant that never runs out of seed. Birds are so mobile and aware of the presence of others of their species that they probably have little trouble finding food if one feeder in a neighborhood of many feeding stations suddenly dries up. Food storing by chickadees, titmice, nuthatches, jays, and many other birds that winter in northern habitats is another effective adaptation for surviving temporary food shortages.

One good reason to keep your feeders full is that once you stop, it may be difficult to attract a variety and number of birds later in the winter if birds have learned to feed elsewhere. But if you live in a neighborhood where there are other feeders, a stop in feeding for a few days in midwinter is unlikely to cause death for backyard feeder birds.

FEEDING SEED TO WILD BIRDS

Seeds are the preferred foods of vegetarian birds because they contain concentrated nourishment and are often available for extended periods when other foods may be difficult to find. Birds have strong preferences for certain types of seeds because of differences in nutritional quality, taste, availability, and ease of opening.

Opening Seeds

Small birds with seed-cracking beaks, varying from the tiny beak of the siskin to the massive beaks of the grosbeaks, use subtle movements of their mandibles to first crush and then open seeds.

Small birds, such as finches, open seeds by rolling the seed back and forth over a projection on the lower mandible while the seed balances in a ridge in the upper mandible. The sharp mandible edges, powered by strong jaw muscles, apply crushing pressure until the seed coat opens. Then lateral movements of the mandibles separate the seed from the coat, dropping the seed contents into the mouth and expelling the seed coat onto the ground. This all happens in a split second, and the great piles of sunflower hulls under feeders are testimony to the efficiency of the technique.

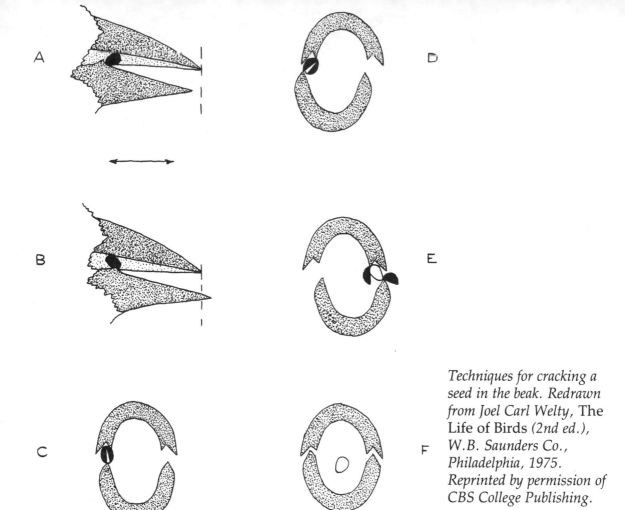

Techniques for cracking a seed in the beak. Redrawn from Joel Carl Welty, The Life of Birds *(2nd ed.), W.B. Saunders Co., Philadelphia, 1975. Reprinted by permission of CBS College Publishing.*

Seed-eating birds that do not have crushing beaks (i.e., chickadees, nuthatches, titmice) are usually also insect eaters and must therefore use other techniques for cracking seeds. These birds usually place the seed in a bark crevice (nuthatches) or hold it in their feet (titmice and chickadees) and pound away until they break through the seed coat.

Grit

Once seed-eating birds break through outer protective shells, the seeds are broken into digestible form by the muscular gizzard. Birds, such as wild turkey, are especially impressive because they can crush whole hickory nuts and acorns in their gizzards. Small seed-eating birds also grind and crush seeds in their muscular, gravel-packed gizzards and require a supply of tiny gravel or grit throughout the year for this purpose.

Birds can usually find plenty of grit along gravel roadsides and other sandy places. Winter is probably the only season when grit is scarce, as snow may cover most supplies. At this season birds often feed along roadsides searching for seeds and gravel, and infrequently they become casualties to passing cars as a result.

You can reduce this hazard by mixing 5 to 10 pounds of grit to every 100 pounds of bird seed mixture. Beach sand or similar-sized quartz sand mixed with ground oyster shell is the ideal grit mixture. Hard quartz sand gives excellent abrasion for grinding seed and the crushed oyster shell (available from poultry feed suppliers) provides calcium, a mineral that is often deficient in northern soils. Calcium is especially important in the spring, as the female needs a great deal of calcium in order to produce adequate eggshells. Eggshells from chicken eggs are an excellent calcium source. They are most readily eaten when crushed and mixed with grain.

FOOD PREFERENCES

Birds show definite, predictable preferences for certain foods. Their choices are certainly influenced by both abundance and availability, but when given choices of equally abundant, available foods, it is interesting to see what different species will select. In general, more nutritious or energy-rich foods are quickly selected over less sustaining options. Although most birds are generally thought to have a poorly developed sense of taste compared to mammals, most feeder birds probably first detect differences between foods by tasting various samples. Later they probably make their choices by noting subtle differences in color, size, and texture and other visual cues.

Foods that are high in fat and protein are especially preferred by most wild birds. The high fat and protein content of sunflower seeds probably explains why this favorite is in a class of its own as the preferred seed choice of most feeder birds. Sweet foods, such as sugar water, provide a ready source of fructose and sucrose, forms of sugar that provide quick energy. After consumption, these sugars break down into glucose, which readily provides calories for maintaining high body temperatures and levels of activity. The high demand for sugar is apparent from the fact that the average concentration of glucose in bird blood is about twice that found in mammalian blood. The need for fat and sugar helps to explain why some unlikely foods such as doughnuts are a special favorite of many birds. This sweetened, deep-fried bread dough provides a ready source of carbohydrate, fat, and sugar. In general, birds eat foods that will give them the greatest amount of energy for the least expenditure of effort.

Seed Preferences

While sunflower seed, millet, and fine cracked corn are highly preferred seeds for attracting birds, there are at least a dozen other grains that find their way into the commercial bird seed trade. Some, such as milo, wheat, oats, and rice, are well known as human foods, but studies of bird stomach contents confirm that

SEED PREFERENCES OF SOME COMMON FEEDER BIRDS

	Mourning Dove (P)	Red-Bellied Woodpecker (S)	Blue Jay (S)	Carolina Chickadee (S)	Tufted Titmouse (S)	Starling (S)	Cardinal (S)	Evening Grosbeak (S)	Tree Sparrow (P)	White-Throated Sparrow (P)	White-Crowned Sparrow (S)	Song Sparrow (S)	Dark-Eyed Junco (P)	Common Grackle (P)	Brown-Headed Cowbird (P)	Purple Finch (S)	House Finch (S)	American Goldfinch (S)	House Sparrow (P)
Buckwheat	2	—	—	—	—	—	1	—	—	—	—	—	—	—	1	—	—	—	1
Canary Seed	3	0	0	1	0	—	0	0	1	2	1	1	2	—	2	1	1	1	2
Cracked Corn Fine	2	—	—	0	—	—	1	—	2	2	—	1	2	3+	1	—	—	—	2
Coarse	2	—	—	—	—	—	—	—	—	—	—	—	—	3+	1	—	—	—	1
Flax Seed	1	—	0	—	—	—	0	0	—	0	—	—	—	—	—	—	—	—	0
Millets German	3	—	0	—	—	—	1	—	—	—	—	—	—	—	3	—	—	—	3
White Proso	3	1	1	1	1	2	2	1	3	3	3	3	3+	2	3+	2	1	1	3+
Red Proso	3	0	1	0	1	1	1	0	3+	3	3	3	3	2	3	2	0	1	2
Japanese	—	—	—	0	—	—	0	—	1	1	—	—	1	—	—	—	0	—	1
Milo (Grain Sorghum)	2	—	1	1	0	1	1	1	0	2	—	—	—	—	1	—	1	—	1
Oats Hulled	2	—	—	—	—	3+	1	—	—	2	—	—	1	—	2	—	1	0	1

3+ = 100 percent more attractive than the standard seed or very highly preferred.
3 = more than 50 percent as attractive as the standard seed.
2 = 15–50 percent as attractive as the standard grain.
1 = less than 15 percent as attractive as the standard grain.
0 = ignored
— = not tested

SEED PREFERENCES OF SOME COMMON FEEDER BIRDS

	Mourning Dove (P)	Red-Bellied Woodpecker (S)	Blue Jay (S)	Carolina Chickadee (S)	Tufted Titmouse (S)	Starling (S)	Cardinal (S)	Evening Grosbeak (S)	Tree Sparrow (P)	White-Throated Sparrow (P)	White-Crowned Sparrow (S)	Song Sparrow (S)	Dark-Eyed Junco (P)	Common Grackle (P)	Brown-Headed Cowbird (P)	Purple Finch (S)	House Finch (S)	American Goldfinch (S)	House Sparrow (P)
Whole	—	—	—	—	—	1	0	—	—	—	—	—	—	—	—	—	0	0	—
Peanuts:																			
Hearts	1	—	1	2	—	3+	1	0	—	1	1	—	1	—	1	0	1	1	0
Kernels	1	—	3+	2	3+	—	1	1	—	3+	—	—	—	—	1	—	1	0	1
Rape Seed	0	—	0	—	0	—	0	0	0	0	—	—	—	—	0	0	0	0	0
Rice	1	—	1	0	—	1	0	—	1	1	—	—	1	—	1	—	0	1	1
Sunflower Seeds																			
Black-Striped	2	3	3	3	3	1	3	3	1	3	3	1	2	—	1	3	3	3	2
Gray-Striped	—	—	3	2	3	—	3	3+	—	—	—	—	—	—	1	3	2	2	—
Hulled	2	—	1	3	0	—	2	—	—	—	—	—	—	—	1	—	3+	3+	2
Oil-Type	3+	1	2	3+	3	—	3+	3+	—	3	3	2	2	3	1	3+	3+	3+	2
Wheat																			
New	—	—	0	—	—	—	1	0	—	—	—	—	—	—	—	—	—	—	—
Old	2	—	1	1	—	—	1	0	—	2	—	—	—	—	1	—	1	0	2
Niger Seed	2	0	0	1	0	0	1	1	0	1	1	1	2	—	1	2	2	3+	1

(S) = Compared to black-striped sunflower seed.
(P) = Compared to white proso millet.

Adapted from Aelred D. Geis, "Relative Attractiveness of Different Foods at Wild Bird Feeders." Special Scientific Report—Wildlife No. 233, U.S. Fish and Wildlife Service, Washington, D.C., 1980, 11 pp.

these grains are also readily eaten by a wide variety of wild birds. It would seem, therefore, that they would be logical additions to bird seed mixtures, especially since they are grown in enormous quantity and prices are often low because of surplus stocks.

Recently, Dr. Aelred D. Geis of the U.S. Fish and Wildlife Service, conducted a detailed, comparative study of the food preferences of 19 common feeder birds of the northeastern United States for 23 different kinds and forms of bird seed.[3] These findings were later substantiated by follow-up studies conducted in Maine, Ohio, and California.[4] By offering food from identical feeders and rotating these in a random way, he compared various seeds to black-striped sunflower and white proso millet to determine preferences. This carefully performed study confirmed what many have long noticed. Some common grains in bird seed mixtures are rarely eaten and are so unappealing that they are usually discarded. His studies have also shown that even superfoods, such as sunflower seed, will not attract all desirable species. In fact, two of the most useful foods, cracked corn and white millet, are rejected by many of the most desirable species.

Among the least desirable seeds are the common cereal grains: milo, wheat, oats, and rice. Although many birds will glean these grains from cultivated fields where they have few other choices, these seeds are soundly rejected when offered at bird feeders.

Undesirable bird seed mixes are often easy to identify because of the distinctive reddish color of milo (grain sorghum). Even at a glance, the largely reddish background color of certain low-priced mixes is evidence of a large proportion of milo. Milo is generally less expensive because it is grown in large quantities for other agricultural markets. In contrast, blends with a light yellow color consist primarily of fine cracked corn and white millet, two of the most popular grains. When prices for sunflower, white millet, and other preferred seeds increase, certain bird seed blends, especially low-priced grocery store mixes, become increasingly loaded with milo, oats, and other commercial grains that have little value as wild bird foods.

Dr. Geis's study also shows promise for selectively attracting desired species over such nuisance birds as starlings. For example, while most feeder birds will not eat milo and hulled oats, these are two of the favorite foods of starlings. Similarly, wheat is a favorite food of the brown-headed cowbird and house sparrow, but few other birds prefer this grain.

[3]Aelred D. Geis. "Relative Attractiveness of Different Foods at Wild Bird Feeders." Special Scientific Report—Wildlife No. 233, U.S. Fish and Wildlife Service, Washington, D.C., 1980, 11 pp.

[4]Aelred D. Geis. "Results of Nation-Wide Tests of Wild Bird Feeding Preferences." Unpublished summary report, U.S. Fish and Wildlife Service, Washington, D.C., 1983, 16 pp.

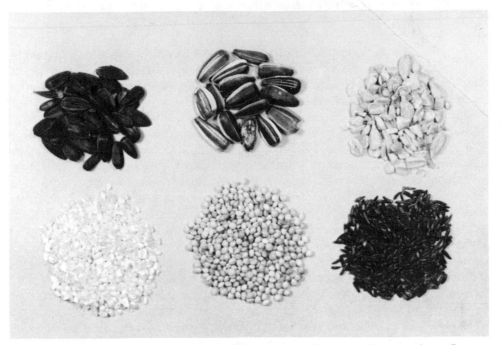

Preferred bird seeds: top row, left to right—oil sunflower seed, striped sunflower seed, hulled sunflower seed (kernels); bottom row, left to right—fine cracked corn, white proso millet, and niger seed ("thistle").

PREFERRED SEEDS

SUNFLOWER SEED
Helianthus annuus

Sunflower seeds are the favorite seed of chickadees, evening grosbeaks, tufted titmice, blue jays, American goldfinches, house finches, purple finches, and cardinals. As long as sunflower seed is available, these birds will eat little else at feeders. Sunflower seed is also readily eaten by at least another 40 species, including wild turkey, nuthatches, scrub jay, black-headed grosbeak, and downy and hairy woodpeckers. Sunflower seeds may have such broad appeal because they have higher proportions of fat and protein than other common grains, such as Japanese millet, proso millet, milo, cracked corn, and oats.

Sunflower seed specialists are so eager to get their favorite food that it is best to offer pure sunflower seed in separate feeders to prevent sunflower-seed-eating birds from spilling large quantities of blended grain while they search through less-preferred seed. In contrast, most true sparrows and mourning doves rarely eat sunflower seed, even when it is hulled.

For years the black-striped sunflower seed (confectioner's sunflower) was the only type sold for bird seed. Then, in about 1975, an especially large crop of the smaller, black oilseed found its way to the bird seed market. Previously, this high-oil-content seed was grown only for production of sunflower seed oil. Studies by Dr. Geis and the Cornell Laboratory of Ornithology have demonstrated that certain birds greatly prefer the smaller oilseed over the larger striped seed. For example, in Dr. Geis's study, chickadees found the oilseeds 3.5 times as attractive as the larger striped sunflower seeds. In addition, evening grosbeak, American goldfinch, house finch, and purple finch also showed strong preference for the oilseeds. Only tufted titmouse, common grackle, and blue jay selected the striped seed over oilseed. Perhaps birds prefer the oilseed because it has a comparatively thinner hull that is easier to remove. It is also smaller and easier to manipulate by small birds and has more oil for its weight than the striped seed.

Sometimes seed companies stock the extra large gray-striped sunflower seeds. These imported African seeds have no advantage over black-striped sunflower seeds and are not nearly as attractive as the small, all-black oilseed.

Hulled sunflower seeds (broken and whole kernels) are by far the most attractive food for American goldfinch—even more attractive than the expensive imported niger seed. The manageable size of the hulled kernels makes them more attractive to white-throated sparrows, but most other birds do not favor them over the seed with its hull. As with shelled grains, hulled sunflower seed is more vulnerable to deterioration in the weather than is the unhulled seed, but since the seed is so attractive, birds generally do not give it a chance to spoil. Hulled sunflower seed is an excellent choice for those wishing to avoid the accumulation of sunflower hulls under their feeder.

Over 70 percent of the 300 million pounds of sunflower seed grown in the United States comes from North Dakota. Minnesota, South Dakota, and Texas are also important sunflower producing states.

PROSO MILLET
Panicum miliaceum

There are two color types of proso millet—white and red. Although both red and white proso millet are readily eaten, most species preferred white proso millet in Dr. Geis's study. It is especially favored by ground-feeding birds, such as sparrows and mourning doves. The following species are listed in order of their preference for this useful and inexpensive grain: tree sparrow, song sparrow, brown-headed cowbird, dark-eyed junco, house sparrow, mourning dove, and white-throated sparrow.

Red proso millet looks much like white millet except for color. As with white millet, it is readily eaten, but it is not as attractive to most birds. In addition to sparrows and doves, proso millet is also eagerly eaten by northern bobwhite, painted bunting, dickcissel, rufous-sided towhee, and several species of waterfowl, including mallard, redhead, shoveler, American widgeon, and green-winged teal.

In 1979 about 2 million acres of millet were planted in North Dakota, South Dakota, and Colorado. This planting produced about 4 billion pounds of grain. In addition to wild bird feed, millet is used for cattle and poultry feed and cereals for human consumption.

A distinct advantage of proso millet as a bird food is that its hard seed coat resists swelling and rotting and, therefore, it may be dispensed from hopper feeders without concern that it will readily clog feeders.

CORN
Zea mays

Whole grain corn kernels, either on or off the cob, are favorite foods of several medium-sized feeder birds, such as mourning dove, blue jay, common grackle, and red-bellied woodpeckers. Whole grain corn is much more readily eaten by larger ground-feeding birds, such as quail, pheasant, and wild turkey, which have powerful gizzards capable of cracking the kernels. Whole corn is a favorite food of at least 16 species of ducks, geese, crows, and sandhill cranes. Whole grain is much more resistant to weather deterioration than cracked corn, but the large kernel size and tough seed coat discourage most smaller birds.

Whole grain corn, with its large kernel and resilient seed coat, is a favorite food of red-bellied woodpeckers and other medium to large birds. Display whole corn in conspicuous places by mounting it on sharp spikes.

Cracked corn is much more readily consumed by smaller birds, but it deteriorates relatively quickly in wet weather. Fine cracked corn is eaten by white-throated sparrows, dark-eyed juncos, cardinals, mourning doves, tree sparrows, and other desirable feeder birds, but it is also a favorite food of squirrels, house sparrows, and blackbirds. Finely cracked corn (also called chick corn) is eaten by more species than coarse cracked corn. Cracked and whole corn make inexpensive feeds for luring squirrels, house sparrows, and blackbirds away from feeders offering more expensive, preferred foods, such as sunflower seed, white millet, and niger seed. Cracked corn is best offered on table feeders or the ground. Because it is soft and water absorbent, it is not a useful grain for dispensing from hanging hopper feeders, as it easily molds and cakes, resulting in clogged feeders.

NIGER (THISTLE) SEED
Guizotia abyssinica

Sometimes known as "thistle" seed, this is an imported seed from the hot tropical environments of India, Nigeria, and Ethiopia. It is not even closely related to the familiar prickly thistles of pastures and roadsides, and will not become a nuisance in gardens. Niger seed is an excellent, though very expensive, food for finches. American goldfinches consume thistle seed almost as readily as they eat sunflower seed. Purple finch, house finch, redpoll, pine siskin, mourning doves, song sparrow, white-throated sparrow, and dark-eyed junco also readily consume the tiny black seeds. Special "niger" feeders with tiny holes help reduce spillage and competition from "nonfinches" whose beaks are too large to extract seeds from the tiny holes. House sparrows, however, will sometimes enlarge "niger" feeder holes by nibbling at plastic and in this way they may gain access to seed. Especially constructed niger mesh bags are not as selective as tube feeders and often spill substantial amounts of seed.

OTHER SEEDS

BUCKWHEAT
Fagopyrum sagittatum

Buckwheat is an occasional additive to low-priced bird foods. As with wheat and oats, wild birds often glean it from cultivated cropland and it is known from the stomachs of at least 21 different wild birds. Among these it is most readily eaten by game birds, such as ring-necked pheasant and greater prairie chicken. However, when it is placed on the feeding table with highly preferred foods, such as white proso millet and cracked corn, it is almost always ignored. In Dr. Geis's study, brown-headed cowbird and mourning doves showed some interest in buckwheat, but even these were much more readily attracted to white millet.

A niger ("thistle") feeder houses this imported tiny black seed, a favorite food of the common redpoll and other small-beaked winter finches.

CANARY SEED
Phalaris canariensis

Canary seed is an annual, introduced grass whose seeds are a common addition to bird seed mixtures. The seed is eaten by most of the species that eat white millet, such as mourning doves, dark-eyed junco, rufous-sided towhee, and most sparrows, but comparative studies show that most of these birds prefer proso millet over canary seed. Since canary seed may be as much as 70 percent more expensive, it does not pay to offer it at feeders.

GERMAN MILLET
Setaria italica

Also known as foxtail or golden millet, German millet is not nearly as attractive to feeder birds as white proso millet. At feeders, it is eaten mainly by white-throated and white-crowned sparrows, brown-headed cowbird, mourning

Other food seeds: top row, left to right—red proso millet, peanut hearts, milo; bottom row, left to right—safflower seed, canary seed, oats, and wheat.

doves, and house sparrows. When planted near wetlands, it is a favorite waterfowl food.

HULLED OATS
Avena sativa

Analyses of stomach contents reveal that oats are an important food for at least 72 kinds of wild birds. Most of these glean discarded oats from cultivated fields. In this way, oats are especially important to greater prairie chicken, blackbirds (Brewer's, red-winged, yellow-headed, and bobolink), horned lark, western meadowlark, and many sparrows (especially grasshopper, white-crowned, and lark). Yet when compared to proso millet, the only birds that preferred hulled oats in Dr. Geis's study were starlings. In this study, whole oats were totally ignored. For this reason, it appears that oats are an undesirable addition to grain mixtures.

JAPANESE MILLET
Echinochloa crusgalli var. *frumentacea*

Japanese millet, also known as duck millet, is an annual, cultivated strain of barnyard grass. Dr. Geis found it less attractive than white proso millet for the species in his studies, but it is known to be a choice food for bobolink, bobwhite, indigo bunting, blue grosbeak, and several species of waterfowl, including gadwall, mallard, pintail, and American widgeon.

MILO (GRAIN SORGHUM)
Sorghum vulgare

Milo, also known as grain sorghum, is an introduced grass from Africa. Each year, approximately 13 million acres are planted with sorghum in Kansas, Texas, and Nebraska, accounting for an annual production of about 45 billion pounds of grain. Most of the milo crop is used for livestock forage and cereals for human consumption, but such mass production makes milo available as an ingredient in low-priced bird seed mixtures. Milo is often substituted for corn and millet when the prices for these grains increase. It is a favorite food of many large game birds, such as ring-necked pheasant, northern bobwhite, wild turkey, and mallard. However, with the exception of starlings, mourning doves, and brown-headed cowbirds, it is seldom eaten by most feeder birds. Perhaps the large size, thick seed coat, and relatively low fat content all contribute to the low desirability of this seed. White sorghum may be eaten more often than the usual reddish seed, but milo of any color should generally be avoided unless it is to be used for feeding mallards, pheasants, and other game birds.

RAPE SEED
Brassica napus

These tiny black seeds are sometimes added to bird seed mixtures. Rape seed is eaten by northern bobwhite, mourning doves, American goldfinch, and common redpoll. However, when offered with other, more preferred choices at bird feeders, Dr. Geis found that rape seed was totally ignored.

SAFFLOWER
Carthamus tinctorius

Safflower seed is most notable as a favorite food for cardinals and is sometimes even sold as "cardinal bait." It is, however, only about one-third as attractive as the cardinal's favorite food, sunflower oilseed. Safflower seed is also readily eaten by white-winged dove, purple finch, and evening grosbeak. It is also eaten, but with less favor, by mourning dove, blue jay, ring-necked pheasant, and tufted titmouse. An advantage of safflower seed is that it is not readily eaten by gray squirrels.

WHEAT
Triticum aestivum

Wheat, as with oats, is one of the most important wildlife foods because of the extent to which it is planted. No fewer than 76 different kinds of wild birds feed on wheat by gleaning it out of farmers' fields after cultivation. However, when wheat is offered as part of a mixed blend, few birds will eat it as long as white

Stellar's jay (above) and blue jays demonstrate a hearty appetite for whole peanuts, high in both fat and protein. Here, the unshelled peanuts are threaded on galvanized wire and hung from a tree branch.

proso millet, cracked corn, and sunflower seed are available. Wheat is readily eaten by house sparrows and makes an inexpensive alternate food for luring sparrows away from higher priced grains.

PEANUTS
Arachis hypogaea

Whole peanut kernels are a favorite food of tufted titmouse, blue jay, Carolina chickadee, and white-throated sparrow. They are also readily eaten by red-winged blackbird, indigo bunting, catbird, black-capped chickadee, crow, American goldfinch, slate-colored junco, ruby-crowned kinglet, warblers (yellow-rumped, orange-crowned, and pine). Whole peanuts probably appeal to both insect- and seed-eating birds because of their high fat and protein content.

Peanut hearts are a common peanut product used in certain seed mixtures. They are the embryos removed from the seed in the manufacture of peanut butter. Although peanut hearts are a relatively inexpensive food, Dr. Geis's study showed that they are a preferred food for starlings, which consumed peanut hearts in preference to all other choices. Where starlings are aggressive competitors at feeders, it is best to eliminate peanut hearts from your feeder menu.

An entertaining way to offer whole peanuts is to thread them onto a section of fishing line or skewer them onto a length of galvanized wire. Bend the bottom end of the wire to hold the peanuts and shape a hook at the other end to hang it in a squirrel-safe place. Jays and woodpeckers will hang on the peanut skewer, skillfully balancing as they shred the shells to retrieve the nuts. Although titmice and blue jays enjoy whole peanuts, they ignore peanut hearts.

SUPPLEMENTAL FOODS

Wild birds will eat a remarkable variety of foods at backyard bird feeders. In fact, what makes feeding birds so much fun is that there is no end of surprises. The greater the variety of choices offered through the seasons, the more kinds of birds will visit your feeders. For example, overwintering yellow-rumped warblers are known to eat grape jelly, brown creepers will eat boiled potato, and robins are said to eat vermicelli (wormlike, cooked spaghetti). I have even heard of an enterprising soul who offers road-killed animals atop a tree platform for his resident flock of black vultures. Several everyday foods make excellent wild bird foods, so save your kitchen scraps when it comes to the foods listed here.

Fruit

To attract a greater variety of birds to your feeders in the summer, try offering apples, oranges, grapefruits, and bananas at backyard feeders. These are favorite foods for many tropical migrants such as tanagers, orioles, and warblers. Sliced apple is especially favored by red-bellied and hairy woodpeckers, and it is also readily eaten by jays, bluebirds, American robin, and Swainson's and hermit thrushes. Sectioned grapefruit and oranges are one of the best ways to lure mockingbirds, catbirds, and thrashers to your feeders.

Currants and Raisins

Currants and raisins are most useful for attracting wild birds in late winter when preferred natural foods have long since been consumed. Raisins and currants may be eaten by blue jays, bluebirds, American robin, varied thrush, and Bohemian and cedar waxwings. The best way to display the fruit is to scatter it on table feeders or other open, conspicuous places.

Bread and Doughnuts

At least 83 different kinds of North American birds are known to eat bread scraps. Certainly the high number of species known to eat bread reflects its availability as a bird food, but it may seem surprising that it is sometimes consumed by such diverse species as red-headed woodpecker, brown creeper, cactus wren, eastern bluebird, and cedar waxwing. Even kestrels and shrikes are known to eat bread sometimes. This wide popularity most likely results because bread consists of both finely ground grains and shortening (fats). Doughnuts, with their higher fat and sugar contents, are also highly attractive to a wide variety of birds. Bread scraps and day-old doughnuts are readily eaten by house sparrows, grackles, starlings, and many other birds that seem to be just as satisfied with these scraps as with such expensive foods as sunflower seeds.

Melon Seeds

The seeds of pumpkin, cantaloupe, watermelon, and squash are readily consumed by at least 20 different kinds of seed-eating birds including mourning dove, blue jay, white and red-breasted nuthatches, northern cardinal, and rose-breasted grosbeak. The list of birds that will eat these seeds might be as long as that for sunflower seed if melon seeds were used as frequently. Smaller birds such as chickadees and yellow-rumped warblers can more readily obtain the nutritious seed hearts if melon seeds are first passed through a meat grinder before they are offered at feeders.

Nutmeats

Nutmeats exposed from the thick hulls of acorns, walnuts, hickory nuts, coconuts, and pecans offer especially nutritious high-energy foods for wild birds. If you can save these nutmeats from squirrels, they may be eaten by such birds as red-headed and pileated woodpecker, blue jay, chickadees, nuthatches, and wrens. Even ruby-crowned kinglets and eastern bluebirds will sometimes eat nutmeats.

Further information about the foods eaten by North American birds can be found in:

Ken Burke, ed. *How to Attract Birds.* Ortho Books of Chevron Chemical Company, San Francisco, Calif. 1983.

Verne E. Davison. *Attracting Birds: From the Prairies to the Atlantic.* Thomas Y. Crowell Company, New York, 1967.

John V. Dennis. *A Complete Guide to Bird Feeding.* Alfred A. Knopf, New York, 1976.

Lanny H. Fish and David A. Steen. "Additional Exploiters of Nectar." *Condor,* vol. 78, 1976, pp. 269–271.

A.D. Geis. "Relative Attractiveness of Different Foods at Wild Bird Feeders." U.S. Fish and Wildlife Service, Special Scientific Report—Wildlife No. 223, Washington, D.C., 1980.

Sally Hoyt Spofford and Lanny H. Fish. "Additions to the List of Nectar Feeding Birds." *Western Birds.* vol. 8, 1977, pp. 109–112.

Species names and order follow the thirty-fourth supplement to the American Ornithologists' Union checklist of North American birds. Supplement to the AUK, vol. 99, no. 3, July 1982.

PRECAUTIONS FOR OPERATING FEEDING STATIONS

Because feeders may create unnaturally large concentrations of birds, certain dangers often crop up. These take their toll and may dampen some of the fun that would otherwise result from feeding birds. Here are a few of the problems that birders should be alert to, with suggestions for reducing the risks.

Window Accidents

Birds usually crash into windows for one of the following three reasons:

1. The angle of the window reflects an expansive scene such as a large lawn, woodland, or other open space. This is probably the most common cause of window accidents.
2. Your windows may be aligned so that birds see an apparent open passage through your home.
3. Spring and summer territorial birds may see their reflections in the window and take chase.

To reduce the frequency of window accidents, do what you can to block "open passageways" and scenic reflections in windows. You can hang a piece of stained glass or other obstruction inside hazardous windows; you can also hang a mobile, wind chime, or other reflection-breaking object outside problem windows. One creative solution is the silhouette of a diving falcon[5] taped to the inside of the window, although silhouettes of any shape would probably be just as effective at breaking up reflections. Accidents can also be reduced by moving feeders to windows that have fewer reflections.

If a bird hits a window and is only stunned, place it inside a cardboard box with a secure lid and then take it indoors to a warm, quiet place. If the bird is going to survive, you'll hear it walking around in the box within a few hours. This simple "box treatment" gives the bird a chance to recover without the added dangers of prowling neighborhood cats and dogs. After recovery, release the bird near a dense thicket or hedge where it can find cover.

If you find a freshly killed bird under your window, put the bird in a plastic bag along with the date, location, and apparent cause of death. Then freeze the

[5]Available from the Crow's Nest Bookshop, Cornell Laboratory of Ornithology, Sapsucker Woods Road, Ithaca, NY 14850

bird and call a local museum, nature center, or university zoology department to see whether any of them would like to add it to their teaching or research collections. Some outstanding collections have grown almost entirely from accidentally killed birds. With the exception of introduced birds, such as starling, house sparrows, and domestic pigeon, it is illegal to keep birds (alive or dead), their feathers, parts, nests, or eggs without both state/provincial and federal permits.

Preservation

Bird feeders built from cedar, redwood, or exterior plywood will have the longest life expectancy. To protect pine and other soft woods, coat the wood with linseed oil or an exterior latex paint. Do not use creosote, as it is extremely toxic.

Peanut Butter

Pure peanut butter is readily eaten by at least 50 kinds of birds. Yet, in 1961, the late Charles K. Nichols, a research associate of the Department of Ornithology of the American Museum of Natural History, reported autopsies on several birds he found dead at his feeders that showed that the esophagus of each was crammed so full of peanut butter that in his opinion, the birds must have choked to death. Ever since, most authors on bird feeding have cautioned readers not to feed pure peanut butter even though, to my knowledge, there has not been another documented fatality. Until someone proves that pure peanut butter is not a hazard, it is best to mix peanut butter with cornmeal at proportions of 1 cup peanut butter to 5 cups of cornmeal. This will ease your conscience and stretch relatively expensive peanut butter supplies.

Salt

Birds sometimes eat salty soils and not infrequently pick up salt along with grit at roadsides. Such northern birds as crossbills and other finches are especially eager salt eaters. Road salt sometimes causes fatalities among turkeys, crossbills, and other birds by paralyzing their central nervous systems and giving them a tame appearance. Generally, however, birds seem to tolerate the low-salt contents of peanut butter and bacon grease. Poultry growers find that approximately 1 percent salt in grain seems to meet the needs of chickens; they can tolerate up to 4 percent salt without obvious ill effects. This low level is usually available from soil, gravel, and natural foods. To avoid possible salt poisoning, do not add salt to grain mixtures.

Freezing to Metal

A common concern at feeders is that birds will freeze to metal perches and other parts. This idea probably is based on the fact that human skin will stick to subfreezing bare metal. The concern, however, has little relevance to birds because their feet, unlike our skin, do not have sweat glands. The horny scales that cover bird feet are perfectly dry, as evidenced by the fact that birds can safely perch on wire fences at the coldest winter temperatures. In *A Complete Guide to Bird Feeding*, John V. Dennis reports one incident of a purple finch that was found with its eye frozen to a metal feeder, but such observations are extremely uncommon. The reflex reactions of healthy birds are so fast that their moist eyes rarely touch anything. Freezing to metal feeders is not a serious hazard for healthy wild birds.

Feeder Diseases

The unusually crowded conditions at feeding stations increase the probability of spreading contagious diseases, especially where uneaten food and bird droppings accumulate. Also, regular food supplies at feeders may permit diseased birds to survive longer than they would without supplemental food, and the longer they reside at feeders, the more likely they are to spread their problems to healthy birds. The bird diseases described here are not contagious to human beings, but they are deadly serious to birds and everything should be done to prevent their occurrence or spread at your feeders.

A common disease problem at bird feeders results from accumulating wet grain that serves as a medium for the growth of the mold, *Aspergillus fumigatus*. The spores of this mold are widely distributed in nature and will readily grow on wet grain. Feeder birds such as juncos, cowbirds, grackles, and many others can contract aspergillus by inhaling mold and spores while eating moldy grain. It can also be a very serious problem for ducks and other waterfowl.

Aspergillus usually attacks the lungs, air sacs, and occasionally the windpipe. To recognize this disease, watch for birds at your feeders that gasp and wheeze or sit quietly for long periods with fluffed feathers. Birds that are about to die from the disease are easy to approach. In the final days of the sickness, they may develop diarrhea and become increasingly lethargic.

Mourning doves and domestic pigeons are especially susceptible to trichomoniasis, a disease caused by the flagellated protozoan *Trichomonas gallinae*. This protozoan lives in the throat, and causes ulcers and swelling that obstruct the esophagus, crop, or pharynx, eventually leading to starvation. Adult birds spread the disease through their excrement or courtship behaviors (regurgitation feeding), and they usually contaminate their young at feeding time. This disease can reach epidemic proportions. In 1951, an outbreak of trichomonas in Alabama led to the deaths of 25,000–30,000 mourning doves. The disease also spreads to hawks and owls that feed on sick birds.

Avian pox is another disease that sometimes infects birds at feeding stations. As with the diseases mentioned above, avian pox will not spread to humans, but it is contagious and can easily contaminate other birds. This virus produces warty protuberances on the feet or head and/or damage to the lining of the throat and respiratory tract.

The best way to reduce the danger of diseases at your feeding stations is to keep grain dry and to clean up spilled grain before it has a chance to begin rotting. By feeding preferred seeds, such as sunflower, white proso millet, and fine cracked corn, there will be less waste at feeders and less opportunity for molds to grow in wet grain. In winter, it is best to feed birds from hopper feeders or other enclosed feeders rather than spreading grain on open feeding tables or the ground, where it is likely to be covered by snow. Clean areas under feeders are also less likely to attract nuisance squirrels, rats, and raccoons.

If you do find sick or dead birds at your feeders, it is best to stop feeding for at least a few days. Let the birds disperse from your property and rake up rotting grain and discarded seed hulls, then bury this accumulation far from the feeding area. Early each fall, carefully scrub all feeders and birdbaths under running water and rinse thoroughly with a disinfectant. If you find birds that you suspect have died from disease, they should be burned or buried. Report injured or sick birds to your local wildlife conservation department. They may know of a nearby licensed rehabilitation program that has the specialized skills and treatments necessary for healing birds. Without appropriate state/provincial or federal permits, it is illegal to keep wild birds, with the exception of introduced species, including starlings, house sparrows, and domestic pigeons.

Predators

Large concentrations of birds at backyard feeders are likely to attract the attention of bird-eating hawks. Cooper's hawk, sharp-shinned hawk, American kestrel, and goshawk, among others, specialize in eating smaller birds, which may be put at a disadvantage at feeders by presenting an unusually large number of potential prey. Predators tend to go after the slow or sick, however, so they can fill a useful role by removing problem birds from feeder populations. Screech and great horned owls may also take their share of feeder birds, but the activities of these nocturnal predators are much less apparent and are rarely observed.

If hawks habitually snag birds at your backyard feeders, the best approach is to let the feeders go empty for a few days. This will temporarily lower feeder populations and decrease vulnerability to hawks. With their prey dispersed, hawks will probably move on to feed elsewhere.

Consider yourself fortunate, though, to witness hawks in action. Their predatory skills are a thrill to observe, as they are masters of coordination and agility. It is interesting to note that feeding stations may also be a hazard for hawks, by exposing them to large windows. It is not unusual for a hawk and its prey to have a fatal window accident in the excitement of the chase.

Healthy birds can usually evade predators at feeders if there is suitable escape cover within approximately 15 to 20 feet of feeders. Dense, thorny hedges, such as rose, hawthorn, holly, or juniper, are ideal for this purpose. Dense cover too close to feeders can be a hazard where lurking house cats are a problem. By placing feeders in open areas within easy flight to shelter, cats will have little chance to catch birds at your feeders.

House cats are a common threat to birds during the nesting season because they can climb to nests or catch fledglings that have not yet learned to fly. Feral cats are the greatest problem, as wild birds may be one of their principal foods at nesting season. To keep cats from climbing trees after nesting birds, wrap a layer of galvanized sheet metal around the trunk about 4 to 5 feet off the ground, overlapping and securing the metal tight to the trunk with self-tapping metal screws. A 1 foot width of metal is enough to keep cats from climbing the tree.

Whenever possible, report feral cats to humane societies or trap them in Hava-hart traps (see the figure in the following subsection). Humane societies will usually collect trapped cats. Whenever possible, do not let pet cats roam freely during the nesting season, especially at night when nests and nestlings are most vulnerable. Because birds feed most in early morning and late afternoon, these are also times when they are most vulnerable to roaming house cats. If cats are a problem, avoid putting feed on the ground (large table feeders will attract the same species), and provide bell collars for free-roaming neighborhood cats.

Squirrels and Raccoons

While most people who feed birds are probably smarter than the average gray squirrel or raccoon, the resolute determination and success of these animals when raiding bird feeders is enough to make one wonder about comparative intelligence. Squirrels will challenge even the most ambitious bird feeding enthusiasts by their remarkable gymnastic talents. Gray squirrels can leap 8 feet from a nearby tree or house onto a feeder or drop 11 feet down to a feeder from an overhanging tree. They may also have the expensive habit of gnawing through wood or plastic to obtain the last bit of grain in a feeder.

Gray squirrels cause the most problems, but in the midwestern and southern states, fox squirrels do their share of mischief. Red squirrels are the principal grain grabber of the northern and mountain coniferous forests, and even the nocturnal flying squirrel can make a significant dent in sunflower seed supplies when feeders are within their capable reach. Raccoons are not as agile as squirrels, but they make up for this on their night raids with abilities to use their paws to open feeders and surprising strength to rip open feeders that are not otherwise accessible.

There are really only two basic tactics for dealing with squirrels and raccoons. The direct approach is to live-trap or kill the nuisance animal. Live traps, such as the Havahart trap, are very effective for capturing both squirrels and raccoons and they will not endanger household pets. However, while trapping and re-

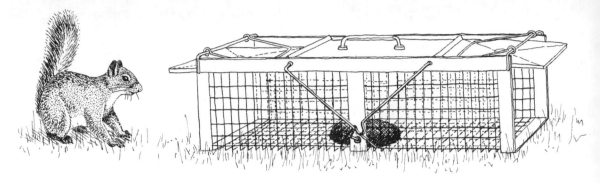

One means of temporarily controlling nuisance raccoons and squirrels is the humane Havahart trap, which allows the animals to be captured alive and released at a distant location. These animals may find themselves competing for scarce food and space as most suitable habitat is already occupied to capacity. Havahart traps are available from Woodstream Corp., Dept. HT, Box 327, Lititz, PA 17543.

moval will alleviate problems caused by specific individuals, new arrivals will soon fill in vacancies. Also, mammals that are trapped and released in new territory with the thought that they will lead a happy future, actually may have a grim chance of surviving because habitats that can support squirrels or raccoons are usually already occupied to capacity.

Shooting nuisance animals is no doubt the most direct approach to control, but it is not usually a legal option. Squirrels and raccoons are game animals protected by hunting laws and may be taken legally only during short seasons in the fall. Further, it is illegal to shoot wildlife inside city limits.

A second, and more satisfying approach to squirrel and raccoon problems is to change our view of these intelligent and interesting natives from nuisance to entertaining. The best way to stop squirrel and raccoon raids on bird feeders is to make whole corn available from ground feeders, well isolated from bird feeders. Then feed birds only from specially designed squirrelproof feeders or from feeders protected by squirrel and raccoon baffles. Deterring squirrels and raccoons from high-priced grains is not only a challenge, but it can be as entertaining as feeding birds.

Among the commercially available bird feeders, there are at least two time-tested varieties that stand out as squirrelproof. The Hylarious feeder and the Animated feeder are built of heavy, squirrelproof steel and work on the principle that the weight of the squirrel or large bird on the feeder platform will drop a protective shield over the grain supply.

Where possible, place bird feeders on 5- to 6-foot-tall poles away from trees or other perches from which squirrels can leap or drop onto feeders. Although homemade baffles above hanging feeders, such as a stack of wobbly 33$\frac{1}{3}$ rpm phonograph records separated by large thread spools, or commercial plastic baffle domes, will deter some of the squirrels part of the time, a truly determined squirrel will often keep trying until its efforts to reach the feeder succeed.

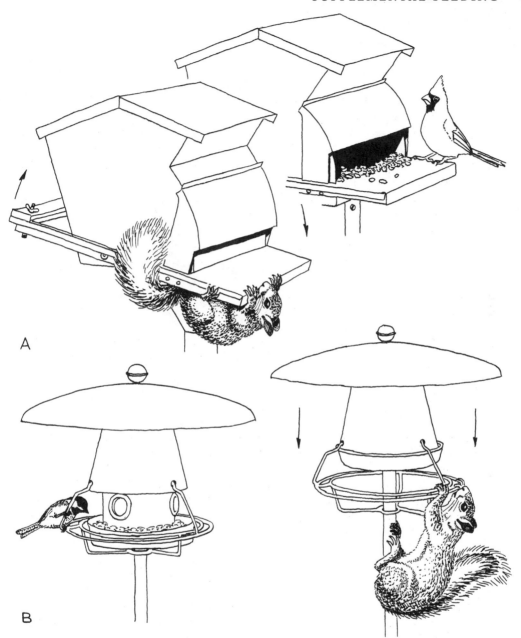

The Hylarious Feeder (A) and the Animated Feeder (B), so-named for the viewing entertainment they provide, prevent aggressive squirrels from dining on expensive grain by blocking feeding portals with metal shields. Both are available from Audubon Workshop, 1501 Paddock Drive, Northbrook, IL 60062.

Merrill Wood of State College, Pennsylvania, experimented with horizontal wires of various weights to find the thinnest weight that a squirrel could walk. He found that gray squirrels could not walk upright on a #9 wire, but they could reach his feeders by clinging upside down, like a very fast sloth. Horizontal wires can be squirrelproofed with elaborate baffles and other devices to stumble even surefooted squirrels. Pat Ellis of Columbus, Ohio, has successfully deterred gray squirrels by lacing thread spools onto a wire and placing flat metal baffles at either end of the spool lineup. She reports that squirrels will climb upside down on the spools without the baffles, but the combination has kept her feeders squirrel-free. Such elaborate efforts suggest that it is much more difficult to baffle squirrels effectively from above feeders than it is to keep them from climbing up to feeders from the ground.

Feeders on poles positioned in open sites restrict squirrels to climbing rather than leaping and dropping from overhead perches. There are several ways to prevent access from the ground. One commercial solution to the problem is the squirrel Spooker Pole, a specially designed feeder pole that repels squirrels with a moveable sleeve that quickly slides to the ground under the weight of a squirrel and then returns to the top of the pole by means of an internal counterweight. It is available from Duncraft, Penacook, NH 03303 (see Appendix D).

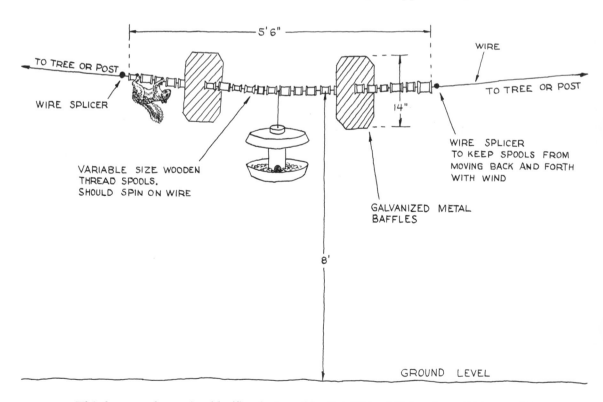

This homemake squirrel baffle, designed by Pat Ellis of Columbus, Ohio, combines the use of thread spools and flat metal baffles to provide an effective deterrent for gray squirrels.

Several less expensive homemade alternatives for deterring squirrels are also available. One of the simplest homemade baffles was designed by Dick Tuttle of Delaware, Ohio. His squirrel baffle consists of a 12-inch length of 4-inch-diameter PVC sewer pipe positioned just under the feeder with hooks. Squirrels climbing the pole find themselves inside of the wobbly pipe, with no way to get around this slippery baffle. A similar idea is to cut the bottom off a gallon milk jug, bleach bottle, or whatever, and then secure it just under the feeder. Squirrels can climb the feeder pole, but are unable to get around the walls of this easy to construct baffle.

Cone-shaped baffles are a commonly used device for keeping squirrels, raccoons, and cats from climbing feeder poles. The success of this device rests on constructing a cone large enough to keep the nuisance mammals from reaching out and pulling themselves around the lip of the cone. Ben Lapin of Montreal, Quebec, has experimented with different sized metal cones and has found that gray squirrels cannot make their way around a 20-inch-diameter cone.

To construct a cone with a 20-inch diameter at its base, use tin snips to cut a circle with a 15-inch radius from galvanized sheet metal. Then cut a wedge with a 31-inch arc from the circle, and snip a circular opening in the center of the piece. Form the cone by overlapping the metal by an inch and securing the joint with self-tapping metal screws. To mount the cone on the feeder pole, first attach 1 × 6 inch strips of metal to the narrow end of the cone to create a collar; then nail the collar to the pole or use a tight-fitting radiator clamp.

Dana Buckelen of Bethany, West Virginia, has successfully baffled squirrels and even house cats from climbing the poles to his feeders by securing a garbage can lid to the feeder pole. He does this by using a tin snip to cut a circular hole in the center of the lid, leaving the cut-out flap attached at one side. The garbage-can handle is cut at one end and used along with the cutout to secure the lid onto a wooden pole (see page 279, Figure D).

David Cooper of Lewiston, New York, has devised an equally simple squirrel baffle. He suggests cutting out a 24-inch circular piece of sheet metal with a central hole large enough to slide over the feeder pole. This flat baffle is free to wobble, tilt, and rotate, as the only thing holding it in place is a ball of duct tape wound beneath it around the pole (see page 279, Figure E). Marjorie Edelen of Lambertville, Michigan, has a similar technique that has also proved successful. She simply took a child's sliding saucer and inverted it between the feeder and the top of a wooden post, completely baffling her gray squirrels (see page 279, Figure F).

In addition to baffles, the poles that support feeders may be coated with various lubricants to impede squirrels from climbing to feeders. Van Voigt of New Castle, Delaware, uses a liberal coating of Crisco shortening smeared on the metal pole under her squirrel baffles. She finds that when squirrels climb the pole, they hesitate under the baffles and soon begin to slide back to the ground.

Daniel Turner of Ypsilanti, Michigan, sanded, burnished, and polished a 1½-inch steel pipe, but still found that gray squirrels could climb 6 feet to his feeders. He then coated the pipe with automobile grease, but found as temperatures dropped, the grease became tacky, and squirrels once again climbed to his feeders. He solved the problem by cleaning the pipe with gasoline and coating it with No. 10 weight motor oil, and this foiled the squirrels. Grease may be a satisfactory pole lubricant for southern latitudes, but for the frigid winters of the north, motor oil appears to be the best choice.

E. Stuart Mitchell of Portland, Connecticut, was having trouble with squirrels chewing on his feeders. In retaliation, he discovered an ingenious deterrent. To "cure" squirrels of their chewing mischief, he applies a thin coat of clear silicone bathtub caulk to trouble spots on his feeders and imbeds a thick coating of red pepper or chili powder into the caulking. He finds that several layers of the mixture are excellent protection to his feeders.

Of all the suggestions received for baffling squirrels, the ultimate squirrel trap illustrated by cartoonist, Creig Flessel of Huntington, New York, suggests the lengths that some feeder enthusiasts will go in their minds, if not in their yards, to keep grain from the grasp of persistent squirrels.

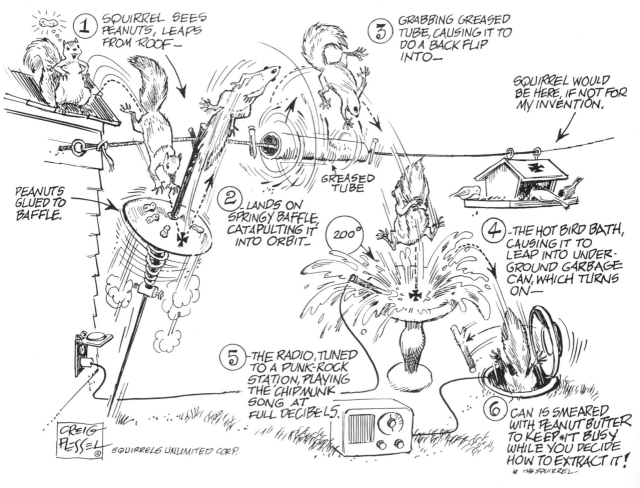

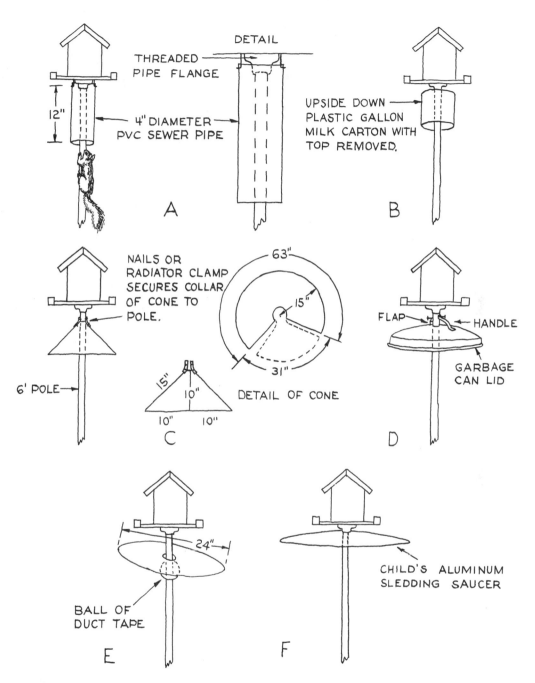

DETAIL

THREADED PIPE FLANGE

12"

4" DIAMETER PVC SEWER PIPE

A

UPSIDE DOWN PLASTIC GALLON MILK CARTON WITH TOP REMOVED.

B

NAILS OR RADIATOR CLAMP SECURES COLLAR OF CONE TO POLE.

6' POLE

63"

15"

31"

DETAIL OF CONE

15"

10"

10" 10"

C

FLAP

HANDLE

GARBAGE CAN LID

D

24"

BALL OF DUCT TAPE

E

CHILD'S ALUMINUM SLEDDING SAUCER

F

SQUIRREL BAFFLES FOR POLE FEEDERS   A. SEWER PIPE BAFFLE. B. MILK JUG BAFFLE.   C. SHEET METAL CONE. D. GARBAGE CAN LID BAFFLE.   E. WOBBLY SHEET METAL DISK. F. SLEDDING SAUCER BAFFLE.

Rats and Mice

Rats and mice will find their way into grains stored in paper bags, and will even chew through plastic garbage cans. Only metal garbage cans with tight-fitting lids will keep rats and mice out of stored grain. These should be stored inside a shed or garage to discourage raccoons from lifting off lids and helping themselves.

Rats and mice may be quick to discover spilled grain under bird feeders, and will climb up feeder poles and into feeders that are not equipped with squirrel baffles. Burrows with 2- to 3-inch openings in the ground near feeders are likely to be rat dens. If you discover rats using such burrows, clean up spilled grain, baffle your feeders, and for final measure, pour Warfarin rat poison down the burrows. To minimize danger to birds, do not spread this on the ground.

Rats can also be trapped with rat-sized snap traps. These should be placed at each burrow entrance with a ring of additional traps circling the entrance. To avoid having birds accidentally trip the traps, put them out at dusk, remove captured rats, and set off unsprung traps before going to bed. Rats are seldom trapped late at night or in the morning. Most rats killed in traps are caught between dusk and 10 P.M.

FEEDER DESIGNS

Mounting Feeders on Living Trees

Whenever possible, avoid nailing bird feeders and houses onto living trees. Nails often cause sapwood to die and may create an avenue for either internal rot or external infection to spread through the tree's living tissues. Also, bark will eventually grow over exposed nails, hiding them from woodcutters' saws. One hidden nail can destroy a chain-saw blade and will greatly decrease the value of prime lumber trees.

A technique commonly used for hanging feeders and birdhouses in Sweden is recommended by Bob Burrell of Arlington, Illinois. This method consists simply of a wooden strut attached to the back of the feeder or bird house. This supports the feeder in a tree crotch without using nails. The length of the strut is cut to fit specific trees.

Since squirrels can easily chew through cotton or nylon line, it is best to suspend hanging feeders with wire or small-link chains. This, however, can seriously damage living tree limbs, for the wire will eventually cut into growing tissue as the tree limb matures. To avoid this problem on narrow branches, thread the wire through a split section of garden hose.

Suet Feeders

Whole suet and suet mixtures are easy to provide for winter birds. Press suet into 1-inch holes drilled in hanging suet logs (food sticks) or pack it into holes drilled in dead snags. Other ways to provide suet are in hanging lobster bait bags

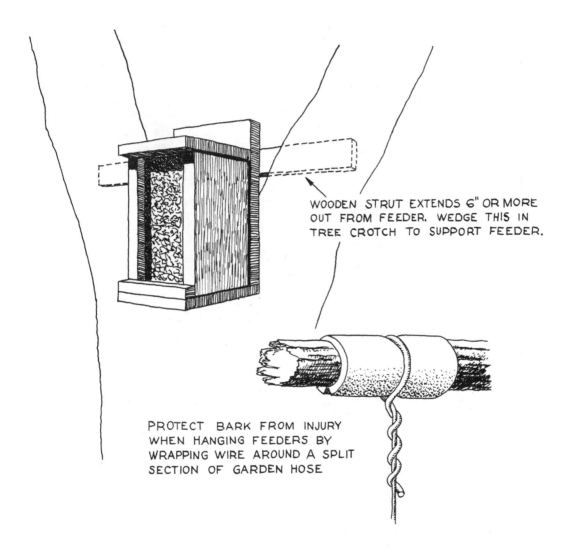

WOODEN STRUT EXTENDS 6" OR MORE OUT FROM FEEDER. WEDGE THIS IN TREE CROTCH TO SUPPORT FEEDER.

PROTECT BARK FROM INJURY WHEN HANGING FEEDERS BY WRAPPING WIRE AROUND A SPLIT SECTION OF GARDEN HOSE

Tree-protecting devices for mounting feeders and nest boxes lower the risk of rot and infection.

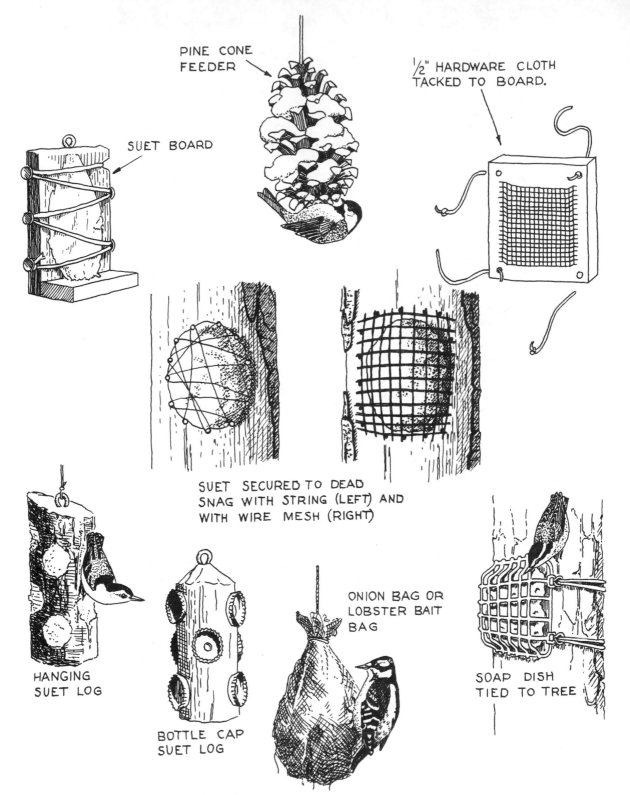

PINE CONE FEEDER

½" HARDWARE CLOTH TACKED TO BOARD.

SUET BOARD

SUET SECURED TO DEAD SNAG WITH STRING (LEFT) AND WITH WIRE MESH (RIGHT)

HANGING SUET LOG

BOTTLE CAP SUET LOG

ONION BAG OR LOBSTER BAIT BAG

SOAP DISH TIED TO TREE

A variety of methods to provide suet for birds.

(these are very sturdy), onion/citrus bags, soap dishes strapped to trees, and a variety of other simple and more elaborate dispensers. The selection of which design to use depends more on available materials and carpentry skills than on differences in attractiveness to birds.

Although squirrels do not usually have a taste for suet, it is a favorite of raccoons, dogs, and starlings, all of which can rob and destroy feeders in their eagerness to get at suet.

To protect suet feeders, hang them well above the reach of the largest neighborhood dog or serve suet only from raccoon-baffled feeders (see previous section). Starlings are probably the most difficult suet eaters to discourage. One way to shield suet from starlings is to serve it only to small birds, such as chickadees and titmice, from a dispenser completely protected by a square chicken-wire cage through which only small birds can enter. Be sure to use 1½-inch chicken wire, as starlings can squeeze through the 2-inch openings of larger mesh chicken wire. Although this technique excludes starlings, it also keeps woodpeckers out.

Remember also that chickadees, titmice, nuthatches, and woodpeckers can feed upside down by using their sharp toenails. Woodpeckers can also balance with their stiff, proplike tails. A suet feeder designed by Richard Tuttle of Delaware, Ohio, selectively excludes starlings while giving woodpeckers, chickadees, and nuthatches ready access. First attract suet-eating birds to a couple of display holes in the upright log section of the feeder. After birds have become familiar with the feeder, suet is then offered only from holes underneath the horizontal top section. Woodpeckers, nuthatches, titmice, and chickadees will cling upside down to obtain suet, but starlings cannot.

Frederick Sweet of Manchester, Connecticut, designed another innovative starlingproof feeder. This hanging feeder is based on the fact that starlings cannot climb vertical logs. To reach the suet basket in Sweet's feeder, birds must either cling to the suspended log and hike their way up to the feeder basket or be small enough (as are chickadees) to hop through the 1½-inch-mesh chicken-wire cage.

Grain Feeders

In addition to many excellent commercial feeder designs (see Appendix D for suppliers), there are dozens of suitable ideas for dispensing grain from homemade feeders. There is a special satisfaction in luring birds to homemade feeders. Perhaps it is the idea that one can build something that works as well as expensive commercial products, or perhaps it is just the pleasant notion of using "throwaway" items, such as milk cartons, soda bottles, and scrap wood, for a good purpose. Here is a sampling of the best ideas that came from my call for feeder projects. I also include project ideas and detailed plans for some of the standard, time-proven feeder designs.

Of course, birds do not really care how much a feeder costs or what it looks like. Cost and aesthetics aside, the only thing that is really important is that food

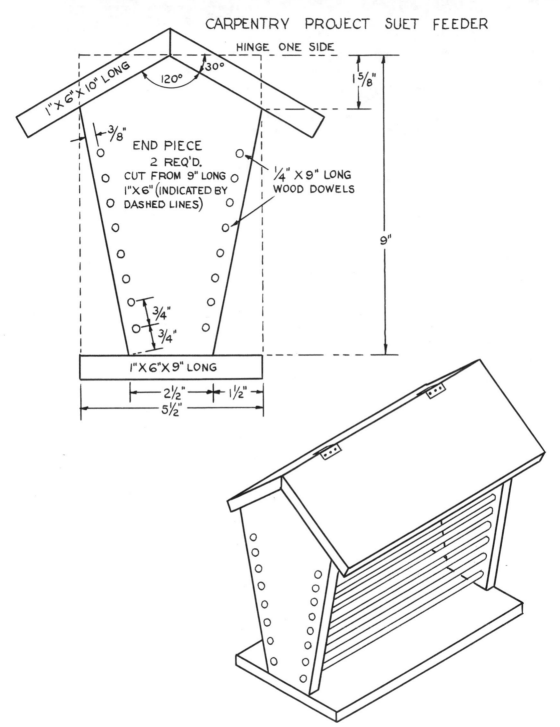

CARPENTRY PROJECT SUET FEEDER

HINGE ONE SIDE

1⅝"

1" X 6" X 10" LONG

120°   30°

3/8"

END PIECE
2 REQ'D.
CUT FROM 9" LONG
1" X 6" (INDICATED BY
DASHED LINES)

¼" X 9" LONG
WOOD DOWELS

9"

3/4"

3/4"

1" X 6" X 9" LONG

2½"   1½"

5½"

Three carpentry project suet feeders.

CARPENTRY PROJECT SUET FEEDERS

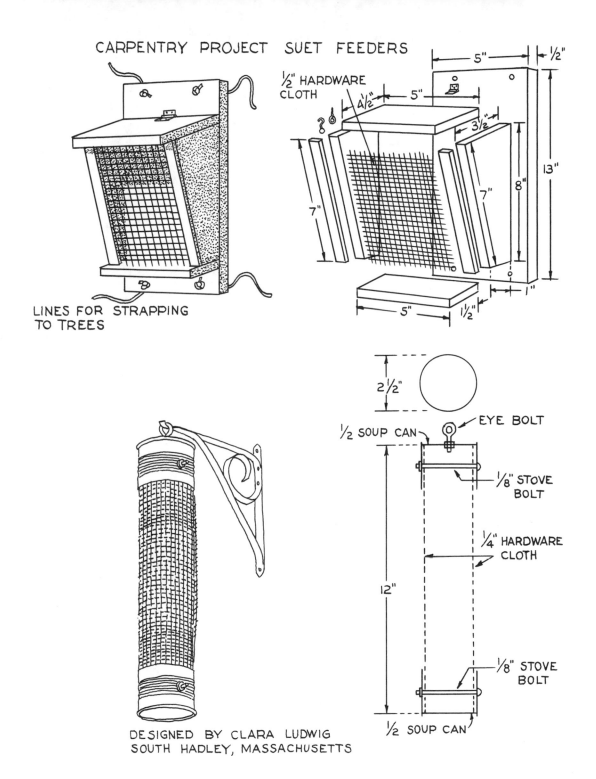

½" HARDWARE CLOTH

5"

½"

5"

4½"

3½"

13"

8"

7"

7"

1"

5"

½"

LINES FOR STRAPPING TO TREES

2½"

½ SOUP CAN

EYE BOLT

⅛" STOVE BOLT

¼" HARDWARE CLOTH

12"

⅛" STOVE BOLT

½ SOUP CAN

DESIGNED BY CLARA LUDWIG
SOUTH HADLEY, MASSACHUSETTS

285

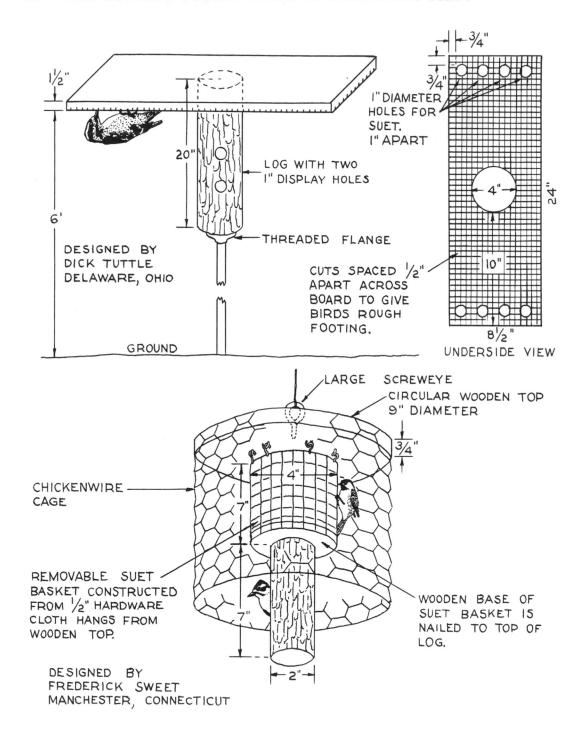

1½"

20"

LOG WITH TWO
1" DISPLAY HOLES

THREADED FLANGE

6'

DESIGNED BY
DICK TUTTLE
DELAWARE, OHIO

CUTS SPACED ½"
APART ACROSS
BOARD TO GIVE
BIRDS ROUGH
FOOTING.

GROUND

¾"

¾"

1" DIAMETER
HOLES FOR
SUET.
1" APART

4"

24"

10"

8½"

UNDERSIDE VIEW

LARGE SCREWEYE

CIRCULAR WOODEN TOP
9" DIAMETER

¾"

CHICKENWIRE
CAGE

4"

7"

REMOVABLE SUET
BASKET CONSTRUCTED
FROM ½" HARDWARE
CLOTH HANGS FROM
WOODEN TOP.

7"

WOODEN BASE OF
SUET BASKET IS
NAILED TO TOP OF
LOG.

2"

DESIGNED BY
FREDERICK SWEET
MANCHESTER, CONNECTICUT

does not deteriorate before the birds have an opportunity to eat it. Moisture is the greatest problem in bird feeders, as it can turn grain to mush in a matter of hours, creating a medium for mold that could prove fatal to birds.

Feeders with roofs are especially important during winter, when snow readily covers and soaks into grain. Even feeders with secure lids may take on excessive moisture through feeding portals, so some drainage is important in nearly all feeders. The weathervane feeder uses another way to keep birds and grain out of direct wind and precipitation.

Feeders that exclude larger birds, such as jays and grackles, permit smaller birds access to grain without waiting for leftovers from the larger, more aggressive species. Such selective feeders as the coffee can feeder or hanging soda bottle with 1-inch holes in its ends are excellent ways to provide choice food only for chickadees and titmice, which can duck into the tiny holes. Perch length can also help to attract one species over another. For example, American goldfinches will perch on feeders with 3/4-inch-long perches, but this is usually too small for the competitive house finches.

The stacked bowl feeder with varying entrances can provide food for small and large birds at the same time by varying feeding level and size of entrances to grain. Likewise, the "harmony feeder" permits hundreds of flocking birds, such as grosbeaks, to feed at the same time by providing many feeding levels and expansive surfaces for displaying grain.

Of all the ideas received, a letter from June Osborne of Waco, Texas, offered the most basic feeder idea combined with a fundamental concept underlying supplemental feeding. Osborne tried for years to attract goldfinches to her yard with sunflower and thistle seeds, but could not lure them to her feeders, even though her neighbor fed many goldfinch. Apparently, one of the main differences between Osborne's yard and her neighbor's was the presence of mature sycamore trees near her neighbor's home. These were heavy with sycamore fruit, a favorite goldfinch food. Within 3 days of tying dozens of sycamore balls to a barren mimosa tree, Osborne finally lured goldfinch to her yard. First they visited the sycamore fruits, then discovered her feeders.

June Osborne's experience emphasizes that feeders placed in unsuitable habitat will attract few birds, and the presence of certain bird species is usually explained by the presence of specific plants and plant communities. Although bird feeders may attract birds to your property for brief visits, long-term improvements will occur only when feeding is part of general landscaping made with birds in mind.

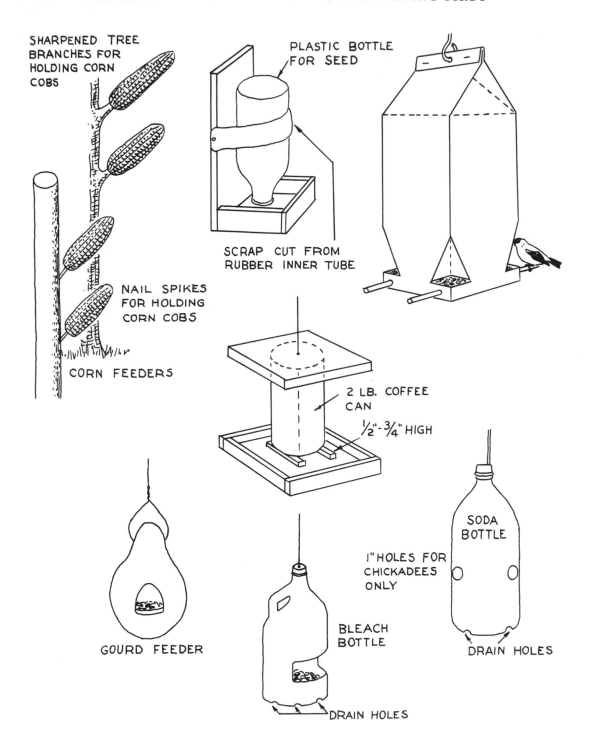

SHARPENED TREE BRANCHES FOR HOLDING CORN COBS

PLASTIC BOTTLE FOR SEED

NAIL SPIKES FOR HOLDING CORN COBS

CORN FEEDERS

SCRAP CUT FROM RUBBER INNER TUBE

2 LB. COFFEE CAN

½"-¾" HIGH

GOURD FEEDER

1" HOLES FOR CHICKADEES ONLY

BLEACH BOTTLE

DRAIN HOLES

SODA BOTTLE

DRAIN HOLES

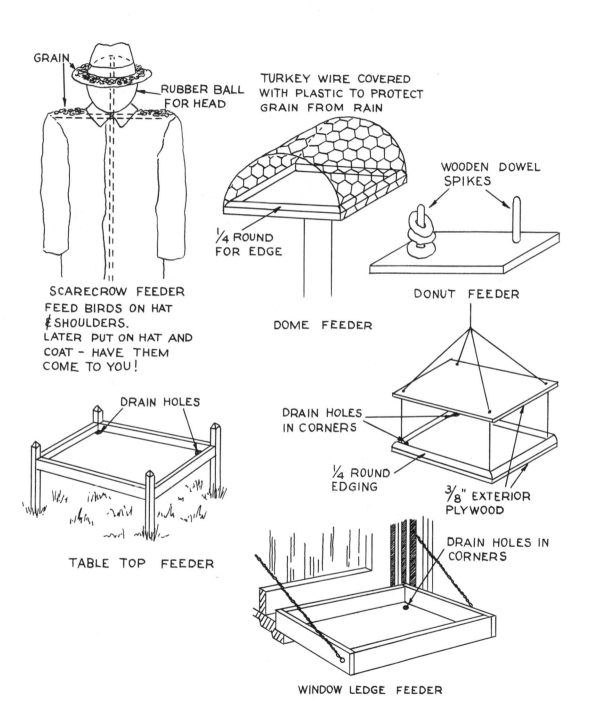

GRAIN

RUBBER BALL FOR HEAD

SCARECROW FEEDER
FEED BIRDS ON HAT & SHOULDERS.
LATER PUT ON HAT AND COAT – HAVE THEM COME TO YOU!

TURKEY WIRE COVERED WITH PLASTIC TO PROTECT GRAIN FROM RAIN

¼ ROUND FOR EDGE

DOME FEEDER

WOODEN DOWEL SPIKES

DONUT FEEDER

DRAIN HOLES

TABLE TOP FEEDER

DRAIN HOLES IN CORNERS

¼ ROUND EDGING

⅜" EXTERIOR PLYWOOD

DRAIN HOLES IN CORNERS

WINDOW LEDGE FEEDER

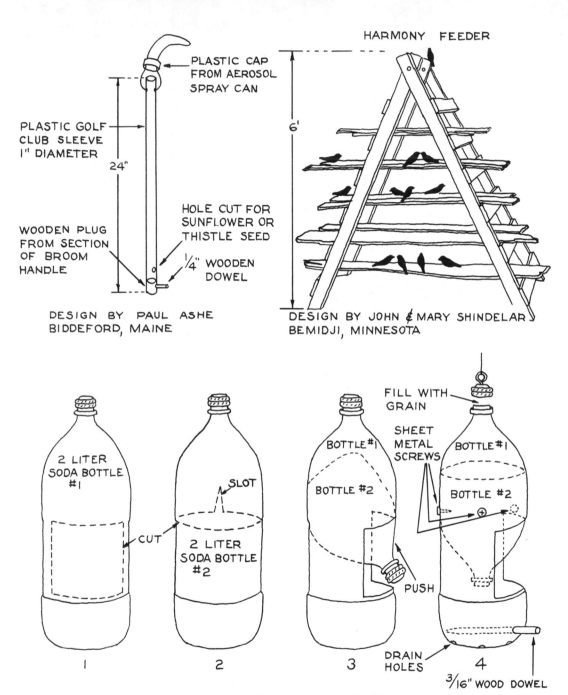

PLASTIC CAP
FROM AEROSOL
SPRAY CAN

PLASTIC GOLF
CLUB SLEEVE
1" DIAMETER

24"

WOODEN PLUG
FROM SECTION
OF BROOM
HANDLE

HOLE CUT FOR
SUNFLOWER OR
THISTLE SEED

1/4" WOODEN
DOWEL

DESIGN BY PAUL ASHE
BIDDEFORD, MAINE

HARMONY FEEDER

6'

DESIGN BY JOHN & MARY SHINDELAR
BEMIDJI, MINNESOTA

2 LITER
SODA BOTTLE
#1

CUT

1

SLOT

2 LITER
SODA BOTTLE
#2

2

BOTTLE #1

BOTTLE #2

PUSH

DRAIN
HOLES

3

FILL WITH
GRAIN

SHEET
METAL
SCREWS

BOTTLE #1

BOTTLE #2

4

3/16" WOOD DOWEL

DESIGN BY DAVID L. WHITE
WILLIAMSPORT, PENNSYLVANIA

THISTLE SEED FEEDER

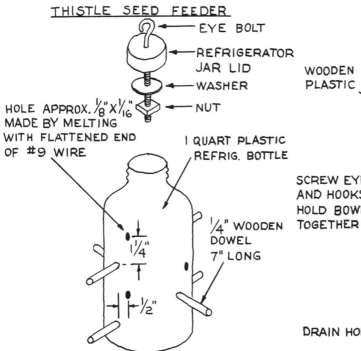

EYE BOLT

REFRIGERATOR JAR LID

WASHER

NUT

HOLE APPROX. 1/8" X 1/16" MADE BY MELTING WITH FLATTENED END OF #9 WIRE

1 QUART PLASTIC REFRIG. BOTTLE

1/4" WOODEN DOWEL 7" LONG

1 1/4"

1/2"

DESIGN BY RICHARD WASON
LISLE, ILLINOIS

WOODEN DOWEL SPACERS PERMIT DIFFERENT SIZE BIRDS TO OBTAIN FOOD

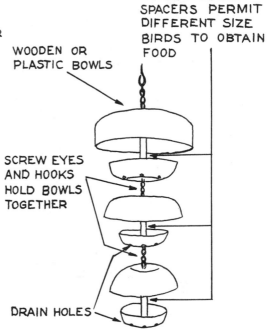

WOODEN OR PLASTIC BOWLS

SCREW EYES AND HOOKS HOLD BOWLS TOGETHER

DRAIN HOLES

DESIGN BY ALEXANDER HILLIARD
ORANGE PARK, FLORIDA

DONUT FEEDER

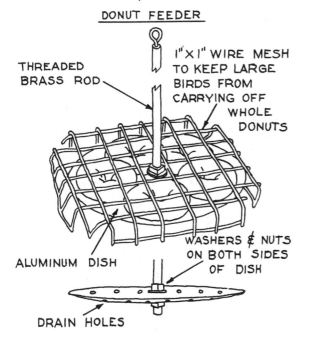

THREADED BRASS ROD

1" X 1" WIRE MESH TO KEEP LARGE BIRDS FROM CARRYING OFF WHOLE DONUTS

ALUMINUM DISH

WASHERS & NUTS ON BOTH SIDES OF DISH

DRAIN HOLES

DESIGN BY LISA VON BOROWSKY
BROOKSVILLE, FLORIDA

SUNFLOWER SEED FEEDER
FOR CHICKADEES & TITMICE

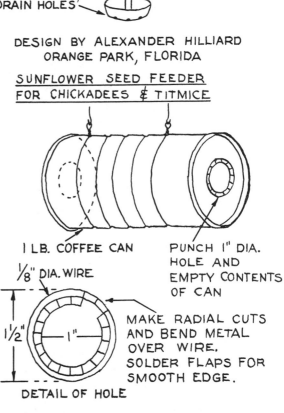

1 LB. COFFEE CAN

PUNCH 1" DIA. HOLE AND EMPTY CONTENTS OF CAN

1/8" DIA. WIRE

1 1/2"

1"

MAKE RADIAL CUTS AND BEND METAL OVER WIRE. SOLDER FLAPS FOR SMOOTH EDGE.

DETAIL OF HOLE

DESIGN BY CHRIS CHRISTIANSEN
MURRAY HILL, NEW JERSEY

LEAN-TO GROUND FEEDER

PREVAILING WIND

CONIFER BRANCHES
FOR SHELTER

CORN ON SPIKES
IN FEEDING TRAY

RIM ON FEEDING
TRAY TO CONTAIN
GRAIN

HOPPER FEEDER

DOUBLE HOPPER FEEDER

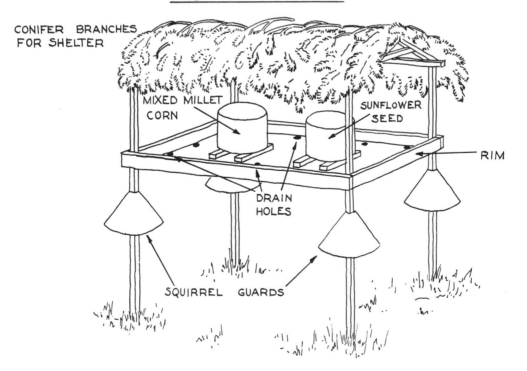

CONIFER BRANCHES
FOR SHELTER

MIXED MILLET
CORN

SUNFLOWER
SEED

RIM

DRAIN
HOLES

SQUIRREL GUARDS

CARPENTRY PROJECT GRAIN FEEDERS
HOPPER FEEDER

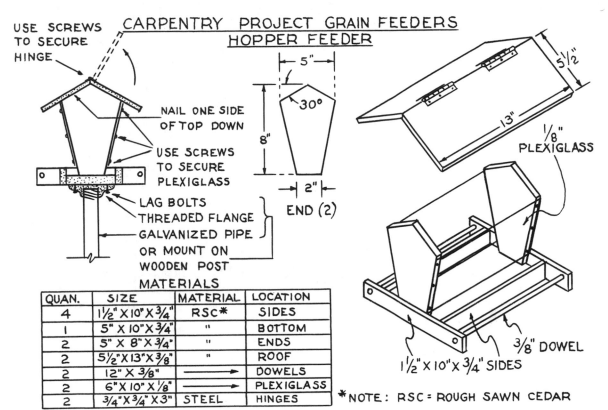

USE SCREWS TO SECURE HINGE

NAIL ONE SIDE OF TOP DOWN

USE SCREWS TO SECURE PLEXIGLASS

LAG BOLTS
THREADED FLANGE
GALVANIZED PIPE
OR MOUNT ON
WOODEN POST

5"
30°
8"
2"
END (2)

5½"
13"
⅛" PLEXIGLASS

3/8" DOWEL

1½" X 10" X ¾" SIDES

MATERIALS

QUAN.	SIZE	MATERIAL	LOCATION
4	1½"X10"X¾"	RSC*	SIDES
1	5"X10"X¾"	"	BOTTOM
2	5"X8"X¾"	"	ENDS
2	5½"X13"X⅜"	"	ROOF
2	12"X⅜"	→	DOWELS
2	6"X10"X⅛"	→	PLEXIGLASS
2	¾"X¾"X3"	STEEL	HINGES

*NOTE: RSC = ROUGH SAWN CEDAR

WEATHER VANE BIRD FEEDER

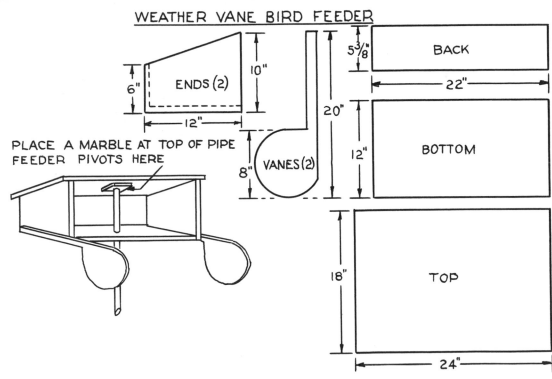

PLACE A MARBLE AT TOP OF PIPE
FEEDER PIVOTS HERE

6"
10"
ENDS (2)
12"

8"
VANES (2)

20"

5⅜"
BACK
22"

12"
BOTTOM

18"
TOP
24"

CARPENTRY PROJECT GRAIN FEEDERS
GROUND FEEDER

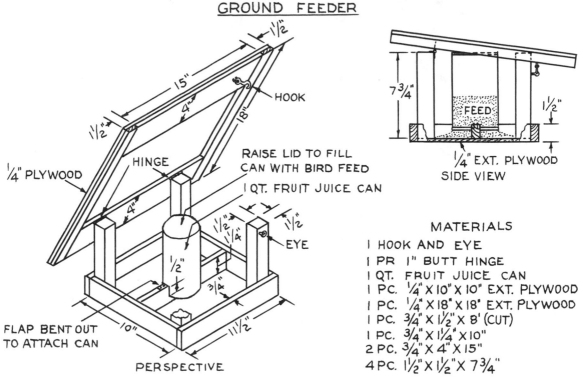

1½"

15"

4"

18"

1½"

HOOK

¼" PLYWOOD

HINGE

4"

RAISE LID TO FILL
CAN WITH BIRD FEED

1 QT. FRUIT JUICE CAN

1½" 1½"
¼" EYE

½"

¾"

FLAP BENT OUT
TO ATTACH CAN

10"

1½"

PERSPECTIVE

7¾"

FEED

1½"

¼" EXT. PLYWOOD
SIDE VIEW

MATERIALS

1 HOOK AND EYE
1 PR 1" BUTT HINGE
1 QT. FRUIT JUICE CAN
1 PC. ¼" X 10" X 10" EXT. PLYWOOD
1 PC. ¼" X 18" X 18" EXT. PLYWOOD
1 PC. ¾" X 1½" X 8' (CUT)
1 PC. ¾" X 1¼" X 10"
2 PC. ¾" X 4" X 15"
4 PC. 1½" X 1½" X 7¾"

ONCE-A-WEEK FEEDER

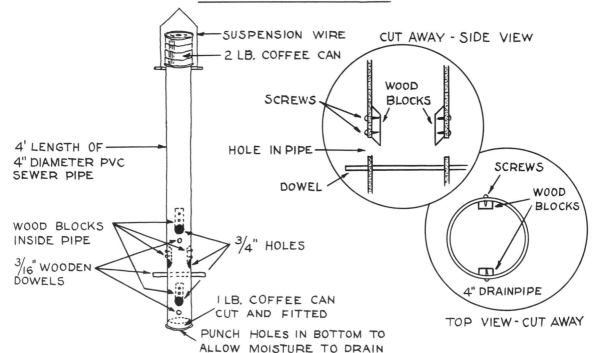

SUSPENSION WIRE

2 LB. COFFEE CAN

CUT AWAY - SIDE VIEW

SCREWS

WOOD
BLOCKS

4' LENGTH OF
4" DIAMETER PVC
SEWER PIPE

HOLE IN PIPE

DOWEL

SCREWS

WOOD
BLOCKS

WOOD BLOCKS
INSIDE PIPE

¾" HOLES

3/16" WOODEN
DOWELS

4" DRAINPIPE

TOP VIEW - CUT AWAY

1 LB. COFFEE CAN
CUT AND FITTED

PUNCH HOLES IN BOTTOM TO
ALLOW MOISTURE TO DRAIN

REFERENCES FOR ATTRACTING BIRDS

Of all the books and booklets written on attracting birds and wildlife management, I recommend the following three titles for their thoroughness and readable style. (Books in this section are listed alphabetically, in order of their authors' last names.)

Dennis, John V. *A Complete Guide to Bird Feeding*. Alfred A. Knopf, New York, 1976, 288 pages (hardcover and paperback). This is an excellent guide to setting up and maintaining a bird feeding station. As its title conveys, it does not treat landscaping or housing. Because of its focused approach, Dennis is able to include abundant but not redundant detail about his personal experiences feeding birds. The first half of the book offers recommendations for setting up the feeding station, and the second consists of species accounts describing the behavior of common feeder birds. These include various techniques and foods useful for attracting or dispersing different species.

Leopold, Aldo. *A Sand County Almanac—With Other Essays on Conservation from Round River*. Oxford University Press, New York, 1966, 269 pages (hardcover and paperback). Aldo Leopold was the founder of game management and as such laid both the technical information and philosophical background for how we should serve as stewards for the land. He was remarkably prophetic 50 years ago when Scribners published his *Game Management* text, the first wildlife management book ever published. *A Sand County Almanac* contains the essence of Leopold's conservation philosophy, in which he explains in elegant language that until the land is loved and thus respected, there is no chance for it (and wildlife) to survive mechanized land-use.

Terres, John K. *Songbirds in Your Garden,* 3rd ed. Hawthorne Books, Inc., New York, 1977, 299 pages (hardcover and paperback). This is the most complete reference to feeding, housing, and landscaping for backyard birds of North America. John Terres presents information in a conversational way that shares his enthusiasm for attracting birds. His many years of firsthand experience and his remarkable ability to assemble facts, ranks this as basic reading for anyone interested in improving his property for wild birds.

GOOD CHOICES ON SUBJECT AREAS

General Bird Attracting

Burke, Ken, Ed. *How to Attract Birds.* Ortho Books, San Francisco, 1983, 96 pages (paperback). This well-illustrated book contains color photos and illustrations. These accompany an abundant informative text about how to provide food, water, and nest sites for both eastern and western birds. About one-third of the book consists of species accounts with range maps that briefly describe nesting and feeding habits of 75 types of bird that respond to attracting techniques.

Gellner, Sherry, ed. *Attracting Birds to Your Garden.* Lane Magazine and Book Co., Menlo Park, Calif., 96 pages (paperback). The emphasis of this book is on western landscape plants that are attractive to birds. It also contains brief accounts for 33 bird species that inhabit the far western states. This paperback is especially useful because of the paucity of literature on attracting western birds.

Harrison, George H. *The Backyard Bird Watcher.* Simon and Schuster, New York, 1979, 284 pages (hardcover and paperback). This conversation-toned book discusses some of the basics of feeding, housing, and landscaping for birds. As the title suggests, the emphasis is definitely on small properties, though some of the suggestions can have broader application. Of special value is the chapter on planning and planting backyard habitats, in which Harrison describes backyards in various U.S. regions that have successfully increased bird variety through creative landscaping.

McElroy, Thomas P., Jr. *The New Handbook of Attracting Birds,* 2nd ed. Alfred A. Knopf, New York, 1975, 262 pages (hardcover). In addition to the basics of bird attracting, such as feeders, houses, water supplies, and plantings, this book also discusses projects for attracting birds to farms, care of young and injured birds, laws protecting birds, and the importance of predators.

Pistorius, Alan. *The Country Journal Book of Birding and Bird Attracting*. W.W. Norton and Co., New York, 1981, 274 pages (hardcover). This is by far one of the most readable and entertaining treatments of bird attracting. Alan Pistorius provides excellent discussion of topics including feeding, planting, and housing with a refreshing ability to blend substantial findings from scientific research with his own often wry observations about birds and the people who care about them.

Habitat Management Techniques

Billard, Ruth Sawyer. "Birdscaping Your Yard." Connecticut Department of Environmental Protection, Hartford, undated, 47 pages (paperback). This guide emphasizes bird management through vegetation manipulation. It includes useful tips for pruning to encourage nest sites in shrubs, creating improved cover through vegetation plantings, propagation through cuttings, and other plant propagation techniques.

Bourne, Russell, Ed. *Gardening with Wildlife*. National Wildlife Federation, Washington, D.C., 1974, 190 pages (hardcover). This well-illustrated book is a basic guide to developing a backyard wildlife sanctuary. Its central theme is that planned plant succession can bring diverse life to an otherwise sterile lot. In addition to brief sections about feeding, housing, and landscaping, it includes a design for a wildlife pool and an appendix listing North American flowers, shrubs, and trees for attracting birds.

Briggs, Shirley A., ed. "Landscaping for Birds." Audubon Naturalist Society of the Central Atlantic States, Inc., Washington, D.C., 1973, 62 pages (paperback). This multiauthored booklet is a wealth of information about such topics as landscaping principles, ornamental trees for wildlife, and landscaping the bulldozed lot. An especially informative chapter is titled "The Bird Garden," adapted from the *Journal of the British Trust for Ornithology*. This gives a delightful perspective to British "bird gardening."

Gillespie, John, ed. *Garden Pools, Fountains and Waterfalls*. Lane Publishing Co., Menlo Park, Calif., 1974, 80 pages (paperback). This helpful guide to constructing garden pools, fountains, and waterfalls contains a wide range of ideas from simple birdbaths to gushing fountains. The emphasis is on naturalistic designs enhanced by appropriate plantings. Installation of a backyard pool can help to increase bird populations, and this easy to follow guide provides much practical help.

Decker, Daniel J., and John W. Kelley. "Enhancement of Wildlife Habitat on Private Lands." *Information Bulletin 181*, Cooperative Extension Service, Ithaca, N.Y., undated, 40 pages (paperback). This booklet describes 10 wildlife enhancement projects for small and large properties that will benefit birds and other wildlife. Attractive line drawings and well-written text encourage the reader to pick a project and start working to improve wildlife habitat.

Leopold, Aldo. *Game Management*. Charles Scribner's Sons, New York, 1933, 481 pages. Leopold's classic *Game Management* has many lessons as relevant today as when he first published this first text to "the art of cropping land for game." Certainly there is much in common about improving the land for the production of both game and nongame animals. *Game Management* remains an excellent review of the history of wildlife management and the principles of wildlife biology.

Schemnitz, Sanford D., ed. *Wildlife Management Techniques Manual*, 4th ed. The Wildlife Society, Washington, D.C., 1980, 686 pages (hardcover). For serious amateurs and professional wildlife managers, this authoritative, multiauthored manual includes many of the current techniques for managing wild bird and mammal populations. Some of the relevant chapters include making observations and records, wildlife nutrition, and capturing and marking wild animals.

Shomon, Joseph J., Byron L. Ashbaugh, and C.D. Tolman. "Wildlife Habitat Improvement." National Audubon Society, New York, 1974, 96 pages (paperback). This manual provides techniques for improving habitats for wild birds through vegetation planning on small and large properties. It also includes techniques for arid habitats and wetlands.

Plants for Attracting Birds

Davison, Verne E. *Attracting Birds: From the Prairies to the Atlantic*. Thomas Y. Crowell Co., New York, 1967, 251 pages (hardcover). This book contains extensive lists of food preferences for over 400 species of birds. These lists are divided into two sections, the first lists bird species, plant and animal foods eaten by each, and nest locations. The second list provides plant names, followed by the birds that eat each species. This is a very impressive collection of food habit information for eastern birds.

DeGraaf, Richard M., and Gretchin M. Witman. *Trees, Shrubs and Vines for Attracting Birds—A Manual for the Northeast*. University of Massachusetts Press, Amherst, 1979, 194 pages (hardcover and paperback). This excellent treatment of plantings for attracting birds contains 136 descriptions of trees, shrubs, and vines that are important food and cover plants for birds. Each species account contains a plant description, habitat type, landscape notes, and suggestions for propagation. Most species are illustrated with excellent line drawings and accompanied by a list of birds that use the plant for food, cover, or nest sites. It is hoped this book will inspire similar treatments for other North American regions.

Martin, Alexander C., Herbert S. Zim, and Arnold L. Nelson. *American Wildlife and Plants—A Guide to Wildlife Food Habits*. Dover Publications, Inc., New York, 1951, 500 pages (paperback). This important reference summarizes some of the extensive studies conducted by the U.S. Biological Survey on food habits of North American wildlife. Most of the data were compiled by laborious studies of stomach contents. Data are compiled first by species account for birds and mammals, including range maps and measures of seasonal importance. The same data are then reorganized in the second half of the book, where the reader finds a listing of important woody plants, upland weeds, aquatic plants, and cultivated plants. The birds and mammals that eat each plant are ranked by measures of importance of the plant to the animal.

McKenny, Margaret. *Birds in the Garden and How to Attract Them.* The University of Minnesota Press, Minneapolis, 1939, 349 pages (hardcover). The first two-thirds of this book on attracting birds has much better modern equivalents, but the final third contains a listing of important bird-attracting plants by region. This is based on the important work of W. L. McAtee of the U.S. Biological Survey, who conducted extensive stomach analysis work on bird food habits. Margaret McKenny's review of the importance of various plants to wild birds remains a very useful reference, especially for western birds.

Gardening with Native Plants

Anon. "North Carolina Native Plant Propagation Handbook." North Carolina Wild Flower Preservation Society, Inc., Wilson, 79 pages (paperback). This booklet covers the basics of site preparation for woodland gardens, bog gardens, and sunny habitat plantings. It also discusses seed collection, storage, and germination techniques. Two dozen recommended native plants for cultivation are described.

Bruce, Hal. *How to Grow Wildflowers and Wild Shrubs and Trees in Your Garden.* Alfred A. Knopf, New York, 1976, 294 pages (hardcover). This lively discussion of native plants for backyard horticulture provides suggestions primarily from an aesthetic view rather than a bird-attracting purpose, but the abundant suggestions of color combinations and planting associations will provide useful ideas for encouraging bird-attracting plants, many of which are described in this book.

duPont, Elizabeth N. "Landscaping with Native Plants in the Middle Atlantic Region." Brandywine Conservancy, Chadds Ford, Pa., 1978, 72 pages (paperback). This booklet discusses the rationale for using native plants over exotics, and shows how whether planting a small or large garden, the use of native plants can create a pleasing, natural look. Considerations for planting in swampy habitats, dry areas, and various forest types are discussed, as are techniques for transplanting and propagation. The second half of the book consists of detailed tables listing growth characteristics of selected native northeast plants that have food value for songbirds and other wildlife.

Kenfield, Warren G. *The Wild Gardener in the Wild Landscape.* Hafner Publishing Co., New York, 1970, 232 pages (hardcover). Here is a practical guide to natural landscaping. It covers subjects such as perpetuating existing plant communities, eliminating plants, and the art of adding and aiding selected plants. This book contains many useful techniques for selectively improving land for wildlife use.

Keough, Jane S., Project Director. *North American Horticulture—A Reference Guide.* Compiled by the American Horticultural Society. Charles Scribner's Sons, New York, 1982, 367 pages (hardcover). This reference lists horticultural organizations, horticultural libraries, conservation groups, local garden clubs, as well as arboretums that specialize in native plantings. Such collections are excellent places to visit to see which bird-attracting plants grow in your vicinity and to better appreciate what mature specimens look like.

Kiekelmann, John, and Robert Schuster. *Natural Landscaping—Designing with Native Plant Communities.* McGraw-Hill, New York, 1982, 276 pages (hardcover). As alternatives to expansive lawns with their dreary monotony, Kiekelmann and Schuster have looked for inspiration in native plant communities to help them offer suggestions for modifying human communities with designs from nature. The book offers specific landscaping designs for various landscapes that reflect the structure of native plant communities. This is a refreshing and imaginative approach to bringing the feeling of native plants into the urban and suburban settings.

Mooberry, F.M., and Jane H. Scott. "Grow Native Shrubs in Your Garden." Brandywine Conservancy, Chadds Ford, Pa., 1980, 68 pages (paperback). This useful booklet describes the growing conditions of native shrubs, offering suggestions for planting combinations to make best use of the aesthetic characteristics of selected shrubs. It also includes tips on propagation.

Perry, Bob. *Trees and Shrubs for Dry California Landscapes.* Land Design Publishing, San Dimas, Calif., 1981, 184 pages (hardcover). This very useful guide for the southwestern states describes trees and shrubs that are adapted for this dry climate. As water becomes increasingly scarce in this region, it makes sense to plant trees and shrubs that can flourish without copious watering. Illustrated by 490 color photographs, it is a welcome reference for anyone interested in landscaping in the southwest.

Stokes, Donald W. *The Natural History of Wild Shrubs and Vines—Eastern and Central North America.* Harper & Row, Publishers, New York, 1981, 246 pages (hardcover). This very readable book provides interesting natural history information about 49 species of native shrubs and vines. Many of the plants described in this book, such as juniper, greenbrier, bayberry, shadbush, and trumpet vine are very useful for attracting birds.

Workman, Richard W. *Growing Native Plants for Landscape Use in Coastal South Florida.* The Sanibel-Captiva Conservation Foundation, Inc., Sanibel, Fla., 1980, 137 pages (paperback). The often forgotten native plants of south coastal Florida are especially adapted to the temperature and salt demands of this unique North American habitat. *Growing Native Plants* helps to familiarize the reader with some of the native trees and shrubs of south Florida. Although it contains little information about attractiveness to birds, there is abundant general natural history information. This book is organized into beach, forest, wetland, and mangrove habitats and contains black and white photos of most plants.

Managing Woodlands for Birds

DeGraaf, Richard M., Technical Coordinator. "Management of Southern Forests for Nongame Birds." USDA Forest Service Technical Report SE-14, Southeast Forest Experiment Station, Asheville, N.C., 1978, 176 pages (paperback). This multiauthored technical report discusses the effects of management practices on nongame birds in southern forest communities, and details specific management options for snag-nesting birds, raptors, and wading birds.

DeGraaf, Richard M., Technical Coordinator. "Management of North Central and Northeastern Forests for Nongame Birds." USDA Forest Service General Technical Report NC-51, North Central Forest Experiment Station, St. Paul, Minn., 1979, 268 pages (paperback). This additional title in the nongame bird management series presents management techniques for central and eastern forest habitats. It also reviews selected nongame bird habitat programs in several states.

DeGraff, Richard M., Technical Coordinator. "Management of Western Forests and Grasslands for Nongame Birds." USDA Forest Service General Technical Report INT-86, Intermountain Forest and Range Experiment Station, Ogden, Utah, 1980, 535 pages (paperback). This weighty volume pulls together a great variety of topics concerning western nongame bird management, such as effects of grazing, strip-mining, and fire on several western bird communities. Specific papers by many authors discuss management of birds in lodgepole pine forests, birds in aspen forests, birds in montane meadows, and much more.

Gutierrez, R.J., R.A. Howard, Jr., and J.P. Lassoie. "Managing Small Woodlands for Wildlife." *Information Bulletin 157*, Extension Publication of the New York State College of Agriculture and Life Sciences, Ithaca, N.Y., undated, 32 pages (paperback). This useful booklet first defines wildlife management terminology, and then continues on to present woodland management suggestions that favor birds and other small animals. The booklet includes several tables of wildlife food preferences.

Hassinger, Jerry, Lou Hoffman, Michael J. Puglisi, Terry Rader, and Robert G. Wingard. "Woodlands and Wildlife." The Pennsylvania State University, College of Agriculture, University Park, 1979, 67 pages (paperback). This primer discusses how to develop a management plan for small woodlands and offers specific management suggestions for a variety of birds and mammals.

Minckler, Leon S. *Woodland Ecology—Environmental Forestry for the Small Owner*, 2nd ed. Syracuse University Press, Syracuse, N.Y., 1980, 241 pages (paperback). This book provides practical suggestions for how good forest management can also improve habitat for wildlife. Minckler discusses some of the principles of ecology and economics of managing small forests.

Smith, Dixie R., Technical Coordinator. "Management of Forest and Range Habitats for Nongame Birds." USDA Forest Service General Technical Report WO-1, USDA Forest Service, Washington, D.C., 1975, 343 pages (paperback). This multiauthored proceeding contains papers on various management approaches to western deciduous and coniferous forests and rangelands for nongame birds.

Nesting Structures

Grussing, Don. *How to Control House Sparrows*. Roseville Publishing House, Roseville, Minn., 1980, 52 pages (paperback). This booklet covers basic techniques for eliminating house sparrows, including shooting, live-trapping, placing snap traps in boxes (must be constantly supervised), etc. Although the booklet deals with house sparrows as "enemies," it avoids seeing them as evil, a tone that should be basic to any control effort. There is also an interesting historical section, reviewing the introduction of house sparrows and starlings, as well as justification for control programs.

Harrison, Hal H. *A Field Guide to Birds' Nests*. Houghton Mifflin Company, Boston, 1975, 257 pages (hardcover and paperback). This member of the Peterson Field Guide Series contains color photos of 285 species found breeding in the United States east of the Mississippi River. Eggs are visible in most nests, and cavity-nesting birds are usually photographed in excavated cavities. Each species account contains headings describing breeding range, habitat, nest, eggs, and general notes.

Layton, R.B. *30 Birds That Will Build in Bird Houses*. Nature Books Publishers, Jackson, Miss., 1977, 225 pages (paperback). This introductory reading features about 30 common residents of nest boxes in eastern North America. For each species there is a range map, sonogram of the song, silhouette, and photograph of the bird and its egg. The last 55 pages of the book contain simple line drawings of 39 nest box designs.

Sawyer, Edmund J. "Homes for Wildlife Baths and Feeding Shelters." *Bulletin No. 1*, 6th ed. Cranbrook Press, Bloomfield Hills, Mich., 1974, 36 pages (paperback). This very readable booklet begins with the premise that the best birdhouse is a woodpecker cavity. Learning from woodpeckers, the author shows how to construct cavities with chisel, hammer, and drills. The booklet contains plans for constructing houses for wrens, martins, wood duck, robin, and many other birds, mostly using natural materials.

Wade, J.L. *What You Should Know about the Purple Martin*. Trio Manufacturing Co., Griggsville, Ill., 1966, 240 pages (paperback). Although somewhat dated, this remains the most useful single title on the subject of attracting purple martins. The book contains chapters about martin biology, but mostly describes various kinds of homes, with a strong emphasis toward aluminum multiple-compartment designs.

Zeleny, Lawrence. *The Bluebird*. Indiana University Press, Bloomington, Ind., 1976, 170 pages (paperback). This is an excellent review of bluebird nesting behavior, with emphasis on building up bluebird populations through use of artificial nesting boxes. From his years of experience, Zeleny explains how to avoid various problems, such as parasites, predators, and nest competitors. The book contains a calendar of events during the bluebird nesting season, and includes several bluebird box designs.

Supplemental Feeding

Arbib, Robert, and Tony Soper. *The Hungry Bird Book*. Taplinger Publishing Co., New York, 1971, 126 pages (hardcover). Adapted from Tony Soper's British book titled *The Bird Table Book*, this delightful little guide to bird feeding gives many useful suggestions about setting up a feeding station. It also briefly reviews the importance of providing water, plantings, and nesting structures. The book ends with a brief guide to 99 species that visit eastern feeders. Each account includes at least one reference in the scientific literature.

Benneward, Patrice. "Banquets for Birds." National Audubon Society, New York, 1983, 24 pages (paperback). Emphasizing the importance of bird-attracting plantings, this useful guide covers the basics of setting up a bird feeding area.

Crook, Beverly Courtney. *Invite a Bird to Dinner*. Lothrop, Lee and Shepard Co., New York, 1978, 63 pages (hardcover). This is a children's book about feeding birds. It has large type, clever cartoons, and an abundance of good ideas for making feeders out of everyday materials.

Kress, Stephen W. "Bird Feeding Manual," 2nd ed. Country Foods Division of Agway, Syracuse, N.Y., in press. This concise review of how to set up a feeding station discusses feeder hazards, predators, and selective feeders for attracting a greater variety of species while minimizing wasted seed. It also includes a table showing the times of the year that you might expect various species to visit feeders in the northeast.

PERIODICALS

Around the Bird Feeder. P.O. Box 225, Mystic, CT 06355. *Around the Bird Feeder* is the quarterly magazine of the Bird Feeders Society. This publication is for the beginning bird watcher. Light, but interesting articles feature various birds that come to feeders.

Native Plant Sources. P.O. Box 515, Windsor, CA 95492. This annual publication, appearing each October, lists California nurseries and their supplies of native California plants. For those interested in gardening with native plants on the West Coast, this publication will prove a great asset in locating appropriate plant stock.

Nature Society News. Purple Martin Junction, Griggsville, IL 62340. This quarterly newsprint periodical features articles mainly about purple martin, but it usually also has features about other cavity-nesting birds, good bird-watching sites, and other appropriate news.

Organic Gardening. Rodale Press, 33 E. Minor St., Emmaus, PA 18049. Although this publication contains few articles about birds, it is a rich source for gardening tips and suppliers.

Restoration and Management Notes. University of Wisconsin-Madison, Arboretum, 1207 Seminole Highway, Madison, WI 53711. This biannual magazine is a forum for news, views, and information among ecologists, landowners, naturalists, and others interested in the area of restoration and wise stewardship of plant and animal communities. Each issue contains articles about restoration of wetlands, prairies, lakes and streams, and much more. Also includes a review of current research and publications.

Sialia. North American Bluebird Society, Box 6295, Silver Spring, MD 20906-0295. This is the quarterly journal of the North American Bluebird Society. It contains articles about managing native birds through use of nest boxes, control of parasites, nest competitors, and much more. It is not restricted to bluebirds, but also includes articles about innovative attraction techniques for other native birds.

Wild Bird Guide. Bird Friends Society, Essex, CT 06426. This is a quarterly magazine for those with a beginning interest in birds. Each issue contains 2 or 3 short articles about common birds, some interesting facts, and a list of books, feeders, and other bird-attracting supplies available from Bird Friends Society.

U.S. GOVERNMENT PUBLICATIONS

The following publications are for sale from the Superintendent of Documents. To order and obtain a current price list, write to Superintendent of Documents, U.S. Government Printing Office, Washington, DC 20402.

"Invite Birds to Your Home: Conservation Plantings for the Northeast." Anon. USDA Soil Conservation Service, PA-840, 1969, 16-panel foldout. Includes a wildlife plan for a large or small suburban lot and an illustrated discussion of wildlife-attracting techniques, such as food plots, living fences, and water areas. Nineteen useful shrubs and small trees are described, nine with color photos.

"Invite Birds to Your Home: Conservation Plantings for the Southeast." Olan W. Dillon, Jr. USDA Soil Conservation Service, Program Aid 1093, 1975, 15 pp. (Stock No. 0100-00316). Landscaping suggestions from the Carolinas to Texas that will help attract birds. Includes descriptions of 20 useful bird-attracting shrubs for this region, with color photos.

"Invite Birds to Your Home: Conservation Plantings for the Midwest." Wade H. Hamor. USDA Soil Conservation Service, PA-982, 1971, 16-panel foldout (Stock No. 0100-1450). Describes 17 shrubs useful for attracting birds from Michigan and Indiana west to the Dakotas and Kansas. Includes a landscape design for a suburban property and other landscaping suggestions for attracting birds.

"Invite Birds to Your Home: Conservation Plantings for the Northwest." L. Dean Marriage. USDA Soil Conservation Service, Program Aid 1094, 1975, 19 pp. (Stock No. 0100-03307). This booklet describes 20 shrubs and small trees useful for attracting birds to suburban properties in Washington, Oregon, and in California north of San Francisco. Several species of birds and some of the plants are illustrated in color drawings and photos. This colorful brochure also includes a landscape design for a suburban house and a table of food preferences of some common northwest birds.

"Making Land Produce Useful Wildlife." Wallace L. Anderson. USDA Farmer's Bulletin. 2035, 1975, 29 pp. (Stock No. 001-000-0021-7). Practical wildlife management projects for farmers and other large property owners. Includes a general discussion of wildlife requirements, followed by specific improvement projects for wetlands, ditch banks, odd areas, ponds, fencerows, and windbreaks.

"More Wildlife through Soil and Water Conservation." Wallace L. Anderson and Lawrence V. Compton. USDA Soil Conservation Service Agriculture Information Bulletin No. 175, 1977, 15 pp. (Stock No. 001-000-01425-1). Mostly black and white photos, this is a general interest publication with little detail, but some useful wildlife management practices, such as windbreaks, hedgerows, stream protection, and odd-areas management.

"Conservation Practices—Signs of Good Hunting and Fishing." Lawrence V. Compton, Felix Summers, and Philip F. Allan. USDA Soil Conservation Service Program Aid 1012, 1972, 31 pp. (Stock No. 0100-2573). This booklet is for those looking for a simple overview of farm and other large-property management for wildlife. It contains line drawings and brief descriptions of various farming practices that benefit both game and nongame species.

"Conservation Plants for the Northeast." W. Curtis Sharp. USDA Soil Conservation Service Program Aid No. 1154, 1977, 40 pp. (Stock No. 001-000-03605-0). This booklet contains recommended plants for disturbed areas, ornamental ground cover, plants for coastal dunes and sandy inland areas, wildlife food and cover plants, and plants for screens, hedges, and windbreaks. All are illustrated with color photos.

"Plant Materials for Conservation." Anon. USDA Soil Conservation Service Program Aid No. 1219, 1979, 31 pp. (Stock No. 001-000-03867). This booklet describes the work of the USDA plant materials centers and illustrates some of the more than 140 plant varieties developed for use in solving conservation problems, such as stopping soil erosion, reclaiming strip-mined areas, and developing range and pasture plants. The booklet also describes several varieties of wildlife food plants. Contains many color photos.

Recommended wildlife plant leaflets from USDA Soil Conservation Service: " 'Rem Red' Amur Honeysuckle," Program Aid Number 1245, 1980; " 'Roselow' Sargent Crabapple," Program Aid Number 1279, 1980-0-328-354; "VA-70 Shrub lespedeza," Program Aid Number 1277, 1980-0-328-355, "Autumn Olive," leaflet No. 458. Stock No. 001-000-02607-1.

"Cavity-Nesting Birds of North American Forests." Virgil E. Scott, Keith E. Evans, David R. Patton, and Charles P. Stone. (illustrations by Arthur Singer). *USDA Forest Service Agriculture Handbook 511,* 1977, 112 pp. (Stock No. 001-000-03726). This informative booklet reviews current research into managing forests for birds, and then reviews for each of 85 cavity-nesting birds their habitat, nest, and food requirements. Nesting discussions include preferred location for nests and recommended dimensions and height above the ground for nest boxes. This useful booklet is well-referenced with a list of cited literature.

"Planning for Wildlife in Cities and Suburbs." Daniel L. Leedy, Robert M. Maestro, and Thomas M. Franklin. USDI Fish and Wildlife Service, FWS/OBS-77/66, 1978, 64 pp. (Stock No. 024-010-00471). A thorough discussion of such topics as site planning to include wildlife needs, principles of wildlife management, and special wildlife planning concerns, such as wildlife management in streams, impoundments, parks, cemeteries, streets, highways and airports. It also includes a useful review of sources of information (especially appropriate for professional wildlife managers).

"Homes for Birds." E.R. Kalmbach and W.L. McAtee. (Revised in 1979 by D. Daniel Boone). Conservation Bulletin 14, USDI Fish and Wildlife Service, 22 pp. (1980-0-301-753). This very readable guide to building nest boxes covers all the basics for construction, placement, maintenance, and protection from predators. Several box designs are illustrated, including several natural-looking boxes.

"Attracting and Feeding Birds." Thurman W. Booth, Jr., and Donald W. Pfitzer. (Revised 1973). Conservation Bulletin No. 1, USDI Fish and Wildlife Service, 10 pp. (1973-727-375/202-3-1). This basic introduction to bird attracting gives some tips for feeding birds and lists some of the most popular trees and shrubs for attracting birds.

"Relative Attractiveness of Different Foods at Wild Bird Feeders." Aelred D. Geis. USDI Fish and Wildlife Service Special Scientific Report—Wildlife No. 233, 1980, 11 pp. (Stock No. 024-010-00587). A detailed study of the food preferences of 19 common feeder birds that visited experimental feeders in Laurel, Maryland. This report also offers recommendations for including various seeds in supplemental feeding programs.

"Establishment of Seeded Grasslands for Wildlife Habitat in the Prairie Pothole Region." Harold F. Duebbert, Erling T. Jacobson, Kenneth F. Higgins, and Erling B. Podoll. USDI Fish and Wildlife Service Special Scientific Report—Wildlife No. 234, 1981, 21 pp. (Supt. of Docs. No.: I 49.15/3:234). This publication describes techniques for establishing grasslands for waterfowl nesting in the prairie pothole region of the northcentral United States and adjacent Canada. Management of grasslands for wildlife is an important wildlife management activity in this region.

The following publication is available from: North Central Forest Experiment Station, 1992 Folwell Ave., St. Paul, MN 55108, or Northeastern Area State and Private Forestry, 370 Reed Rd., Broomall, PA 19008.

"How to Attract Cavity-nesting Birds to Your Woodlot." Anon. Undated. Six-panel folder that gives practical suggestions for managing woodlot snags for common cavity-nesting birds. Includes steps to take for creating snags and offers recommended snag density per acre for northcentral and northeastern forests.

MISCELLANEOUS PUBLICATIONS

"Helping Wildlife: Working with Nature." Delwin E. Benson. 1977, 26 pp. Published by Wildlife Management Institute, 709 Wire Building, 1000 Vermont Ave., N.W., Washington, DC 20005 ($1.00). An introductory guide to wildlife management concepts, emphasizing the importance of habitat quality in determining wildlife populations. This well-illustrated booklet explains some of the basics of population dynamics, role of predators, and endangered species management.

"Invite Wildlife to Your Backyard." Jack Ward Thomas, Robert O. Brush, and Richard M. DeGraaf. (Reprinted from April/May 1973 *National Wildlife Magazine*). 12 pp. National Wildlife Federation, 1412 16th St., N.W., Washington, DC 20036. This colorful reprint illustrates how to change a sterile suburban lot into a backyard wildlife sanctuary. The article shows three stages in the development of good habitat and gives suggestions on how to improve your property for wildlife by providing food, cover, water, and nesting sites.

"Placing American Wildlife Management in Perspective." Anon. 1974, 29 pp. ($0.50). Wildlife Management Institute, 1000 Vermont Ave., N.W., 709 Wire Building, Washington, DC 20005. This clearly written booklet discusses the importance of preserving habitat as the key to successful wildlife management. It exposes the problems of isolating emotionalism from wise management and points out that protection alone is usually not good management. Very clever cartoons illustrate the text.

"Wildlife Habitat—A Handbook for Canada's Prairies and Parklands." H.J. Poston and R.K. Schmidt. Canadian Wildlife Service Environment 1981, 51 pp. (Catalogue No. CW66-511/1981E). Available from Information Services, Agriculture Canada, Ottawa, Ont., Canada KIA OC7. This handbook is for farmers and managers of large properties who want to improve the quality of their land for wildlife. This well-illustrated guide offers many excellent techniques for improving the diversity and abundance of both game and nongame wildlife in the provinces of central Canada. An underlying emphasis is that habitat improvement for wildlife also helps to conserve soils and improves the appearance of the landscape.

BIBLIOGRAPHIES

"A Selected Bibliography of Books on Wild Flowers, Trees, Shrubs, and Ferns of North America." Anon. 1973, 3 pp. USDA Agricultural Research Service Northeastern Region, United States National Arboretum, Washington, DC 20002. A list of 70 references to the identification of North American flora.

"An Annotated Bibliography on Planning and Management for Urban-Suburban Wildlife." Daniel L. Leedy. USDI Fish and Wildlife Service Biological Services Program FWS/OBS-79/25, 1979, 256 pp. Available from Office of Biological Services, Fish and Wildlife Service, USDI, Washington, DC 20240. This bibliography contains 464 annotated references pertaining to wildlife management in urban and suburban habitats. References are compiled from the scientific literature, proceedings from symposia, annual reports, and other references that may not otherwise be readily available.

"A Bibliography of Cooperative Extension Service Literature on Wildlife, Fish, and Forest Resources." Compiled by Robert L. Ruff. Dept. of Wildlife Ecology, Cooperative Extension, Natural Resources Unit, Extension Service and Office of Extension Education, Fish and Wildlife Service, 1982, 112 pp. Available from Natural Resources Unit, Extension Service, USDA, Washington, DC 20250. This bibliography reviews available Cooperative Extension Service literature about wildlife, fish, and forest conservation and management. The citations are organized by state under headings from Animal Damage Control to Urban Forestry and Landscaping. A separate chapter lists 4-H and youth literature.

STATE AND PROVINCIAL PUBLICATIONS

The following references were compiled from literature currently available from state and provincial natural resource agencies, state offices of the Soil Conservation Service, and the Cooperative Extension Service. Most of these publications are free on request. Write to determine availability and possible cost. Although these publications vary greatly in quality, they contain abundant local information on such topics as planting recommendations and plans for constructing birdhouses, feeders, and ponds.

UNITED STATES

Alabama

Soil Conservation Service, P.O. Box 311, Auburn 36830

"Habitat Management for Birds." Anon. Guide No. A1-11-H, 1983, 2 pp. Includes some recommended plants for attracting nongame birds in Alabama and suggestions for planting food plots and providing cover and water.

"Habitat Management for Doves." Anon. Guide No. Al-11-D, 1983, 2 pp. Recommendations for increasing dove production on farmlands through planting food plots (browntop millet is favored) along with rows of corn, dove proso, and sunflower.

"Habitat Management for Ducks (Beaver Ponds)." Anon. Guide No. Al-11-I, 1983, 2 pp. Instructions for draining beaver ponds and planting them with foods that will attract wild ducks.

"Habitat Management for Quail." Anon. Guide No. Al-11-A, 1983, 2 pp. Recommendations for improving quail habitat by retaining natural food and cover plants and by creating new cover and food plot plantings.

"Habitat Management for Wild Turkeys." Anon. Guide No. Al-11-C, 1983, 2 pp. Suggested plantings and cover for developing wild turkey habitat.

"Nest Boxes for Non-game Birds." Anon. Guide No. AL-11-K, 1983, 3 pp. Discussion of materials for building nest boxes and predator guards, with box dimensions and notes for 17 types of cavity-nesting birds.

"Planting Guide." Anon. Guide No. AL-6, 1975, 4 pp. Gives recommended planting zones in Alabama, planting dates, quantities, and depths for 42 recommended legumes and grasses that stabilize soil and benefit wildlife.

Alaska

Alaska Department of Fish and Game, Nongame Wildlife Program, 1300 College Road, Fairbanks 99701

"Birdhouses for Alaska." Susan E. Quinlan. Vol. 1, no. 3, 1982, 8 pp. Discussion of considerations for building and placing nest boxes. Includes a table of nest box dimensions for 19 species of cavity-nesting Alaskan birds. Also includes plans for nesting ledges and winter roost boxes, and describes the value of dead tree snags to wildlife.

"Landscaping for Wildlife in Alaska." Susan E. Quinlan and Sal Cuccarese. Vol. 1, no. 2, 1982, 12 pp. Provides six steps for creating wildlife habitat. Gives suggestions for preparing a landscape design, transplanting plant materials, and recommendations for wildlife plantings in Alaska.

"Winter Bird-Feeding in Alaska." Susan E. Quinlan. Vol. 1, no. 1, 1982, 4 pp. Recommendations for setting up and maintaining a feeding station, with plans for six simple homemade feeders. This leaflet also includes a winter distribution map for 28 common feeder birds, with notation about their food preferences.

Cooperative Extension Service, Extension Editor, University of Alaska, Fairbanks 99701

"Alaska's Birds—Their Identification, Biology and Conservation." Susan Quinlan and Lori Quakenbush. Publication #BIR/AK-M-11, 1982, 81 pp. Book written as a guide for 4-H/Youth Program, but useful for anyone with a beginning interest in Alaskan birds. Most of the book describes common Alaskan birds, habitat, migration, and methods of attracting birds. Includes recommended activities for studying birds.

"A Key to Flower Growing in Alaska." A. C. Epps. 1977, 25 pp. Provides information on flower propagation, planting dates, and tips for beginning gardeners in Alaska.

"Landscape Plant Materials for Alaska." A. C. Epps. 1980, 66 pp. Provides information about transplanting techniques, selection and placement of plants, and availability and suitability of a variety of trees and shrubs for landscaping in Alaska. Lists and describes 227 species of trees, shrubs, and vines.

"Soil Sampling." A. C. Epps and T. E. Loynachan. 1980, 6 pp. Detailed instructions on how to take soil samples to ensure accurate results, and specific addresses to send soil samples for analysis in Alaska.

Soil Conservation Service, Professional Center, Suite 129, 2221 E. Northern Lights Blvd., Anchorage 99504

"A Revegetative Guide for Alaska" Anon. Alaska Rural Development Council, 1983, 74 pp. Provides useful information for revegetating large areas, including seed-broadcast rates (pounds/acre), fertilizer amounts and plant viability by region of Alaska. Information on planting methods. Also available from Cooperative Extension Service.

U.S. Government Printing Office, Washington, DC 20402

"Alaska Trees and Shrubs." L.A. Vierick and E.L. Little. Agricultural Handbook
No. 410. U.S. Forest Service, 1972 (Stock No. 001-000-01344-1). Specific identification and distribution information on Alaska trees and shrubs.

Arkansas

Cooperative Extension Service, State Leader—Commun., University of Arkansas, P.O. Box 391, Little Rock 72203

"Farm Pond Management." Anon. Leaflet 248, undated, 8-page folder. Describes
how to locate, construct, stock, and fertilize farm ponds.
"Homes for Purple Martins." R.A. Price. Undated, 10 pp. Discussion of martin
life history, including arrival dates in Arkansas and maintenance of houses.
Includes excellent detailed plans for a mounting pole, ranchhouse style, and
two-level martin houses.
"Shade Trees." Anon. Leaflet 261, undated, 6-panel foldout. Discusses how to
select, locate, plant, and care for shade trees.
"Wood Ducks and Wood Duck Nest Boxes." Anon. Leaflet 523, undated, 6-panel
foldout. Natural history description of wood duck nesting habits with detailed plans for how to build both wooden and metal wood duck nest boxes.
Also discusses how to reduce predation from raccoons, and illustrates predator guards.

Soil Conservation Service, P.O. Box 2323, Little Rock 72203

"Attracting Wildlife to Your Back Yard." R.G. Price. AR-BIOL-Management
Guide 3, 1980, 6 pp. Discussion of the needs of wildlife and how to incorporate these into developing a backyard wildlife management plan. Includes
a list of suggested plantings.
"Bluebird House Plans and Instructions." R.G. Price. AR-BIOL-Management
Guide 2, 1980, 2 pp. A detailed plan for building a wooden bluebird house
with instructions for locating, mounting, and maintaining.
"Fencerow Development for Wildlife in Arkansas." P.M. Brady. AR-BIOL-Management Guide 1, 1980, 4 pp. Discusses the value of developing fencerows
for wildlife, and describes seven shrubs that make ideal fencerows. Includes
a list of sources for plant materials and a reference list.
"Nongame Birds in Arkansas." R.G. Price. AR-BIOL-Management Guide 6,
1980, 8 pp. Wildlife management projects for agricultural land and large-
acreage landowners. Includes a list of birdhouse specifications for 11 common Arkansas cavity-nesting birds.

California

State of California, The Resources Agency, Department of Forestry, 1416 Ninth St., Sacramento 95814

"Establishing Woody Plants for Upland Habitat in California." L. McKibben and R. Slayback. Wildlife Habitat Leaflet No. 6, 1977, 7 pp. Recommended plants for attracting wildlife (much more than game birds) to six different California habitats, ranging from coastal valleys to the Sierra Nevada range. Also contains planting and maintenance procedures.

"The Hip Pocket Urban Tree Planter." Anon. Undated, 35 pp. Booklet in hip pocket size that discusses how to start a successful planting program. Includes information on how to organize, get people involved, select plants, planting technique, and additional references.

Cooperative Extension Service, Agricultural Sciences Publications, University of California, 1422 Harbour Way South, Richmond 94804-3688. Request price list.

"California Birds and How to Improve Their Habitat." Lewis Nelson, Jr., and Jon K. Hooper. Leaflet 2707, 1976, 32 pp. Illustrated guide to common California birds with plans for homemade feeders and houses.

"California Waterfowl and Their Management." L. Nelson, Jr., and J.K. Hooper. Leaflet 2247, 1976, 33 pp. Abundantly illustrated with line drawings, this booklet reviews the characteristics of waterfowl, methods for identification, and gives 30 suggestions for improving land for waterfowl.

"Wildlife Project Idea Book." Lewis Nelson, Jr., William G. Schneeflock, Richard D. Teague, Lee Fitzhugh, and Paul Gorenzel. Leaflet 2940, 1981, 42 pp. Booklet containing 20 wildlife projects for elementary school age students. Included are nine projects related to bird study, including plans for building mourning dove nest supports, and Canada goose and wood duck nest sites.

Other leaflets useful for attracting birds:

"Direct Seeding Woody Plants in the Landscape." No. 2577.
"Fertilizing Wood Plants." No. 2958.
"A Guide to Shrubs for Coastal California." No. 2584.
"Growing Coast and Sierra Redwoods Outside Their Natural Ranges." No. 2706.
"Landscape Trees for the Great Central Valley of California." No. 2580.
"Native California Plants for Ornamental Use." No. 2831.
"Oaks for Home Grounds." No. 2783.
"Ornamentals for California's Middle Elevation Desert." No. 1839.
"Planting Landscape Trees." No. 2576.

Cooperative Extension Service, Visual Media, University of California, Davis 95616. Write for rental and sale information.

"Distribution and Habitats of Western Upland Birds" is a 7:18-minute 54-slide–tape program with silent slide advance markers. It presents the items that constitute bird habitat, beginning with major climatic and vegetation zones in the western United States and progressing to more specific examples of feeding and nesting requirements. Changing the arrangement and spacing of vegetation will help people attract locally adapted birds by better meeting their specific habitat needs.

"Easy Living for Western Upland Birds" is a 8:44-minute 55-slide–tape program with silent slide advance markers. It stimulates ideas for local bird-enhancement projects by presenting examples of food, cover, water, and nesting requirements of rural and urban, game and nongame birds throughout the western United States.

Colorado

Division of Wildlife, Colorado Department of Natural Resources, 6060 Broadway, Denver 80216

"Bird Feeders You Can Build." E.J. Sawyer. Undated. One page of plans for building five easily constructed feeders.

"Make a Home for Wildlife." Anon. Circular 127, undated. One-page review of several birdhouse projects that children can easily construct.

Cooperative Extension Service, Extension Editor, College of Agriculture, Colorado State University, Fort Collins 80523

"Songbirds and Birds of Prey." Jon K. Hooper and Dwight R. Smith. 4H unit 6, M 52506B Members Manual, undated, 26 pp. Guide to bird study projects, including designs for simply constructed feeders and feeding adaptations of many common song- and predatory birds of Colorado. Well-illustrated with a checklist of common birds.

Connecticut

State of Connecticut, Department of Environmental Protection, Wildlife Bureau, State Office Building, Hartford 06106

"Connecticut Bluebird Project." Anon. Undated, 5 pp. Notes on construction of bluebird boxes and instructions for their placement in Connecticut.

"Wood Duck Nesting Box." Anon. Undated. Detailed plans for the construction of wood duck nest boxes with recommendations for placement. Assistance with placement is available from department personnel.

Department of Environmental Protection, Information and Education, State Office Building, Hartford 06106

"Birdscaping Your Yard." Ruth Sawyer Billard. Undated, 47 pp. Booklet gives recommendations for improving shelter, water, and landscaping on small properties. Appendix gives useful lists of Connecticut plants attractive to wildlife.

Cooperation Extension Service, Head, Agricultural Publications, Box U-35, University of Connecticut, Storrs 06268

"Attracting Birds." R.D. McDowell. 10 pp. This leaflet provides activities for attracting birds all year round. Contains a brief list of wild bird plantings and detailed plans for 14 homemade nest boxes and feeders.
"Trees and Shrubs for Connecticut." E.D. Carpenter. Undated, 47 pp. This booklet does not specify which plants are valuable for wildlife, but provides very useful descriptions of the growth and fruiting habits of most Connecticut trees and shrubs.
"Vines for Connecticut." E.D. Carpenter. Undated, 12 pp. This booklet contains useful tips for growing vines, and presents growth characteristics for 38 vine species that will grow in Connecticut; however, there is no mention of which plants are useful for attracting birds.

Delaware

Cooperative Extension Service, Agricultural Editor, Agricultural Hall, University of Delaware, Newark 19711

"Bird-Attracting Plants for the Home Landscape." David V. Tatnall. Undated, 3 pp. List of recommended plantings to attract birds in Delaware, with comments on the value of selected plantings.

Florida

Soil Conservation Service, P.O. Box 1208, Gainesville 32602

"Management for Wildlife—A Supplement to Wildlife Standard and Specification for Florida." Anon. Undated, 80 pp. Compilation of management recommendations for Florida wildlife, including sections on small nongame birds—bobwhite quail, mourning dove, wading birds (herons, etc.), wild turkey, and wood duck. Also includes an extensive listing of plantings useful for attracting wildlife in Florida.

The Sanibel-Captiva Conservation Foundation, P.O. Drawer S, Sanibel 33957

"Growing Native—Native Plants for Landscape Use in Coastal South Florida." Richard Workman. Undated, 137 pp. An invaluable resource for south Floridians who are interested in landscaping with native plants. Also a useful guide to the ecology and identification of some dominant woody plants native to beach, forest, wetlands, and mangrove communities. Includes wildlife use, propagation methods, culture, and adaptability for landscaping purposes.

Georgia

Department of Natural Resources, 270 Washington St., S.W., Atlanta 30334

EASILY CONSTRUCTED FEEDER DESIGNS

"Feeder Plans." Anon. Undated, 4 pp.
"Plants Important to Hummingbirds" and "Flowering Plants Used by Birds." Anon. Undated, 1 page each. Each summarizes some of the common garden plants recommended for attracting birds in Georgia.
"Possible Wildlife Habitat Improvements." Anon. Undated, 2 pp. A list of 42 projects for improving wildlife habitat.

Department of Natural Resources, Non-Game/Endangered Species Program, Game and Fish Division, Route 2, Box 119, Social Circle 30279

Films, video tapes, and pamphlets on Georgia endangered species. Write for a complete list.

Cooperative Extension Service, Publications Editor, College of Agriculture, University of Georgia, Athens 30602

"Annuals Are for the Birds." Anon. Undated, 2 pp. Brochure listing suggested annuals for attracting birds in Georgia.
"Attracting Birds to Your Home." Robert L. Carlton. Bulletin 727, 1974, 19 pp. Booklet presenting general guidelines for attracting birds and plans for homemade feeders, bathing pools, and nest boxes. Also includes food preferences for 52 bird species.
"Birds and Shrubs." Anon. Undated, 2 pp. List of recommended shrubs for attracting birds in Georgia.

"Birds and Vines." Anon. Undated, 2 pp. List of recommended vines and helpful tips for planting vines.

"Bring Ducks to Your Land." J. J. Jackson. Circular 718, 1980, 15 pp. Booklet offering suggestions for managing ponds and marshes for waterfowl.

"Georgia Outdoors." J. J. Jackson. Undated, 1 page. Summaries of the following topics: "How to Bring Birds into Your Life," "The Martins Are Good Neighbors," "The Bird That Lives in the Fast Lane," "A Visitor Comes Down the Chimney (Swifts)," "Why Birds Attack Windows," and "Best Food Patch for Deer and Quail."

"Managing Timber and Wildlife in the Southern Piedmont." J. J. Jackson, C. D. Walker, R. L. Shell, and D. Heiges. 1981, 51 pp. Booklet describes techniques for managing upland pines, mixed pine and hardwood stands, bottomland, and cove hardwoods for wood production and wildlife.

"Selected Practices and Plantings for Wildlife." R. L. Carlton. Bulletin 733, 1974, 11 pp. Booklet provides annotated recommendations for wildlife plantings (including aquatic and marsh plants). Growing conditions for 26 plant species are included. The booklet also describes water-control techniques, and gives management recommendations for quail and turkey.

"Wanted: More Wood Ducks in Georgia." David Almand. 1970, 11 pp. Discussion of habitat requirements for wood ducks in Georgia, with photos and descriptions of habitat, nest, eggs, and predators. Includes plans for building a wooden nest box, and details on how to locate and maintain boxes.

"Woodpeckers and Houses." J. J. Jackson. Leaflet 239. 1982, 2 pp. Describes why woodpeckers drum on houses and what can be done to deter them.

Hawaii

State of Hawaii, Department of Land and Natural Resources, Division of Forestry and Wildlife, 1151 Punchbowl St., Honolulu 96813

"Attracting Birds." Anon. Division of Forestry and Wildlife, undated, 3 pp. Leaflet describing general considerations for placing birdhouses and tending bird feeders.

Idaho

Soil Conservation Service, Room 345, 304 N. Eighth St., Boise 83702

"Appar Lewis Flax," "Delar Small Burnet," "Magnar Basin Wildrye," "Nezpar Indian Ricegrass." Anon. Undated, 4 pp each. Leaflets describing plant characteristics of these important wild bird foods.

"Landscaping for Birds in Southwestern Idaho." Golden Eagle Audubon Society and USDA, Soil Conservation Service, undated, 20 pp. A guide to planning landscaping, with lists of recommended trees, shrubs, vines, flowers, and wetland plants. Includes a list of 59 common Idaho birds, indicating food preference, seasonal status, and nest location. Also includes a checklist of southwestern Idaho birds. Similar booklets on landscaping for birds are planned for northern and eastern Idaho.

"Management and Uses of . . ." series. Anon. Undated, 2–3 pp. each. Illustrated. Each contains physical descriptions, uses, and management of the following wildlife food and cover plants for Idaho: snowberry, chokecherry, service-berry, black sagebrush, salt-marsh bulrush, silky dogwood, sago pondweed, proso millet, tall wheatgrass, widgeon grass, dwarf purple willow, smart-weed, bird's-foot trefoil, bluebunch wheatgrass, Sandberg bluegrass, buck-wheat, antelope bitterbrush, barley, Japanese millet, foxtail millet (bristle grass), Idaho fescue, redtop, barnyard-grass willows, quaking aspen, bear-berry.

"Plant Materials for Use on Surface-Mined Lands in Arid and Semiarid Regions." Ashley A. Thornburg. 1982, 88 pp. This booklet describes and maps the plant growth regions of the arid and semiarid areas of the western United States, and describes recommended trees, shrubs, and herbaceous plants that have wildlife value.

Illinois

Cooperative Extension Service, Head, Office of Agricultural Communications, College of Agriculture, University of Illinois, Urbana 61801

"Farmstead Windbreaks." W. L. Fix. No. FNR-38, 1978, 4 pp. Discussion of the importance of windbreaks, with techniques for planting and sources for ob-taining planting stocks. Includes description of recommended trees and shrubs, and a schematic drawing illustrating the conversion of an exposed farmstead to a protected environment through the use of windbreak plant-ings.

"Planting Forest Trees and Shrubs in Indiana." W. L. Fix. No. FNR-36, 1980, 8 pp. Discussion and recommendations for planting trees in old fields, wood-land openings, and windbreaks, and for wildlife habitat improvement. In-cludes planting techniques and a table showing the soil properties, erosion tolerance, and exposure requirements for 25 trees and shrubs recommended for Indiana.

"Woodlot Wildlife Management." H. C. Krauch. No. FNR-102, 1980, 7 pp. Gen-eral discussion about the importance of including wildlife in wood lot man-agement plans. Includes discussion and photos that illustrate the importance of good soils, shrubs, and mast crops. Lists 16 recommended woodland wildlife management practices.

Illinois Department of Conservation, Lincoln Tower Plaza, 524 S. Second St., Springfield 62706

"An Easily Made Bluebird House." Paul W. Woodward. Undated, 3 pp. Leaflet describing construction of a bluebird house from milk carton, and also a plan for a standard wooden design.

"Guide to Backyard Bird Feeding." Sally F. Stone. Undated, 4 pp. Leaflet that details general feeding considerations, such as placement of feeders, when to feed, and maintenance.

"How to Become a Purple Martin Landlord." Anon. Undated, 1 page. Review of nesting requirements, nest site location, and other helpful hints for attracting martins. From *Purple Martin Capital News*.

"Nest Houses for Wood Ducks." Anon. Undated. 4 pp. Leaflet describing construction of a wooden duck box, with recommendations for placement.

"Small Lakes and Ponds—Their Construction and Care." James S. Allen and Alvin C. Lopinot. Fishery Bulletin No. 3, undated, 23 pp. Booklet describes recommendations for constructing small ponds.

Illinois Department of Conservation, Mining Program, 524 S. Second St., Springfield 62706

"Illinois Plants for Habitat Restoration." Anon. 1981, 61 pp. Species descriptions of 142 trees, shrubs, vines, ground covers, aquatic plants, and prairie plants that are useful for restoring or improving the quality of Illinois lands. Each account presents, in table format, notes on height, wildlife use, habitat, and recommended planting techniques. Also includes an Illinois county map with local records for each species, as well as commercial suppliers. An excellent resource.

Soil Conservation Service, Springer Federal Building, 301 N. Randolph St., Champaign 61820

"Building Brushpiles for Wildlife." Anon. No. J.S. 812, undated, 2 pp. Contains illustrations for how to construct brush piles.

"Field Border Strips." Anon. No. J.S. 233, 1975, 2 pp. This leaflet describes how to create wildlife habitats in usually unproductive agricultural areas, such as edges of fields, borders of drainage ditches, and power line right-of-ways. Includes suggestions for planting perennial grasses and legumes.

"Wildlife Planning in Rural Areas." Anon. No. J.S. 215, undated, 2 pp. This leaflet makes the case for planning wildlife habitats in rural areas through planting hedgerows, leaving brushy areas, and planting eroded areas. Gives some specific planting suggestions.

"Wood Duck Nest Boxes." Anon. No. J.S. 234, 1975, 2 pp. Detailed plans for constructing wooden and sheet metal wood duck nest boxes, with recommendations for placement.

Indiana

Indiana Department of Natural Resources, Publications, Division of Fish and Wildlife, 607 State Office Building, Indianapolis 46204

"Artificial Homes for Wildlife." Anon. Management Series No. 2, undated, 10 pp. Plans for constructing nest sites for wood ducks, Canada goose, purple martin, and many small cavity nesters. Also plans for a rabbit burrow.

"Back Yard Wildlife Management." Anon. Management Series No. 2, undated, 16 pp. Suggestions for improving suburban lots into productive wildlife areas through landscaping and providing artificial nest boxes and feeders. This booklet includes a schematic drawing for a 100 × 200 foot lot, and lists recommended trees and shrubs for Indiana, with soil, light, and spacing requirements.

"Winter Bird Feeding." Anon. Management Series No. 14, undated, 7 pp. Suggestions for construction of feeders and planting sorghum food plots.

Additional management leaflets are available on the following topics: "Use of Herbicides in Establishing Woody Plantings," "Managing Woodlands for Wildlife," "Wildlife Management with Herbaceous Cover," "Wildlife Management with Trees and Shrubs," "Marsh Development for Wildlife." Write for a complete list.

Soil Conservation Service, Suite 2200, 5610 Crawfordsville Rd., Indianapolis 46224

"Building Brushpiles for Wildlife." Anon. No. JS-IN-BI-19, undated, 2 pp. Plans for building brush piles.

"Developing Pond Areas for Wildlife." Anon. No. JS-IN-BI-19, undated, 2 pp. Suggestions for landscaping the immediate area around farm ponds to prevent excessive trampling and to achieve maximum benefit for wildlife.

"Feeding Songbirds." Anon. No. JS-IN-BI-24, undated, 1 page. General suggestions for feeding birds, and plans for the construction of a simple window-shelf feeder.

"Field Border Strips." Anon. 1968, 1 page. Techniques for planting a grassy strip of wildlife cover and food at the edge of a farm field.

"Land Management for Non-Game Birds." Anon. No. JS-IN-BI-14, undated, 2 pp. This list of suggested habitat improvements gives specific examples of projects that will provide more food and shelter for small birds.

"Odd Area Development and Management." Anon. 1968, 1 page. Suggestions for how to plant odd areas, such as rock outcrops, to benefit wildlife.

Iowa

Iowa Conservation Commission, Wildlife Research Station, R.R. #1, Boone 50036

"Attracting Back Yard Wildlife." Anon. Undated. Eight-panel color foldout providing specific shrub recommendations for Iowa. The leaflet also includes a sample landscape design, as well as Iowa district forester and wildlife management biologist addresses.

"Iowa Bird Study." Anon. Undated, 16 pp. Booklet contains checklist of Iowa birds, plans for constructing a wood duck box, and specifications for building birdhouses for cavity-nesting birds.

"Iowa's Farm Ponds." Kay Hill and Joe Schwartz. Undated, 16 pp. Booklet has recommendations for pond construction, vegetation control, and general suggestions for improving the wildlife value of the pond through plantings.

Cooperative Extension Service, Extension Editor, Morrill Hall, Iowa State University, Ames 50011

"A House for Bluebirds." Anon. No. WL-41, 1975, 1 page. Detailed plan for construction.

"A Four Room Martin House." Anon. No. WL-31, 1968, 1 page. Construction design.

"A Robin Nesting Shelter." Anon. WL-23, 1963, 1 page. Construction design.

"A Weather Vane Bird Feeder." Anon. No. WL-20, 1966, 1 page. Detailed construction plan.

Kansas

Kansas Fish and Game, Pratt Headquarters, Box 54A, Rural Route 2, Pratt 67124

"Who's Who at Kansas Birdfeeders—Guide to a Winter Windowsill." In *Kansas Wildlife*, Jan./Feb. 1981, pp. 25–31. Color photographs and brief text describing the food preferences of 13 common feeder birds in Kansas.

Cooperative Extension Service, Extension Editor, College of Agriculture, Kansas State University, Manhattan 66506

"Mr. Landowner . . . Wildlife Needs Your Help.." Anon. 1975, 12 pp. Discussion of the importance of plantings to wildlife.

"Naturalistic Landscaping." Gustaaf A. van der Hoeven. No. C-581, 1977, 27 pp. Improving the appearance of landscape through natural design. Gives specific recommendations for how to place plantings with aesthetics in mind. Appendices include descriptions of useful wildlife plantings and several "naturalistic feeders."

"Shrubs That Attract Songbirds and Wildlife." James J. Nighswonger. 1981, 2 pp. List of preferred shrubs for songbirds in Kansas.

"Trees and Shrubs for Conservation Plantings." Anon. 1977, 7 pp. Annotated list of the trees and shrubs available from the Kansas State nursery.

"Trees That Attract Songbirds and Wildlife." James J. Nighswonger. 1981, 2 pp. Listing of trees attractive to Kansas songbirds.

Kentucky

Kentucky Department of Fish and Wildlife Resources, Arnold L. Mitchell Bldg., #1 Game Farm Road, Frankfort 40601

"How to Have Both Firewood and Wildlife." Jim Durell. In *Kentucky Happy Hunting Ground*, Sept./Oct. 1980, 4 pp. Recommendations for managing forest lands to produce abundant wildlife.

"Wildlife Management Practices." Anon. 1978, 14 pp. Discussion of recommended plantings for improving wildlife habitat. Includes a table of 18 recommended food plants for wildlife, giving pounds of seed per acre, planting dates, width or spacing, and recommended fertilizer and cultivation methods.

Soil Conservation Service, 333 Waller Ave., Lexington 40504

"Developing Farm Pond Areas for Wildlife." Anon. 1962, 2 pp. Guidelines for planting vegetation around a farm pond to benefit wildlife.

"Land Management" series. Anon. Undated, 2 pp. each. Guidelines for improving wildlife habitat for the following birds: nongame birds, mourning doves, wild turkey, ducks, ruffed grouse, and bobwhite quail.

Louisiana

Louisiana Department of Wildlife and Fisheries, P.O. Box 15570, Baton Rouge 70895

"The Barn Owl." Leslie L. Glasgow. Undated, 7 pp. Booklet describing the feeding habits of the barn owl, demonstrating its value in controlling rodent populations.

"The Birds and Their Feed." Hannah M. Yates. Wildlife Education Bulletin No. 27, undated, 8 pp. Discussion of food for nongame birds.

"Common Birds of Louisiana." Anon. Wildlife Education Bulletin No. 71-1976, revised 1981, 67 pp. Illustrated booklet providing natural history information about 47 Louisiana bird species. General comments on birdhouses, birdbanding, and attracting birds.

"Food for Wildlife." Robert Murry. Wildlife Education Bulletin No. 60, undated, 7 pp. Review of some of the important foods for Louisiana game birds.

"Louisiana Bobwhite Basics." Tommy Prickett. Wildlife Education Bulletin No. 113, undated, 35 pp. Booklet showing ways to increase bobwhite populations through habitat management.

"The Wood Duck in Louisiana." Hugh A. Bateman. Wildlife Education Bulletin No. 29, undated, 31 pp. Booklet providing plans for construction of wood duck houses, and suggestions for maintaining the boxes and deterring predators. Also life history and migration information.

Cooperative Extension Service, Communications Division, Center for Agricultural Science & Rural Development, Knapp Hall, University Station, Louisiana State University, Baton Rouge 70803

"Build a Bird a Home." Anon. Undated, 10 pp. Booklet for upper elementary age students, containing plans for construction of nest boxes for wrens, purple martins, wood duck, and screech owl.

Soil Conservation Service, 3737 Government St., Alexandria 71301

"A Supplement to Biology Standards and Specifications for Louisiana." Anon. Undated, 110 pp. A guide to game management for fish, mammals, and birds in Louisiana. Includes suggestions for improving habitat for quail, ducks, geese, mourning dove, wild turkey, and snipe. Includes a useful 23-page illustrated appendix to Louisiana aquatic plants.

Maine

Cooperative Extension Service, Director of Public Information, College of Life Sciences and Agriculture, University of Maine, Orono 04473

"Flowering Crabapples in Maine." Lyle Littlefield. Bulletin No. 593, Univ. of Maine at Orono, 1981, 10 pp. A guide to planting and selecting flowering crabapples, presenting information on 78 varieties that will grow in Maine. This helpful booklet describes the colors of flowers and fruits, presents information on which are preferred by birds, and much more.

Soil Conservation Service, USDA Office Building, University of Maine, Orono 04473

"Attracting Songbirds with Plants." Anon. ME-B-41, 1981, 4 pp. Discussion of general requirements and specific plants that are useful for attracting songbirds in Maine. Lists include grasses and legumes, herbaceous flowering plants, trees, shrubs, and vines, with indications of the number of songbirds known to feed on each species.

"Control of Bird Damage to Agricultural Crops." Robert J. Wengrzynek. ME-B-38, 1981, 9 pp. Discussion of control methods for crows, ravens, pigeons, gulls, sparrows, starlings, and blackbirds.

"50 Suggestions for Improvement of Maine Wildlife Habitat." Anon. ME-B-43, 1981, 4 pp. Fifty habitat improvement ideas, ranging from developing more edge to providing dusting areas for songbirds.

"Hedges for Conservation." Robert J. Wengrzynek, Jr. ME-B-5, 1974, 5 pp. Recommended shrubs for building fencerows in Maine, with illustrations of various planting configurations.

"How to Graft Fruit Trees for Wildlife." E.A. Swenson. ME-645-24, 1968, 2 pp. Detailed directions on how to graft useful crabapple selections onto wild apple trees.

"Land Management for Woodcock in New England." Robert J. Wengrzynek and William Krohn. ME-645-34, 1980, 4 pp. Natural history of woodcocks in the northeast, with suggestions for managing habitat for their benefit.

"Planting Shrubs in Maine." Anon. ME-645-8, 1963. List of seven popular wildlife shrubs that thrive in Maine, with recommendations on how to plant them.

"Plants for Conservation in the Northeast." Anon. ME-645-11, Conservation Plant Sheet-38 "Crabapples," undated. Description and uses of crabapples for wildlife foods, with recommendations of three important species for the northeast—Siberian, Japanese, and Sargent crabapples.

"Trees That Have Important Wildlife Value in Maine." Howard L. Burpee. ME-BO4, 1974, 4 pp. Annotated list of 31 trees with particular benefits for Maine wildlife.

Massachusetts

Massachusetts Division of Fisheries and Wildlife, Field Headquarters, Westboro 01581 (send SASE)

"The Chickadee—Massachusetts State Bird." Anon. Undated, 2 pp. Discussion of the natural history habits of black-capped chickadee, with emphasis on feeding behavior and how to attract this popular bird.

"Housing Project for Wood Ducks." Anon. Undated, 8 pp. Recommended plans for building wood duck nest boxes and predator guards.

"Massachusetts Martin House." Anon. Undated, 2 pp. List of materials and detailed plans for constructing a 12-compartment wood martin house.

"Purple Martin Program." Anon. Undated, 3 pp. Discussion of the nesting requirements of the purple martin, with suggestions for attraction.

Cooperative Extension Service, University of Massachusetts, Amherst 01003

"Popple Partridge." F. Greeley, Reprinted from *Massachusetts Wildlife*, Sept./Oct. 1975, 7 pp. Discussion of the importance of aspen trees as food for ruffed grouse, with suggestions for managing forests to favor aspen.

Michigan

Department of Natural Resources, Stevens T. Mason Building, Box 30028, Lansing 48909

"Birdhouses: A Guide for Building and Placing Houses for Birds." Anon. DNR Reports, undated, 12 pp. Birdhouse designs for the following species, among others: wood duck, robin, black-capped chickadee, kestrel/screech owl, tree swallow, purple martin, and bluebird.

Cooperative Extension Service, Manager, Extension & Research Information, 109 Agricultural Hall, Michigan State University, East Lansing 48824

"Cut-Back Borders Provide Wildlife Habitat." Anon. J.S.-823, 1982, 2 pp. Discussion of the practice of thinning woodland borders to increase shrub growth, which favors many wild bird species.
"Developing Odd Areas for Wildlife." Anon. J.S. 814, 1981. Suggested planting plans for "odd areas," such as corners of agricultural fields, rock-outcrop areas, and ponds. Includes a list of recommended grasses, shrubs, and trees, with information on recommended planting procedures.
"Developing Odd Areas for Wildlife." Anon. 1981, 2 pp. Discussion of landscaping ideas that will benefit wildlife. Includes selection of grasses, trees, shrubs, and vines for wild birds, with notes on planting procedures.
"Establishing Vegetation on Utility Rights-of-Way." Anon. J.S. 539, 1975, 2 pp. Recommended planting procedures and plant species for planting under utility power lines.
"Feeding and Attracting Wildlife." Anon. Extension Bulletin E-759, 1982, 12 pp. Booklet gives plans for construction of homemade feeders, water supplies, and birdhouses.
"Field Border Strips for Wildlife Use." Anon. J.S. 824, 1982, 2 pp. Recommendation to plant a strip of low-growing perennial vegetation at the edge of a crop field. Includes some recommended plants for this purpose.
"Land Management for Mourning Doves." Anon. BI-12, undated, 2 pp. Suggestions for improving agricultural land for mourning doves by providing shelters, watering areas, and food supplies.
"Land Management for Non-Game Birds." Anon. BI-14, undated, 2 pp. Projects

for managing agricultural lands and forests for increased production of song-birds. Includes discussion of such management practices as hedgerows, fencerows, roadsides, and ditch banks.

Minnesota

Minnesota Department of Natural Resources, Bureau of Information and Education, Box 46, Centennial Office Building, St. Paul 55155

"Attract Wildlife to Your Back Yard." Charles A. Wechsler. DNR Reports, Number 92, undated, 4 pp. Discussion of recommended trees and shrubs for attracting wildlife in Minnesota. Includes a planting plan and discusses the value of wildlife for teaching ecological concepts to the family.

"Birdhouses in Minnesota." Carol Henderson. DNR Reports, Number 77, undated, 8 pp. Pamphlet with detailed plans for building nest boxes for house wren, wood duck, black-capped chickadee, kestrel/screech owl, tree swallow, purple martin, and bluebird. Also plans for mourning dove, robin, and phoebe nest platforms. Includes general guidelines for placement.

Cooperative Extension Service, Head of Department, Information & Agricultural Forestry & Home Economics, 433 Coffey Hall, University of Minnesota, St. Paul 55108

"Snags for Wildlife." James R. Kitts. Extension Folder 581-1981, undated, 4 pp. Discussion of the value of dead trees and tree cavities for attracting wildlife. Presents guidelines for maintaining an ample number of snags as part of a woodlot management program.

"Woody Plants That Attract Birds." Mervin Eisel. Arboretum Review No. 13-1972, undated, 4 pp. List of recommended trees, shrubs, and vines for attracting birds of Minnesota. The list includes relative wildlife value, fruiting season, and general remarks.

Soil Conservation Service, 316 N. Robert St., Rm. 200, Federal Bldg., St. Paul 55101

"Minnesota Plant Adaptations and Limitations for Plants Used for Recreation or Non-Agricultural Uses." Anon. Tech. Guide Section II-1, 1980, 25 pp. Detailed list of recommended grasses, shrubs, and trees used for wildlife and landscape plantings in table form, with notes on growth form, tolerance to trampling and flooding, uses, and so forth.

"Steps in Managing Land for Ruffed Grouse." Anon. 1979, 4 pp. Discusses the cause of cycles in grouse populations, and points to the management of aspen groves as the most important approach. Includes a distribution map showing the range of the ruffed grouse in Minnesota.

"Windbreak Species with Good Wildlife Fruits by Times When Fruits Are Available." Anon. 1980, 1 page. List of selected trees and shrubs that can double for windbreaks and improvement of wildlife habitat. The list gives height of each shrub after 20 years.

"Wood Duck Nest Box." Anon. 1978, 2 pp. Plan for construction of a wood duck nest box, with comments on the placement of the boxes and suggestions for predator deflectors.

Mississippi

Mississippi Dept. of Wildlife Conservation, Mississippi Museum of Natural Science, 111 N. Jefferson St., Jackson 39202

"How to Attract Songbirds in Mississippi." Anon. Undated, 1 page. Guide to providing food, housing dimensions for cavity-nesting birds, and plantings.

Cooperative Extension Service, Leader, Extension Information, College of Agriculture, Mississippi State University, Mississippi 39762

"Attracting Birds." Anon. Undated, 1 page. Discussion containing useful tips for feeding birds.

"Building a Bird Feeder." Anon. Undated, 2 pp. Plan for building a Hooper bird feeder.

"Raising Red Worms in a Tub." Anon. Undated, 2 pp. Tells how anyone can raise fishing worms. Beneficial for attracting worm-eating birds, such as robins.

Missouri

Missouri Department of Conservation, P.O. Box 180, Jefferson City 65102

"Back Yard Birds." John Wylie. Undated, 4 pp. Discussion of techniques for attracting more birds to backyard habitat through use of feeders and plantings. This brochure also includes recommended birdhouse dimensions for 14 species of cavity-nesting birds.

"Hopper Feeder Plan." Anon. Undated, 1 page. Detailed plan for construction of a weather-resistant hopper-type bird feeder.

"Winter Birds." James D. Wilson, Reprint from the Dec. 1979 issue of *Missouri Conservationist*, 4 pp. Discussion of favored foods for 21 bird species that frequent Missouri feeders in winter. Includes color illustrations.

Montana

Cooperative Extension Service, Editor, Extension Information, Hamilton Hall, Montana State University, Bozeman 59717

"Trees and Shrubs for Montana." Anon. Bulletin 323, 1977, 73 pp. Descriptions and range maps for 75 species of trees and shrubs that grow in Montana. Most species descriptions contain photographs and line drawings. Includes notes on the value of certain trees and shrubs for wildlife.

Soil Conservation Service, P.O. Box 970, Federal Building, Bozeman 59715

"Do Something Wild—Landscape for Wildlife." Anon. Undated, 13 pp. Describes Montana's Back Yard Wildlife Program, and provides addresses of several local nurseries and a useful list of recommended plants for attracting wildlife. The publication also includes dimensions and illustrations for many homemade houses and feeders.

Nebraska

Nebraska Game and Parks Commission, 2200 N. 33rd St., P.O. Box 30370, Lincoln 68503

"Cultivated Foods for Wildlife." Anon. Planting Series No. 3, undated, 4 pp. Suggestions for planting food plots, including cultivation procedures for corn, milo, sunflowers, and millet.
"Legumes for Wildlife." Anon. Planting Series No. 6, undated, 4 pp. Recommendations for planting legumes that favor wildlife. This brochure describes planting technique and the value of these plants for wildlife.
"Nut Seeding for Wildlife." Anon. Planting Series No. 5, undated, 4 pp. Recommendations for increasing nut production through planting more nut- and berry-producing trees.
"Shrubs for Wildlife." Anon. Planting Series No. 2, undated, 4 pp. Discussion that gives recommended shrubs and their growth characteristics. Includes suggestions for planting technique.
"Sources for Bird Seed." Anon. Undated, 1 page. List of commercial grain suppliers and the prices and availability of various seeds.
"Trees for Wildlife." Anon. Planting Series No. 4, undated, 4 pp. Includes growth characteristics and planting procedures for 22 recommended trees.
"Warm Season Grasses for Wildlife." Anon. Planting Series No. 1, undated, 4 pp. Discussion presenting recommendations for selecting grass seed, ground preparation, seeding, and weed control.
"Wildlife Habitat: Planning and Planting for the Future." Anon. Undated, 16 pp.

Booklet with abundant color photographs. General discussion about what can be done to favor wildlife through habitat management. Specific recommendations detail how winter cover, travel lanes, shelter belts, and other management techniques can make a real difference in wildlife. The booklet includes specific suggestions for trees, shrubs, and vines.

Cooperative Extension Service, Extension Editor, Publications, Institute of Agricultural & Natural Resources, Agriculture Hall, East Campus, University of Nebraska, Lincoln 68583

"Broadleaf Trees for Nebraska." Neal E. Jennings *et al.* 1978, 55 pp. Color photographs illustrate 57 different broadleaf trees that grow in Nebraska. Each species entry includes a description of the tree, Nebraska range map, and points of interest, including soil type, disease resistance, and value to birds.

"Guides to Clarke-McNary Shrubs, Broadleaf Trees, and Conifers." Anon. Undated, 4 pp. Leaflets include color photographs, tables of growth characteristics, soil suitability, and additional information about the trees and shrubs available from the Nebraska state tree nursery.

"How to Plant Landscape Trees." Dennis M. Adams and Richard J. Gavit. Neb. Guide No. G77-347, 1981. Presents techniques for selection, planting, pruning, staking, and other maintenance tips for getting landscape trees off to a good start.

"Planting for Wildlife." Jon Farar, Ed. Nebraska Game and Parks Commission, undated, 14 pp. Attractively illustrated color booklet showing 6 projects for improving rural land for wildlife. The booklet includes tables of recommended trees, shrubs, and vines, with growth characteristics, and gives suggestions for managing urban habitats for wildlife.

"Ponds for Nebraskans." Philip S. Gipson, Darrell E. Feit, and Jerry W. Morris. No. EC75-1427, undated, 14 pp. Discusses where and how to build farm ponds so that they can provide maximum value for wildlife. Includes recommended plants for landscaping and a farm pond design. Abundantly illustrated with color photos.

Nevada

Cooperative Extension Service, Publications Editor, Agricultural Community Services, University of Nevada, Reno 89507

"Conservation Plantings for Rangeland, Windbreaks, Wildlife, Soil Conservation Cover." H.M. Kilpatrick, *et al.* 1978, 24 pp. Booklet presents growth characteristics for recommended trees, shrubs, and ground-cover plants to aid wildlife in Nevada. Describes planting procedures for conservation plantings.

New Hampshire

Soil Conservation Service, Box G, Durham 03824

"Attracting Songbirds with Plants." Anon. Biology NH-38, 1981, 4 pp. Recommended grasses, herbs, and shrubs for attracting birds in New Hampshire, with notes on parts of the plant consumed, seasonal use, and the number of songbird species known to use the plant in the northeast.

"Plants with a Purpose." D.N. Alan. 1978, 16 pp. Description and maps showing the locations of 33 different plant species in locations throughout New Hampshire that serve as long-term study plots. Includes notes on the growth performance of each species under different local conditions. A unique, nicely documented publication.

New Mexico

Cooperative Extension Service, Agricultural Editor, Drawer 3AI, New Mexico State University, Las Cruces 88003

"Recommended New Mexico Evergreen and Deciduous Trees." Anon. Undated, 2 pp. List of 16 recommended coniferous and deciduous trees for New Mexico, including descriptions, soil preference, elevation range, and uses.

New York

Department of Natural Resources, New York State College of Agriculture and Life Sciences, Cornell University, Ithaca 14850

"Back Yard Improvements of Wildlife Habitat." J.N. Briggs. Conserv. Circ. 12(4), 1974, 4 pp. Discussion of the value of certain plants for improving backyard landscape for wildlife. Includes recommendations.

"Bird Damage Control Guide for Homeowners." Anon. Conserv. Circ. 19(1), 1981, 4 pp. Includes a list of addresses for repellents and netting. Also gives control recommendations for solving bird damage problems.

"Guide to Deer-Resistant Ornamental Plants." J.W. Caslick. Conserv. Circ. 20(2), 1982, 3 pp. List of 65 deer-resistant plants, including trees, shrubs, vines, and ground covers.

"A New Technique for Planting Multiflora Rose Hedges for Wildlife." J.W. Caslick. Conserv. Circ. 9(2), 1971, 2 pp. Describes how black polyethylene plastic can greatly increase the survival of newly planted multiflora rose hedges. Technique also shows promise for planting other hedge plants.

"Plants for Improving Wildlife Habitat Around Your Home." C.P. Dawson and D.J. Decker. Conserv. Circ. 16(7), 1978, 8 pp. Includes guidelines for selection and placement of wildlife plantings, an annotated bibliography, and a list of selected plants for enhancing wildlife habitat in New York.

"The Purple Martin and Mosquitoes." J. Tate, Jr. Conserv. Circ. 9(3), 1971, 3 pp. Discussion of the controversy about the martin's proclaimed food preference for mosquitoes. According to this leaflet, there is no evidence that mosquitoes comprise a significant portion of the martin's diet.

"What Should I Do With This Bird?" J. Tate, Jr. Conserv. Circ. 10(2), 1972, 4 pp. Discussion of basic care for orphaned birds.

"Woodpecker Damage and the Homeowner." J. Tate, Jr. Conserv. Circ. 8(3), 1970, 3 pp. Discussion of why woodpeckers drum and feed on houses, with several suggestions for displacing problem birds.

Soil Conservation Service, James M. Hanley Federal Building, 100 S. Clinton St., Rm. 771, Syracuse 13260

"Cottontail Rabbits." Anon. Tech. Guide Section IV, No. 645, 1975. Habitat requirements and management specifications for improving land for rabbits in New York; the same management techniques are also very helpful to many songbirds. Lists recommended plantings for food and cover, and optimum percentage of cover for grasses, herbaceous perennials, and hardwood plantings.

"How to Plant Wildlife Shrubs." 1979. Inform. Sheet NY-64, Anon, 4 pp. Illustrated directions for soil preparation and planting techniques for wildlife shrubs.

"Maintaining Open Areas." Inform. Sheet NY-66, 1971, 2 pp. Describes the value of maintaining open land, and various techniques, such as moving, selective cutting, and grubbing.

"Supplement for Wildlife Wetland Habitat Management." Anon. No. 644-1, 1983, 15 pp. Defines various wetland habitats, and describes specifications for water-control structures, such as dams and spillways. This paper describes the size of wetlands and the vegetation and other requirements necessary for attracting wildlife, such as ducks, geese, songbirds, and muskrats.

"Wild Plants and Their Value to Upland Wildlife." Anon. Inform. Sheet NY-59, 1982, 4 pp. Recommendations for improving land for wild birds and mammals. Includes a list of recommended trees, shrubs, vines, grasses, and herbaceous plants, indicating wildlife use.

North Carolina

North Carolina Wildlife Resources Commission, Archdale Building, 512 N. Salisbury St., Raleigh 27611

"Bird Furniture." Anon. Undated, 8 pp. Plans for building birdbaths, houses, and feeders.

Cooperative Extension Service, Head, Department of Agricultural Information, North Carolina State University, P.O. Box 5037, Raleigh 27650

"Pigeon Control," "Blackbird Control in North Carolina," and "Control of English Sparrows." Anon. Zoology Notes, undated, 4 pp each. Leaflets provide recommendations for control of these species.

North Dakota

Soil Conservation Service, P.O. Box 1458, Bismarck 58502

"Hedgerow Planting." Anon. Tech. Guide Notice ND-16, Standards and Specifications Section IV-E, No. 422-1, 1982, 2 pp. Guidelines for establishing a hedgerow–travel lane with recommendations for shrubs and conifers adapted to the North Dakota climate.

"Multirow Wildlife Plantings with Single Species Planted in Blocks." Anon. Undated, 2 pp. Recommended planting pattern for a large wildlife planting creating a rectangular plot of mixed trees and shrubs. Includes specific recommendations.

"Plantings for Small Acreages." Anon. Undated, 10 pp. Designs for planting that consider prevailing wind patterns and snow accumulation trends. Includes designs for single- and multiple-ownership properties.

"Suggested Design for Large Multirow Wildlife Plantings." Anon. Undated. Schematic drawing that suggests an arrangement for a large wildlife planting.

"Suggested Planting Arrangements to Benefit Wildlife Near Pivot Irrigation Systems." Anon. Undated, 4 pp. Recommended ways to benefit wildlife on agricultural lands that use the pivot irrigation system, through various planting patterns.

"Suggested Wildlife Planting for an Open Area." Anon. Undated, 1 page. Planting arrangement for a large, circular wildlife plot for open countryside. Includes specific shrub and tree recommendations for North Dakota.

"Wildlife Upland Habitat Management." Anon. Tech. Guide Notice ND-8, Standards and Specifications Section IV, No. 645-1, 1982, 14 pp. The use of fire, fertilizer, and plantings to improve land for wildlife. Includes procedures for planting food plots and managing agricultural lands.

"Wildlife-Windbreak-Beautification Plantings for Small Rural Acreages and Homesites." D.L. Hintz. Tech. Notes, Woodland No. 16, 1976, 2 pp. Recommendations for selecting trees that have wildlife and beautification qualities when planting windbreaks.

Ohio

Ohio Department of Natural Resources, Division of Wildlife, Fountain Square, Columbus 43224

"Attracting Birds in Ohio." Merrill C. Gilfillan. Publication 37, undated, 25 pp. Plans for construction of houses and feeders, as well as general suggestions for landscaping to favor wildlife. The booklet also includes a list of Ohio birds.

"Bird Feeding." Anon. Publication 345, undated, 2 pp. General guide to food preferences for some Ohio birds and a plan for a hopper-type feeder.

"Wild Food Patch Seed Mixture." Anon. Publication 351, undated, 1 page. Description of how to establish a food patch for wildlife.

Soil Conservation Service, 200 North High Street, Columbus 43215

"Native Ohio Shrubs." M.C. Gilfillan and A.W. Cannon. Undated, 8 pp. Includes 16 color photos of the fruits of common Ohio shrubs, and describes a total of 32 shrubs that are valuable for attracting birds.

"Standards and Specifications for Wildlife Habitat Management." Anon. Ohio SCS Technical Guide, Section IV 6, undated, 3 pp. Recommended crops, herbaceous plants, shrubs, and trees for improving land for wildlife in Ohio, with notes on food and cover preferences for local bird species.

Oklahoma

Soil Conservation Service, State Office, Stillwater 74074

"Plants for a Purpose: Manhattan Plant Materials Center." Anon. Undated, 8 pp. Describes the activities of the Manhattan Plant Materials Center and how its employees develop and select plants for wildlife management and other conservation purposes.

"Windbreaks for Wildlife." Anon. Undated, 4 pp. Discusses the value of windbreaks to wildlife and how to best plant the windbreak. Lists and describes recommended shrubs and trees that are available from the state's forestry division.

Oregon

Information and Education Section, Oregon Department of Fish and Wildlife, 506 S.W. Mill Street, P.O. Box 3503, Portland 97208

"Bird Feeders." Anon. Undated, 2 pp. Illustrations for 17 simple ways to offer grain and suet to birds, with general comments on providing suet, peanut butter, seeds, grit, and hummingbird food.

"Bird House Assembly Using Wood-Fiber Transplanting Pots." Anon. Undated, 2 pp. Illustrated directions for how to construct a nest box from a transplanting pot. Also includes sizes for entrance holes and approximate height above ground for box placement for 10 species of local cavity-nesting birds.

"Wood Duck Nest Box Plan." Anon. Undated, 2 pp. Detailed construction plans and materials list for building a wood duck box, with suggestions for placing the box.

"Wood Duck Nesting Box." Anon. Undated, 2 pp. Suggestions for placing wood duck boxes, and detailed construction plans for building a wood duck nest box.

Pennsylvania

Pennsylvania Game Commission, P.O. Box 1567, Harrisburg 17120

"50 Birds and Mammals of Pennsylvania." Tony Williams and Ned Smith. Undated, 17 pp. Survey of 50 common birds and mammals. Excellent line illustrations and informative natural history notes.

"Nesting Boxes, Feeding Stations, Bird Houses and Wildlife Shelters." Anon. Undated, 4 pp.Well-illustrated designs for a variety of easily constructed feeders and houses.

"Wildlife Notes Series." Chuck Fergus. Undated 2- to 4-page leaflets about the natural histories and habitat needs of the following birds: ruffed grouse, owls, raptors, crows and ravens, woodpeckers, bobwhite quail, heron familly, wild turkey, mourning dove, ring-necked pheasant, Canada goose, woodcock, vultures, eagles, and osprey.

"Wings Out Your Window." P.J. Bell, Undated, 4 pp. Discussion of the importance of food, cover, and water for birds, with suggestions on how to attract more birds. Also a calendar of bird activity, and a list of suggested wildlife plantings, with notes on growth characteristics.

Cooperative Extension Service, Publications Editor, 401 Agricultural Administration Bldg., Pennsylvania State University, University Park 16802

"Aquatic Plants: Management and Control." R. G. Wingard, T. D. Rader, W. K. Hock, and R. B. Hesser. Special Circular 79, undated, 18 pp. Discusses how to control aquatic vegetation in farm ponds. Includes a catalog of aquatic plants that illustrates and describes 30 common aquatic plants in Pennsylvania ponds and lakes.

Cooperative Extension Service, Box 985 Federal Square Station, Harrisburg 17108

"A Guide for Wildlife Food and Cover Plantings in Pennsylvania." Anon. 1969,

4 pp. Tables of recommended wild bird food-crops, with suggestions for rotation plans and seed mixtures.

South Carolina

Cooperative Extension Service, Publications Editor, Clemson University, Clemson 29631

"Single and Multiple Bluebird Boxes." John R. Sweeney and Carroll G. Belser. 1980, 4 pp. Folder about bluebirds, including a design for a wooden, solid-roof house, and layout for how to make 26 bluebird houses out of two 4 × 8 foot plywood sheets.

South Dakota

Cooperative Extension Service, Agriculture Information Editor, South Dakota State University, University Station, Brookings 57007

"Pheasants and Farming in South Dakota." Anon. No. FS 656, undated. Fourteen agricultural practices that benefit pheasant populations in South Dakota (most also apply elsewhere). Also includes a list of six practices that will decrease pheasant populations.

Tennessee

Tennessee Wildlife Resources Agency, Ellington Agricultural Center, P.O. Box 40747, Nashville 37204

"Giving Wildlife an Edge: A Guide to Ornamental Plants for Wildlife Habitat." Valerie S. Powers and Robert M. Hatcher. 1982, 44 pp. Booklet including selected black and white photographs and the growth characteristics of 91 trees, shrubs, vines, and ground covers that are useful for attracting wildlife in Tennessee.

"A 'Lot' for Wildlife." Valerie Powers. Reprint from *Tennessee Wildlife Magazine*, March/April 1981, 8 pp. Discussion of the use of wildlife plantings for improving wildlife habitat around the home. Includes a table listing 20 recommended trees, shrubs, and vines for Tennessee.

"Source List of Wildlife-Related Environmental Education Materials." Anon. 1982, 3 pp. List of films and literature about Tennessee wildlife.

"The Wildlife Plant Source—Materials for Wildlife Habitat Improvement." Anon. 1982, 9 pp. List of mail-order houses and the wildlife plantings that each supplier can provide.

Cooperative Extension Service, Director, Office of Communications, Institute of Agriculture, University of Tennessee, P.O. Box 1071, Knoxville 37901

"A Look At: Bird Problems and Their Control." James L. Byford. Publication 723, 1976, 9 pp. Review of control methods for reducing property damage from blackbirds, house sparrows, pigeons, and crows.
"Tennessee Wildlife Tips." J. Byford. Undated. Detailed plans for constructing a hopper-type feeder, as well as houses for bluebirds, purple martins, and wood ducks.

Texas

Texas Parks and Wildlife Department, 4200 Smith School Road, Austin 78744

"Construction Hints and Preliminary Management Practices for New Ponds and Lakes." C.R. Inman. Booklet 3000-7, 1980, 10 pp. Tips on selecting a pond site, pond construction, and wildlife enhancement.
"Hawk: Friend or Foe?" Jerome Kasten. Reprint from the *Texas Game and Fish Magazine*, April 1961, 4 pp. Discussion of the food habits of common Texas hawks points to the benefits that insect- and rodent-eating hawks have on Texas agriculture.

Cooperative Extension Service, Head, Department of Agricultural Communications, Reed McDonald Building, Texas A&M University, College Station 77843

"Bobwhite Food Development." Charles W. Ramsey and Milo J. Shult. Anon. No. L-1665, undated, 4 pp. Recommendations for improving bobwhite quail food supplies in Texas. Includes a list of important food plants, and discusses techniques for planting six crop plants that are especially favored foods for bobwhite.

Soil Conservation Service, P.O. Box 648, Temple 76503

"Animal Guides for Texas." Anon. Undated. Species accounts that give biological facts, habitat needs, management techniques, and useful references. The following animal guides are available about birds (others are available on mammals): bobwhite quail, mourning dove, wild turkey, ring-necked pheasant, surface-feeding ducks, geese, scaled quail, diving ducks, sandhill crane, lesser prairie chicken, and chachalaca.

Utah

State of Utah Natural Resources and Energy, Wildlife Resources, 1596 W. North Temple, Salt Lake City 84116

"Back Yard Bird Feeding." Bob Walters. Undated, 16 pp. General guidelines for feeding birds, with a discussion of the comparative value of different types of feeders and food. This publication also includes a detailed list of 105 Utah birds and their food preferences at feeders.

"Landscaping Plants Useful for Attracting Birds." Anon. Undated, 1 page. List of recommended trees, shrubs, and vines for Utah wildlife landscaping.

"Project Bluebird." Bob Walters. Undated, 5 pp. Review describing the causes for bluebird population declines in Utah, with a plan for a bluebird house, directions for mounting the house, and a form for reporting nesting activity.

Soil Conservation Service, Federal Building, Rm. 4012, 125 S. State St., Salt Lake City 84138

"Plant Use Guide for Wildlife." Anon. 1982, 4 pp. Includes a table showing the selected wildlife use of 47 recommended grasses, forbs, shrubs, and trees.

Vermont

State of Vermont, Department of Fish and Game, Montpelier 95602

"Basic Birdhouses." Anon. Undated, 8 pp. Detailed plans for building nest boxes for bluebirds, tree swallows, wood duck, goldeneye, phoebe, house wren, and purple martin. Also contains plans for constructing a raccoon guard.

Cooperative Extension Service, Publications Distribution Officer, Morrill Hall, University of Vermont, Burlington 05405

"Flowering Crabapples." Leonard P. Perry. No. OH 16, undated, 2 pp. Describes the values of crabapples and presents a table showing the colors of fruits and flowers for 26 crabapple varieties that will grow in Vermont.

"Landscape Plants for Vermont." Harrison L. Flint. Brieflet 1290 5C-183-VP, 1966, 84 pp. (Revised 1983 by Norman E. Pellett). Discussion of landscape considerations for Vermont, with a detailed hardiness zone for various subregions of Vermont. Most of this useful booklet consists of descriptions of native and cultivated plants adapted to Vermont climates. A valuable resource for the New England wildlife manager, even though it does not include notes on wildlife use.

"Transplanting Trees and Shrubs from the Wild." Norman E. Pellett. No. OH 13,

1979, 1 page. Techniques for transplanting wild trees and shrubs, with suggestions for pruning and timing.

Virginia

Commonwealth of Virginia, Commission of Game and Inland Fisheries, Box 11104, Richmond 23230

"Back Yard Habitats." George H. Harrison. Undated, 4 pp. A discussion (illustrated with black and white photos) that describes the value of building wildlife habitats, how to make a wildlife management plan, and where to receive assistance.

"A Guide to Feeding Birds." Joseph J. Shomon. Reprinted from Jan. 1974 *Virginia Wildlife*, 4 pp. Article describing some guidelines for feeding birds, with discussion about when and where to put feeders. The article includes color illustrations of 19 common Virginia feeder birds.

"More Wildlife on Your Property." Anon. Undated, 28 pp. This booklet discusses basic principles of managing woodland fields and wetlands for wildlife. Also includes several feeder plans, dimensions for nest boxes, and suggested shrubs, trees, and vines.

"Nesting Boxes, Feeding Stations, Bird Houses, Wildlife Shelters and How to Build Them." Anon. Reprint D-1, from *Virginia Wildlife*, Jan. 1955, 4 pp. Illustrated leaflet containing 28 projects for feeding and sheltering birds.

Cooperative Extension Service, Extension Editor, Information Services Division, Virginia Polytechnic Institute & State University, Blacksburg 24061

"Common Water Plants of Virginia." Louis A. Helfrich, Garland B. Pardue, and Diana L. Weigmann. Pub. 844, 1981, 29 pp. Species description of 22 common water plants found in the Virginia region. Most accounts include photos and line illustrations. Wildlife value is included for most.

"Controlling Aquatic Weeds and Improving Quality in Ponds and Lakes." Louis A. Helfrich and Diana L. Weigmann. Pub. 809, 1979, 16 pp. Discusses various methods of control, such as mechanical, biological, and chemical approaches to the problem of excessive pond vegetation.

"Feeding Wild Birds." Peter T. Bromley and Aelred D. Geis. Pub. No. 420-006, 1982, 5 pp. Well-illustrated guide to the food preferences of 16 common Virginia feeder birds.

"How to Do It: Plans for Attracting Birds." Anon. 1974, 5 pp. Guidelines for constructing and locating nest boxes, with plans for building nest boxes, feeders, and watering devices.

"Pond Construction: Some Practical Considerations." Garland B. Pardue and Louis A. Helfrich. No. MT 11 H, 1978, 7 pp. Discusses how to construct a farm pond.

"Solutions to Common Farm Pond Problems." L. A. Helfrich, G. B. Pardue, and P. T. Bromley. 1982, 33 pp. Practical suggestions for solving pond problems and maintaining the proper amount of oxygen, pH, and water in artificial impoundments. Well-illustrated with black and white photos.

Washington

Department of Game, 600 N. Capitol Way, Olympia 98504

"Nesting Structures and Feeders for Birds." Anon. Undated, 6 pp. Suggestions for building and locating feeders and nest boxes. The leaflet includes a plan for a birdhouse, nest box specifications, and suggestions for placing boxes for 15 bird species.

West Virginia

West Virginia Department of Natural Resources, Wildlife Division, Charleston 25305

"Strictly for the Feathered." Anon. Undated. Eight-panel leaflet that provides tips for offering suet, grain, fruit, and grit for birds. Includes recommendations for wildlife plantings.

Wisconsin

Wisconsin Department of Natural Resources, Box 7921, Madison 53707

"Back Yard Wildlife." Anon. Undated, 2 pp. Attracting birds through landscaping, feeding, and watering. Includes a list of 15 projects to help wild birds. Also, nest box specifications for 21 types of cavity nesters.
"Bird Houses and Song Bird Feeders." Anon. Undated, 2 pp. Birdhouse and feeder designs, including nest box dimensions for six bird species. Includes a water-warming device for birdbaths utilizing an electric bulb.
"Woodsman Spare That Snag." Anon. Undated, 2 pp. Discusses the importance of leaving snags in actively managed woodlots and forests. Includes a list of 34 Wisconsin bird species that use snags for nesting and roosting.

Cooperative Extension Service, Publications Editor, 101 Agricultural Journalism Bldg., 440 Henry Mall, University of Wisconsin, Madison 53706

"Bird Feeding: Tips for Beginners and Veterans." Scott R. Craven and Robert L. Ruff. No. G3176, 1982, 11 pp. An exceptionally well-illustrated guide to the subject, with discussion of feeder placement, designs for feeders, food preference, and the need for water, grit, and sanitation.

"Controlling Woodpecker Damage." Scott Craven, No. G3117, 1981, 2 pp. Provides background on why woodpeckers damage houses and what can be done to prevent such damage. Also suggestions for controlling sapsucker damage to fruit trees.

"Landscape Plants That Attract Birds." Robert Ellarson, No. G1609, 1975, 8 pp. Discussion of habitat preferences of some common birds. Includes landscaping ideas, and a wide selection of recommended wildlife plantings, providing growth characteristics for trees, shrubs, and vines.

"Shelves, Houses and Feeders for Birds and Squirrels." G. Barquest, et al. No. G2091, undated, 32 pp. Detailed plans for 22 birdhouse and 6 feeder designs. Excellent illustrations.

"Wisconsin Woodlands: Wildlife Management." Scott Craven. No. G3097, 1981, 8 pp. Recommendations for increasing wildlife variety through use of plantings, feeding, den trees, brush piles, and nest boxes. Includes sources for professional assistance and further readings.

Soil Conservation Service, 4601 Hammersley Road, Madison 53711

"Farm Pond Improvement for Wildlife." Orrin J. Rongstad and Laverne C. Stricker. No. G2140, 1974, 2 pp. Recommendations for maintaining vegetation around a farm pond to best develop ponds for wildlife use.

"Land Management for Non-Game Birds." Wade H. Hamor. 1961, 2 pp. Recommendations for developing hedgerows, fencerows, woodlands, food patches, and wetland areas to favor use by nongame birds.

CANADA

British Columbia

Provincial Museum, Victoria, B.C., Canada V8W 1A1

"Attracting and Feeding Birds in British Columbia." R. Wayne Campbell and Harold Hosford. Undated, 31 pp. This booklet includes suggested trees, shrubs, and vines for wildlife. Also suggestions for feeding, giving recipes for insect-eating birds, including hummingbirds. The booklet also contains plans for building nest boxes and recommends providing nesting material, such as string, horsehair, and mud. Includes appendices for naturalist clubs, checklists, and journals for bird watchers in British Columbia.

Manitoba

Manitoba Department of Natural Resources, Public Information Services, 1495 St. James St., Box 22, Winnipeg, Man., Canada R3H 0W9

"Enjoying Winter Bird Feeders." Ted Muir. Undated, 8 pp. Attractive line drawings, giving guidelines for setting up and maintaining a feeding station. Includes designs for several homemade feeders.

"A Home for Bluebirds and Swallows." Anon. Undated, 2 pp. Plans for constructing a bluebird/swallow house on the successful bluebird trail project of Dr. John Lane, who placed 4000 bird boxes in southern Manitoba. Includes plan and directions for where to place boxes for best results.

"A Home for Purple Martins." Anon. Undated, 6 pp. Describes some purple martin natural history, with detailed plans for constructing a 9-compartment, 1-level wooden martin house. Includes suggestions for mounting on poles and rooftops.

"Land for Wildlife and People—Manitoba's Wildlife Management Areas." Detailed map showing the locations of 48 wildlife management areas in Manitoba.

"A Nestbox for Wood Ducks." Anon. Undated, 6 pp. Pamphlet containing a plan for construction of a wood duck box. Includes a discussion of this tree-nesting duck's life history.

Ontario

Ontario Ministry of Natural Resources, Wildlife Branch, Whitney Block, Queen's Park, Toronto, Ont., Canada M7A 1W3

"Back Yard Habitat." Gerald B. McKeating and William A. Creighton. Anon. Reprinted from the *Ontario Naturalist Magazine*, vol. 14, no. 2, pp. 21–29, June 1974, 10 pp. Review of basic food and cover needs of backyard birds. Includes a useful schematic plan for developing a suburban backyard with wildlife plantings.

Prince Edward Island

Prince Edward Island, Department of Community Affairs, P.O. Box 2000, 11 Kent St., Charlottetown, P.E.I., Canada C1A 7N8

The P.E.I. Environeer. Anon. Vol. 5, no. 1, Winter 1977, 2 pp. Suggestions for building homemade feeders and displaying them for use by wintering birds on Prince Edward Island.

AGENCIES AND ORGANIZATIONS THAT CAN HELP

Cooperative Extension Service

The Cooperative Extension Service of the U.S. Department of Agriculture has the responsibility of making current research and management about natural resources available to farmers, youth, and homeowners. Cooperative Extension has an office at each state land-grant university and over 3000 local offices, one each in nearly every county in the United States. The county extension office is an excellent place to find free or inexpensive publications about landscaping for birds, pond building, woodlot management, and a vast variety of other information useful for improving land for wildlife. Extension agents are usually available to discuss various resource management problems. Local Cooperative Extension Offices are listed under Cooperative Extension in the white pages of most telephone directories.

Soil Conservation Service

The Soil Conservation Service of the U.S. Department of Agriculture provides soil and water resource data and field technical assistance to land users in both rural and urbanizing habitats. Staff from your local Soil Conservation Service office will visit your propery without charge to assist with planning for construction of ponds and other wetlands. They will inspect soils to help determine the best location for wetlands and can advise on specific wildlife plantings and fertilizer requirements for your property. The Soil Conservation Service is listed in the white pages of telephone directories under U.S. Department of Agriculture.

State and Provincial Wildlife Departments

State and provincial wildlife departments vary greatly in the services that they provide for nongame management. Recently, however, at least 22 states have passed nongame tax checkoffs in which taxpayers contribute to nongame programs. This funding approach is providing much-needed revenues to state game departments so that they may study nongame species and provide materials and assistance to the public. State and provincial wildlife agents can often offer assistance in trapping protected nuisance wildlife, such as squirrels and raccoons. Check your telephone directory under state or provincial listings for your local wildlife department office.

Local Nurseries

The staff of local nurseries can offer a wealth of information about the availability of various wildlife plantings and the specific growing requirements of plants adapted for your vicinity. They can usually offer ready solutions to problems about plant health, planting technique, fertilizer requirements, and other horticultural details.

National Audubon Society, 950 Third Avenue, New York, NY 10022

More than 450 Audubon Society chapters offer abundant contact with local bird-watching enthusiasts. To find the Audubon group nearest your home, check your telephone directory or write the society's national office in New York. National Audubon also sponsors summer workshops and ecology camps in Maine, Connecticut, Wisconsin, and Wyoming that offer resident courses in natural history with classes in ornithology and habitat management.

National Institute for Urban Wildlife, 10921 Trotting Ridge Way, Columbia, MD 21044

The National Institute for Urban Wildlife is a private, nonprofit organization that conducts research on the relationship between man and wildlife in urban and urbanizing settings. It prepares technical reports and public information leaflets about a variety of city wildlife encounters, including leaflets about creating wildlife habitat and feeding birds in the city. It publishes a quarterly newsletter that often includes bird-attracting ideas and reviews current relevant research and publications.

National Wildlife Federation, 1412 Sixteenth St., N.W., Washington, DC 20036

The Backyard Wildlife Habitat Program of the National Wildlife Federation offers a package of materials called the *Gardening with Wildlife Kit.* It provides materials giving specific ideas for improving food, water, cover, and reproductive areas in backyard habitats. The *Gardening with Wildlife Kit* includes planning guides, a wildlife habitat log, graph paper, landscaping template, and much more. Backyard properties that meet the federation's criteria for habitat improvement receive a numbered registration certificate.

Private Consultants

A.E.S. Wildlife Management Consulting, 4320 Bolton Road, Gasport, N.Y. 14067, offers 8- to 10-page management plans for modifying habitat to attract specific birds. Feeders and nest boxes are recommended as appropriate, but the emphasis is on planting and favoring different plant communities. Management plans for the following species are available: American robin, song sparrow, catbird, house wren, chipping sparrow, eastern bluebird, black-capped chickadee, barn swallow, cedar waxwing, and American goldfinch. Each plan includes life history information, a discussion of limiting factors, recommended landscape design, and additional literature. A.E.S. Consulting also provides on-site assistance. Wildlife Systems, Ltd, P.O. Box 1031, Blackfoot, ID 83221, provides on-site consulting services to help private and public landowners develop homes, corporate headquarters, ranches, housing developments, and other construction projects so that these areas will be attractive to wildlife.

ORDERING TREES AND SHRUBS THROUGH THE MAIL

Local plant nurseries are usually the best place to purchase common bird-attracting plants for your property. Here you can select healthy-looking plants that are often larger than those that are available through the mail. Local nurseries also offer potted and balled and burlapped trees and shrubs that are generally not available through the mail. However, although some local nurseries will special order unusual plants on request, their choices are generally much more limited than mail-order nurseries that specialize in particular types or varieties.

The following list summarizes, by category, the plants available from selected mail-order nurseries. Commonly available wildlife plants such as flowering dogwood and autumn olive are usually available from any of the sources that specialize in trees and shrubs, but some of the best bird-attracting plants are often very hard to find. This is especially true for native plants which show promise for attracting birds to arid and far northern regions. To meet this need, the following list of hard-to-find bird-attracting plants includes species that are available from relatively few mail-order nurseries. See Chapter II for descriptions of all listed plants.

Sources for hard-to-find bird-attracting plants were compiled primarily from *An Index to Sources of Cultivated Plants,* derived from current horticultural trade catalogues from the United States and Canada. The *Index* was compiled largely by Ethel Z. Bailey for the Bailey Hortatorium of Cornell University and checked for current availability by a direct mailing to all listed plant sources.

The following directories to plant sources provide many additional sources for a wide variety of useful bird-attracting plants.

"Illinois Plants for Habitat Restoration." Anon. 1981, 61pp., Illinois Dept. of Conservation, Bureau of Program Services, Division of Planning and Information, Lincoln Tower Plaza, 524 S. Second St. Springfield 62706

"Nursery Source Manual." Frederick McGourty, Jr., ed. Pub. 99, 1982. 89pp. Brooklyn Botanic Garden, 1000 Washington Ave., Brooklyn, NY 11225.

"Sources of Planting Stock and Seed of Conservation Plants used in the Northeast." W. Curtis Sharp, compiler. 1981. 15pp. USDA, Soil Conservation Service, Northeast Technical Service Center, Broomall, PA. 19008

"The Wildlife Plant Source-Materials for Wildlife Habitat Improvement." Anon. Undated. 9pp. Tennesee Wildlife Resources Agency, P.O. Box 40707, Ellington Agricultural Center, Nashville 37204

Nurseries that specialize in seed production usually identify themselves as seedsmen or refer to seeds in their company name. Several wholesale sources are also listed for commercial customers only. Since prices and nursery offerings vary from year to year, it is best to write to the nurseries for current catalogues and follow their conditions of sale and instructions when ordering.

SOURCES FOR HARD-TO-FIND BIRD-ATTRACTING PLANTS

Arrowheads *(Sagittaria spp.):* Van Ness Water Garden, 2460 N. Euclid Ave., Upland, CA 91786, Catalog $2

Bearberry *(Arctostaphylos uva-ursi):* Corliss Brothers, 31 Essex Rd., Ipswich, MA 01938; Emlong Nurseries, Inc., Stevensville, MI 49127; Oliver Nurseries, 1159 Bronson Rd., Fairfield, CT 06430; F. W. Schumacher, Co., Inc., Horticulturists, 36 Spring Hill Rd., Sandwich, MA 02563; The Shop in the Sierra, Box 1, Midpines, CA 95345

Beautyberry, American *(Callicarpa americana):* Emlong Nurseries, Inc., Stevensville, MI 49127; J. L. Hudson, Seedsman, P.O. Box 1058, Redwood City, CA 94064, Catalog $1; Oliver Nurseries, 1159 Bronson Rd., Fairfield, CT 06430; Patrick's Vineyard Nursery & Farm Market, P.O. Box 992, Tifton, GA 31794

Bilberry, bog *(Vaccinium uliginosum):* Far North Gardens, 16785 Harrison, Livonia, MI 48154, Catalog $2; J. L. Hudson, Seedsman, P.O. Box 1058, Redwood City, CA 94064, Catalog $1

Bladderbush *(Isomeris arborea):* Yerba Buena Nursery, 19500 Skyline Blvd., Woodside, CA 94062

Blueberry, lowbush *(Vaccinium angustifolium):* The Cummins Garden, 22 Robertsville Rd., Marlboro, NJ 07746, Catalog $1 (minimum order for shipping, $15)

Buckthorn, holly-leaved *(Rhamnus crocea):* Yerba Buena Nursery, 19500 Skyline Blvd., Woodside, CA 94062

Buckthorn, California (coffeeberry) *(Rhamnus californica):* Yerba Buena Nursery, 19500 Skyline Blvd., Woodside, CA 94062

Buffaloberry, silver *(Shepherdia argentea):* Emlong Nurseries, Inc., Stevensville, MI 49127; J. L. Hudson, Seedsman, P.O. Box 1058, Redwood City, CA 94064, Catalog $1; Patrick's Vineyard Nursery & Farm Market, P.O. Box 992, Tifton, GA 31794; F. W. Schumacher, Co., Inc., Horticulturists, 36 Spring Hill Rd., Sandwich, MA 02563

Bunchberry *(Cornus canadensis):* Gardens of the Blue Ridge, P.O. Box 10, Pineola, NC 28662; Far North Gardens, 16785 Harrison, Livonia, MI 48154, Catalog $2; Orchid Gardens, 6700 Split Hand Rd., Grand Rapids, MN 55744, Catalog $0.50; Oliver Nurseries, 1159 Bronson Rd., Fairfield, CT 06430; Siskiyou Rare Plant Nursery, 2825 Cummings Rd., Medford, OR 97501, Catalog $1.50

Buttonbush, common *(Cephalanthus occidentalis):* Charles Fiore Nurseries, 17101 West Highway 22, P.O. Box 67, Prairie View, IL 60069 (wholesale); J. L. Hudson, Seedsman, P.O. Box 1058, Redwood City, CA 94064, Catalog $1; Patrick's Vineyard Nursery & Farm Market, P.O. Box 992, Tifton, GA 31794

Cactus, prickly pear *(Opuntia spp.):* Cactus by Mueller, 10411 Rosedale Hwy., Bakersfield, CA 93308, Catalog $1; Far North Gardens, 16785 Harrison, Livonia, MI 48154, Catalog $2; Henrietta's Nursery, 1345 N. Brawley, Fresno, CA 93711, Catalog $1; Midwest Wildflowers, Box 64, Rockton, IL 61072, Catalog $0.50 (seed only); Panfield Nurseries, 322 Southdown Rd., Huntington, NY 11743 (wholesale)

Caragana, pigmy *(Caragana pygmalea):* Foxborough Nurseries, 3611 Miller Rd., Street, MD 21154; J. L. Hudson, Seedsman, P.O. Box 1058, Redwood City, CA 94064, Catalog $1

Cherry, black *(Prunus serotina):* Earl E. May Seed & Nursery Co., 208 North Elm, Shenandoah, IA 51603; Musser Forests, Box 340M, Indiana, PA 15701-0340; The Plumfield Nurseries, P.O. Box 410, Fremont, NE 68025 (wholesale); F. W. Schumacher, Co., Inc., Horticulturists, 36 Spring Hill Rd., Sandwich, MA 02563; Van Pines, Inc., West Olive, MI 49460 (wholesale)

Cherry, Catalina *(Prunus lyonii):* The Shop in the Sierra, Box 1, Midpines, CA 95345; Yerba Buena Nursery, 19500 Skyline Blvd., Woodside, CA 94062

Cherry, holly-leaved *(Prunus ilicifolia):* The Shop in the Sierra, Box 1, Midpines, CA 95345; Yerba Buena Nursery, 19500 Skyline Blvd., Woodside, CA 94062

Cherry, Manchu *(Prunus tomentosa):* Musser Forests, Box 340M, Indiana, PA 15701-0340

Christmasberry (toyon) *(Photinia arbutifolia):* J. L. Hudson, Seedsman, P.O. Box 1058, Redwood City, CA 94064, Catalog $1; Patrick's Vineyard Nursery & Farm Market, P.O. Box 992, Tifton, GA 31794; The Shop in the Sierra, Box 1, Midpines, CA 95345

Coralberry *(Symphoricarpos orbiculatus):* Eisler Nurseries, 219 E. Pearl St., Box 70,

Butler, PA 16003-0070; J. W. Jung Seed Company, Randolph, WI 53957; Earl E. May Seed & Nursery Co., 208 North Elm, Shenandoah, IA 51603; Shady Oaks Nursery, 700 19th Ave., N.E., Waseca, MN 56093; F. W. Schumacher, Co., Inc., Horticulturists, 36 Spring Hill Rd., Sandwich, MA 02563

Cotoneaster, creeping *(Cotoneaster adpressa):* Corliss Brothers, 31 Essex Rd., Ipswich, MA 01938; Cottage Gardens, Rt. #3, South Waverly and Bishop Rds., Lansing, MI 48910 (wholesale); Foxborough Nurseries, 3611 Miller Rd., Street, MD 21154; Ingleside Plantation Nurseries, P.O. Box 1038, Oak Grove, VA 22443 (wholesale); Monrovia Nursery Co., Box Q, 18331 E. Foothill Blvd., Azusa, CA 91702 (wholesale)

Cowberry *(Vaccinium vitis-idaea):* The Bovees, 1737 S.W. Coronado St., Portland, OR 97219; The Cummins Garden, 22 Robertsville Rd., Marlboro, NJ 07746, Catalog $1 (minimum order for shipping, $15); Far North Gardens, 16785 Harrison, Livonia, MI 48154, Catalog $2; J. L. Hudson, Seedsman, P.O. Box 1058, Redwood City, CA 94064, Catalog $1; Siskiyou Rare Plant Nursery, 2825 Cummings Rd., Medford, OR 97501, Catalog $1.50

Crabapple, flowering "Bob White" *(Malus spp.):* Eisler Nurseries, 219 E. Pearl St., Box 70, Butler, PA 16003-0070; Simpson Orchard Co., 1504 Wheatland Rd., Vincennes, IN 47591 (extra charge for small orders); The Tankard Nurseries, Box 649, Exmore, VA 23350 (wholesale)

Crabapple, flowering "Mary Potter" *(Malus spp.):* Cottage Gardens, Rt. 3, South Waverly and Bishop Rds., Lansing, MI 48910 (wholesale); Simpson Orchard Co., 1504 Wheatland Rd., Vincennes, IN 47591 (extra charge for small orders); Wayside Gardens, 53 Garden Lane, Hodges, SC 29695

Crabapple, Toringo *(Malus sieboldii):* Greenbrier Farms, Inc., 201 Hickory Rd., West, Chesapeake, VA 23320 (wholesale); F. W. Schumacher, Co., Inc., Horticulturists, 36 Spring Hill Rd., Sandwich, MA 02563

Crowberry, black *(Empetrum nigrum):* Siskiyou Rare Plant Nursery, 2825 Cummings Rd., Medford, OR 97501, Catalog $1.50

Currant, buffalo *(Ribes odoratum):* Bailey Nurseries, 1325 Bailey Rd., St. Paul, MN 55119 (wholesale); Charles Fiore Nurseries, 17101 West Highway 22, P.O. Box 67, Prairie View, IL 60069 (wholesale); Sherman Nursery Co., Charles City, IA 50616 (wholesale)

Currant, golden *(Ribes aureum):* Bailey Nurseries, 1325 Bailey Rd., St. Paul, MN 55119 (wholesale); Charles Fiore Nurseries, 17101 West Highway 22, P.O. Box 67, Prairie View, IL 60069 (wholesale); The Plumfield Nurseries, P.O. Box 410, Fremont, NE 68025 (wholesale)

Deerberry, common *(Vaccinium stamineum):* Richter's, Goodwood, Ontario LOC 1A0, Catalog $2

Dogwood, cornelian cherry *(Cornus mas):* Kingwood Nurseries, 2859 Burns Rd., Madison, OH 44057 (wholesale)

Dogwood, Pacific *(Cornus nuttallii):* Far North Gardens, 16785 Harrison, Livonia, MI 48154, Catalog $2; F. W. Schumacher, Co., Inc., Horticulturists, 36 Spring

Hill Rd., Sandwich, MA 02563; The Shop in the Sierra, Box 1, Midpines, CA 95345; Yerba Buena Nursery, 19500 Skyline Blvd., Woodside, CA 94062

Elder, American *(Sambucus canadensis):* Bailey Nurseries, 1325 Bailey Rd., St. Paul, MN 55119 (wholesale); Charles Fiore Nurseries, 17101 West Highway 22, P.O. Box 67, Prairie View, IL 60069; J. L. Hudson, Seedsman, P.O. Box 1058, Redwood City, CA 94064, Catalog $1; Michael Brothers Nursery, Michael Rd., Box 126, R.D. 1, Cheswick, PA 15024; Patrick's Vineyard Nursery & Farm Market, P.O. Box 992, Tifton, GA 31794

Elder, blueberry *(Sambucus cerulea):* Yerba Buena Nursery, 19500 Skyline Blvd., Woodside, CA 94062

Elder, scarlet *(Sambucus pubens):* Bailey Nurseries, 1325 Bailey Rd., St. Paul, MN 55119 (wholesale); Far North Gardens, 16785 Harrison, Livonia, MI 48154, Catalog $2; Orchid Gardens, 6700 Split Hand Rd., Grand Rapids, MN 55744, Catalog $0.50

Farkleberry *(Vaccinium arboreum):* Patrick's Vineyard Nursery & Farm Market, P.O. Box 992, Tifton, GA 31794

Fig *(Ficus carica):* Aldridge Nursery, Rt. 1, Box 8, Von Ormy, TX 78073 (wholesale); Emlong Nurseries, Inc., Stevensville, MI 49127; Logee's Greenhouses, 55 North St., Danielson, CT 06239, Catalog $2.50; Monrovia Nursery Co., Box Q, 18331 E. Foothill Blvd., Azusa, CA 91702 (wholesale)

Fig, Moreton Bay *(Ficus macrophylla):* Aldridge Nursery, Rt. 1, Box 8, Von Ormy, TX 78073 (wholesale); J. L. Hudson, Seedsman, P.O. Box 1058, Redwood City, CA 94064, Catalog $1

Gallberry, large *(Ilex coriacea):* Patrick's Vineyard Nursery & Farm Market, P.O. Box 992, Tifton, GA 31794

Hackberry, common *(Celtis occidentalis):* Eisler Nurseries, 219 E. Pearl St., Box 70, Butler, PA 16003-0070; Earl Ferris Nursery, 811 Fourth St., N.E., Hampton, IA 50441; J. L. Hudson, Seedsman, P.O. Box 1058, Redwood City, CA 94064, Catalog $1; Earl E. May Seed & Nursery Co., 208 North Elm, Shenandoah, IA 51603; F. W. Schumacher, Co., Inc., Horticulturists, 36 Spring Hill Rd., Sandwich, MA 02563

Hawthorn, cockspur *(Crataegus crus-galli):* Eisler Nurseries, 219 E. Pearl St., Box 70, Butler, PA 16003-0070; Earl Ferris Nursery, 811 Fourth St., N.E., Hampton, IA 50441; Greenbrier Farms, Inc., 201 Hickory Rd., West, Chesapeake, VA 23320 (wholesale); D. Hill Nursery Co., Rt. 176, Union, IL 60180 (wholesale); Mount Arbor Nurseries, P.O. Box 129, Shenandoah, IA 51601 (wholesale)

Hawthorn, Washington *(Crataegus spp.):* Emlong Nurseries, Inc., Stevensville, MI 49127; Hess Nurseries, P.O. Box 326, Rt. 553, Cedarville, NJ 08311 (wholesale); Simpson Orchard Co., 1504 Wheatland Rd., Vincennes, IN 47591 (extra charge for small orders); Scarff's Nursery, 411 Dayton Lakeview Rd., New Carlisle, OH 45344 (wholesale); The Tankard Nurseries, Box 649, Exmore, VA 23350 (wholesale)

Holly, Yaupon *(Ilex vomitoria):* Aldridge Nursery, Rt. 1, Box 8, Von Ormy, TX 78073 (wholesale); Greenbrier Farms, Inc., 201 Hickory Rd., West, Chesapeake, VA 23320 (wholesale); Holly Hills, Inc., 1216 Hillsdale Rd., Evansville, IN 47711; F. W. Schumacher, Co., Inc., Horticulturists, 36 Spring Hill Rd., Sandwich, MA 02563; Salter Tree Farm, Rt. 2, Box 1332, Madison, FL 32340

Holly-grape, Oregon *(Mahonia nervosa):* Nature's Garden, Rt. 1, Box 488, Beaverton, OR 97007; Princeton Nurseries, P.O. Box 191, Princeton, NJ 08540 (wholesale); F. W. Schumacher, Co., Inc., Horticulturists, 36 Spring Hill Rd., Sandwich, MA 02563

Honeysuckle, Amur *(Lonicera maackii):* Appalachian Nurseries, Box 87, Waynesboro, PA 17268 (wholesale); Charles Fiore Nurseries, 17101 West Highway 22, P.O. Box 67, Prairie View, IL 60069; Musser Forests, Box 340M, Indiana, PA 15701-0340; The Plumfield Nurseries, P.O. Box 410, Fremont, NE 68025 (wholesale); F. W. Schumacher, Co., Inc., Horticulturists, 36 Spring Hill Rd., Sandwich, MA 02563

Honeysuckle, bearberry *(Lonicera involucrata):* Yerba Buena Nursery, 19500 Skyline Blvd., Woodside, CA 94062

Honeysuckle, Morrow *(Lonicera morrowii):* Eisler Nurseries, 219 E. Pearl St., Box 70, Butler, PA 16003-0070; Charles Fiore Nurseries, 17101 West Highway 22, P.O. Box 67, Prairie View, IL 60069 (wholesale); Greenbrier Farms, Inc., 201 Hickory Rd., West, Chesapeake, VA 23320 (wholesale); Princeton Nurseries, P.O. Box 191, Princeton, NJ 08540 (wholesale); Sherman Nursery Co., Charles City, IA 50616 (wholesale)

Honeysuckle, trumpet *(Lonicera sempervirens):* Mount Arbor Nurseries, P.O. Box 129, Shenandoah, IA 51601 (wholesale); Monrovia Nursery Co., Box Q, 18331 E. Foothill Blvd., Azusa, CA 91702 (wholesale); Wayside Gardens, 53 Garden Lane, Hodges, SC 29695

Huckleberry, evergreen *(Vaccinium ovatum):* Yerba Buena Nursery, 19500 Skyline Blvd., Woodside, CA 94062

Huckleberry, tall red *(Vaccinium parvifolium):* Nature's Garden, Rt. 1, Box 488, Beaverton, OR 97007

Huckleberry, box *(Gaylussacia brachycera):* Oliver Nurseries, 1159 Bronson Rd., Fairfield, CT 06430

Juneberry, roundleaf *(Amelanchier sanguinea):* Patrick's Vineyard Nursery & Farm Market, P.O. Box 992, Tifton, GA 31794

Laurel, California *(Umbellularia californica):* Logee's Greenhouses, 55 North St., Danielson, CT 06239, Catalog $2.50; The Shop in the Sierra, Box 1, Midpines, CA 95345; Yerba Buena Nursery, 19500 Skyline Blvd., Woodside, CA 94062

Lespedeza, shrub *(Lespedeza bicolor):* F. W. Schumacher, Co., Inc., Horticulturists, 36 Spring Hill Rd., Sandwich, MA 02563

Madrone *(Arbutus menziesii):* The Shop in the Sierra, Box 1, Midpines, CA 95345; Yerba Buena Nursery, 19500 Skyline Blvd., Woodside, CA 94062

Manzanita *(Arctostaphylos manzanita):* The Shop in the Sierra, Box 1, Midpines, CA 95345; Yerba Buena Nursery, 19500 Skyline Blvd., Woodside, CA 94062

Manzanita, pine-mat *(Arctostaphylos nevadensis):* Siskiyou Rare Plant Nursery, 2825 Cummings Rd., Medford, OR 97501, Catalog $1.50; The Shop in the Sierra, Box 1, Midpines, CA 95345

Mesquite *(Prosopis juliflora):* Aldridge Nursery, Rt. 1, Box 8, Von Ormy, TX 78073 (wholesale)

Mountain ash, American *(Sorbus americana):* Gardens of the Blue Ridge, P.O. Box 10, Pineola, NC 28662; Charles Fiore Nurseries, 17101 West Highway 22, P.O. Box 67, Prairie View, IL 60069 (wholesale); Greenbrier Farms, Inc., 201 Hickory Rd., West, Chesapeake, VA 23320 (wholesale); Orchid Gardens, 6700 Split Hand Rd., Grand Rapids, MN 55744, Catalog $0.50; F. W. Schumacher, Co., Inc., Horticulturists, 36 Spring Hill Rd., Sandwich, MA 02563

Mulberry, red *(Morus rubra):* Patrick's Vineyard Nursery & Farm Market, P.O. Box 992, Tifton, GA 31794; F. W. Schumacher, Co., Inc., Horticulturists, 36 Spring Hill Rd., Sandwich, MA 02563

Mulberry, Texas *(Morus microphylla):* Patrick's Vineyard Nursery & Farm Market, P.O. Box 992, Tifton, GA 31794

Osoberry *(Osmaronia cerasiformis):* The Shop in the Sierra, Box 1, Midpines, CA 95345

Palmetto, cabbage *(Sabal palmetto):* Aldridge Nursery, Rt. 1, Box 8, Von Ormy, TX 78073 (wholesale); The Banana Tree, 715 Northampton St., Easton, PA 18042, Catalog $0.25 or stamps; J. L. Hudson, Seedsman, P.O. Box 1058, Redwood City, CA 94064, Catalog $1

Palmetto, dwarf *(Sabal minor):* Aldridge Nursery, Rt. 1, Box 8, Von Ormy, TX 78073 (wholesale); J. L. Hudson, Seedsman, P.O. Box 1058, Redwood City, CA 94064, Catalog $1

Peashrub, Siberian *(Caragana arborescens):* Emlong Nurseries, Inc., Stevensville, MI 49127; Foxborough Nurseries, 3611 Miller Rd., Street, MD 21154; Girard Nursery, P.O. Box 428, Geneva, OH 44041; J. L. Hudson, Seedsman, P.O. Box 1058, Redwood City, CA 94064, Catalog $1; Earl E. May Seed & Nursery Co., 208 North Elm, Shenandoah, IA 51603

Pepper tree, Brazilian *(Schinus terebinthifolius):* Aldridge Nursery, Rt. 1, Box 8, Von Ormy, TX 78073 (wholesale); The Banana Tree, 715 Northampton St., Easton, PA 18042, Catalog $0.25 or stamps

Pepper tree, California *(Schinus molle):* J. L. Hudson, Seedsman, P.O. Box 1058, Redwood City, CA 94064, Catalog $1; Richter's, Goodwood, Ontario LOC 1A0, Catalog $2; F. W. Schumacher, Co., Inc., Horticulturists, 36 Spring Hill Rd., Sandwich, MA 02563

Pine, shore *(Pinus contorta):* Girard Nursery, P.O. Box 428, Geneva, OH 44041; Joel W. Spingarn, 1535 Forest Ave., Baldwin, NY 11510, Catalog $1 (minimum order, $25); F. W. Schumacher, Co., Inc., Horticulturists, 36 Spring Hill Rd., Sandwich, MA 02563

Pokeberry, common *(Phytolacca americana):* Far North Gardens, 16785 Harrison, Livonia, MI 48154, Catalog $2; J. L. Hudson, Seedsman, P.O. Box 1058, Redwood City, CA 94064, Catalog $1; Midwest Wildflowers, Box 64, Rockton, IL 61072, Catalog $0.50 (seed only); Richter's, Goodwood, Ontario LOC 1A0, Catalog $2

Pondweeds *(Potamogeton spp.):* Kester's Wild Game Food Nurseries, Inc., P.O. Box V, Omro, WI 54963, Catalog $2; Wildlife Nurseries, P.O. Box 2724, Oshkosh, WI 54903-2724

Possumhaw *(Ilex decidua):* Aldridge Nursery, Rt. 1, Box 8, Von Ormy, TX 78073 (wholesale); Simpson Orchard Co., 1504 Wheatland Rd., Vincennes, IN 47591 (extra charge for small orders); F. W. Schumacher, Co., Inc., Horticulturists, 36 Spring Hill Rd., Sandwich, MA 02563

Serviceberry, Allegheny *(Amelanchier laevis):* Bailey Nurseries, 1325 Bailey Rd., St. Paul, MN 55119 (wholesale); Gardens of the Blue Ridge, P.O. Box 10, Pineola, NC 28662; Congdon & Weller, Mile Block Rd., North Collins, NY 14111 (wholesale); Emlong Nurseries, Inc., Stevensville, MI 49127; Eisler Nurseries, 219 E. Pearl St., Box 70, Butler, PA 16003-0070

Serviceberry, downy *(Amelanchier arborea):* Charles Fiore Nurseries, 17101 West Highway 22, P.O. Box 67, Prairie View, IL 60069 (wholesale); Princeton Nurseries, P.O. Box 191, Princeton, NJ 08540 (wholesale)

Serviceberry, running *(Amelanchier stolonifera):* Charles Fiore Nurseries, 17101 West Highway 22, P.O. Box 67, Prairie View, IL 60069 (wholesale); Mount Arbor Nurseries, P.O. Box 129, Shenandoah, IA 51601 (wholesale)

Serviceberry, Saskatoon *(Amelanchier alnifolia):* Bailey Nurseries, 1325 Bailey Rd., St. Paul, MN 55119 (wholesale); Congdon & Weller, Mile Block Rd., North Collins, NY 14111 (wholesale); Hess Nurseries, P.O. Box 326, Rt. 553, Cedarville, NJ 08311 (wholesale); Kingwood Nurseries, 2859 Burns Rd., Madison, OH 44057 (wholesale); Patrick's Vineyard Nursery & Farm Market, P.O. Box 992, Tifton, GA 31794

Serviceberry, western *(Amelanchier florida):* Patrick's Vineyard Nursery & Farm Market, P.O. Box 992, Tifton, GA 31794

Silverberry *(Eleagnus commutata):* F. W. Schumacher, Co., Inc., Horticulturists, 36 Spring Hill Rd., Sandwich, MA 02563

Snowberry, common *(Symphoricarpos albus):* Girard Nursery, P.O. Box 428, Geneva, OH 44041; Nature's Garden, Rt. 1, Box 488, Beaverton, OR 97007; Shady Oaks Nursery, 700 19th Ave., N.E., Waseca, MN 56093; The Shop in the Sierra, Box 1, Midpines, CA 95345; Yerba Buena Nursery, 19500 Skyline Blvd., Woodside, CA 94062

Trumpetcreeper, common *(Campsis radicans):* Emlong Nurseries, Inc., Stevensville, MI 49127; Far North Gardens, 16785 Harrison, Livonia, MI 48154, Catalog $2; Earl E. May Seed & Nursery Co., 208 North Elm, Shenandoah, IA 51603; F. W. Schumacher, Co., Inc., Horticulturists, 36 Spring Hill Rd., Sandwich, MA 02563; Wayside Gardens, 53 Garden Lane, Hodges, SC 29695

Tupelo, black *(Nyssa sylvatica):* Eisler Nurseries, 219 E. Pearl St., Box 70, Butler, PA 16003-0070; Greenbrier Farms, Inc., 201 Hickory Rd., West, Chesapeake, VA 23320 (wholesale); Michael Brothers Nursery, Michael Rd., Box 126, R.D. 1, Cheswick, PA 15024; Patrick's Vineyard Nursery & Farm Market, P.O. Box 992, Tifton, GA 31794; F. W. Schumacher, Co., Inc., Horticulturists, 36 Spring Hill Rd., Sandwich, MA 02563

Wax myrtle, Pacific *(Myrica californica):* Yerba Buena Nursery, 19500 Skyline Blvd., Woodside, CA 94062

Whortleberry, grouse *(Vaccinium scoparium):* Far North Gardens, 16785 Harrison, Livonia, MI 48154, Catalog $2; Siskiyou Rare Plant Nursery, 2825 Cummings Rd., Medford, OR 97501, Catalog $1.50

Wild rice *(Zizania aquatica):* Kester's Wild Game Food Nurseries, Inc., P.O. Box V, Omro, WI 54963, Catalog $2

Winterberry, common *(Ilex verticillata):* Gardens of the Blue Ridge, P.O. Box 10, Pineola, NC 28662; Corliss Brothers, 31 Essex Rd., Ipswich, MA 01938; Foxborough Nurseries, 3611 Miller Rd., Street, MD 21154; Oliver Nurseries, 1159 Bronson Rd., Fairfield, CT 06430; Wayside Gardens, 53 Garden Lane, Hodges, SC 94062

	Fee	Aquatic Plants	Berries and Vines	Cultivated Flowers	Garden Supplies	Ground Cover	Seeds	Trees and Shrubs	Wildflowers
Abbey Gardens, 4620 Carpinteria Ave., Carpinteria, CA 93013: (805) 684-5112/1595. Specialty: cactus, succulents									
Beersheba Wildflower Gardens, Beersheba Springs, TN 37305: (615) 692-3575 (day) (615) 692-3460 (night) Specialty: native wildflowers of Tennessee									X
Blackthorne Gardens, 48 Quincy St., Holbrook, MA 02343-1898: (617) 767-0308. Specialty: lilies, bulbs	X			X					X
Bountiful Ridge Nurseries, Inc., Princess Anne, MD 21853: (800) 638-9356; from Maryland and Canada (301) 651-0400. Specialty: fruit trees, berries, vines			X					X	
Breck's, 6523 N. Galena Rd., Peoria, IL 61632. Specialty: bulbs	X			X					
Buntings' Nurseries, Inc., Selbyville, DE 19975: (800) 441-7701. Specialty: fruit trees			X					X	
Burgess Seed & Plant Co., 905 Four Seasons Rd., Bloomington, IL 61701	X		X	X	X		X	X	
Burpee, 300 Park Ave., Warminster, PA 18991.			X	X	X		X	X	
Bussee Gardens, 635 East 7th St., Rt 2, Box 13, Cokato, MN 55321: (612) 286-2654. Specialty: perennials, trees, shrubs, wild flowers, rock gardens	X							X	X
Carroll Gardens, P.O. Box 310, 444 East Main St., Westminster, MD 21157: (301) 848-5422. Specialty: perennials and rock plants, vines, roses, perennial herbs, evergreens, ornamental trees						X		X	X

	Fee	Aquatic Plants	Berries and Vines	Cultivated Flowers	Garden Supplies	Ground Cover	Seeds	Trees and Shrubs	Wildflowers
Clyde Robin Seed Co., Inc., Box 2855, Castro Valley, CA 94546: (415) 581-3467. Seeds for wildflowers, wild trees, shrubs							X		X
Conley's Garden Center, Boothbay Harbor, ME 04538: (207) 633-5020. Specialty: native wildflowers of northern New England						X			X
Daystar, Litchfield–Hallowell Rd., R.F.D. 2, Litchfield, ME 04350: (207) 724-3369. Specialty: rock gardens	X					X		X	X
Dutch Gardens, Inc., P.O. Box 400, Montvale, NJ 07645: (201) 391-4366. Specialty: bulbs				X					
Emlong Nurseries, Inc., Stevensville, MI 49127: Specialty: fruit trees			X	X				X	
Exeter Wildflower Gardens, P.O. Box 976, Exeter, NH 03833: Specialty: native plants of New Hampshire: lilies, orchids, ferns, aquatic plants, wildflowers		X							X
Far North Gardens, 16785 Harrison, Livonia, MI 48154: (313) 422-0747. Specialty: rare flower seeds	X			X			X	X	X
Farmer Seed and Nursery, Faribault, MN 55021: (507) 334-1651			X	X	X		X	X	
Ferris Nursery, 811 Fourth St., N.E., Hampton, IA 50441: (515) 456-2563. Specialty: ornamental trees and shrubs, evergreens			X	X		X		X	
Garden in the Woods, New England Wild Flower Society, Inc., Hemenway Road, Framingham, MA 01701: Specialty: native New England wildflowers	X								X

	Fee	Aquatic Plants	Berries and Vines	Cultivated Flowers	Garden Supplies	Ground Cover	Seeds	Trees and Shrubs	Wildflowers
Garden Place, 6780 Heisley Rd., P.O. Box 83, Mentor, OH 44060: (216) 255-3705. Specialty: perennials	X					X			X
Gardens of the Blue Ridge, P.O. Box 10, Pineola, NC 28662: (704) 733-2417. Specialty: native trees, shrubs and wildflowers of North Carolina								X	X
Gurney's Seed & Nursery Co., Yankton, SD 57079. Specialty: seeds			X	X	X		X	X	
Henry Field Seed & Nursery, Co., Shenandoah, IA 51602.			X	X	X		X	X	
Henry Leuthardt Nurseries, Inc., Montauk Hwy., Box 666, East Moriches, NY 11940: (516) 878-1387. Specialty: berries and vines, fruit trees			X					X	
Holbrook Farm & Nursery, Rt. 2, Box 223B, Fletcher, NC 28732: (704) 891-7790. Specialty: Appalachian wildflowers				X		X		X	X
House of Wesley, 2200 E. Oakland, Bloomington, IL 61701.			X	X		X	X	X	
Illini Gardens, P.O. Box 125, Oakford, IL 62673. (217) 635-5713. Specialty: rock gardens						X			X
J. W. Jung Seed Co., Randolph, WI 53956.			X	X	X		X	X	
Kelly Bros. Nurseries, Inc., Dansville, NY 14437.			X	X			X	X	
Krider Nurseries, Inc., Box 29, Middlebury, IN 46540: (219) 825-5714.			X	X		X		X	
Lakeland Nurseries Sales, Hanover, PA 17331.	X		X	X	X		X		

	Fee	Aquatic Plants	Berries and Vines	Cultivated Flowers	Garden Supplies	Ground Cover	Seeds	Trees and Shrubs	Wildflowers
Lewis Strawberry Nursery, Inc., P.O. Box 24, Rocky Point, NC 28457: (919) 675-9409. Specialty: strawberry plants									
Lilypons Water Gardens, Brookshire, TX 77423-0188: (713) 934-8525; or Lilypons Water Gardens, Lilypons, MD 21717-0010: (301) 874-5133.	X	X							
Louisiana Nursery, Rt. 7, Box 43, Opelousas, LA 70570: (318) 948-3696 or (318) 942-6404. Specialty: magnolia and odd plants, including holly, ferns, cactus and succulents, perennials, fruit trees	X	X	X	X				X	X
May Seed & Nursery Co., Shenandoah, IA 51603: (712) 246-1020.				X	X	X	X	X	
Mellingers, Inc., 2310 W. South Range, North Lima, OH 44452.				X	X	X	X	X	
Midwest Wild Flowers, Box 64, Rockton, IL 61072. Specialty: midwest wildflowers	X								X
Musser Forests, Box 340M, Indiana, PA 15701-0340: (412) 465-5686.								X	
The National Arbor Day Foundation, Arbor Lodge 100, Nebraska City, NE 68410.				X	X			X	
North Carolina Botanical Garden, Chapel Hill, NC 27514. Specialty: North Carolina native wildflower seeds, trees, shrubs								X	X
L. L. Olds Seed Co., P.O. Box 7790, 2901 Packers Ave., Madison, WI 53707-7790.				X	X	X		X	X
Geo. W. Park Seed Co., Inc, S.C. Hwy, 254 N. Greenwood, SC 29647.				X	X	X	X		X

	Fee	Aquatic Plants	Berries and Vines	Cultivated Flowers	Garden Supplies	Ground Cover	Seeds	Trees and Shrubs	Wildflowers
Patrick's Vineyard, Orchard Nursery & Farm Market, P.O. Box 992A, Tifton, GA 31794: (912) 382-6841 or (912) 382-1770. Specialty: fruit trees, berries			X					X	
Plants of the Southwest, 1570 Pacheco St., Santa Fe, NM 87501: (505) 983-1548. Specialty: plants of the southwest, vegetable seeds							X	X	X
Putney Nursery, Inc., Putney, VT 05346: (802) 387-5577. Specialty: perennials									X
Savage Farms Nurseries, P.O. Box 125 PL, McMinnville, TN 37110. Specialty: fruit trees								X	
The Shop in the Sierra, Box 1, Midpines, CA 95345. Specialty: native trees, shrubs, and ground covers for arid climates	X					X		X	
Siskiyou Rare Plant Nursery, 2825 Cummings Rd., Medford, OR 97501. Specialty: native shrubs and ground covers for arid climates						X		X	
Spring Hill, 110 West Elm St., Tipp City, OH 45371.	X		X	X		X		X	
Stark Bro's Nurseries, Louisiana, MO 63353. Specialty: fruit trees, roses				X				X	
Stern's Nurseries, Inc., Geneva, NY 14456. Specialty: new and rare plants									
Sunnybrook Farms Nursery, 9448 Mayfield Rd., P.O. Box 6, Chesterland, OH 44026: (216) 729-7232. Specialty: herbs, ivies, herb garden supplies	X				X				

	Fee	Aquatic Plants	Berries and Vines	Cultivated Flowers	Garden Supplies	Ground Cover	Seeds	Trees and Shrubs	Wildflowers
Sunsweet Berry & Fruit Nursery, Box C, Sumner, GA 31789: (912) 386-8400. Specialty: fruit trees, berries			X					X	
Taylor's Herb Gardens, Inc., 1535 Lone Oak Rd., Vista, CA 92083: (714) 727-3485. Specialty: herbs and hummingbird flowers	X								
Tropexotic Growers, 708-60th St., N.W., Bradenton, FL 33529: (813) 792-3574. Specialty: ivy	X					X			
Van Bourgondien Bros., P.O. Box A, 245 Farmingdale Rd., Rt. 109, Babylon, NY 11702. Specialty: bulbs			X	X				X	
Windrift Prairie Shop, R.D. 2, Oregon, IL 61061: (815) 732-6890. Specialty: prairie seeds and plants	X						X		
Wild Flowers from the Ozark Mountains, Hi-Mountain Farm, Seligman, MO 65745: (417) 662-2641. Specialty: wildflowers from the Ozark mountains									X
Wildlife Nurseries, P.O. Box 2724, Oshkosh, WI 54903: (414) 231-3780. Specialty: wildlife nurseries, original wildlife and game food consultants		X							
Winterthur Museum & Gardens, Winterthur, DE 19735. (302) 656-8591. Specialty: cultivated plants and shrubs									
Wolfe Nursery, P.O. Box 957, Stephenville, TX 76401. Specialty: fruit trees, roses				X				X	

	Fee	Aquatic Plants	Berries and Vines	Cultivated Flowers	Garden Supplies	Ground Cover	Seeds	Trees and Shrubs	Wildflowers
Vermont Bean Seed Co., Garden Lane, Bomoseen, VT 05732: (802) 265-4212.							X		
Vernon Barnes & Son Nursery, P.O. Box 250L, McMinnville, TN 37110.			X	X				X	X
Vick's Wildgardens, Inc., Conshohocken State Rd., Box 115, Gladwyne, PA 19035: (215) 525-6773. Specialty: nursery-grown wildflowers and ferns									X
Waynesboro Nurseries, Waynesboro, VA 22980: (703) 942-4141.								X	
Wayside Gardens, Hodges, SC 29695.				X		X		X	X
Woodlanders, Inc., 1128 Colleton Ave., Aiken, SC 29801. Specialty: native plants of southern Piedmont and coastal plain, trees and shrubs, wildflowers, perennials, exotic shrubs, trees								X	X
A World Seed Service, J. L. Hudson, Seedman, Box 1058, Redwood City, CA 94064. Specialty: cacti and succulent seeds	X						X		
Worttun Ward, Beach St. RFD, West Wareham, MA 02576. (617) 866-4087.									X
Yerba Buena Nursery, 19500 Skyline Blvd., Woodside, CA 94062. Specialty: trees, shrubs and ground covers for arid climates							X		X

STATE NURSERIES

Most states operate nurseries for the production of tree and shrub seedlings for reforestation and wildlife conservation. These are usually very small bare-root seedlings, but such stock is not only less expensive than private nursery plantings, it may also be strains better adapted for local conditions or varieties that are especially good for wildlife plantings. To reduce competition with private nurseries, most states have certain restrictions on sale of their stock, such as minimal size acreage or asking for assurance that the plantings will not be used for ornamental purposes.

If your state has a nursery program, your local office of the Soil Conservation Service or Cooperative Extension Service can provide details and order forms. The Soil Conservation Service is listed in the white pages of your telephone directory under U.S. Department of Agriculture. The Cooperative Extension Service is listed under its own name. Order forms can also be obtained by writing to the following addresses:

Alaska: Alaska State Forest Nursery, Pouch 7-005, Anchorage 99510
Arkansas: Arkansas Forestry Commission, Baucum Nursery, Route 1, Box 515C, North Little Rock 72117
California: Davis Headquarters Nursery, P.O. Box 1590, Davis 95616
Colorado: Colorado State Forest Service, Colorado State University, Fort Collins 80523

Delaware: State Forester, State Department of Agriculture, Dover 19901

Florida: Florida Division of Forestry, Reforestation Forester, Collins Building, Tallahassee 32301 (trees only)

Georgia: Georgia Forestry Commission, Box 819, Macon 31202

Idaho: Seedings, College of Forestry, University of Idaho, Moscow 83843

Illinois: Forestry Division, 403 S. New St., Springfield 62706

Minnesota: Division of Forestry, Minnesota DNR, 300 Centennial Bldg., St. Paul 55155

Missouri: State Forester, Missouri Department of Conservation, Box 1687, Jefferson City 65102-1687

Mississippi: Forestry Commission, 908 Robert E. Lee Bldg., Jackson 39201 (tree seedlings only)

Montana: Forestry Division, Department of State Lands, 2704 Spurgin Rd., Missoula 59801

Nebraska: Contact your local office of the Cooperative Extension Service or Soil Conservation Service

Nevada: Nevada State Tree Nursery, 885 Eastlake Blvd., Carson City 89701

New Hampshire: Department of Resources and Economic Development, Division of Forests and Lands, Prescott Park Building #2, 105 Loudon Rd., Concord 03301 (for trees)

New Jersey: Contact the local Soil Conservation Service office

New Mexico: Department of Natural Resources, Forestry Division, P.O. Box 2167, 87504-2167

New York: Saratoga Nursery, RD 5, Rt. 50, Saratoga Springs 12866

North Dakota: Contact the local Soil Conservation Service office; North Dakota Forest Service, Towner Nursery, Towner 58755; Lincoln Oakes Nursery, Box 1601, Bismarck 58501

Ohio: Department of Natural Resources, Division of Wildlife, Fountain Square, Columbus 43224

Oklahoma: Forestry Division, State Department of Agriculture, Room 122, State Capitol, Oklahoma City 73105

Pennsylvania: Pennsylvania Game Commission Nursery, R.D. #2, Howard 16841

Rhode Island: Rhode Island Division of Forest Environment, Department of Environmental Management, 83 Park St., Providence 02903

Tennessee: Tennessee Division of Forestry, P.O. Box 20, Pinson 38366; Tennessee Department of Conservation, 701 Broadway, Nashville 37203 (shrubs)

Texas: Contact local Soil Conservation Service offices

Vermont: Contact county foresters and Soil Conservation Service offices

Virginia: Contact county forester

Wisconsin: Contact the County Extension offices

SOURCES FOR BIRD-ATTRACTING SUPPLIES

Aspects, P.O. Box 9, Bristol, RI 02809. Clear plastic window feeders

Audubon Workshop, Inc., 1501 Paddock Drive, Northbrook, IL 60062. Squirrel-proof and selective bird feeders, houses, grain, baths, water heaters

Barzen Enterprises, Inc., 455 Harrison St., N.E., Minneapolis, MN 55413. Feeders, houses, grain, water heaters, suet

Bay-Mor Pet Feeds, Bay-Mor Plaza, Cressona, PA 17929. Feeders, grain, water heaters

The Beverly Company, P.O. Box 101, New Harbor, ME 04554. Watering devices for birdbaths

Bird n' Hand Inc., 73 Sawyer Passway, Fitchburg, MA 01420. Feeders, grain, baths, water heaters

Bird Seed Savings Day, 55 North Sillyman St., Cressona, PA 17929. Feeders, grain, water heaters (for nonprofit organizations only)

Bluebird Recovery Committee, Audubon Chapter of Minneapolis, P.O. Box 566, Minneapolis, MN 55440. Sparrow traps

Bower Bird Feeders, P.O. Box 92, Elkhart, IN 46515. Feeders, squirrel guards, hanging hooks and brackets, suet holders

The Crow's Nest Bookshop, Laboratory of Ornithology, 159 Sapsucker Woods Rd., Ithaca, NY 14850. Feeders, houses

Droll Yankees, Inc., Mill Rd., Foster, RI 02825. Feeders

Duncraft, 33 Fisherville Rd., Penacook, NH 03303. Feeders, houses, grain, baths

Heath Manufacturing Co., 140 Mill St., Coopersville, MI 49404. Feeders, houses, suet

Joe Huber, 1720 Evergreen Court, Heath, OH 43055. Bluebird boxes with built-in sparrow traps

Hummingbird Haven, 1255 Carmel Drive, Simi Valley, CA 93065. Hummingbird and oriole feeders

Hyde Bird Feeder Co., 56 Felton St., P.O. Box 168, Waltham, MA 02254. Feeders, houses, grain, water heaters

Jerry Janicki, 6657 W. 111th St., Worth, IL 60482. Feeders, houses, grain, baths, water heaters, water pumps for pools, pine cones for suet

R. Kopecky, 1220A Ridge Road, Hypoluxo, FL 33462. Squirrel- and starlingproof feeders, grain

Little Giant Pump Co., 3810 N. Tulsa, Oklahoma City, OK 73112. Water pumps for pools, water falls, fountains

National Audubon Society Wild Bird Food, Box 207, Bristol, IL 60512. Grain

Nelson Manufacturing Company, 3049 12th Street, S.W., Cedar Rapids, IA 52404. Birdbath heaters

North States Industries, Inc., 3650 Fremont Avenue, North, Minneapolis, MN 55412. Feeders, houses

Rainbow Mealworms, 126 E. Spruce St., P.O. Box 4907, Compton, CA 90224

Ralston Purina Company, Checkerboard Square, St. Louis, MO 63141. Feeders, grain

Trio Manufacturing Co., Griggsville, IL 62340. Aluminum martin houses and mounting poles

Wells L. Bishop Co., Inc., 464 Pratt Street, Meriden, CT 06450. Feeders, houses, hummingbird supplies, suet cakes

Wild Bird Supplies, 4815 Oak Street, Crystal Lake, IL 60014. Feeders, houses, grain, baths, water heaters, suet cakes

Woodstream Corp., Dept. HT, Box 327, Lititz, PA 17543. Havahart mammal and sparrow traps

INDEX